About this time of the day, I get the urge to shout out, "I like this!" That kind of openness can lead to new experiences, and you may find that many other people feel the same way. It can make the world more fun. Simply saying "I like this" is a way to increase spiritual fortitude and make yourself happy.

—Katsura Hoshino

Shiga Prefecture native Katsura Hoshino's hit manga series *D.Gray-man* has been serialized in *Weekly Shonen Jump* since 2004. Katsura's debut manga, "Continue," appeared for the first time in *Weekly Shonen Jump* in 2003.

Katsura adores cats.

D.GRAY-MAN
VOL. 27
SHONEN JUMP Manga Edition

STORY AND ART BY
KATSURA HOSHINO

Translation/John Werry
Touch-up Art & Lettering/Susan Daigle-Leach
Design/J. Yoshioka
Editor/Gary Leach

D.GRAY-MAN © 2004 by Katsura Hoshino. All rights reserved.
First published in Japan in 2004 by SHUEISHA Inc., Tokyo.
English translation rights arranged by SHUEISHA Inc.

The stories, characters and incidents mentioned in this publication are entirely fictional.

Printed in the U.S.A.

Published by VIZ Media, LLC
P.O. Box 77010
San Francisco, CA 94107

10 9 8 7 6 5 4 3 2 1
First printing, July 2021

viz.com

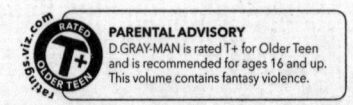

SHONEN JUMP MANGA EDITION

D.Gray-man

vol. 27

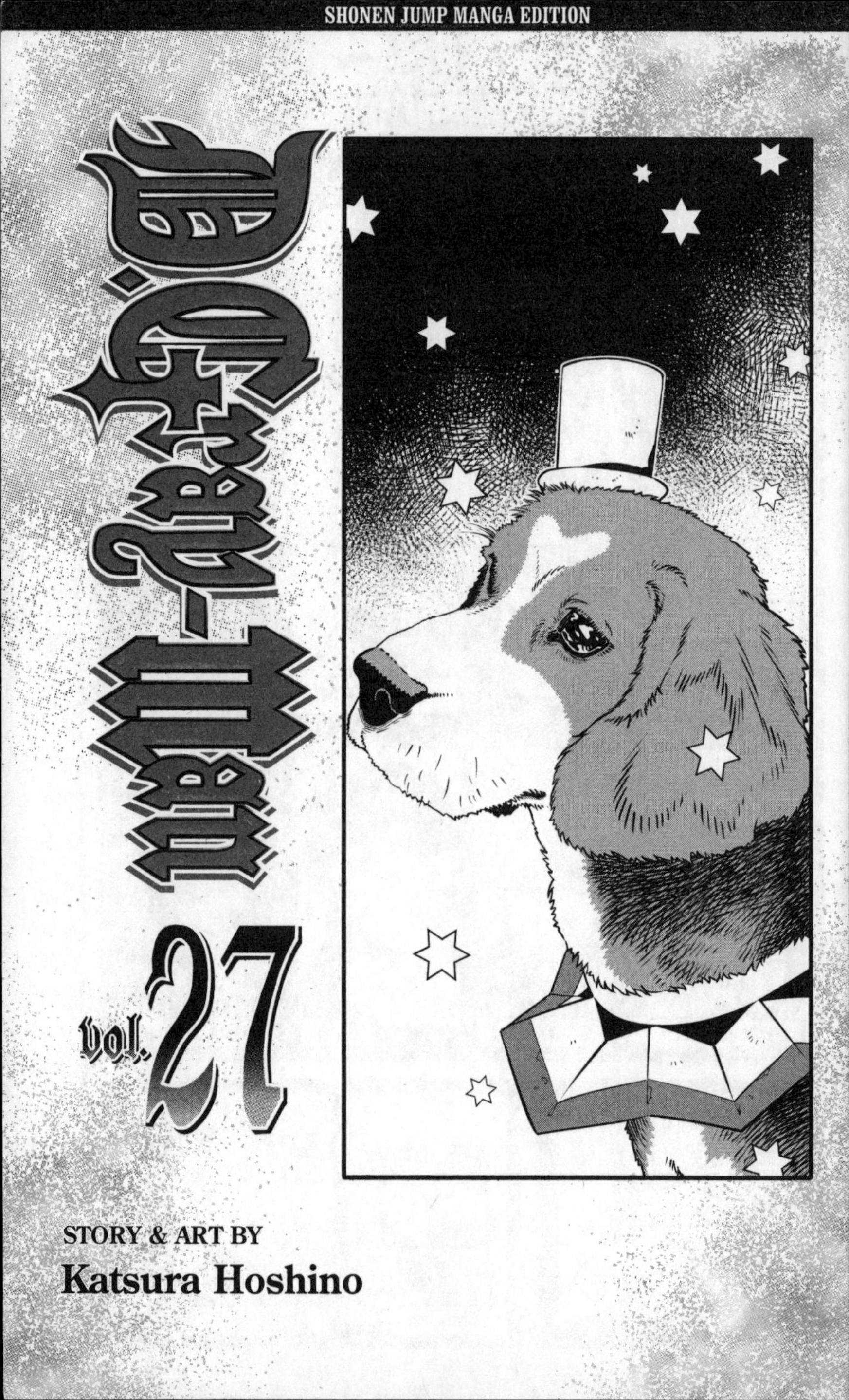

STORY & ART BY

Katsura Hoshino

D.Gray-man
CHARACTERS

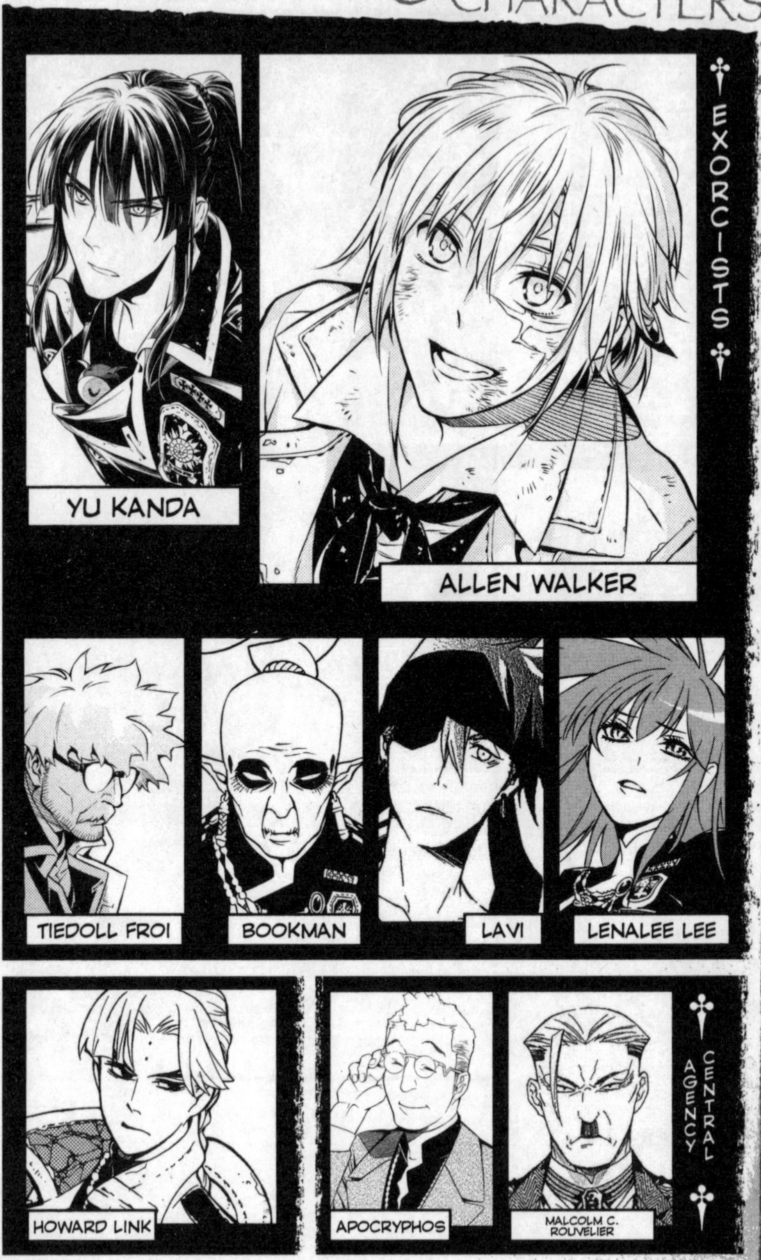
EXORCISTS
ALLEN WALKER
YU KANDA
LENALEE LEE
LAVI
BOOKMAN
TIEDOLL FROI
CENTRAL AGENCY
MALCOLM C. ROUVELIER
APOCRYPHOS
HOWARD LINK

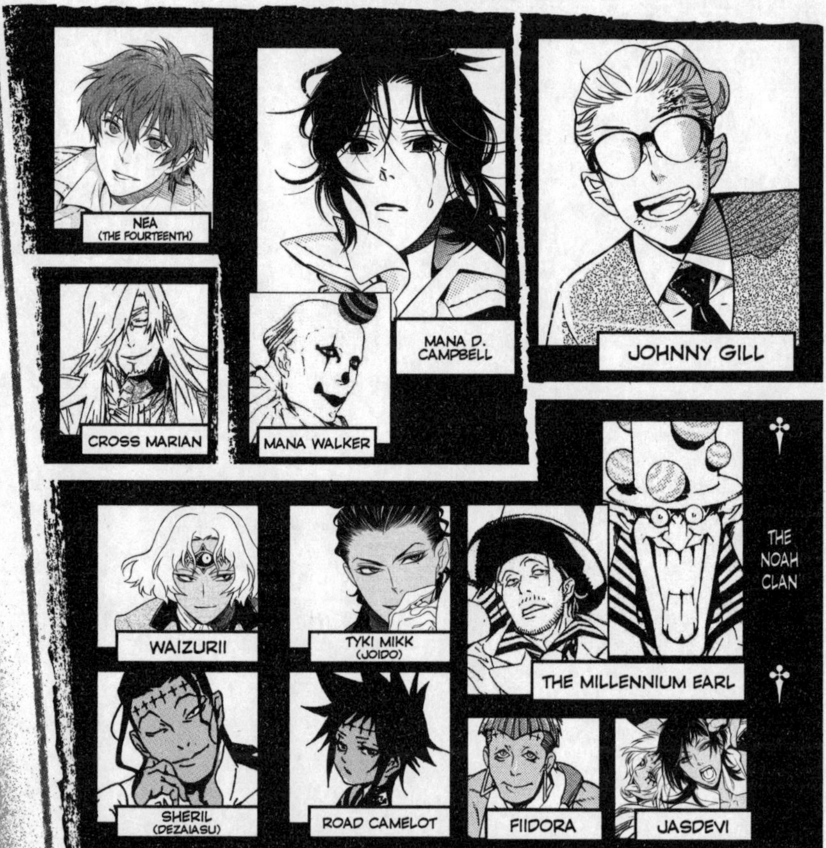
JOHNNY GILL
MANA D. CAMPBELL
NEA (THE FOURTEENTH)
MANA WALKER
CROSS MARIAN
THE NOAH CLAN
THE MILLENNIUM EARL
TYKI MIKK (JOIDO)
WAIZURII
JASDEVI
FIIDORA
ROAD CAMELOT
SHERIL (DEZAIASU)

STORY

THE NOAH CLAN, LED BY THE MILLENNIUM EARL, PLOTS THE END OF THE WORLD, AND THE BLACK ORDER CONTINUOUSLY FIGHTS THEM. EXORCISTS ARE WARRIORS WHO BELONG TO THE ORDER AND HAVE THE ONLY POWER, INNOCENCE, THAT CAN DEFEAT THE EARL'S MINIONS, THE AKUMA.

THE EXORCIST KNOWN AS ALLEN ONCE TURNED HIS OWN ADOPTIVE FATHER INTO AN AKUMA. WHAT'S MORE, HE IS HOST TO THE FOURTEENTH, KNOWN AS NEA—THE NOAH WHO ONCE BETRAYED THE MILLENNIUM EARL.

AS ALLEN'S TRANSFORMATION INTO NEA ADVANCES, THE INDEPENDENT-TYPE INNOCENCE KNOWN AS APOCRYPHOS TRIES TO FUSE WITH ALLEN, FORCING ALLEN TO FLEE FROM THE BLACK ORDER.

WORRIED ABOUT ALLEN, SCIENCE DIVISION MEMBER JOHNNY GILL QUITS THE ORDER AND SETS OUT WITH YU KANDA TO FIND ALLEN. BUT APOCRYPHOS ATTACKS AND DESTROYS ALLEN'S GOLEM TIMCANPY. DURING AN INVASION BY THE NOAH, GENERAL TIEDOLL PROTECTS ALLEN, BUT KANDA GETS INVOLVED AND ALLEN WINDS UP ON THE RUN AGAIN, THIS TIME TOWARD WHAT HE DESCRIBES AS THE "PLACE WHERE 'ALLEN' BEGAN"...

D.GRAY-MAN
Vol. 27

CONTENTS

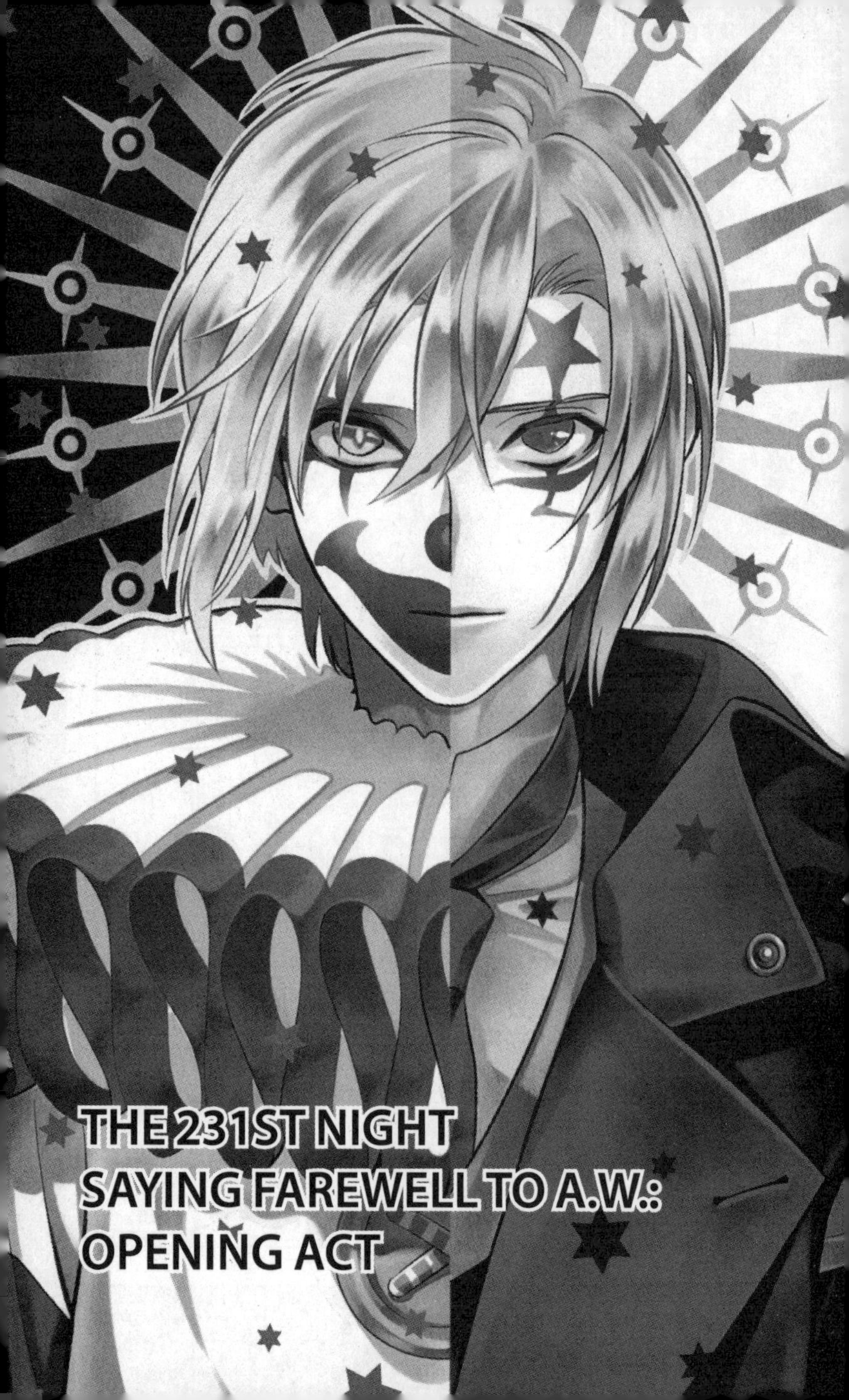
THE 231ST NIGHT
SAYING FAREWELL TO A.W.:
OPENING ACT

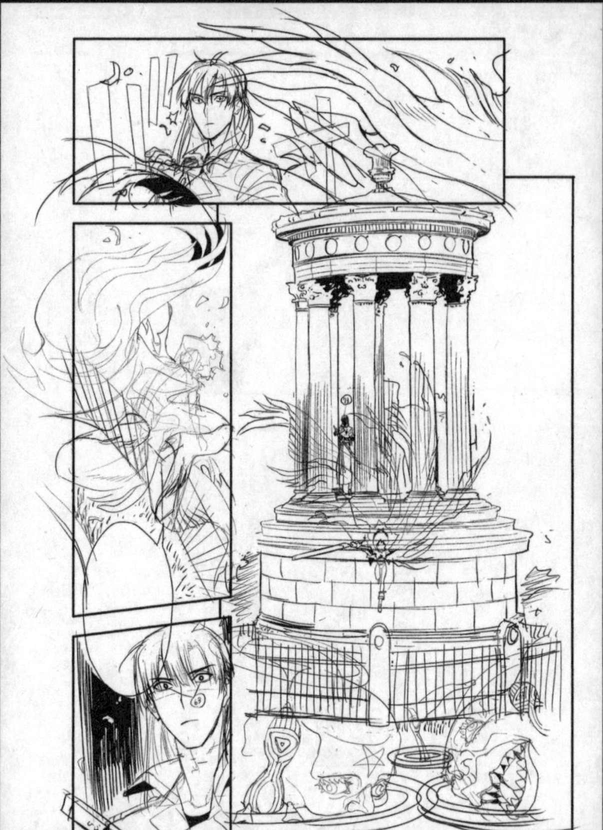

The 231st Night Rough Layout

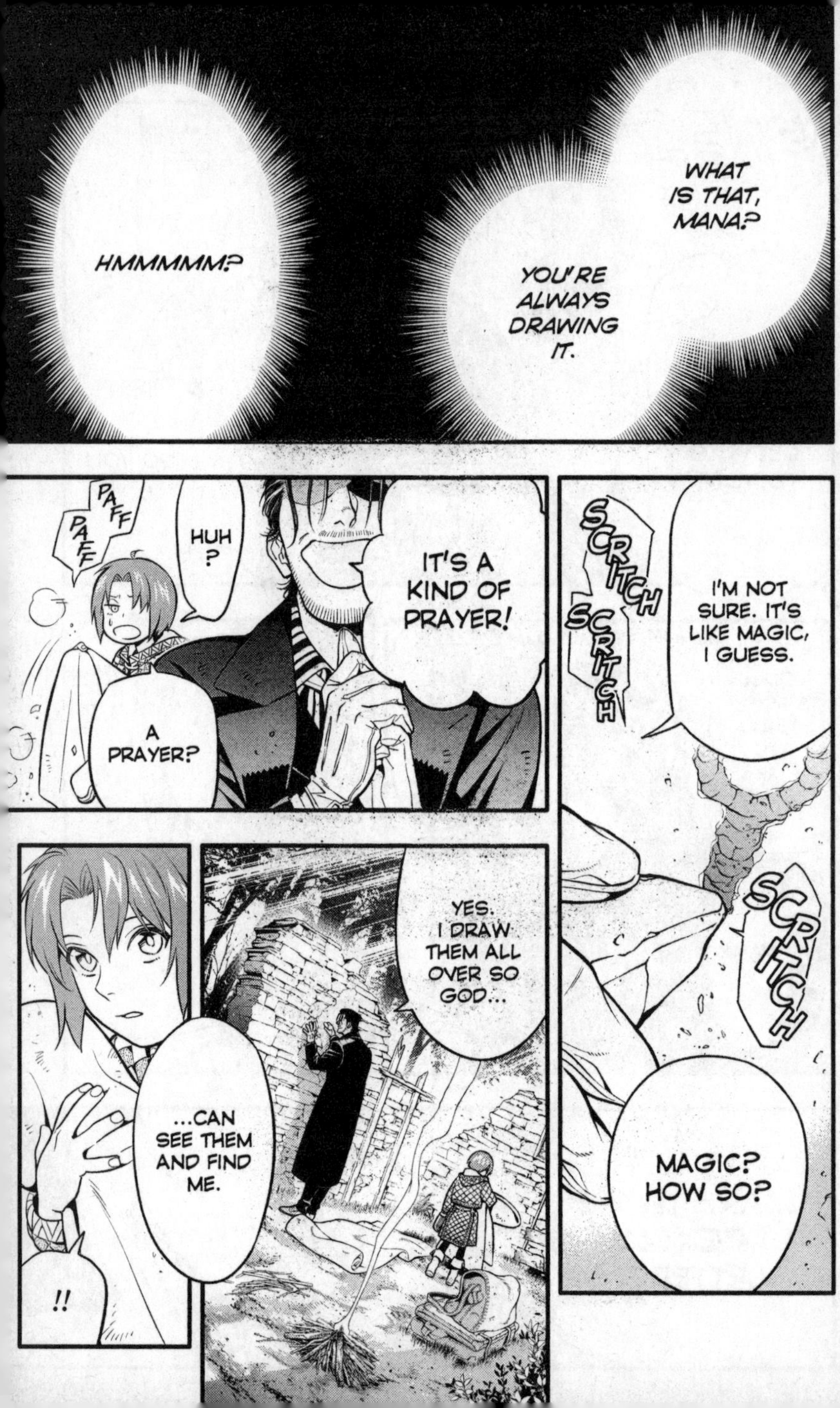
WHAT IS THAT, MANA?
YOU'RE ALWAYS DRAWING IT.
HMMMMM?
I'M NOT SURE. IT'S LIKE MAGIC, I GUESS.
SCRITCH
SCRITCH
SCRITCH
MAGIC? HOW SO?
IT'S A KIND OF PRAYER!
HUH?
PAFF PAFF
A PRAYER?
YES. I DRAW THEM ALL OVER SO GOD...
...CAN SEE THEM AND FIND ME.
!!

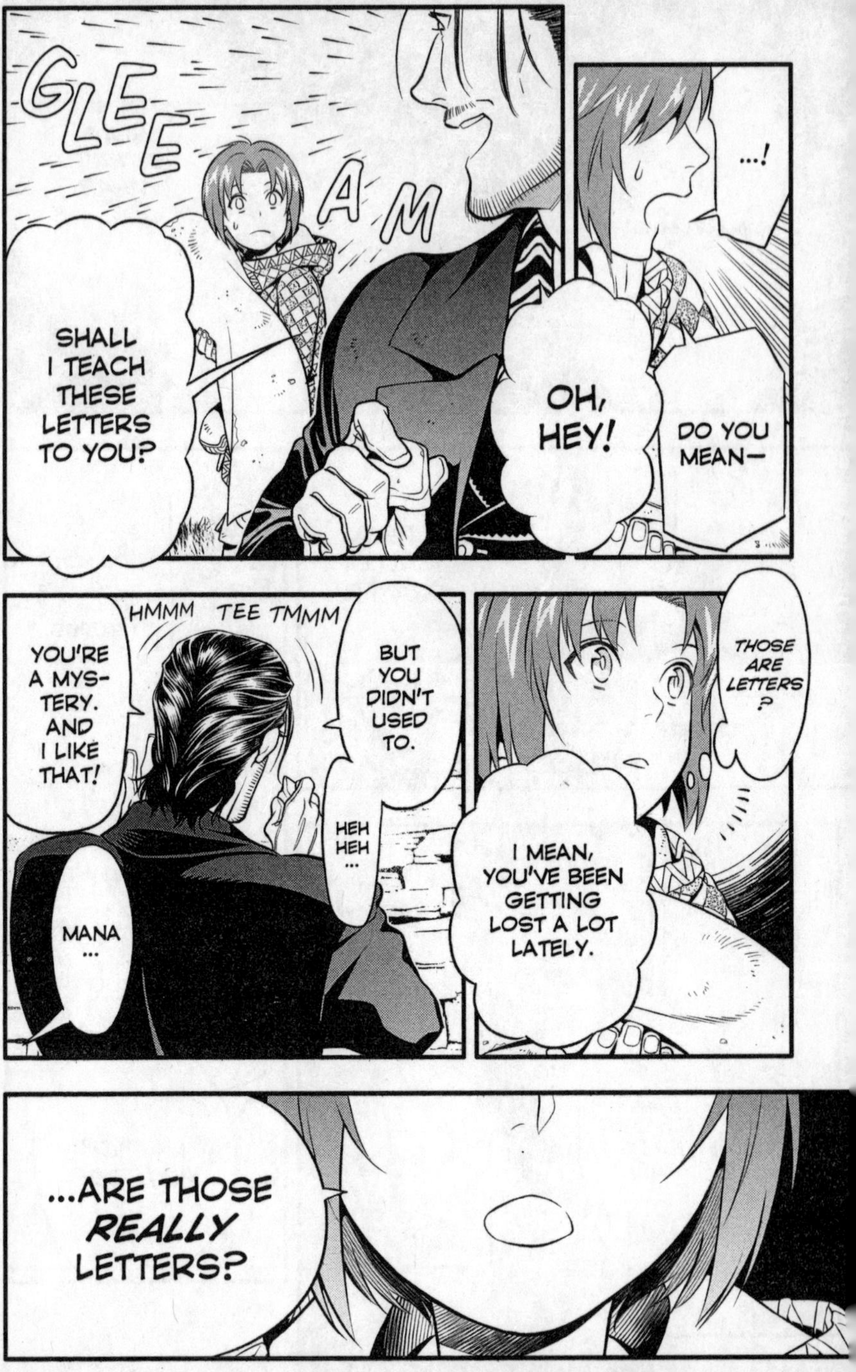
...!
DO YOU MEAN—
OH, HEY!
GLEEAM
SHALL I TEACH THESE LETTERS TO YOU?
THOSE ARE LETTERS ?
I MEAN, YOU'VE BEEN GETTING LOST A LOT LATELY.
BUT YOU DIDN'T USED TO.
HMMM TEE TMMM
YOU'RE A MYS-TERY. AND I LIKE THAT!
HEH HEH ...
MANA ...
...ARE THOSE REALLY LETTERS?

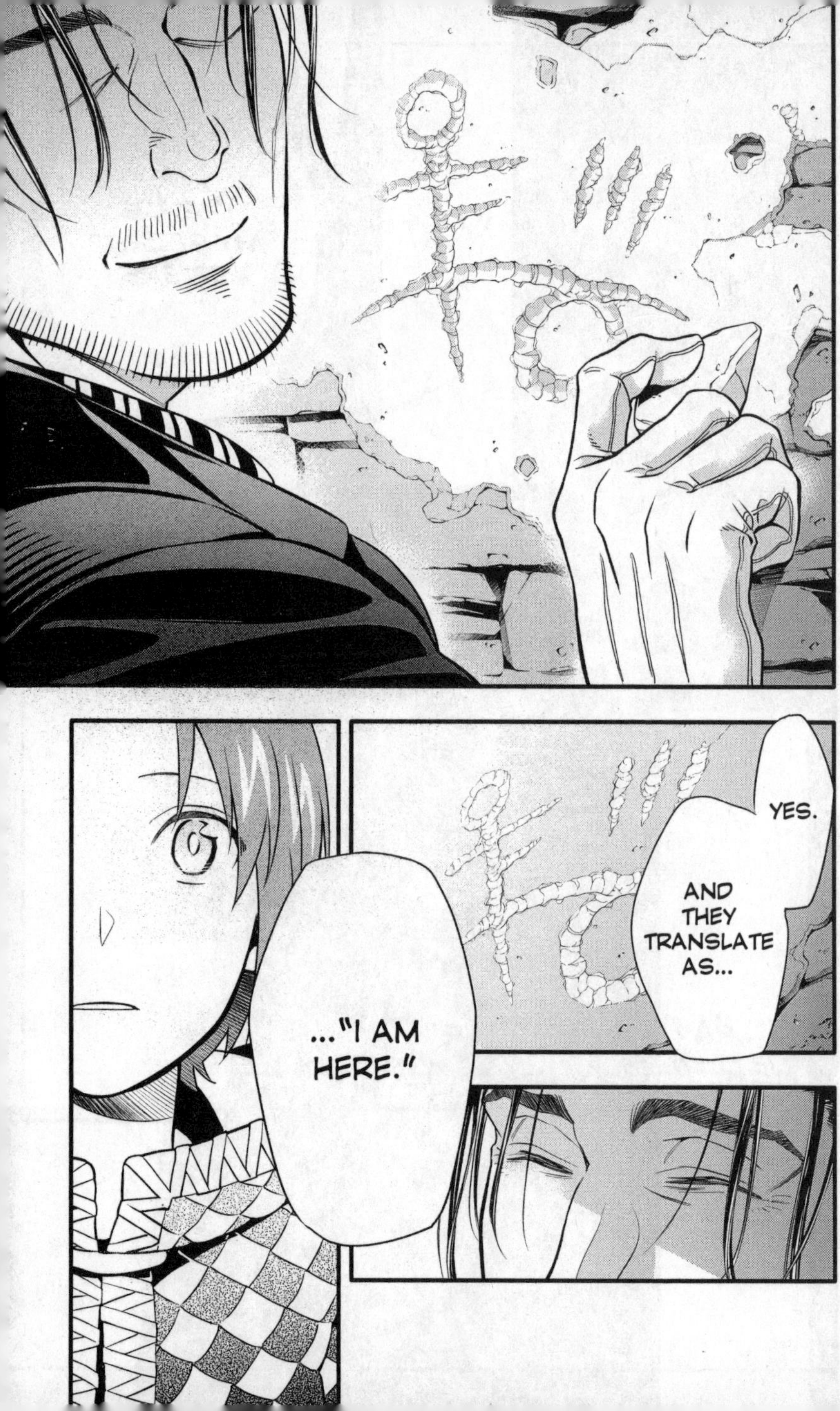
YES.
AND THEY TRANSLATE AS...
..."I AM HERE."

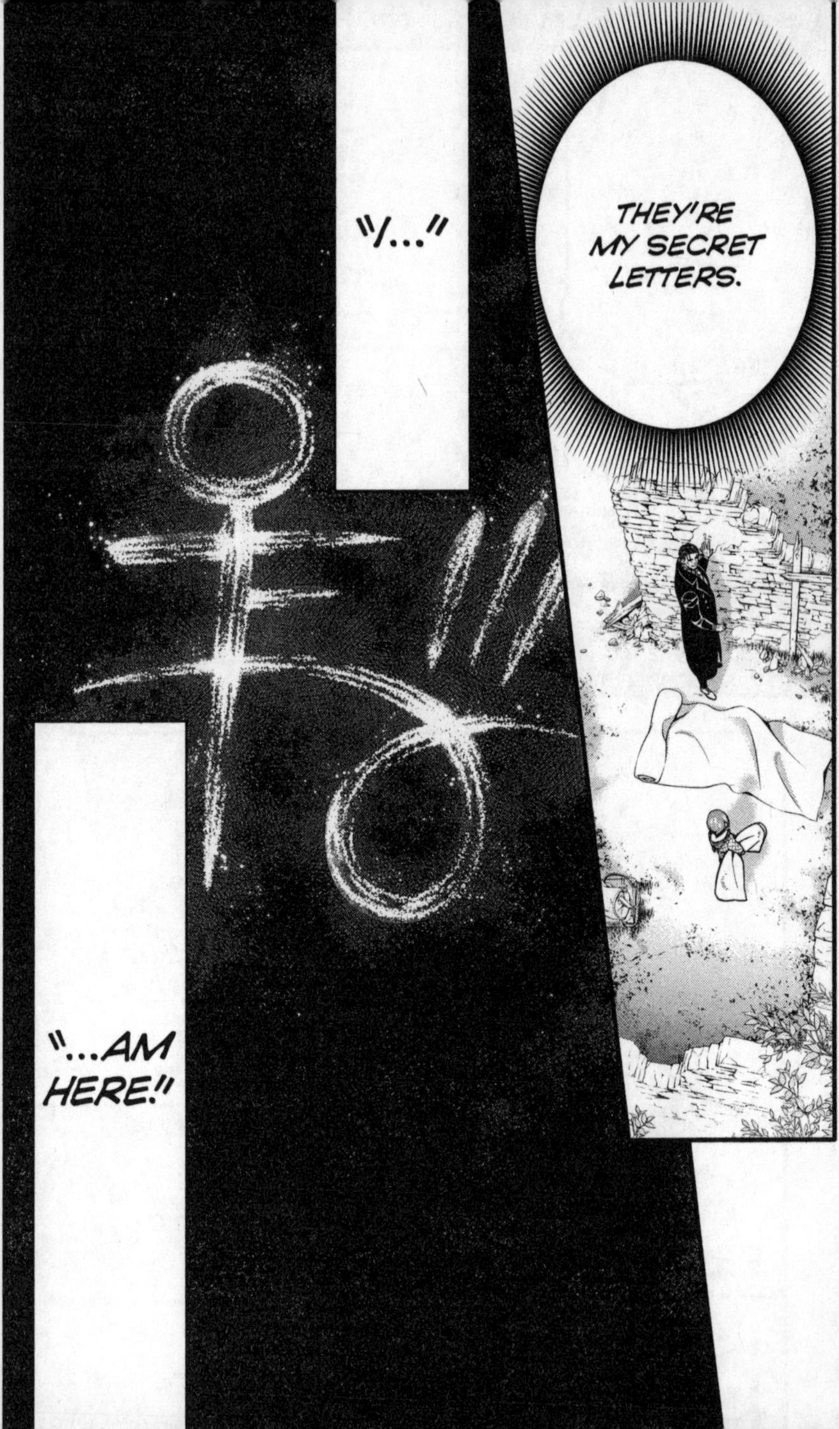
THEY'RE MY SECRET LETTERS.
"I..."
"...AM HERE!"

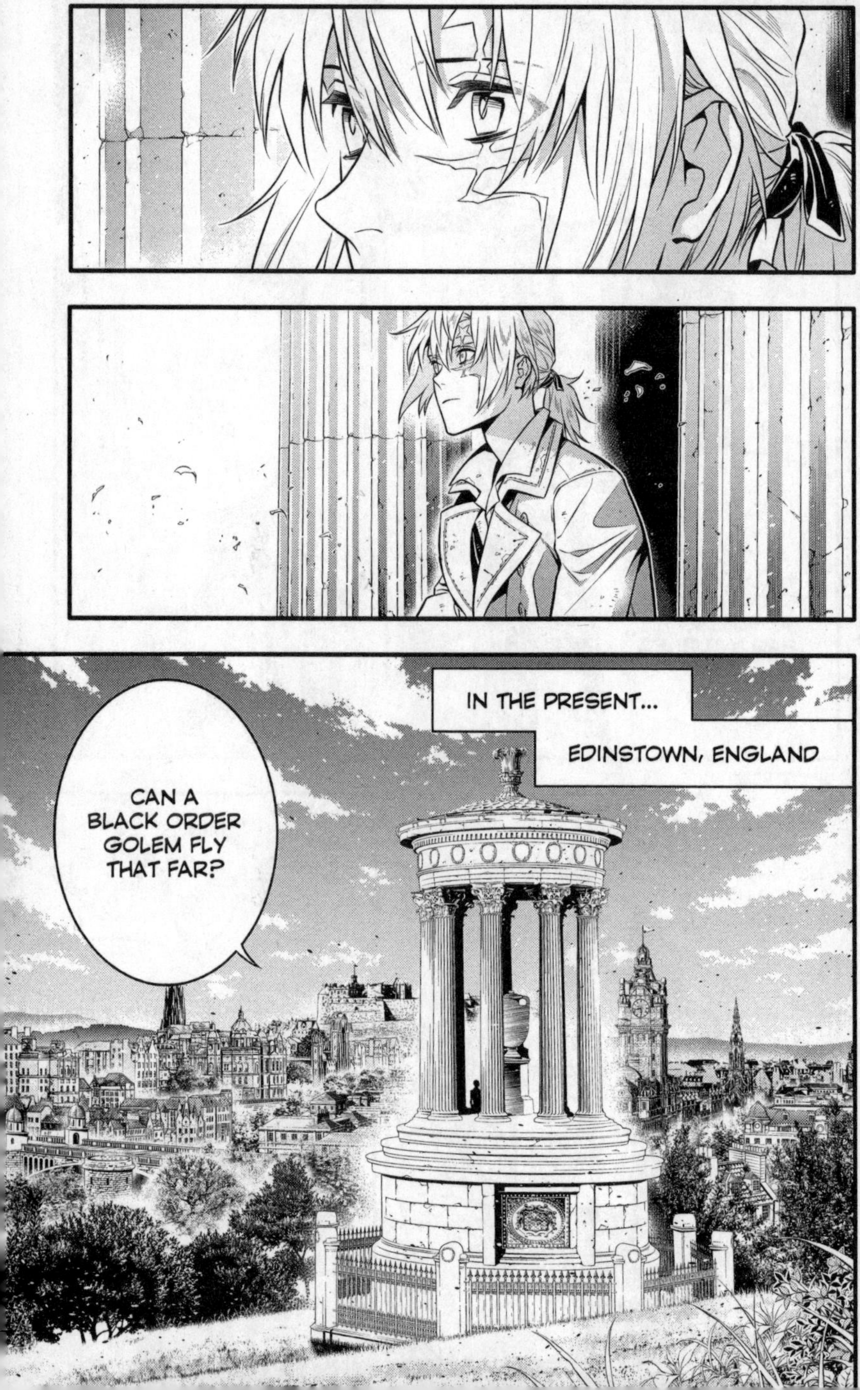
IN THE PRESENT...
EDINSTOWN, ENGLAND
CAN A BLACK ORDER GOLEM FLY THAT FAR?

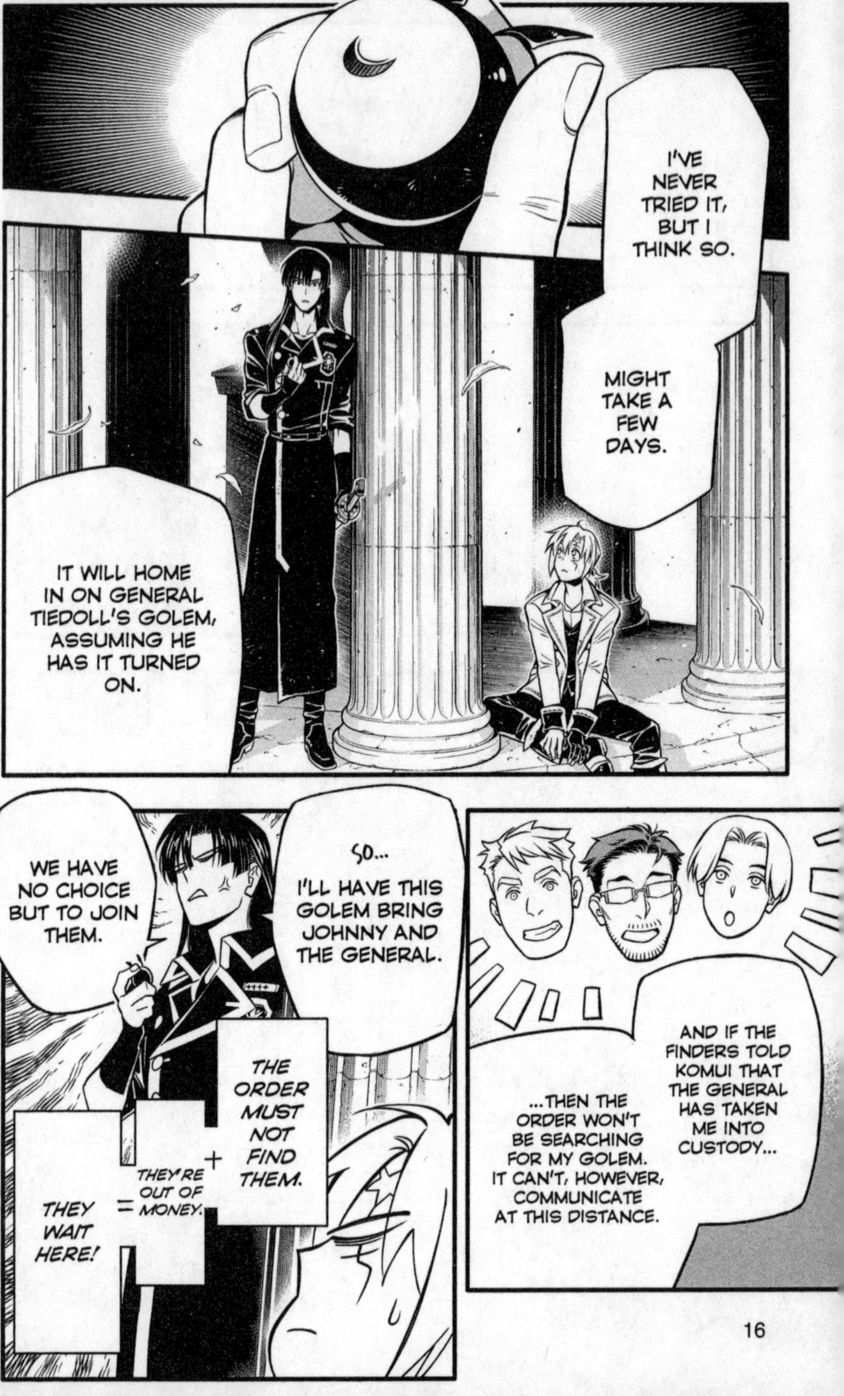
I'VE NEVER TRIED IT, BUT I THINK SO.
MIGHT TAKE A FEW DAYS.
IT WILL HOME IN ON GENERAL TIEDOLL'S GOLEM, ASSUMING HE HAS IT TURNED ON.
AND IF THE FINDERS TOLD KOMUI THAT THE GENERAL HAS TAKEN ME INTO CUSTODY...
...THEN THE ORDER WON'T BE SEARCHING FOR MY GOLEM. IT CAN'T, HOWEVER, COMMUNICATE AT THIS DISTANCE.
SO...
I'LL HAVE THIS GOLEM BRING JOHNNY AND THE GENERAL.
WE HAVE NO CHOICE BUT TO JOIN THEM.
THE ORDER MUST NOT FIND THEM.
+
THEY'RE OUT OF MONEY.
=
THEY WAIT HERE!

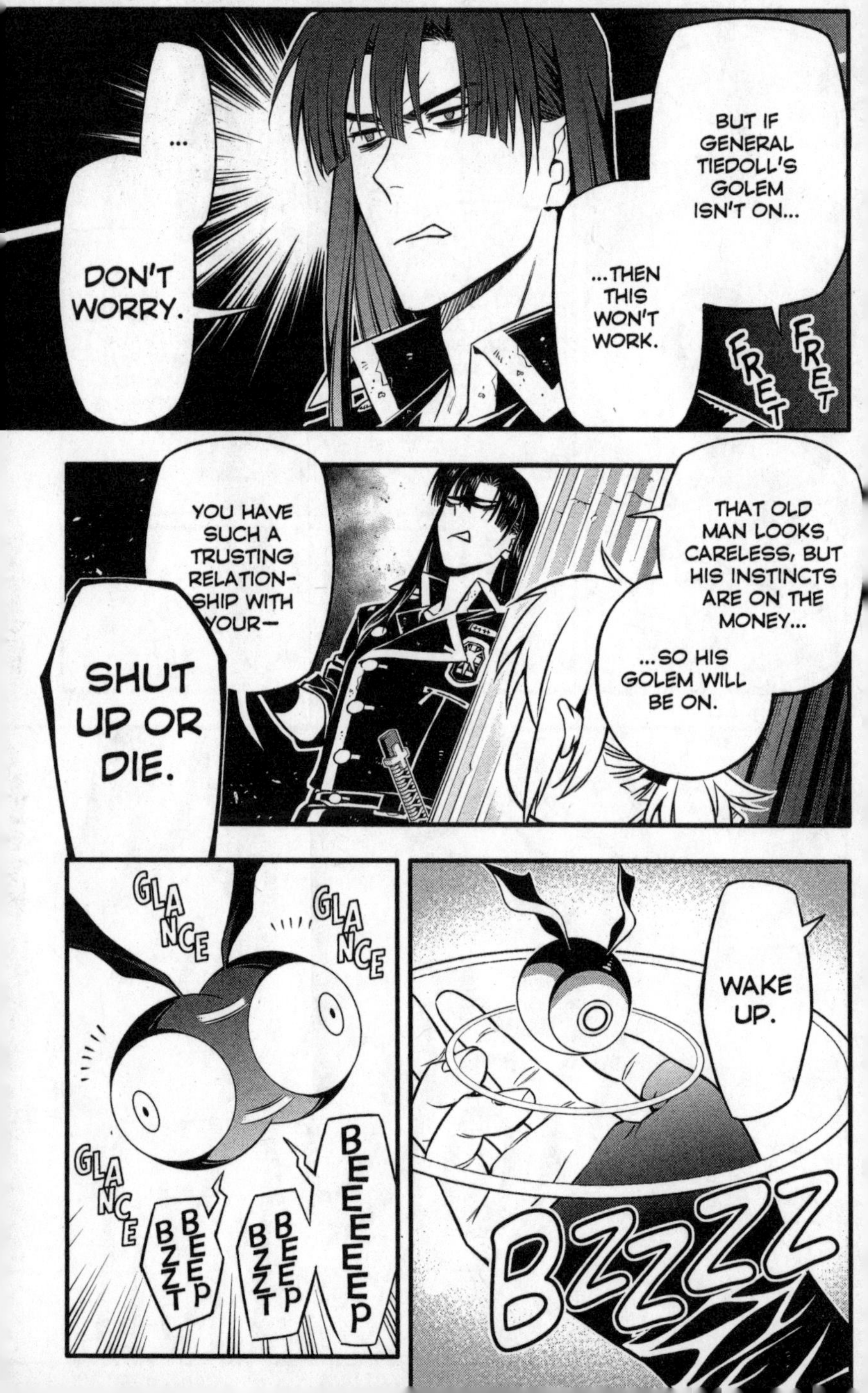
BUT IF GENERAL TIEDOLL'S GOLEM ISN'T ON...
...THEN THIS WON'T WORK.
FRET FRET
...
DON'T WORRY.
THAT OLD MAN LOOKS CARELESS, BUT HIS INSTINCTS ARE ON THE MONEY...
...SO HIS GOLEM WILL BE ON.
YOU HAVE SUCH A TRUSTING RELATION-SHIP WITH YOUR—
SHUT UP OR DIE.
WAKE UP.
BZZZZ
GLANCE
GLANCE
GLANCE
BEEEEEEP
BEEP BZZT
BEEP BZZT

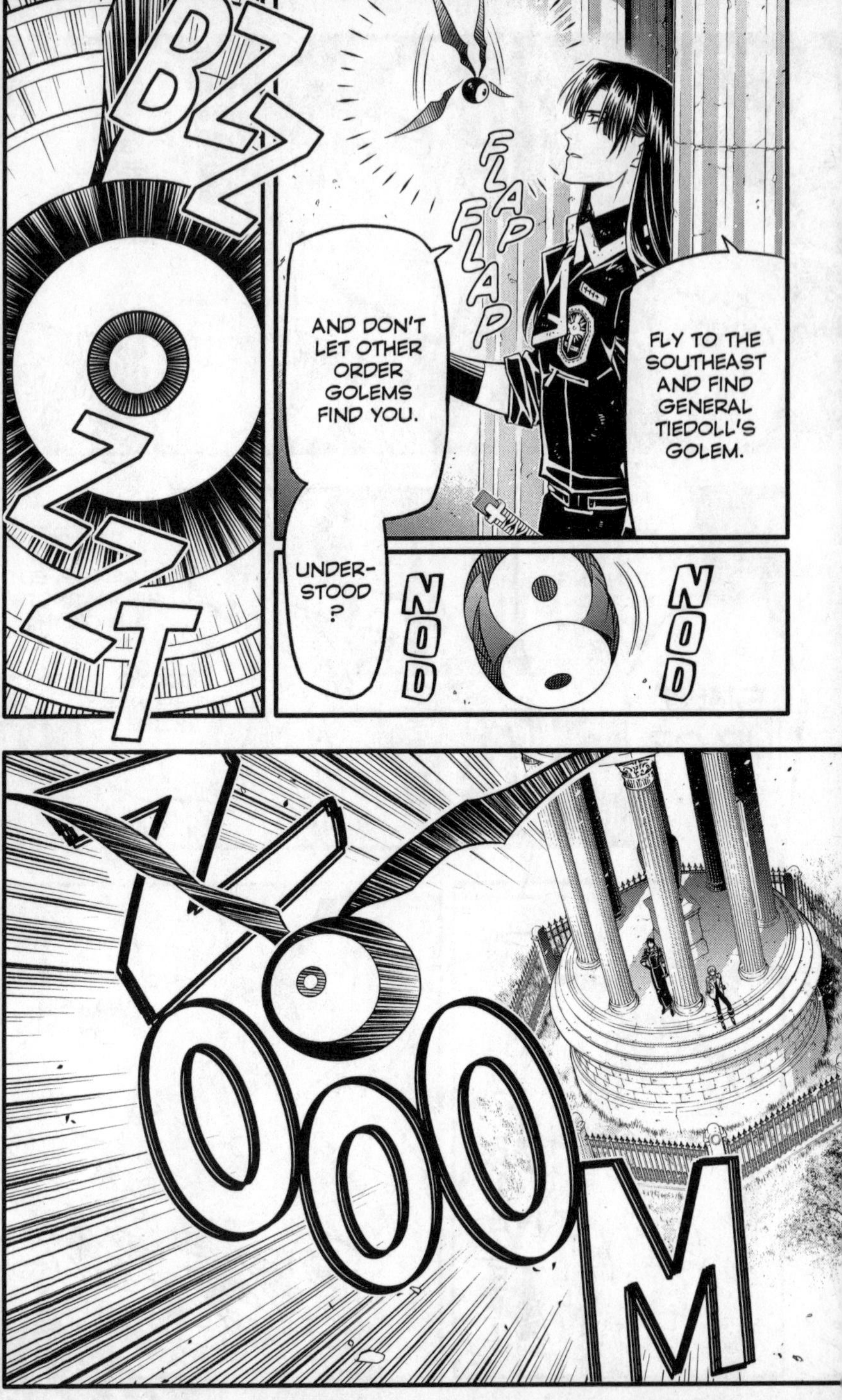
FLY TO THE SOUTHEAST AND FIND GENERAL TIEDOLL'S GOLEM.
FLAP FLAP
AND DON'T LET OTHER ORDER GOLEMS FIND YOU.
BZZZZT
NOD
NOD
UNDER-STOOD?
WOOOOM

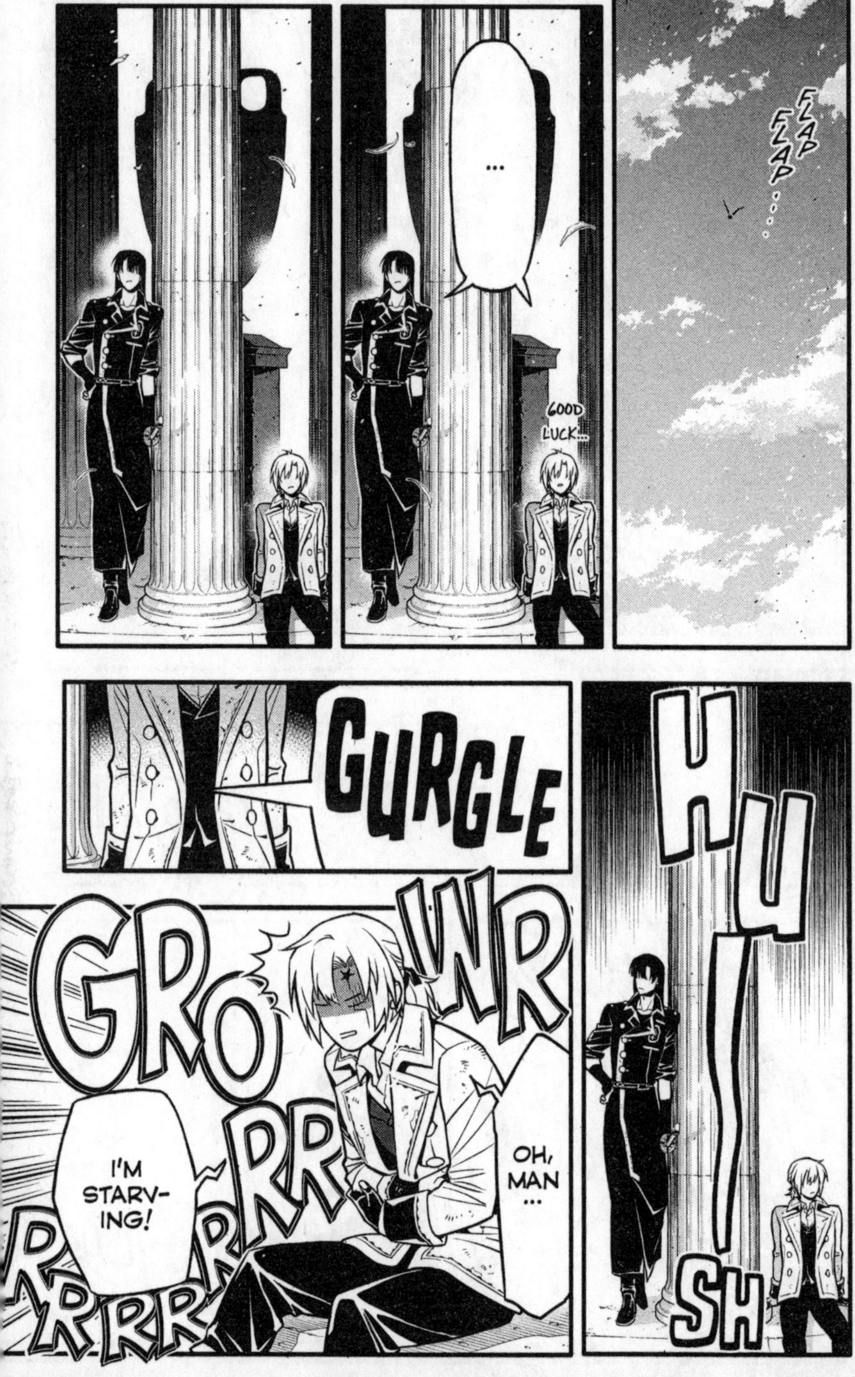
FLAP FLAP...
GOOD LUCK...
...
HUSH
GURGLE
GROWRRRRRRRRRR
OH, MAN...
I'M STARVING!

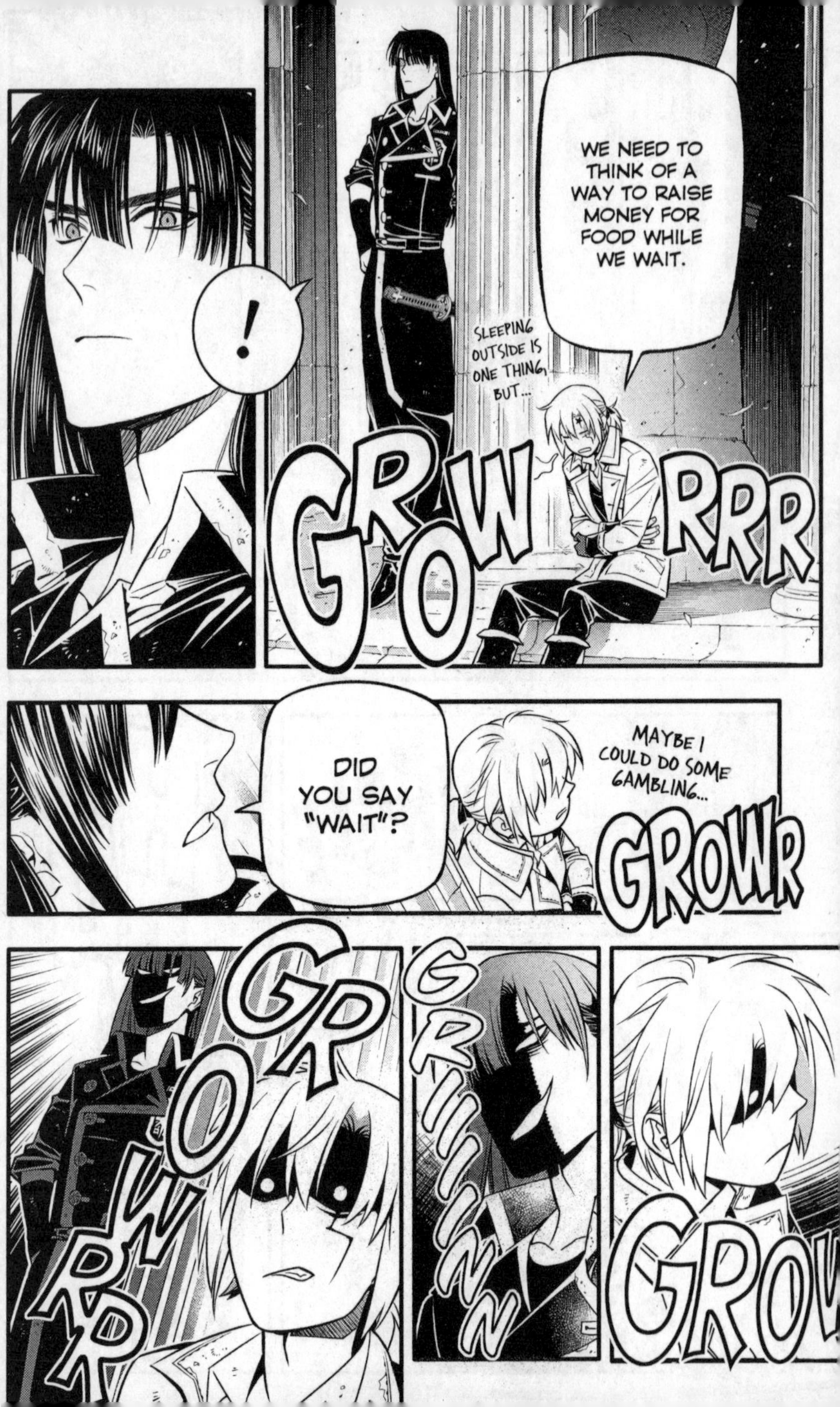
WE NEED TO THINK OF A WAY TO RAISE MONEY FOR FOOD WHILE WE WAIT.
SLEEPING OUTSIDE IS ONE THING, BUT...
GROWRRR
!
MAYBE I COULD DO SOME GAMBLING...
GROWR
DID YOU SAY "WAIT"?
GROU
GRIIIINN
GROWRR

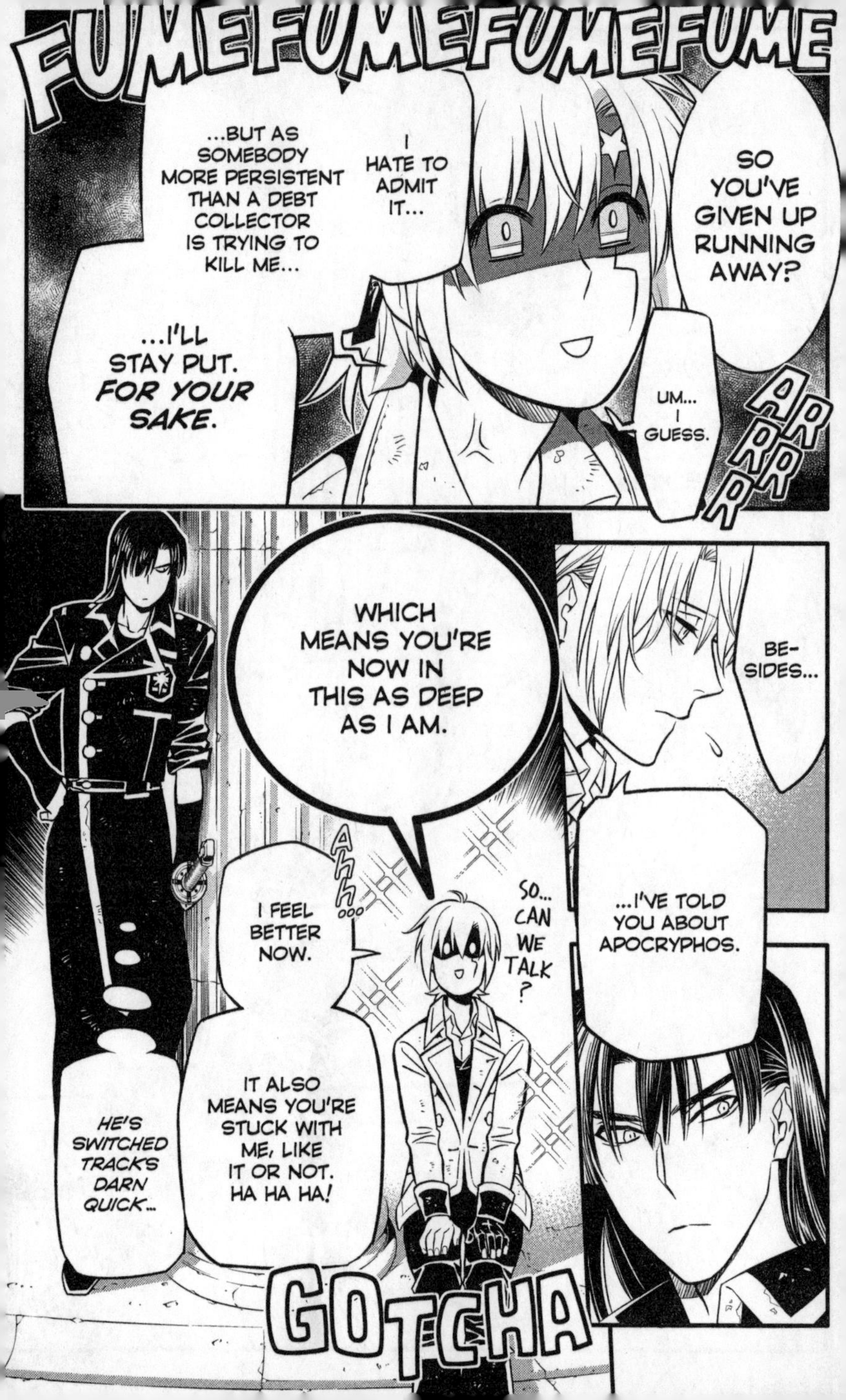
FUMEFUMEFUMEFUME
SO YOU'VE GIVEN UP RUNNING AWAY?
I HATE TO ADMIT IT...
...BUT AS SOMEBODY MORE PERSISTENT THAN A DEBT COLLECTOR IS TRYING TO KILL ME...
UM... I GUESS.
ARRRR
...I'LL STAY PUT. *FOR YOUR SAKE.*
BE-SIDES...
...I'VE TOLD YOU ABOUT APOCRYPHOS.
WHICH MEANS YOU'RE NOW IN THIS AS DEEP AS I AM.
SO... CAN WE TALK?
Ahhooo
I FEEL BETTER NOW.
IT ALSO MEANS YOU'RE STUCK WITH ME, LIKE IT OR NOT. HA HA HA!
GOTCHA
HE'S SWITCHED TRACKS DARN QUICK...

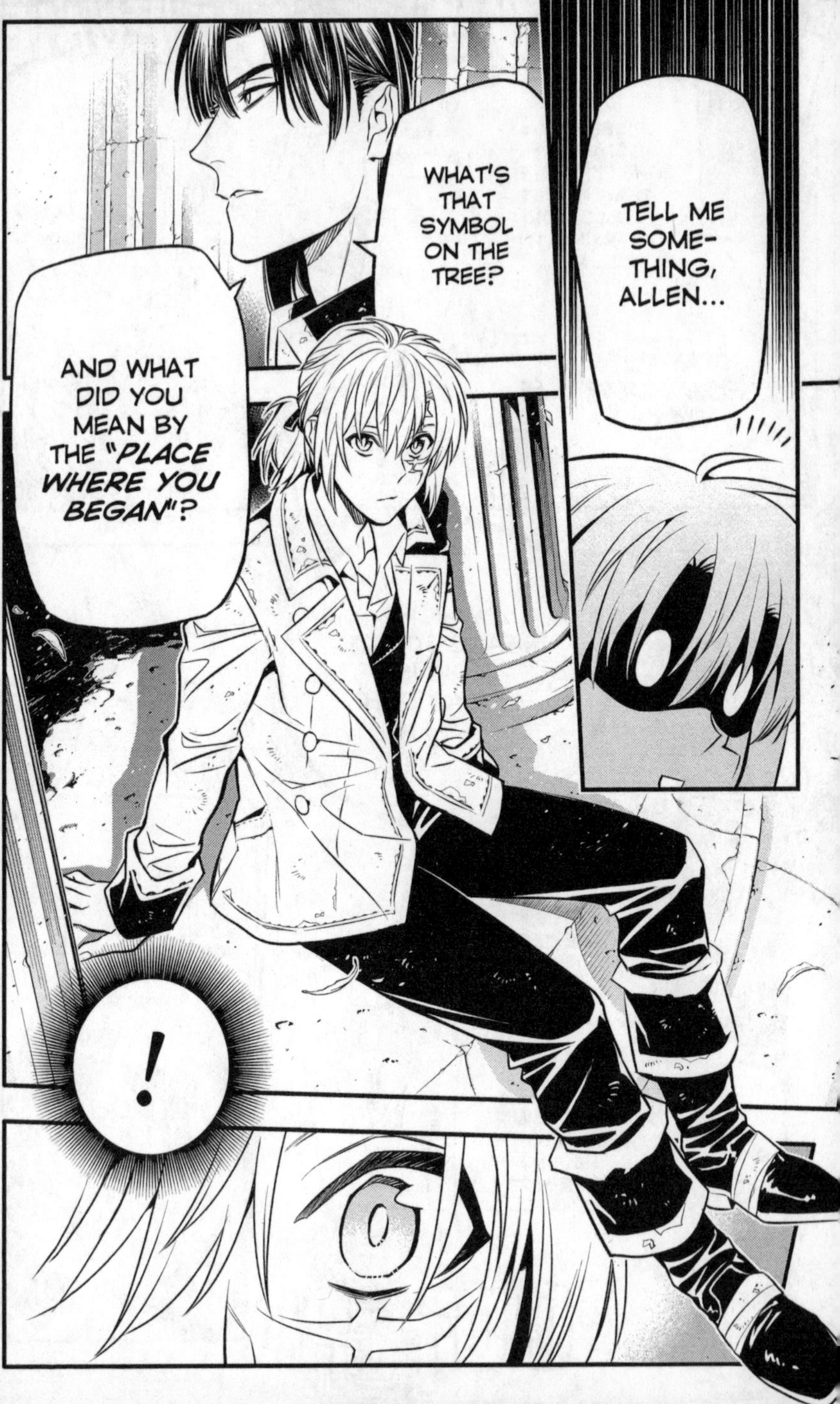
TELL ME SOMETHING, ALLEN...
WHAT'S THAT SYMBOL ON THE TREE?
AND WHAT DID YOU MEAN BY THE "*PLACE WHERE YOU BEGAN*"?
!

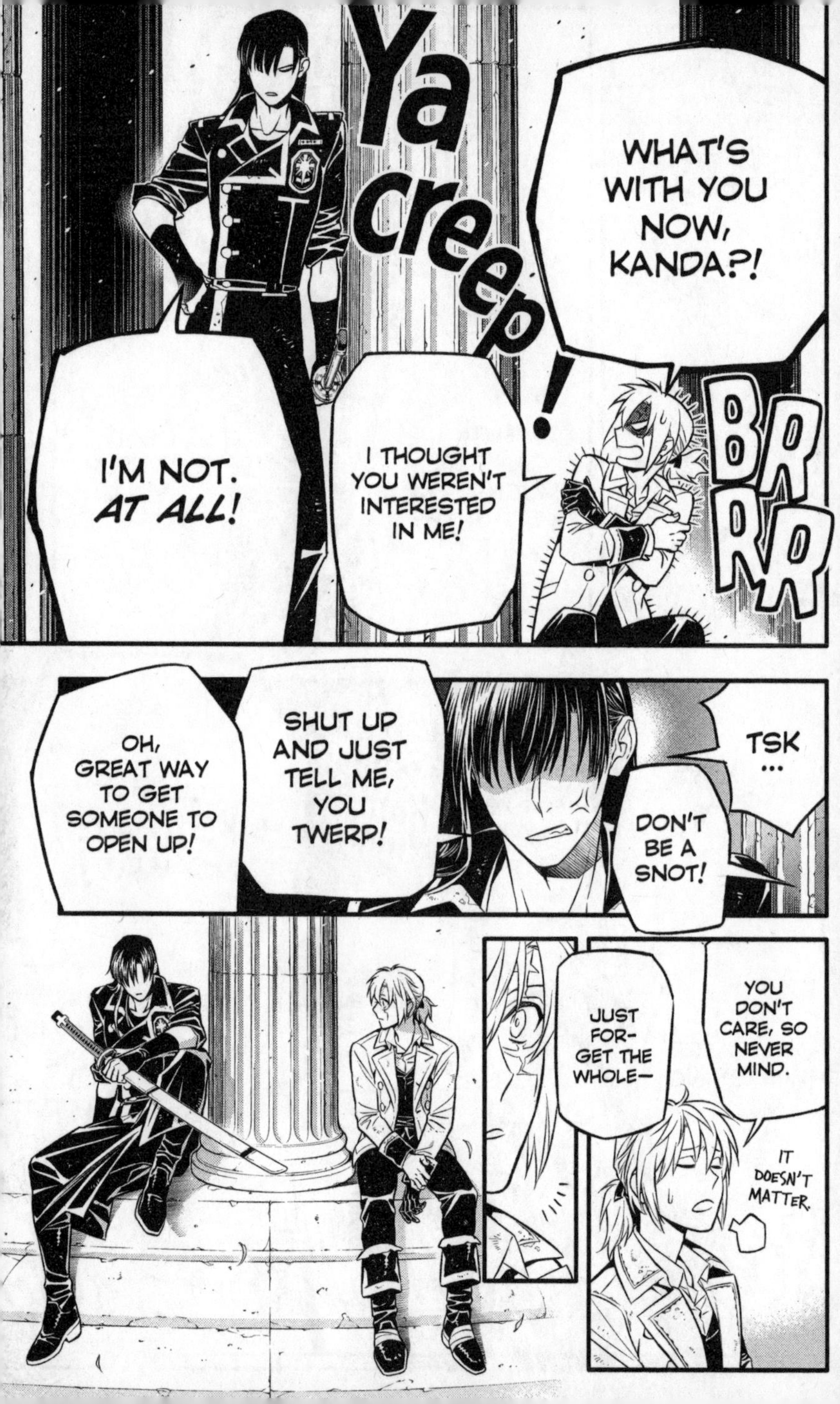
BRRRR
WHAT'S WITH YOU NOW, KANDA?!
Ya creep!
I THOUGHT YOU WEREN'T INTERESTED IN ME!
I'M NOT. AT ALL!
TSK ...
DON'T BE A SNOT!
SHUT UP AND JUST TELL ME, YOU TWERP!
OH, GREAT WAY TO GET SOMEONE TO OPEN UP!
YOU DON'T CARE, SO NEVER MIND.
IT DOESN'T MATTER.
JUST FOR-GET THE WHOLE—

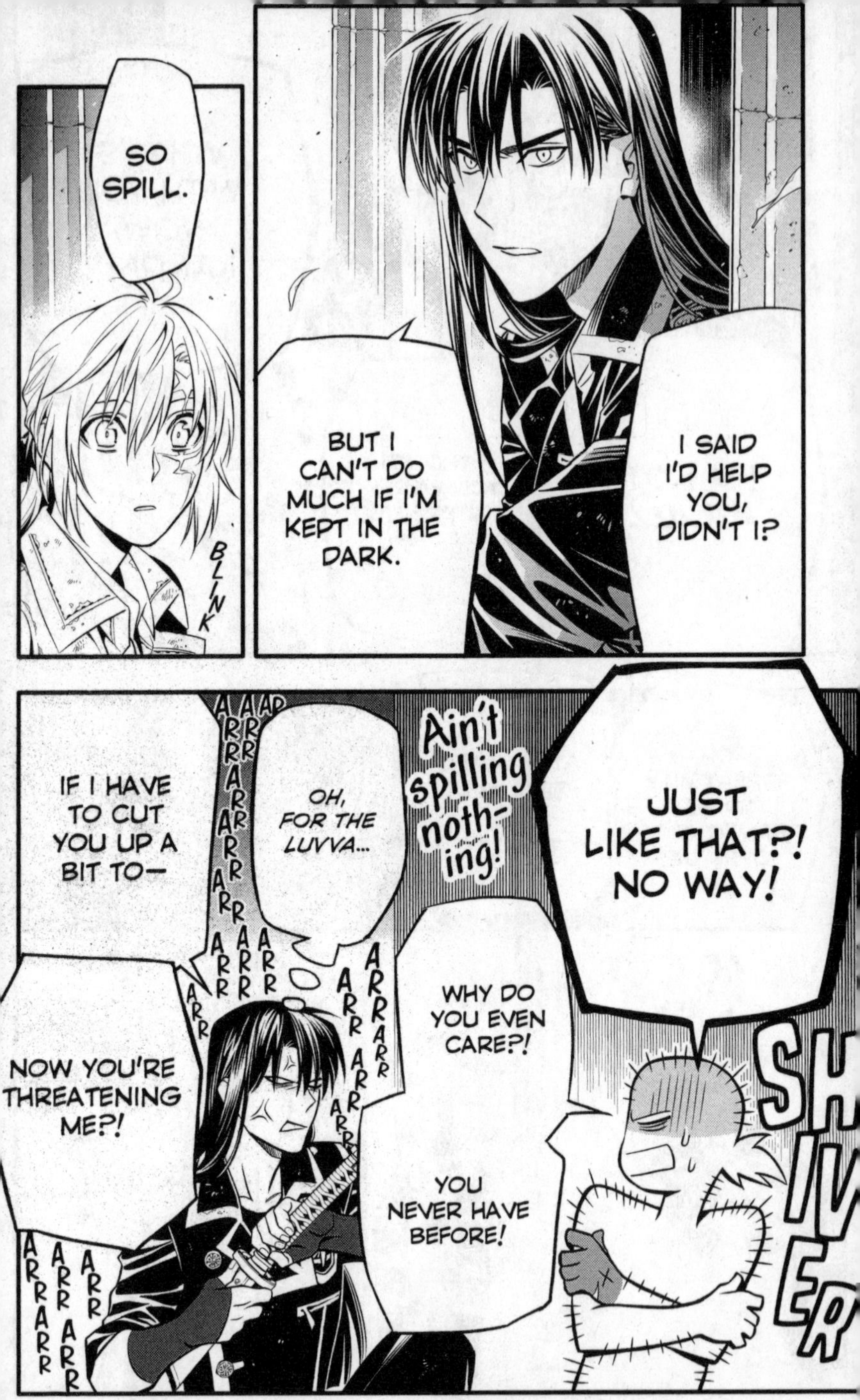
I SAID I'D HELP YOU, DIDN'T I?
BUT I CAN'T DO MUCH IF I'M KEPT IN THE DARK.
SO SPILL.
BLINK
JUST LIKE THAT?! NO WAY!
SHIVER
Ain't spilling noth-ing!
WHY DO YOU EVEN CARE?!
YOU NEVER HAVE BEFORE!
OH, FOR THE LUVVA...
IF I HAVE TO CUT YOU UP A BIT TO—
NOW YOU'RE THREATENING ME?!

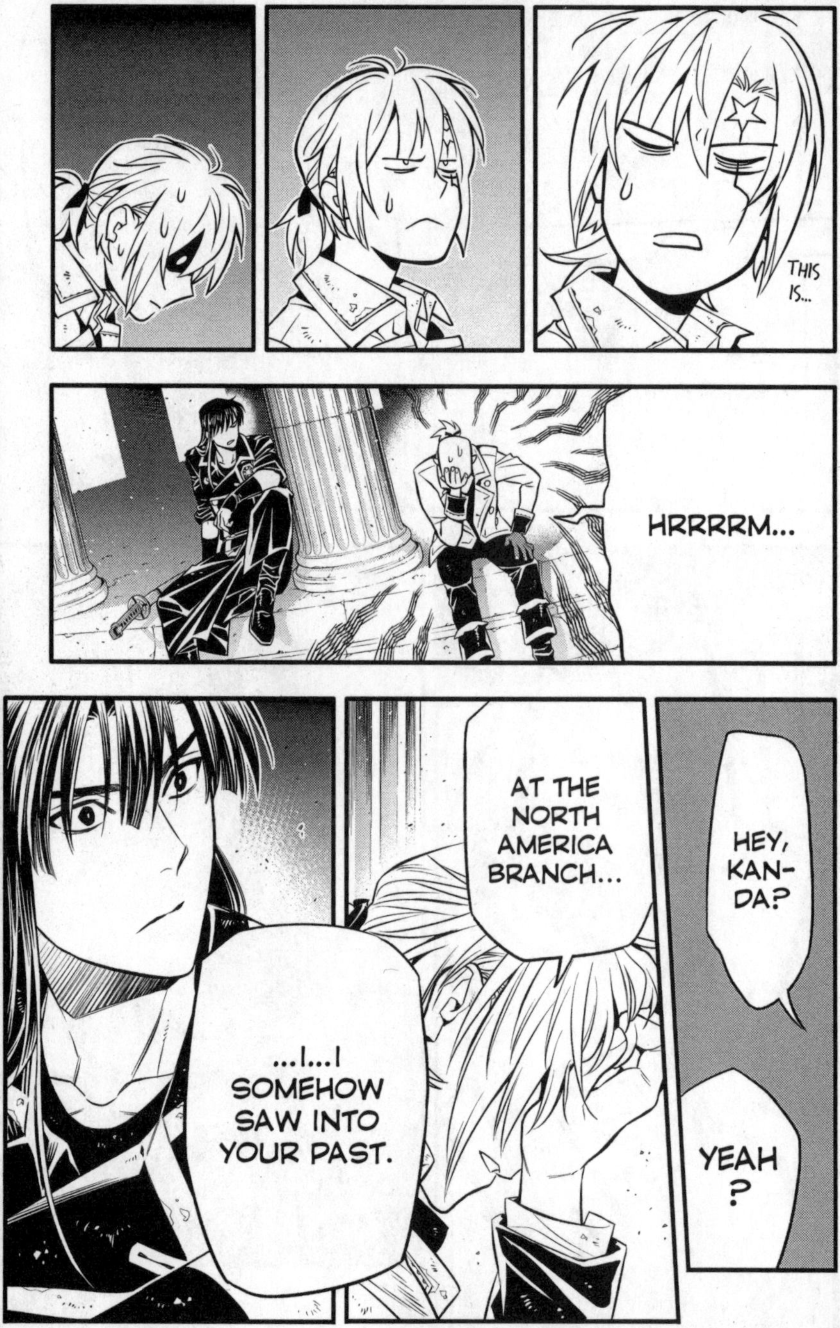
THIS IS...
HRRRRM...
HEY, KAN-DA?
YEAH?
AT THE NORTH AMERICA BRANCH...
...I...I SOMEHOW SAW INTO YOUR PAST.

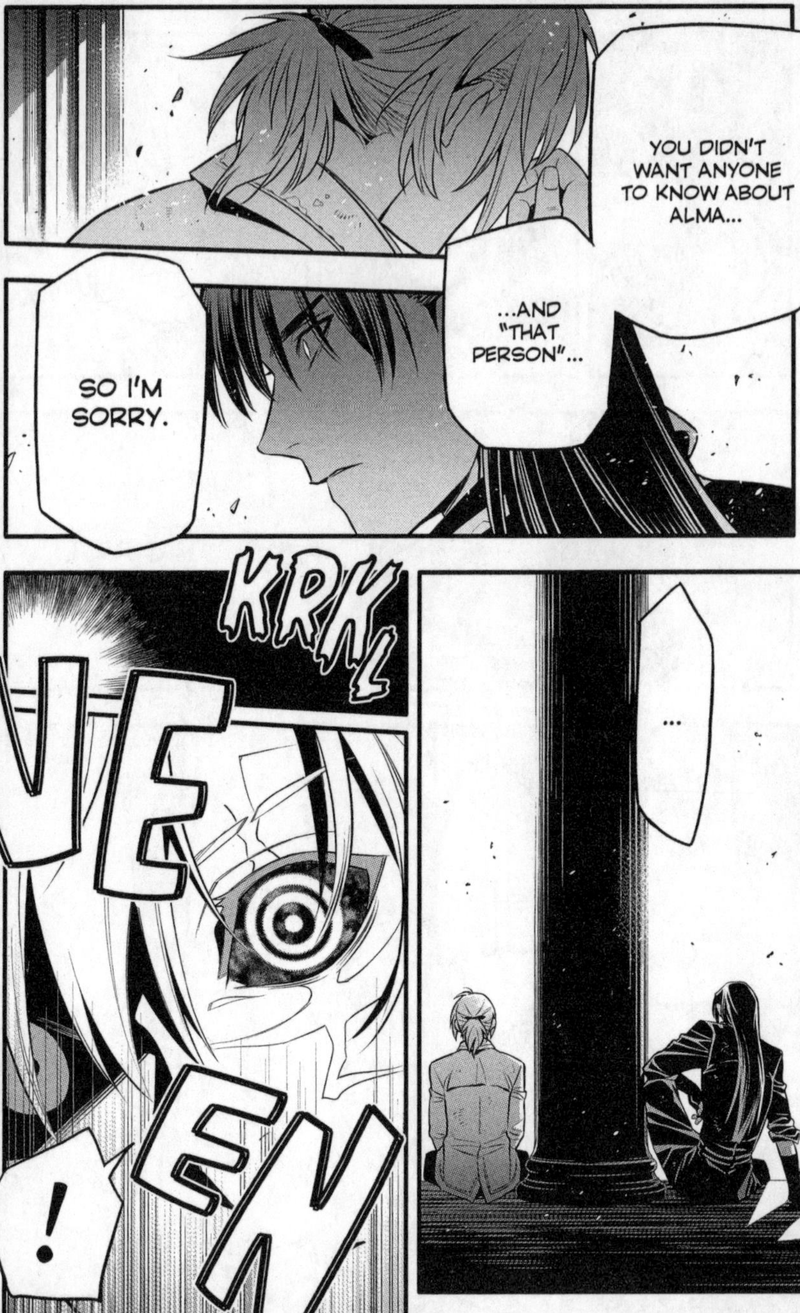
YOU DIDN'T WANT ANYONE TO KNOW ABOUT ALMA...
...AND "THAT PERSON"...
SO I'M SORRY.
...
KRK
VEEEN
!

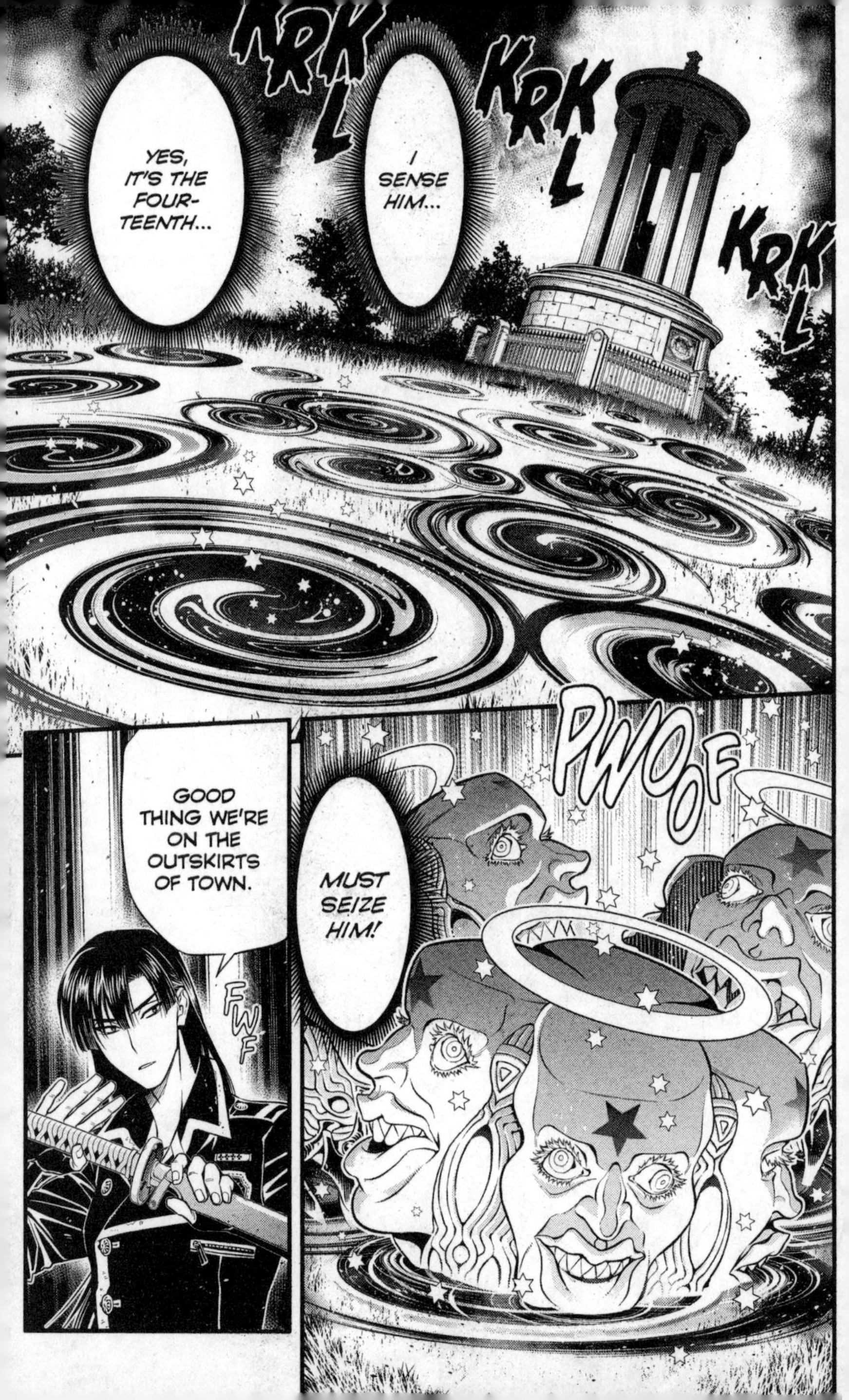
KRKL KRKL KRKL
I SENSE HIM...
YES, IT'S THE FOUR-TEENTH...
PWOOF
MUST SEIZE HIM!
GOOD THING WE'RE ON THE OUTSKIRTS OF TOWN.
FWF

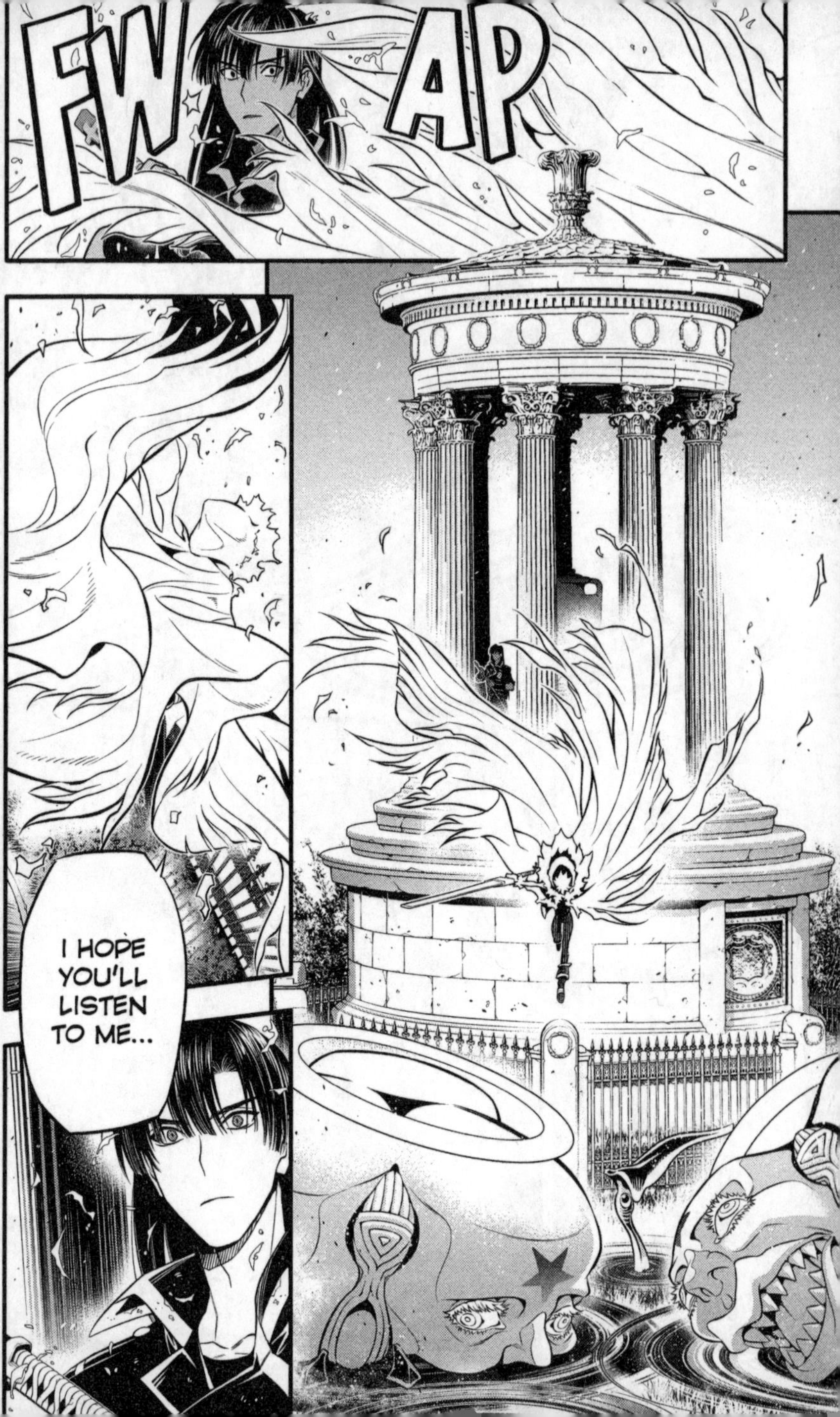
FWAP
I HOPE YOU'LL LISTEN TO ME...

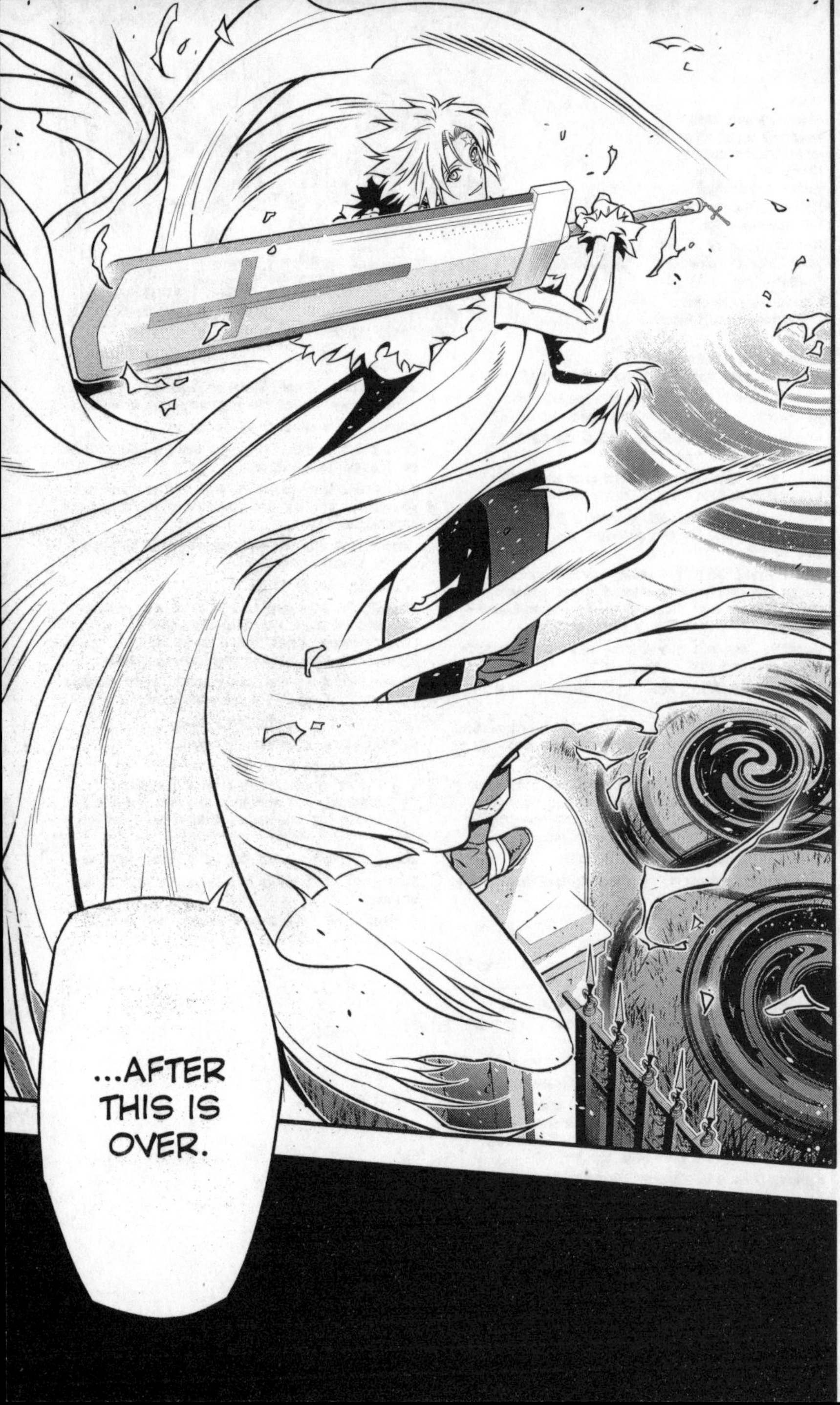
...AFTER THIS IS OVER.

»READ THIS WAY»

KOMUI'S DISCUSSION ROOM 1

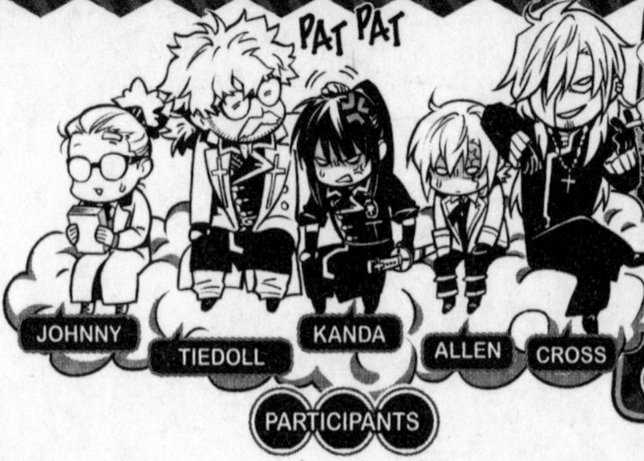
PAT PAT
JOHNNY
TIEDOLL
KANDA
ALLEN
CROSS
PARTICIPANTS

Tiedoll: Hello, and welcome to another session of Komui's Discussion Room without the chief himself. Thanks also for looking after Yu.

Kanda: Stop or I'll hit you. *(blood vessels bulging)*

Cross: Hey, is there any booze here? Fetch some, Allen.

Allen: Nope. There are kids who read this thing, so stay sober!

Cross: Hunh? What's with the 'tude? Who washed the sheets when you peed the bed?!

Allen: What're you talking about, master?! *(blushes beet red)*

Johnny: Looks like a masters and apprentices session this time. Heh... *(worried)*

Kanda: What's the deal, Johnny? There aren't many questions for the generals, so why're these two here?

Allen: Yeah! Don't we usually gather according to those the readers ask about? Most questions are about me and Kanda and Lenalee and Lavi. I thought I'd finally be here with Lenalee!

Johnny: Complain all you like, we have to go with the author's weird ideas.

Cross: Yeah, Allen! Aren't you happy to see me, your master?

Allen: I just didn't want to run into you here. And can't the author stop including people who may or may not be dead...?

Tiedoll: By the power of the ties that bind master and apprentice, let's not go over the word limit this time. We did last time and gave the graphic novel editor and designer a hard time.

Cross: You seem into this, Tiedoll.

Tiedoll: You appear to be too, Marian, despite the lack of booze.

Cross & Tiedoll: Wa ha ha!

Allen & Kanda: *(look miserable)*

Johnny: Hey! Let's get to the questions, okay?!

> **Q** Does Kanda know how good-looking he is? And how does he feel about being told he's handsome?

Cross: What? Who cares?! Next question!

Tiedoll: No, I won't let you table a question for Yu! What's the matter, Marian? Jealous that the first question is for my protégé? But why shouldn't it? Yu's cool and popular!

Kanda: Shut up... *(blood vessels bulging)*

Allen: So answer, Kanda. The sooner we're done with this the better.

Johnny: Is this boring you, Allen...?

Kanda: It's boring me! My looks don't matter!

Tiedoll: Hmm... I wish he wouldn't be so dismissive of his looks. If he'd learn to smile, think of the possibilities. Teach him how to smile, Walker!

Allen: I don't think that's possible.

Cross: Don't even try. If he smiled, you wouldn't be able to tell us apart.

Tiedoll: Hang on, Marian. How in the world are you similar to Yu? Are you saying you're equally handsome?

Cross: Not equally. I ***exceed*** him in all ways. Right, Allen?

Allen: No comment!

Tiedoll: You ***exceed*** him? You, a man whose reckless behavior keeps him in debt?! *(screeching)* I bet that's some kind of mysterious spell making you look so young!

Cross: Ha! An artist like you should appreciate my beauty, Tiedoll! You have no taste!

Johnny: C'mon, no fighting, okay?

Kanda: Let's move on, Johnny.

> **Q** I wear an eyepatch over one eye and basically live with just one eye. I'd like to hear what challenges that has presented.

Johnny: This would be for Lavi, who's not here.

Tiedoll: Oh, but we've got someone who could answer.

Cross: Huh? I'm not one-eyed. I can see.

232ND NIGHT: SAYING FAREWELL TO A.W.: REDARM

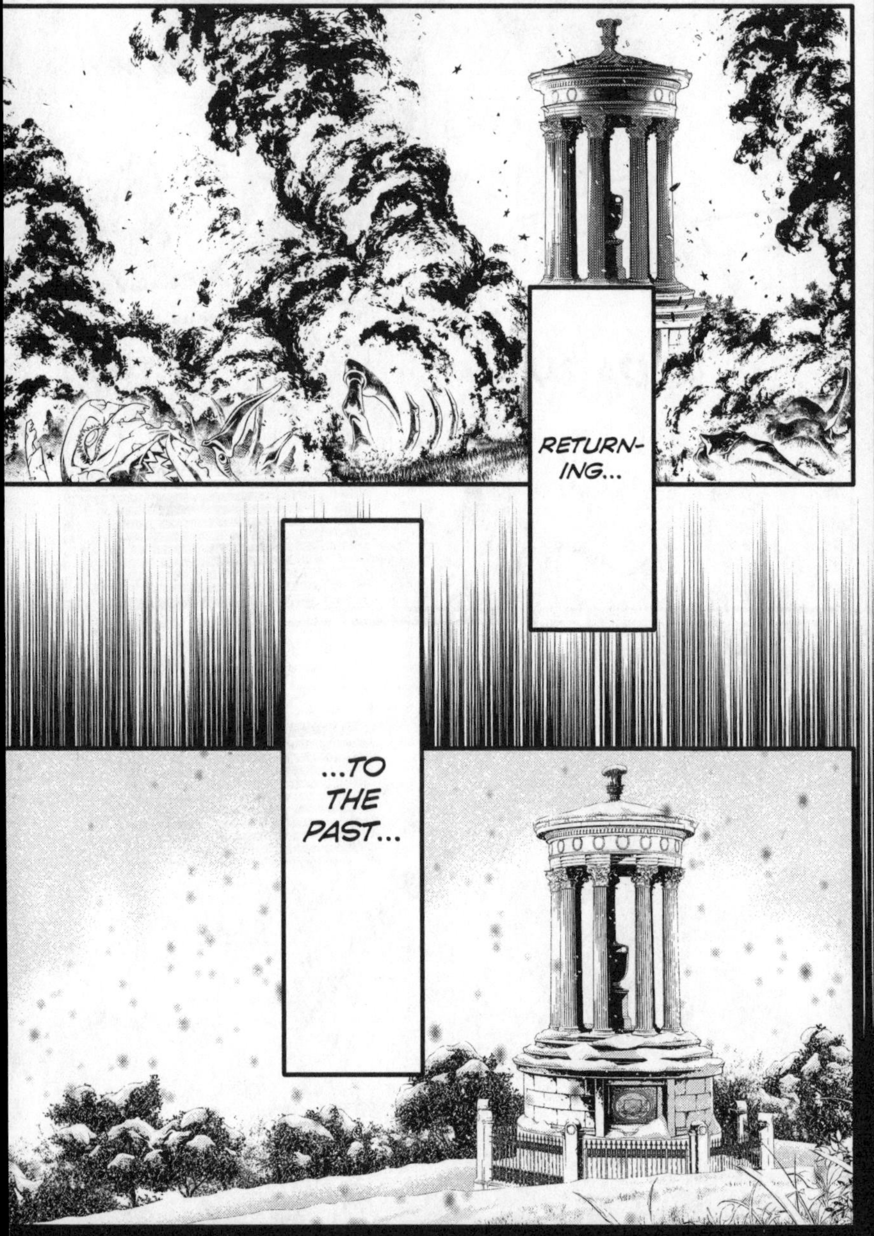
RETURN-ING...
...TO THE PAST...

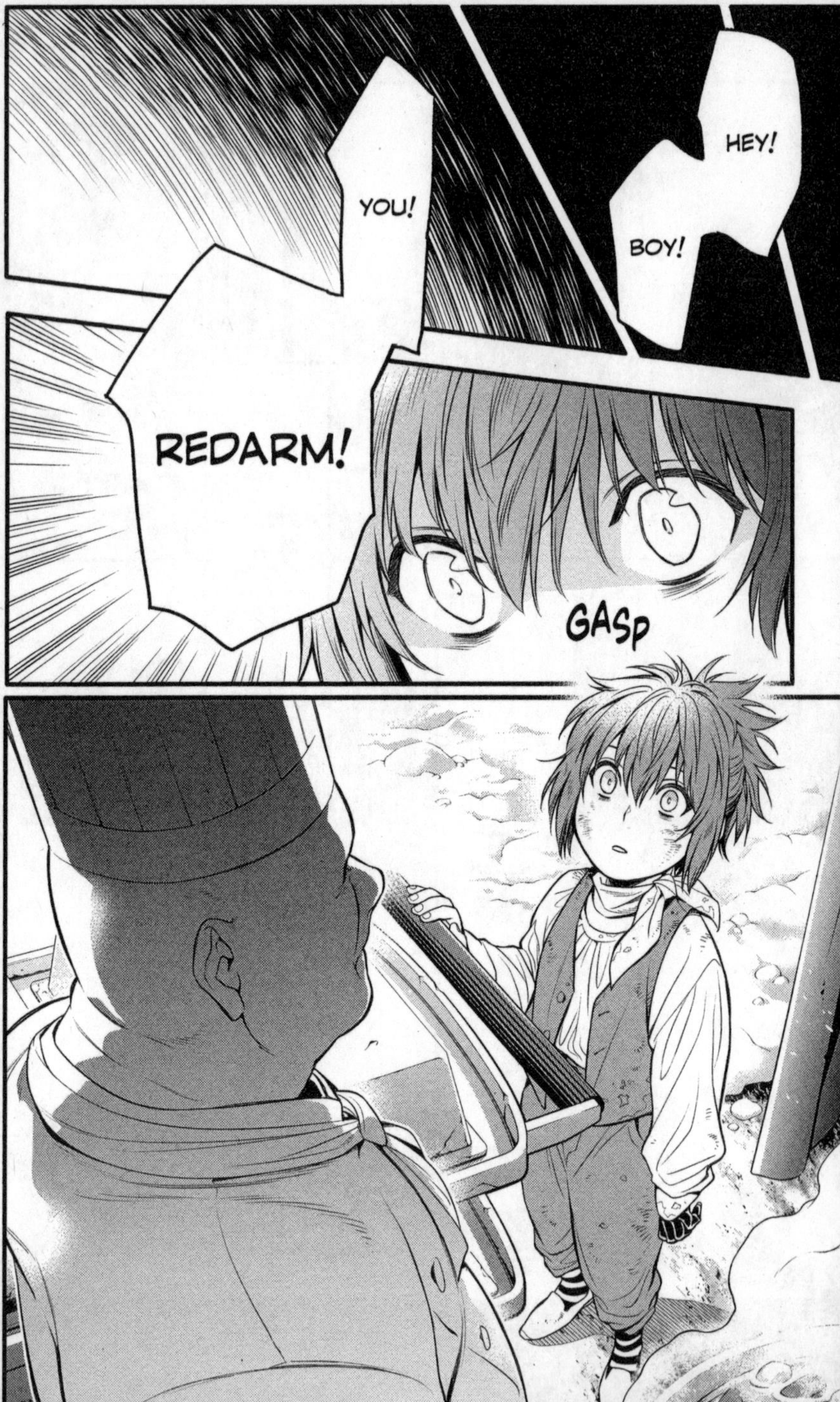
HEY!
BOY!
YOU!
REDARM!
GASP

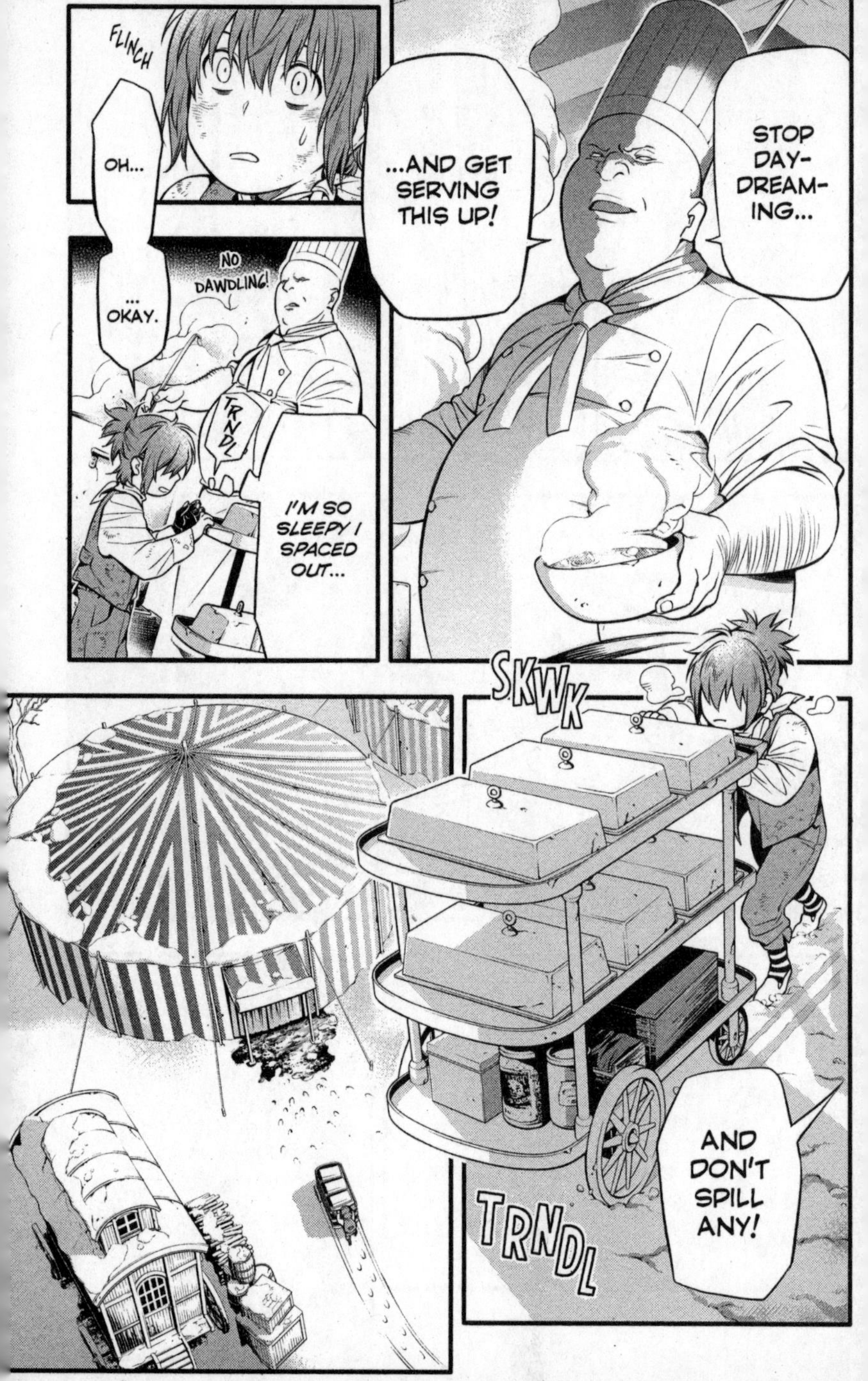
STOP DAY-DREAMING...
...AND GET SERVING THIS UP!
FLINCH
OH...
NO DAWDLING!
... OKAY.
TRNDL
I'M SO SLEEPY I SPACED OUT...
SKWK
AND DON'T SPILL ANY!
TRNDL

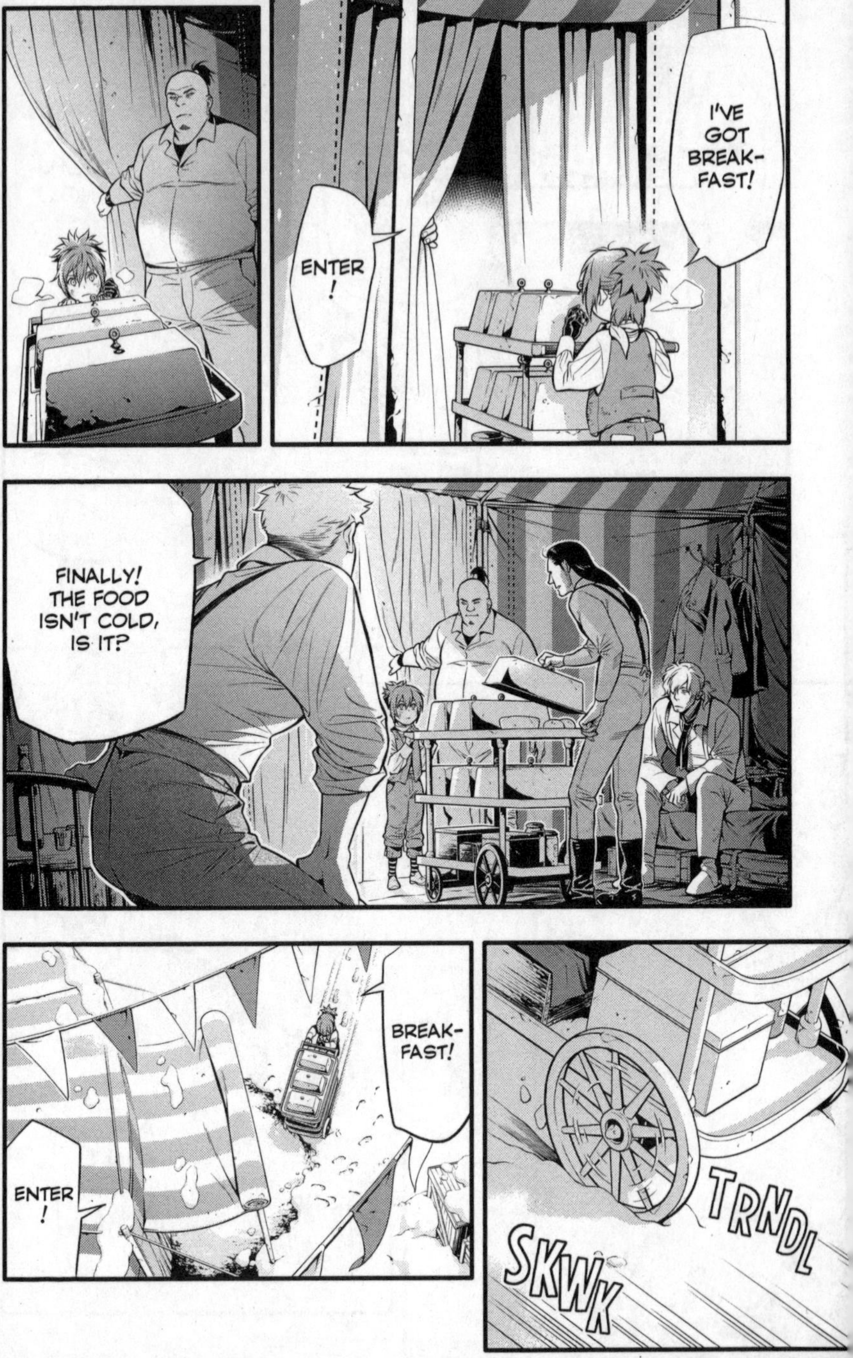
I'VE GOT BREAK-FAST!
ENTER!
FINALLY! THE FOOD ISN'T COLD, IS IT?
TRNDL
SKWK
BREAK-FAST!
ENTER!

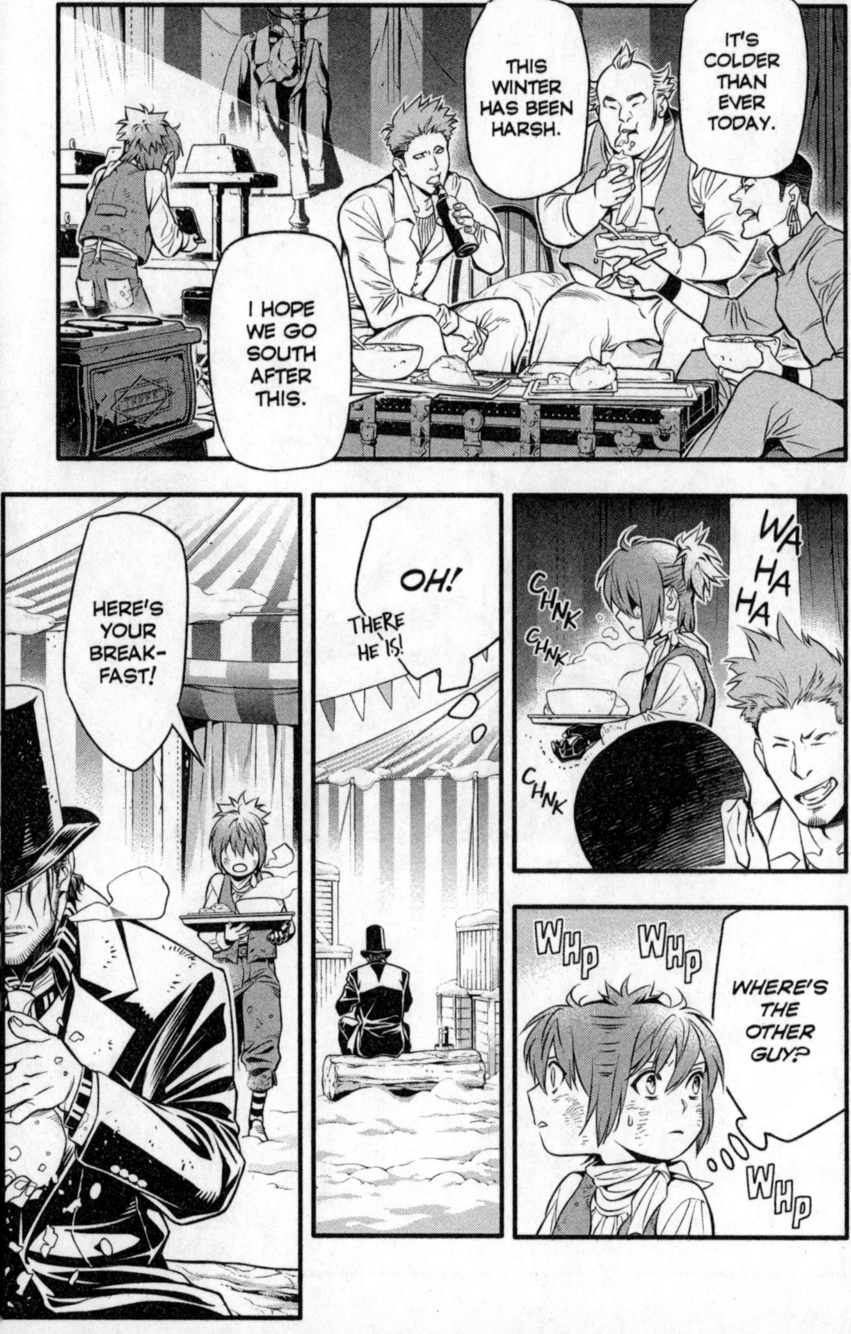
IT'S COLDER THAN EVER TODAY.
THIS WINTER HAS BEEN HARSH.
I HOPE WE GO SOUTH AFTER THIS.
WA HA HA HA
CHNK CHNK
CHNK
WHP WHP
WHERE'S THE OTHER GUY?
WHP
OH!
THERE HE IS!
HERE'S YOUR BREAK-FAST!

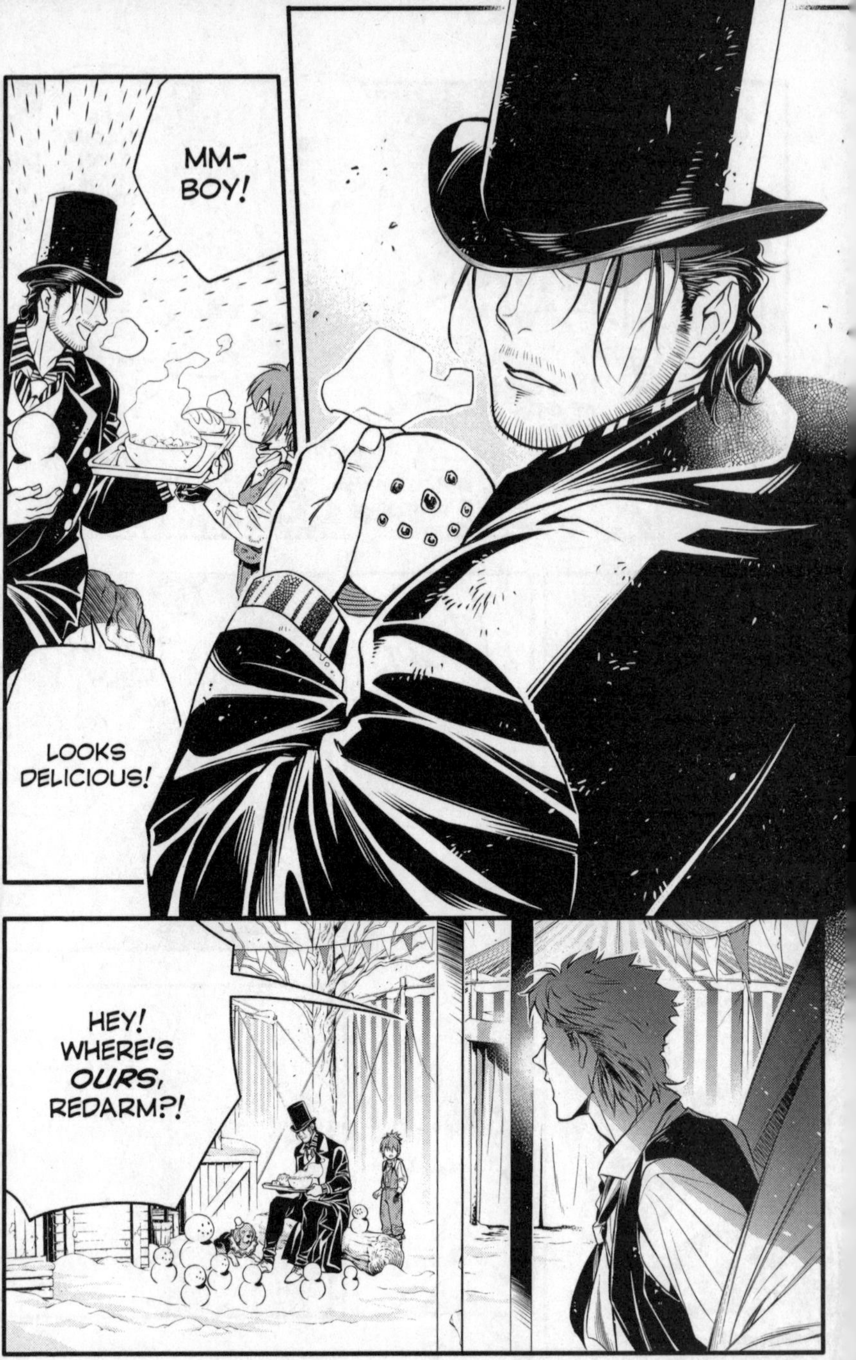
MM-
BOY!
LOOKS DELICIOUS!
HEY! WHERE'S OURS, REDARM?!

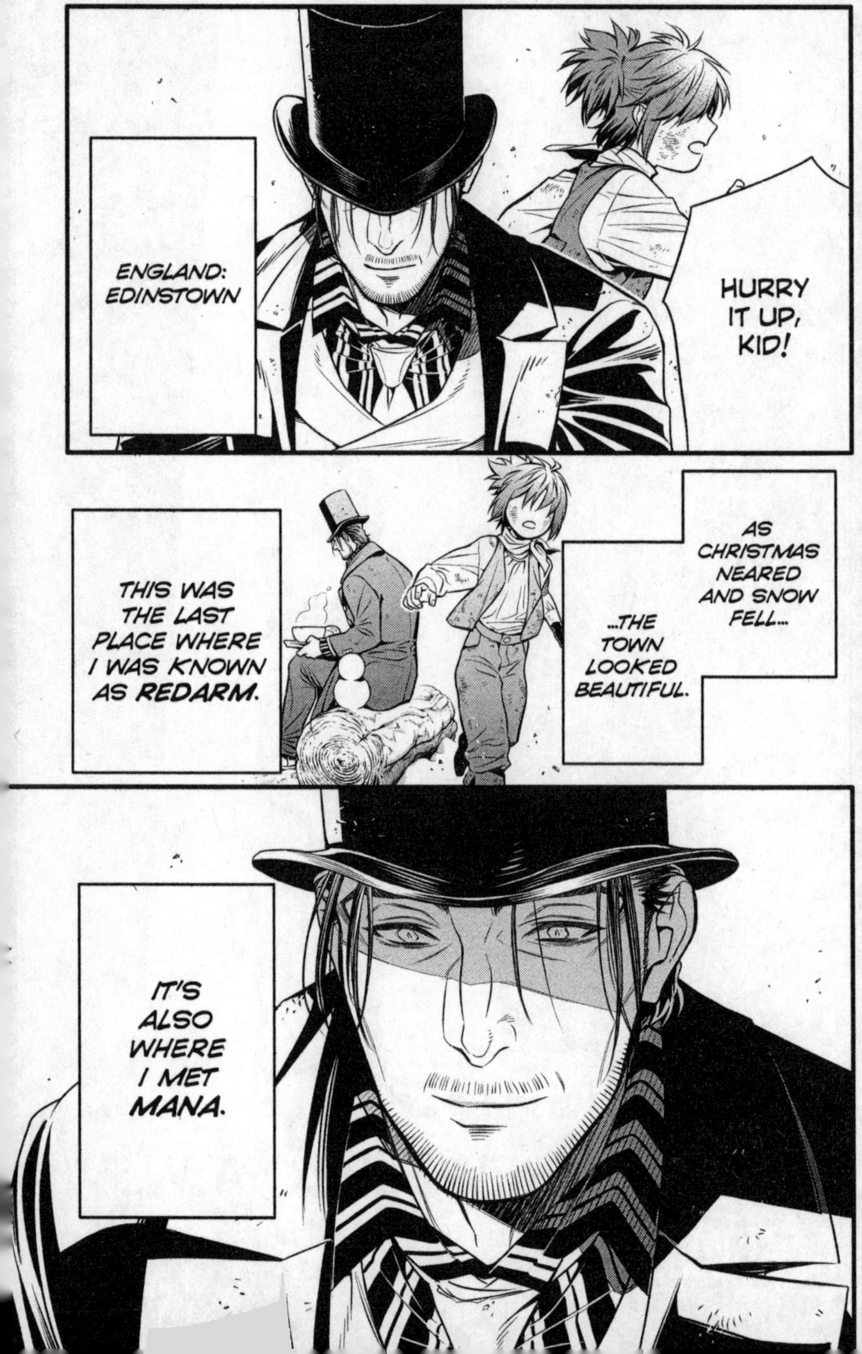
HURRY IT UP, KID!
ENGLAND: EDINSTOWN
AS CHRISTMAS NEARED AND SNOW FELL...
...THE TOWN LOOKED BEAUTIFUL.
THIS WAS THE LAST PLACE WHERE I WAS KNOWN AS REDARM.
IT'S ALSO WHERE I MET MANA.

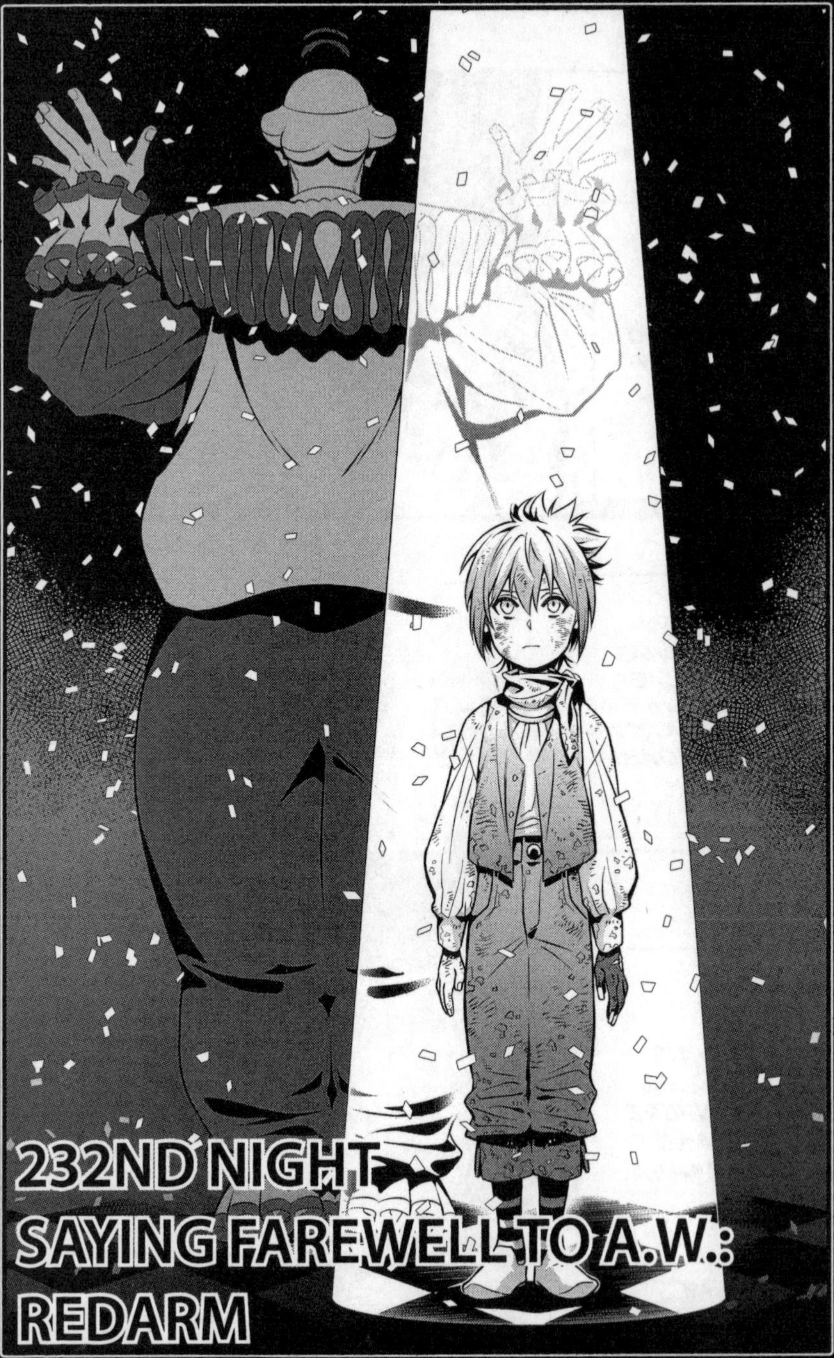
232ND NIGHT
SAYING FAREWELL TO A.W.:
REDARM

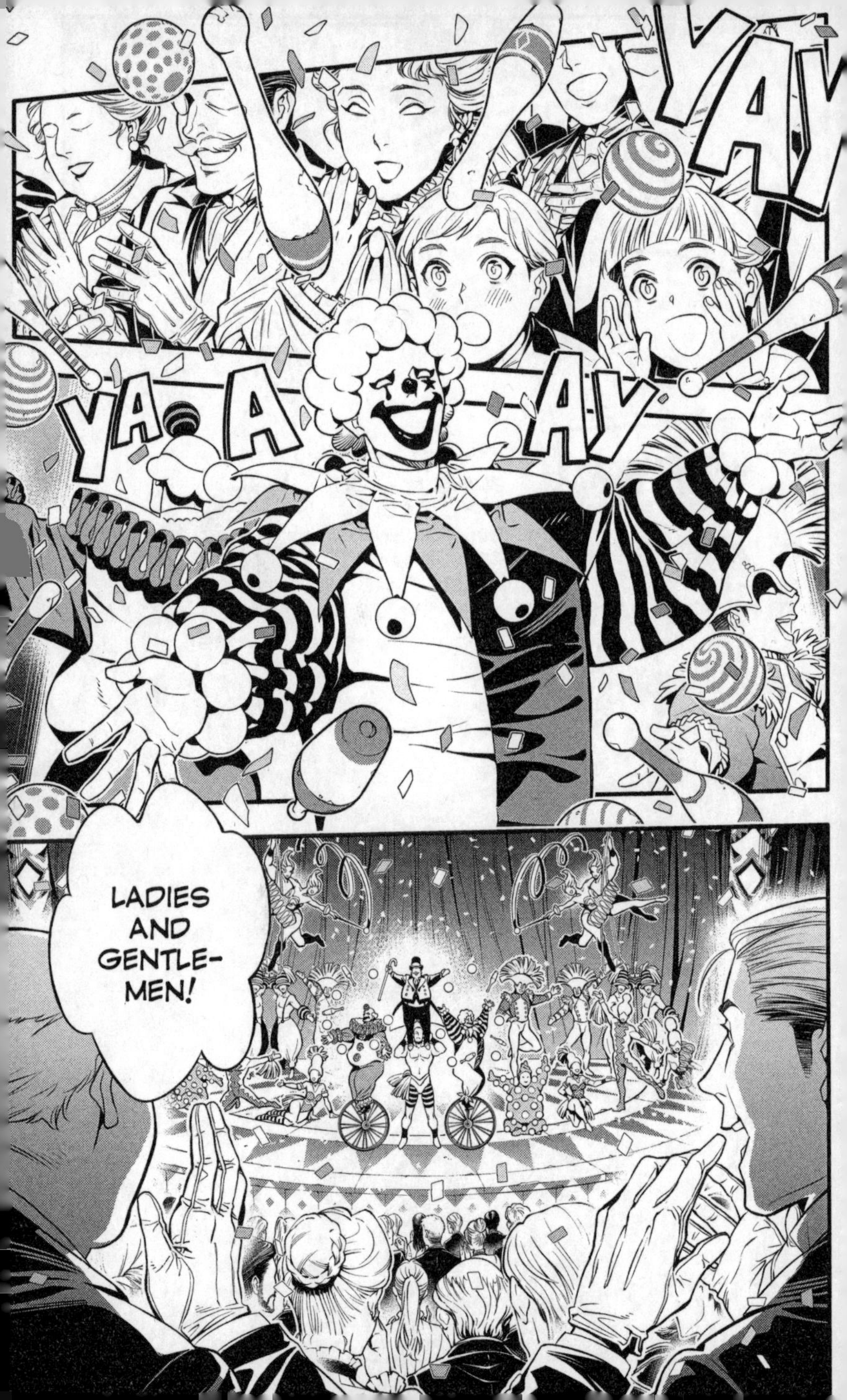
YAY
YA-A-AY
LADIES AND GENTLE-MEN!

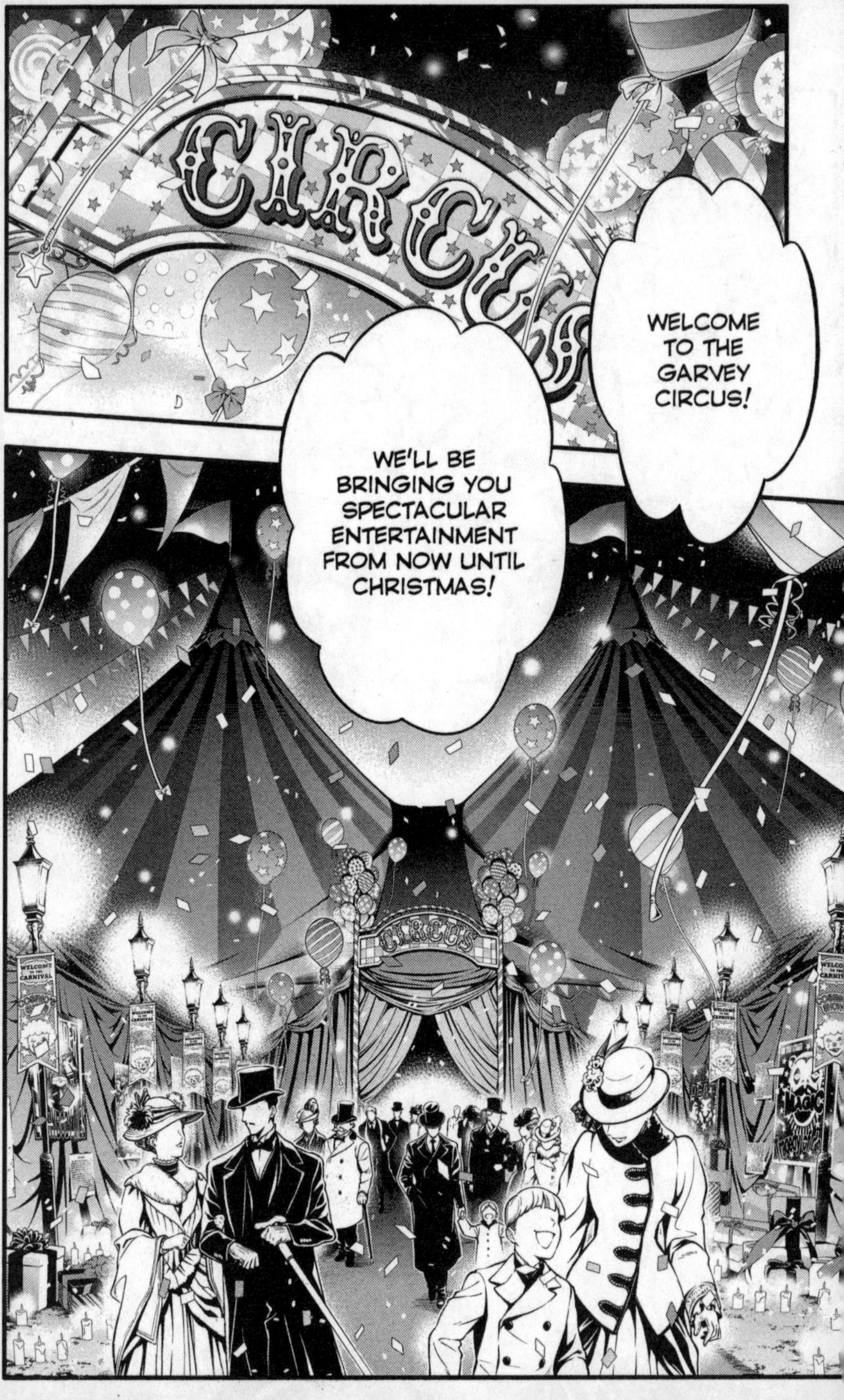
CIRCUS
WELCOME TO THE GARVEY CIRCUS!
WE'LL BE BRINGING YOU SPECTACULAR ENTERTAINMENT FROM NOW UNTIL CHRISTMAS!
CIRCUS
WELCOME TO THE CARNIVAL
MAGIC

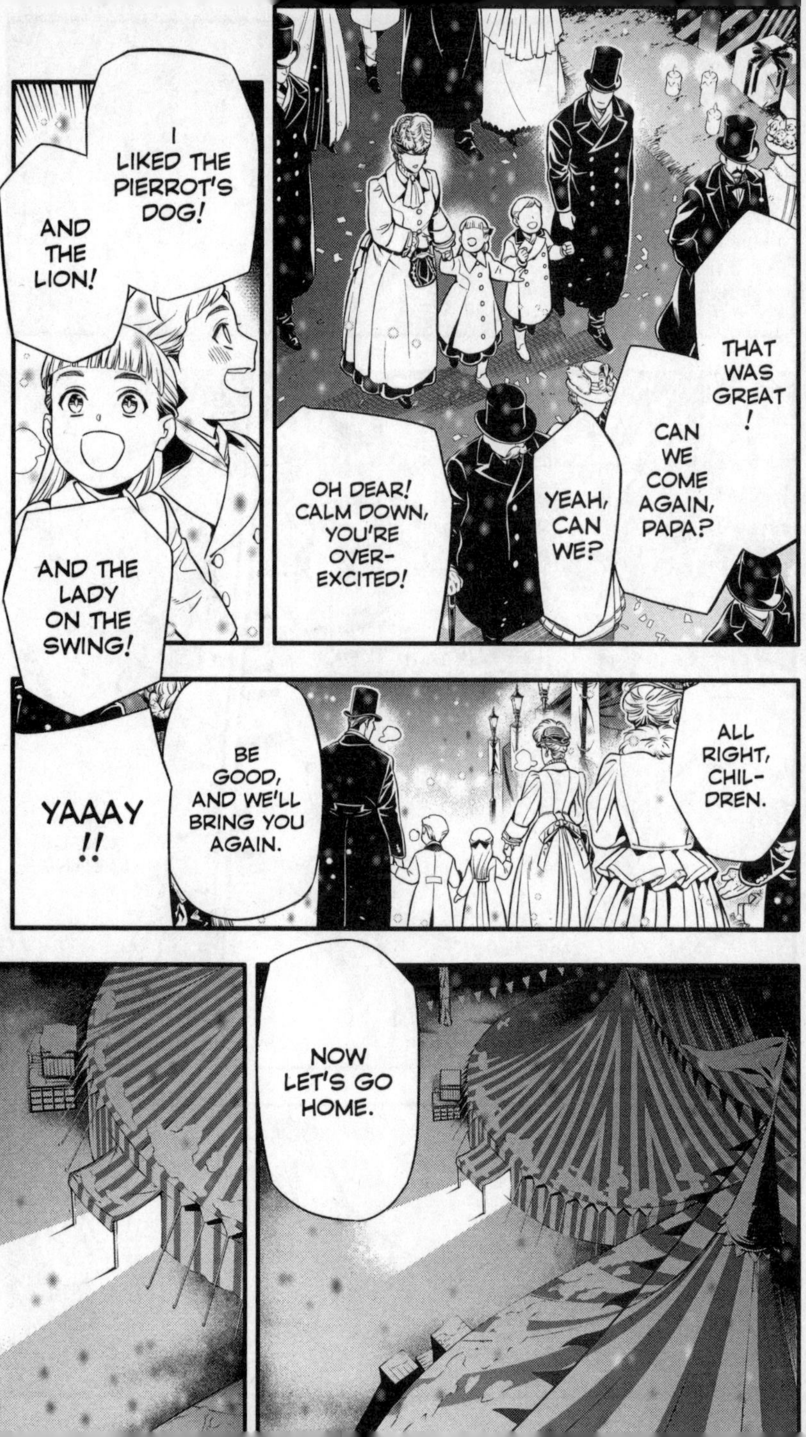
THAT WAS GREAT!
CAN WE COME AGAIN, PAPA?
YEAH, CAN WE?
OH DEAR! CALM DOWN, YOU'RE OVER-EXCITED!
I LIKED THE PIERROT'S DOG!
AND THE LION!
AND THE LADY ON THE SWING!
ALL RIGHT, CHIL-DREN.
BE GOOD, AND WE'LL BRING YOU AGAIN.
YAAAY!!
NOW LET'S GO HOME.

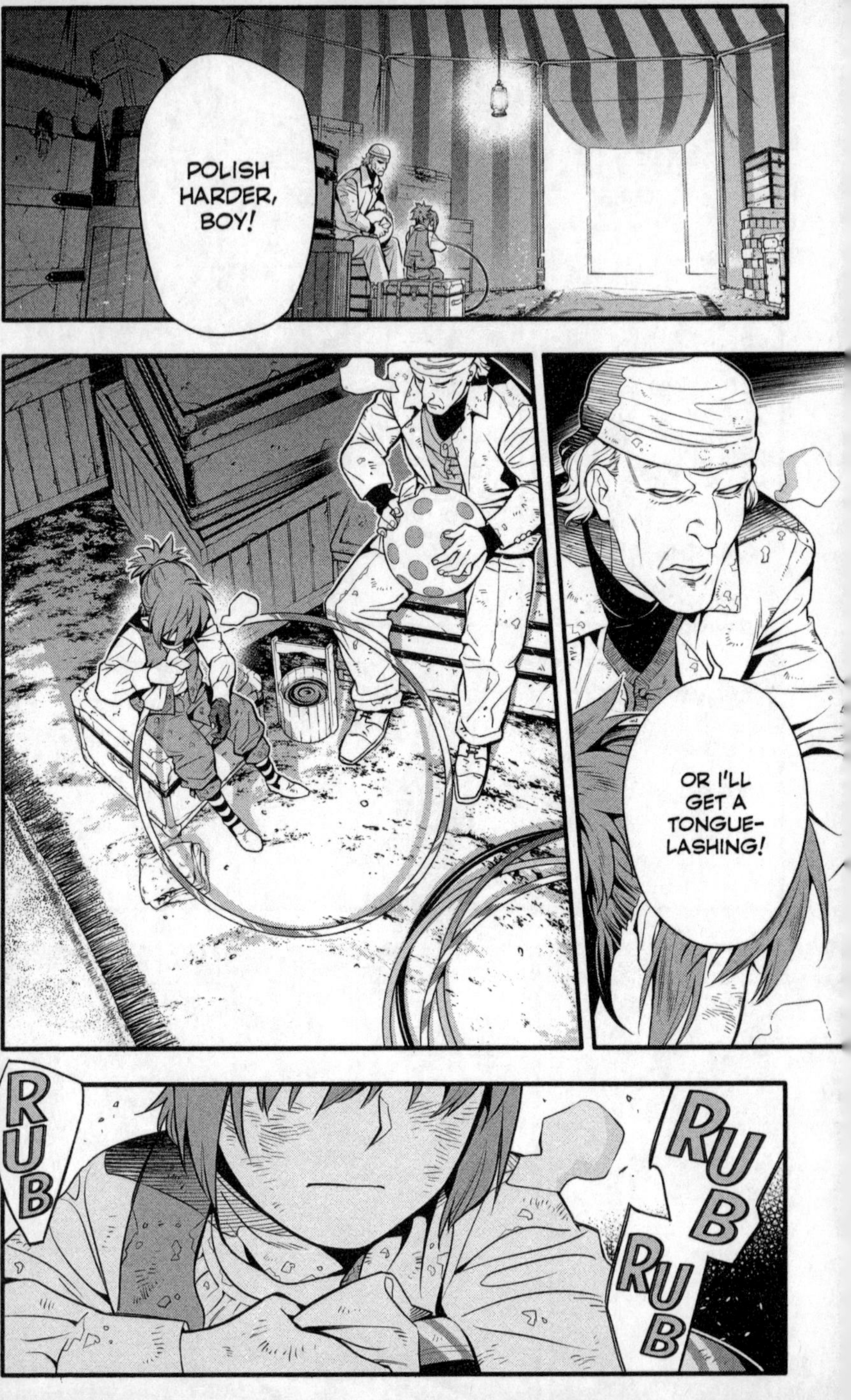
POLISH HARDER, BOY!
OR I'LL GET A TONGUE-LASHING!
RUB RUB
RUB
RUB

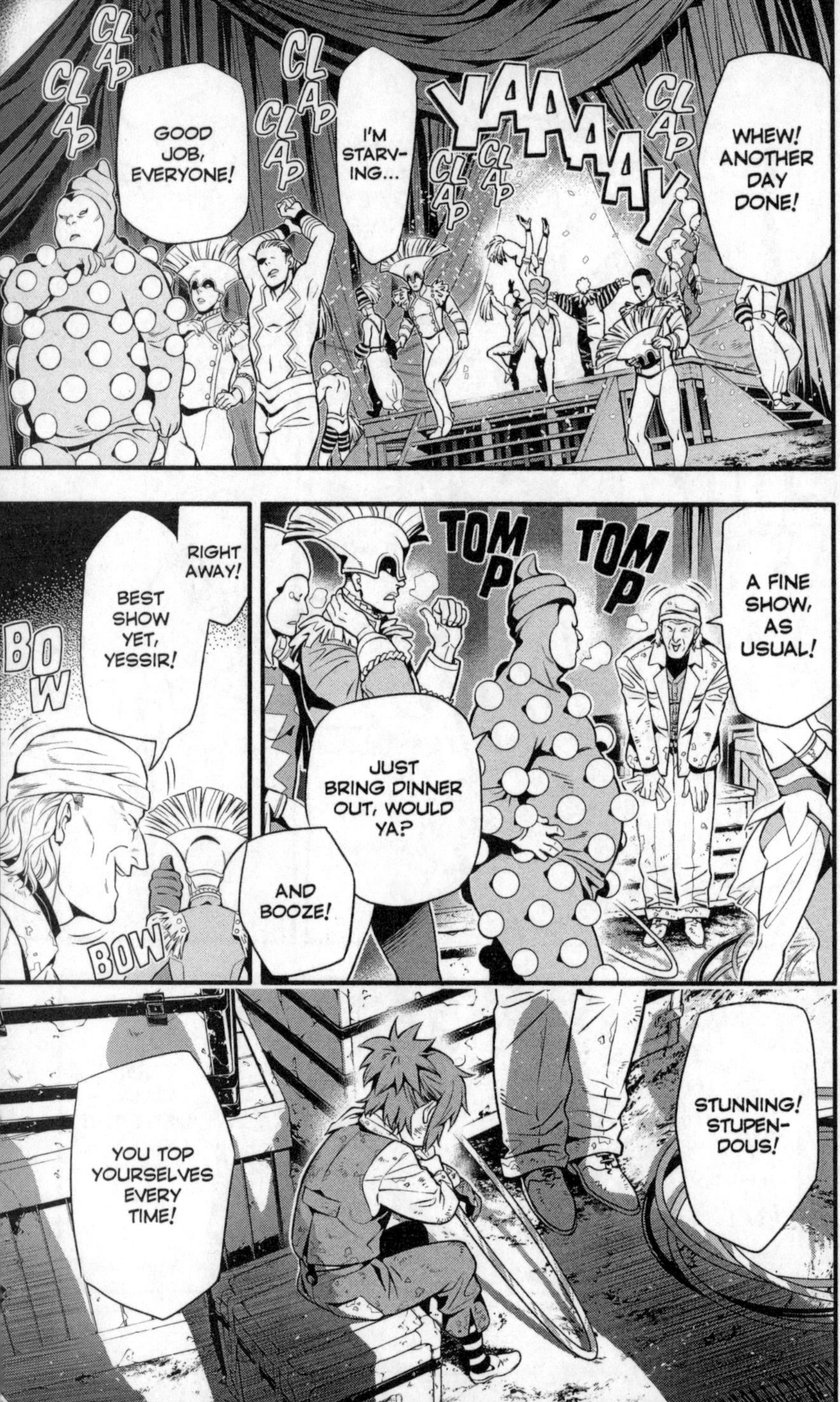
WHEW! ANOTHER DAY DONE!
CLAP CLAP
YAAAAAY
CLAP CLAP
I'M STARVING...
CLAP CLAP
GOOD JOB, EVERYONE!
CLAP CLAP
A FINE SHOW, AS USUAL!
TOMP TOMP
JUST BRING DINNER OUT, WOULD YA?
AND BOOZE!
RIGHT AWAY!
BEST SHOW YET, YESSIR!
BOW
BOW
STUNNING! STUPENDOUS!
YOU TOP YOURSELVES EVERY TIME!

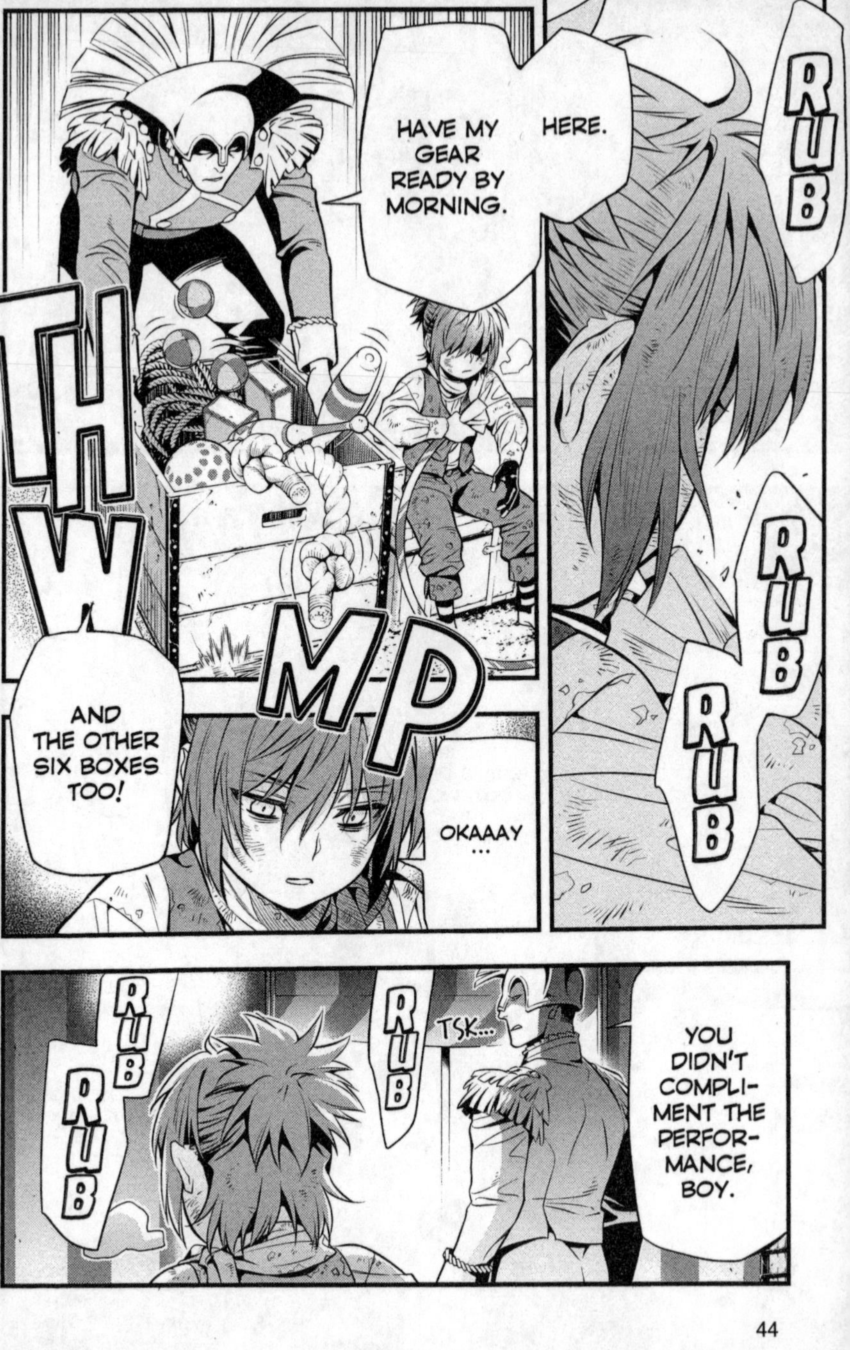

RUB
RUB
RUB
HERE.
HAVE MY GEAR READY BY MORNING.
THWMP
AND THE OTHER SIX BOXES TOO!
OKAAAY ...
YOU DIDN'T COMPLI-MENT THE PERFOR-MANCE, BOY.
TSK...
RUB
RUB
RUB

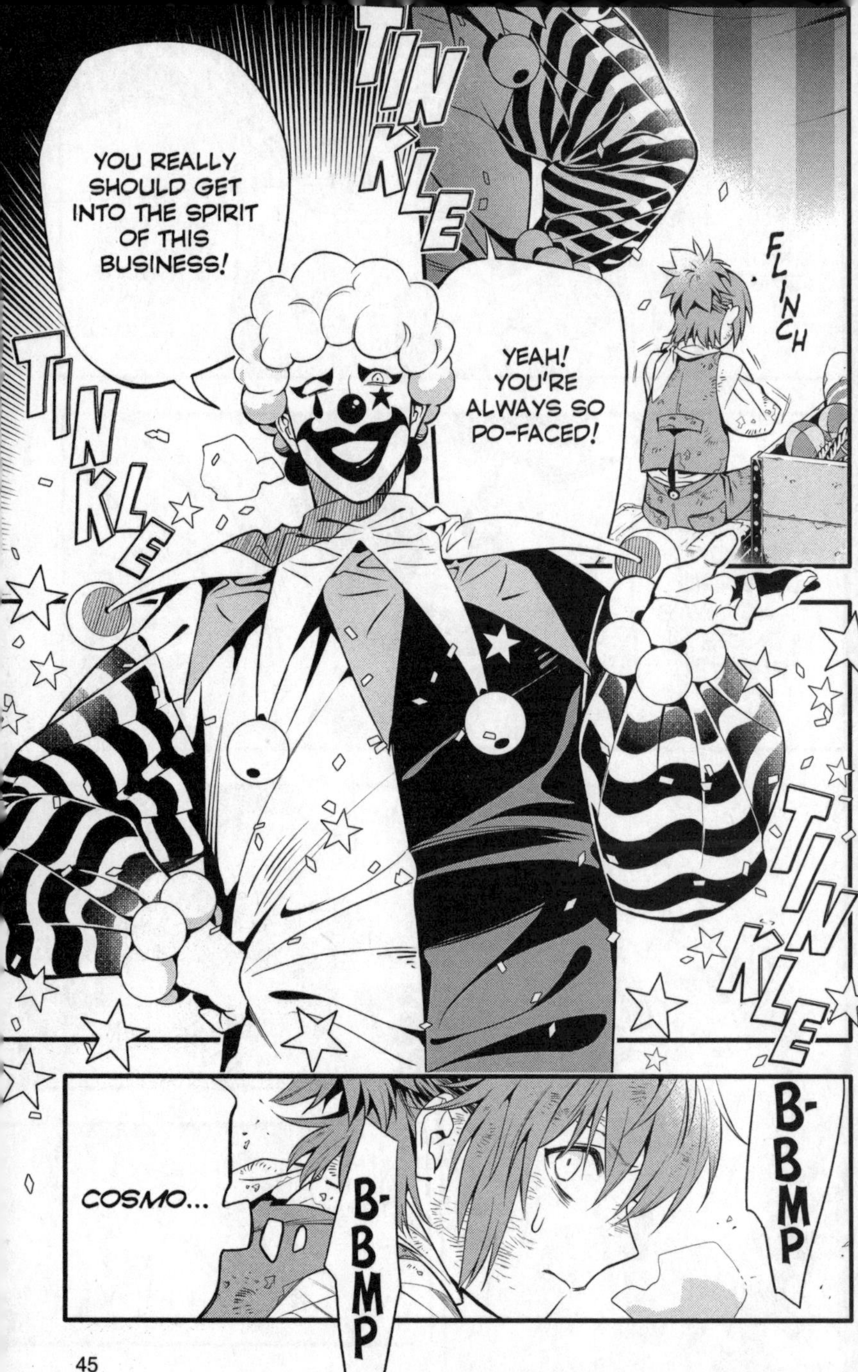
FLINCH
YEAH! YOU'RE ALWAYS SO PO-FACED!
TINKLE
YOU REALLY SHOULD GET INTO THE SPIRIT OF THIS BUSINESS!
TINKLE
TINKLE
B-BBMP
B-BBMP
COSMO...

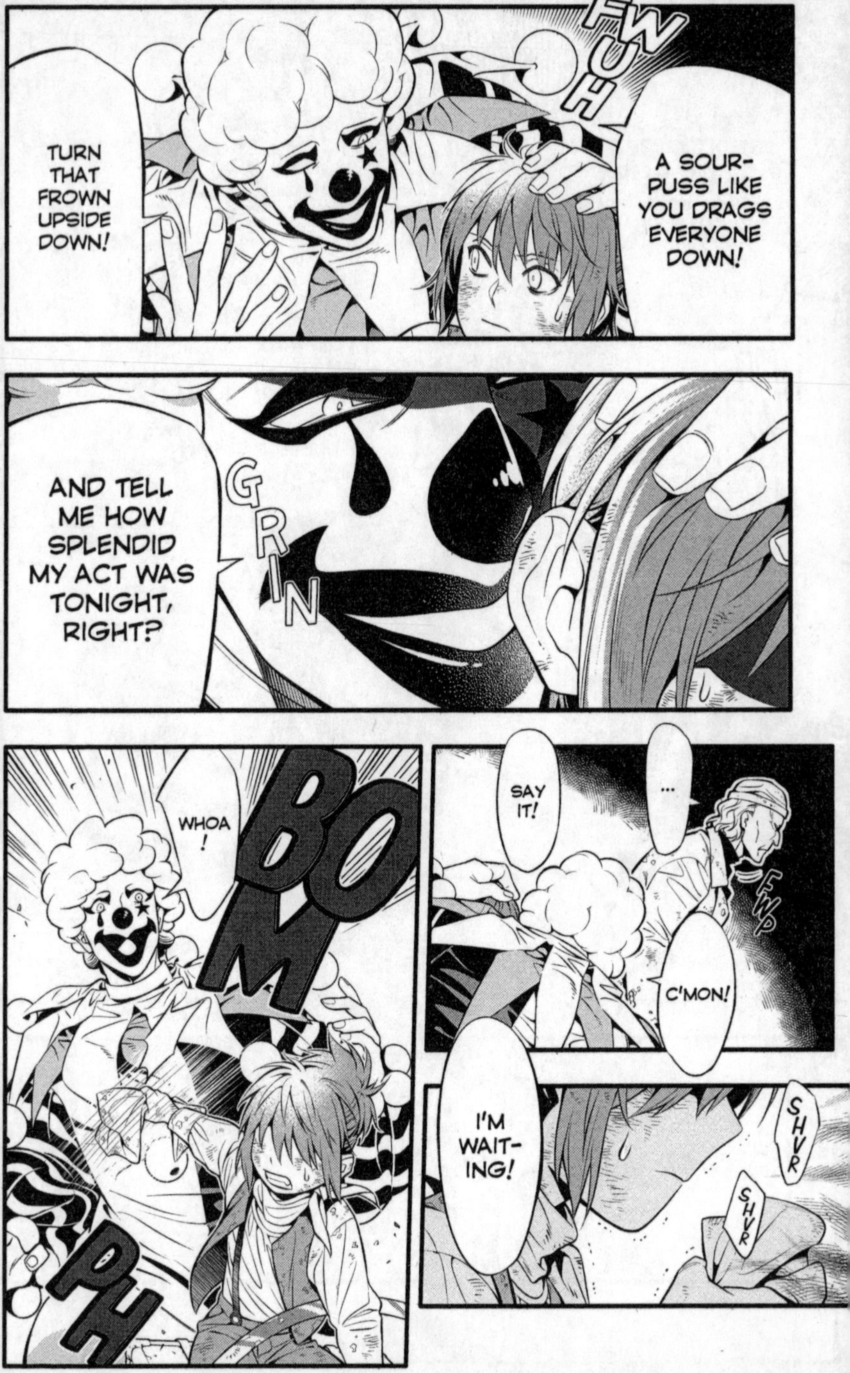
FWUH
A SOUR-PUSS LIKE YOU DRAGS EVERYONE DOWN!
TURN THAT FROWN UPSIDE DOWN!
AND TELL ME HOW SPLENDID MY ACT WAS TONIGHT, RIGHT?
GRIN
...
SAY IT!
FWP
C'MON!
I'M WAIT-ING!
SHVR
SHVR
WHOA!
BOMM
PH

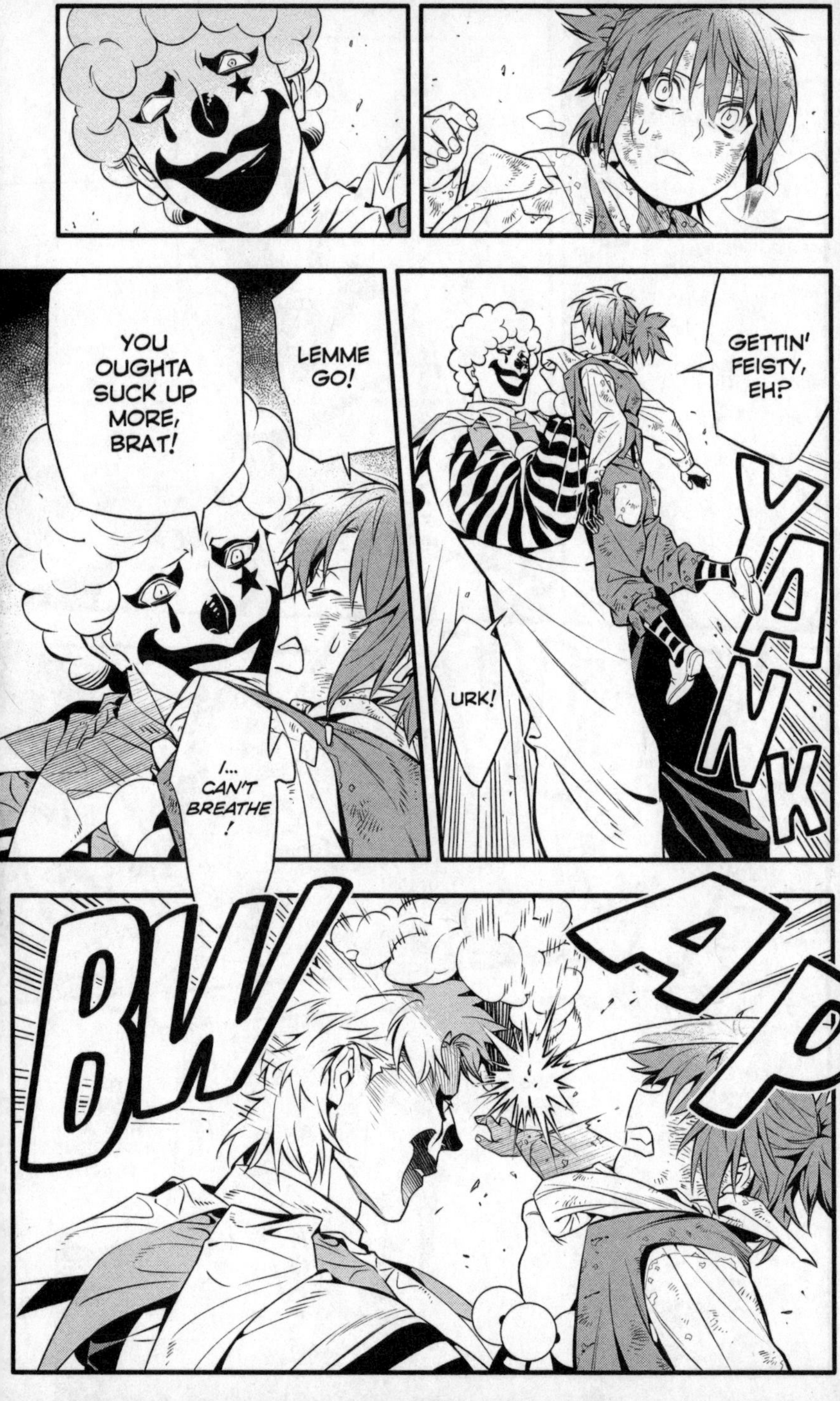
GETTIN' FEISTY, EH?
YANK
URK!
YOU OUGHTA SUCK UP MORE, BRAT!
LEMME GO!
I... CAN'T BREATHE!
BWAP

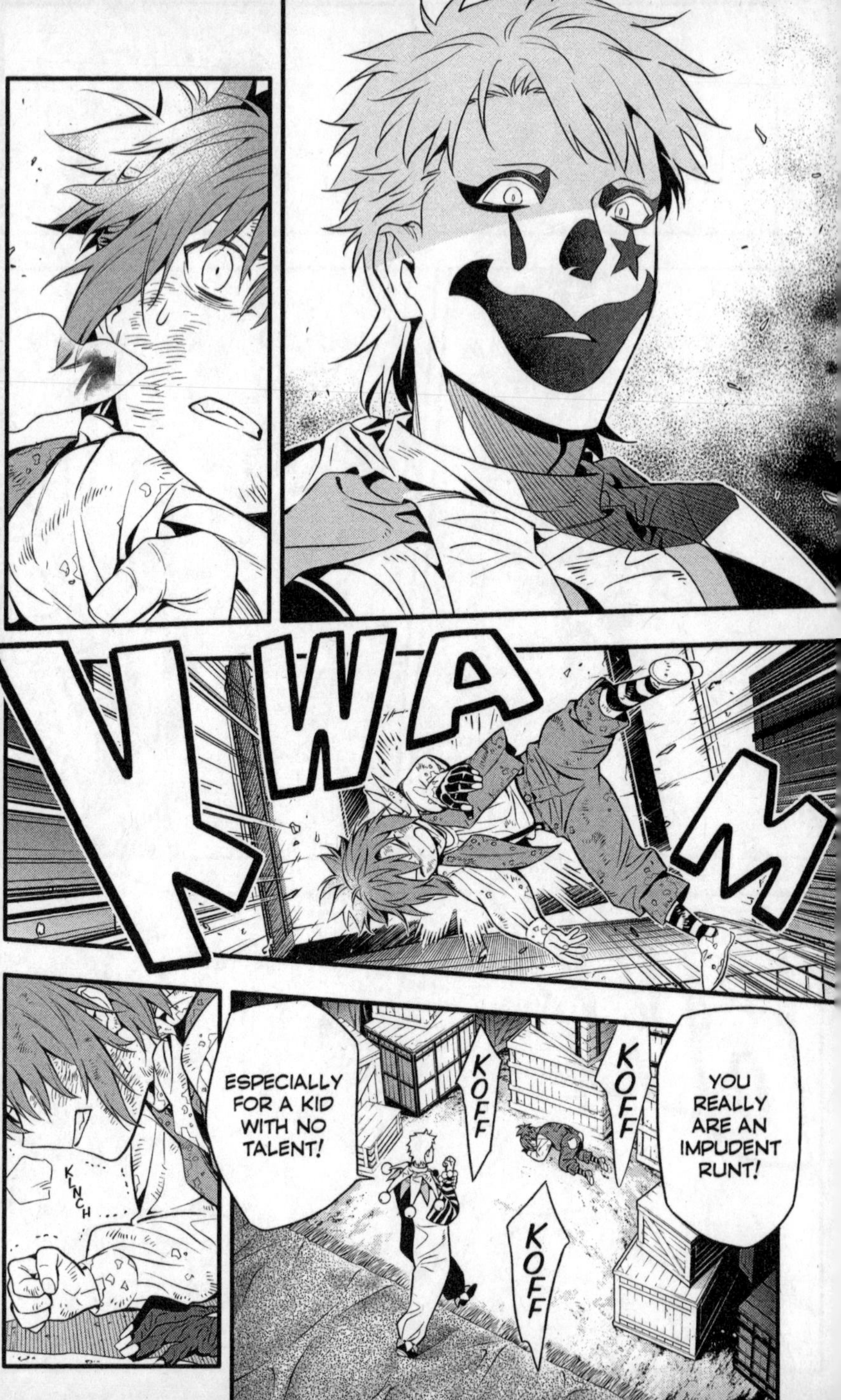
WHAM
YOU REALLY ARE AN IMPUDENT RUNT!
KOFF KOFF
KOFF KOFF
ESPECIALLY FOR A KID WITH NO TALENT!
KLNCH

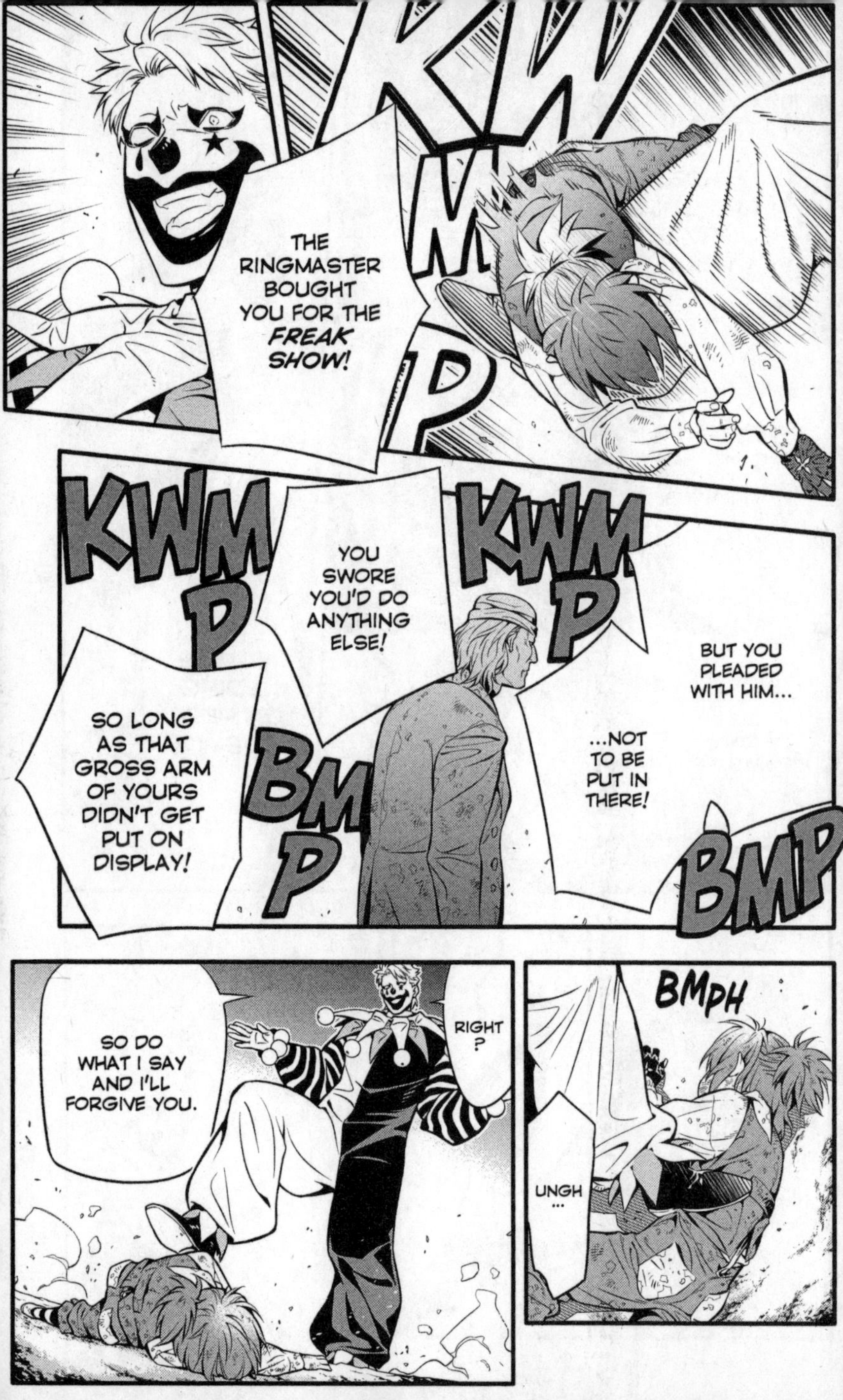
KWM
THE RINGMASTER BOUGHT YOU FOR THE *FREAK SHOW!*
KWMP
BUT YOU PLEADED WITH HIM...
...NOT TO BE PUT IN THERE!
BMP
YOU SWORE YOU'D DO ANYTHING ELSE!
KWMP
BMP
SO LONG AS THAT GROSS ARM OF YOURS DIDN'T GET PUT ON DISPLAY!
BMPH
UNGH...
RIGHT?
SO DO WHAT I SAY AND I'LL FORGIVE YOU.

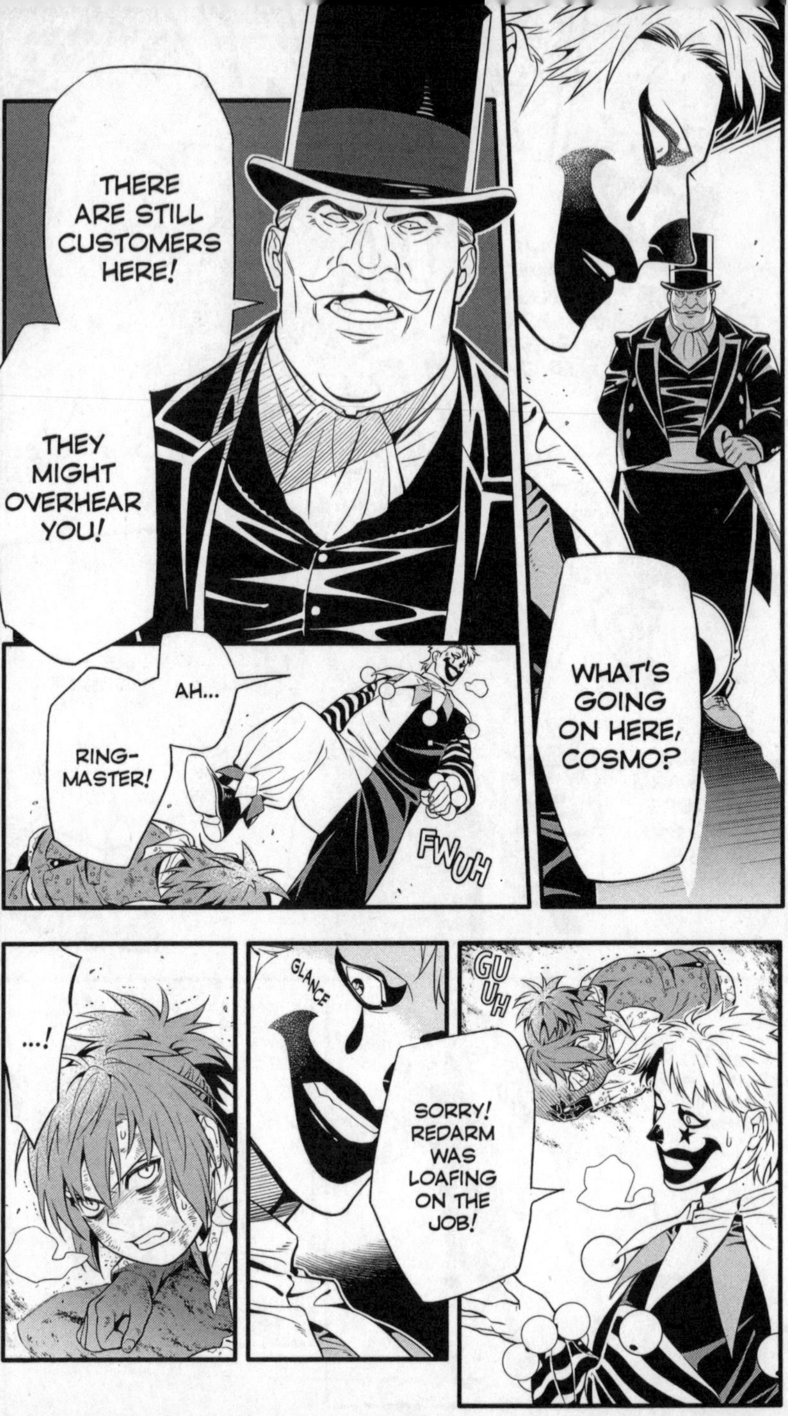
WHAT'S GOING ON HERE, COSMO?
THERE ARE STILL CUSTOMERS HERE!
THEY MIGHT OVERHEAR YOU!
AH... RING-MASTER!
FWUH
GU UH
SORRY! REDARM WAS LOAFING ON THE JOB!
GLANCE
...!

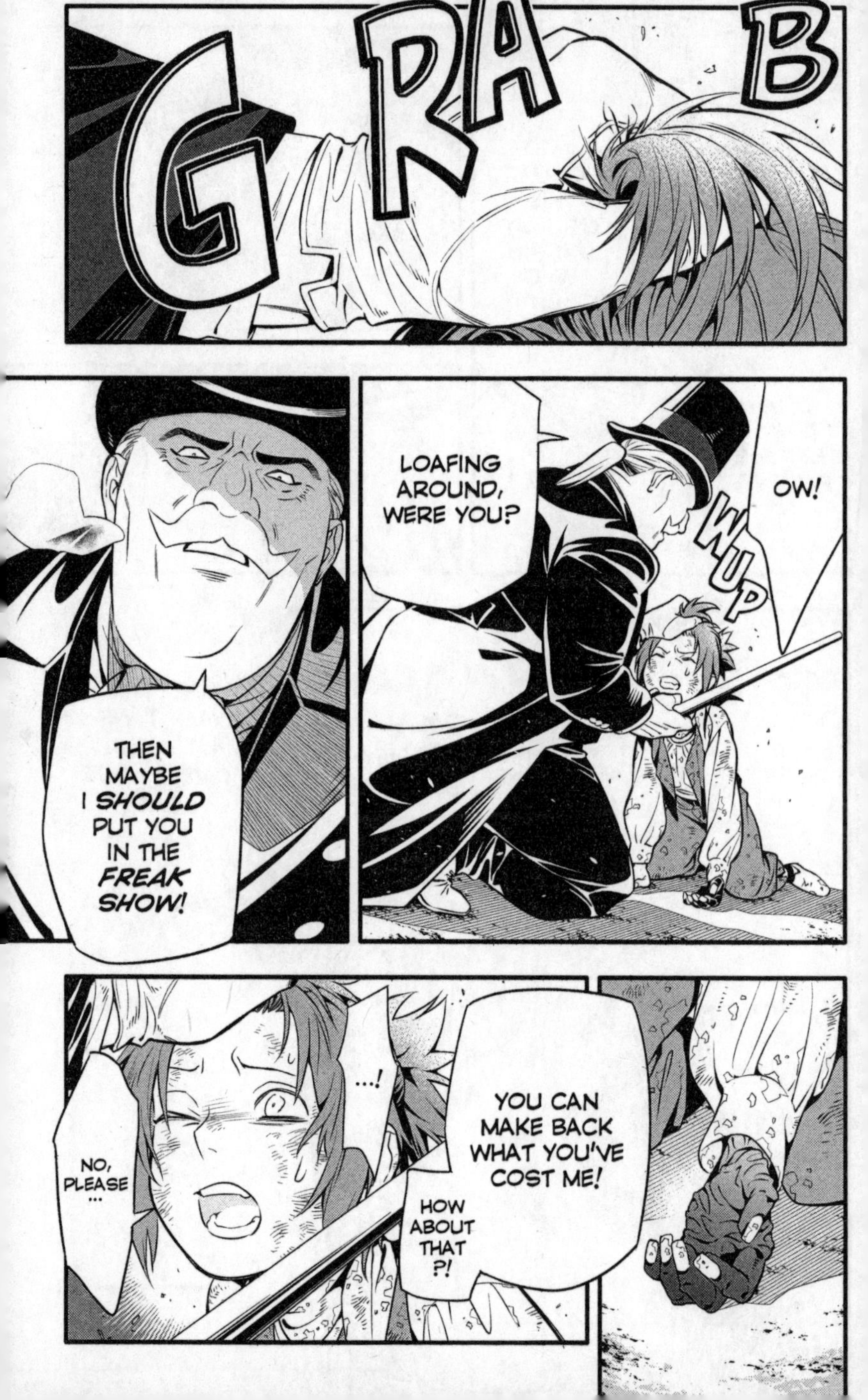
GRAB
LOAFING AROUND, WERE YOU?
OW!
WUP
THEN MAYBE I *SHOULD* PUT YOU IN THE *FREAK SHOW!*
YOU CAN MAKE BACK WHAT YOU'VE COST ME!
...!
HOW ABOUT THAT ?!
NO, PLEASE ...

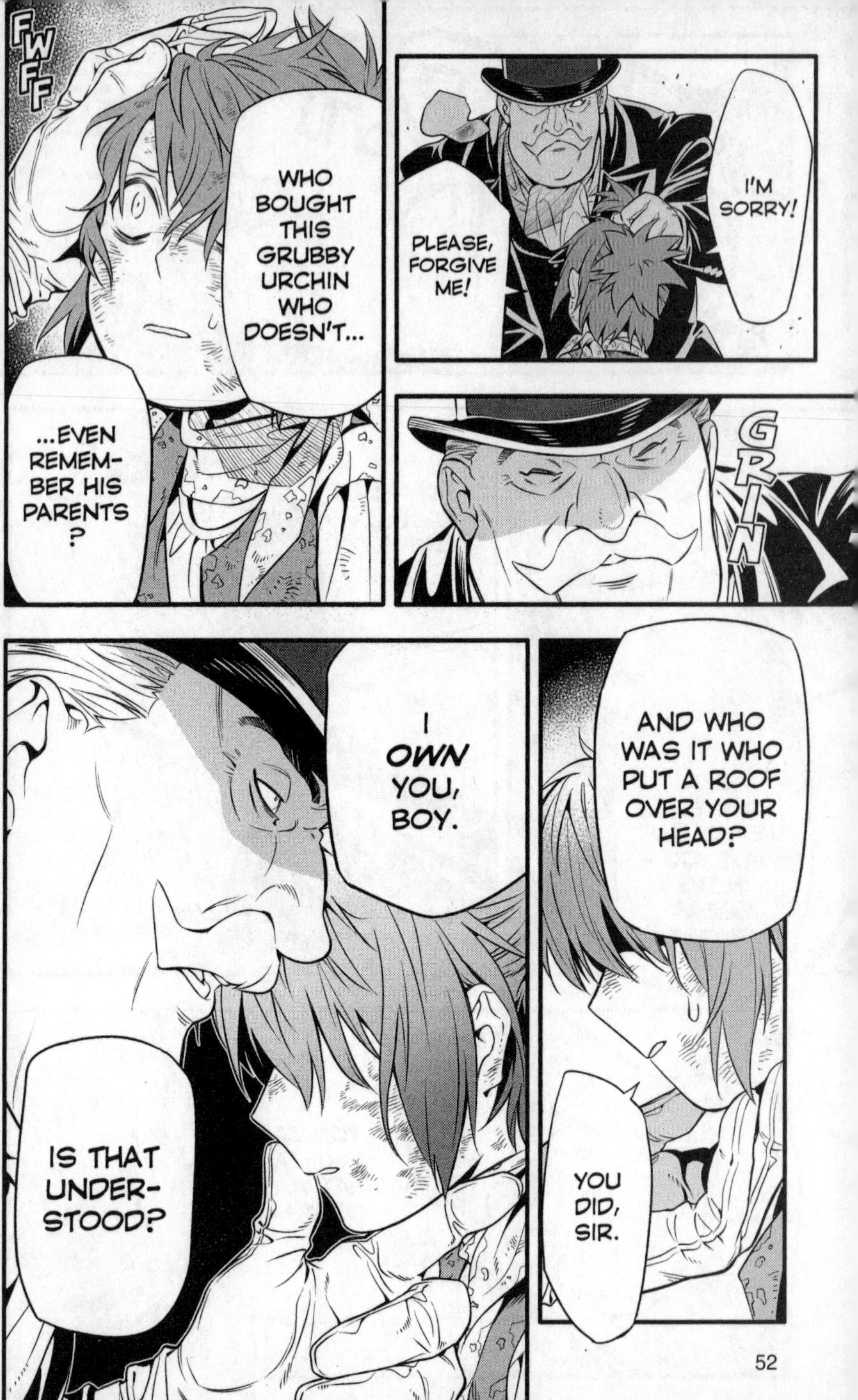
I'M SORRY!
PLEASE, FORGIVE ME!
WHO BOUGHT THIS GRUBBY URCHIN WHO DOESN'T...
FWFF
GRIN
...EVEN REMEMBER HIS PARENTS?
AND WHO WAS IT WHO PUT A ROOF OVER YOUR HEAD?
YOU DID, SIR.
I OWN YOU, BOY.
IS THAT UNDERSTOOD?

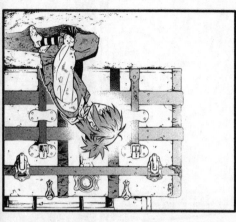

NEXT TIME, I WON'T LEAVE IT AT A FEW WORDS.

BRR

FWS

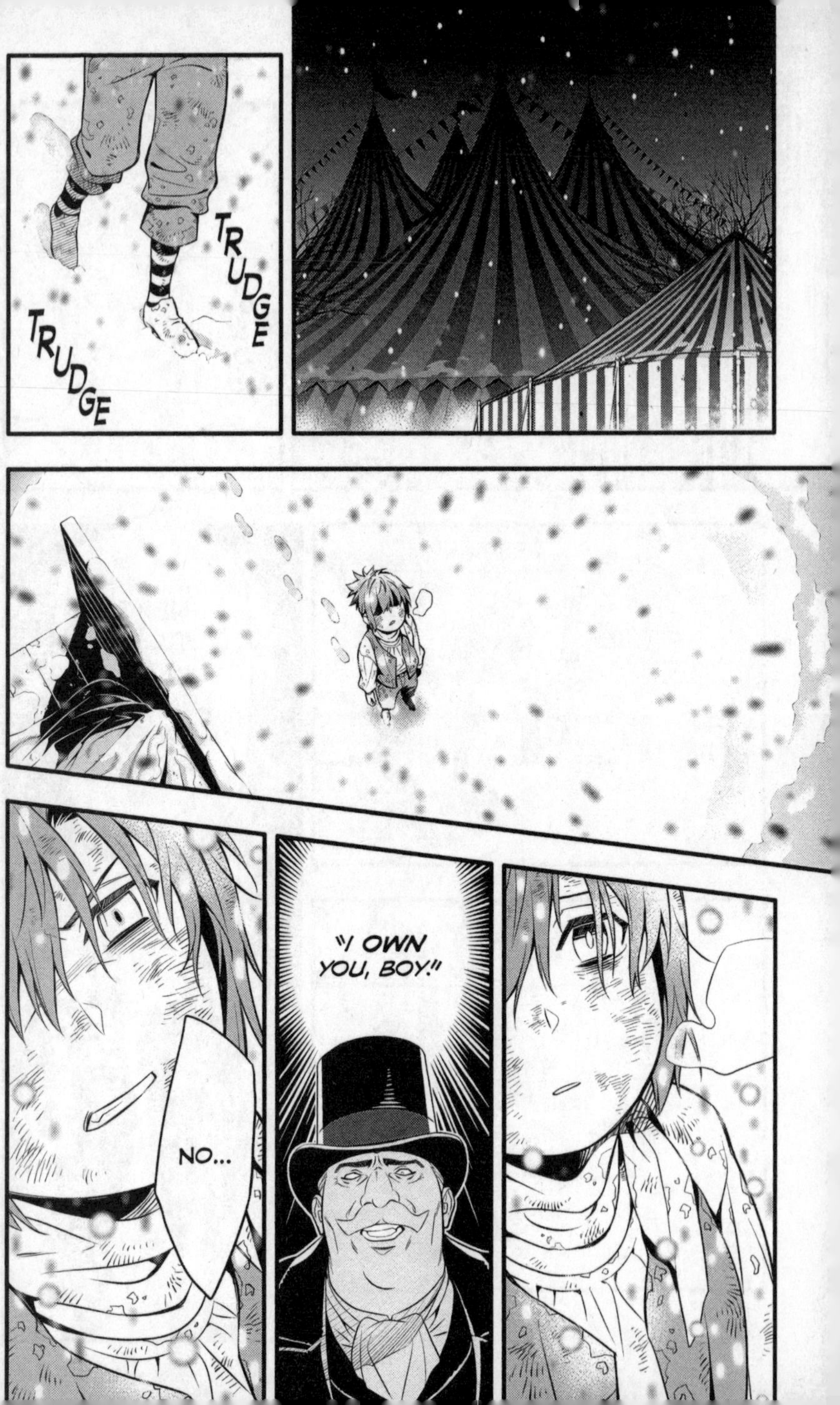
TRUDGE
TRUDGE
"I OWN YOU, BOY!"
NO...

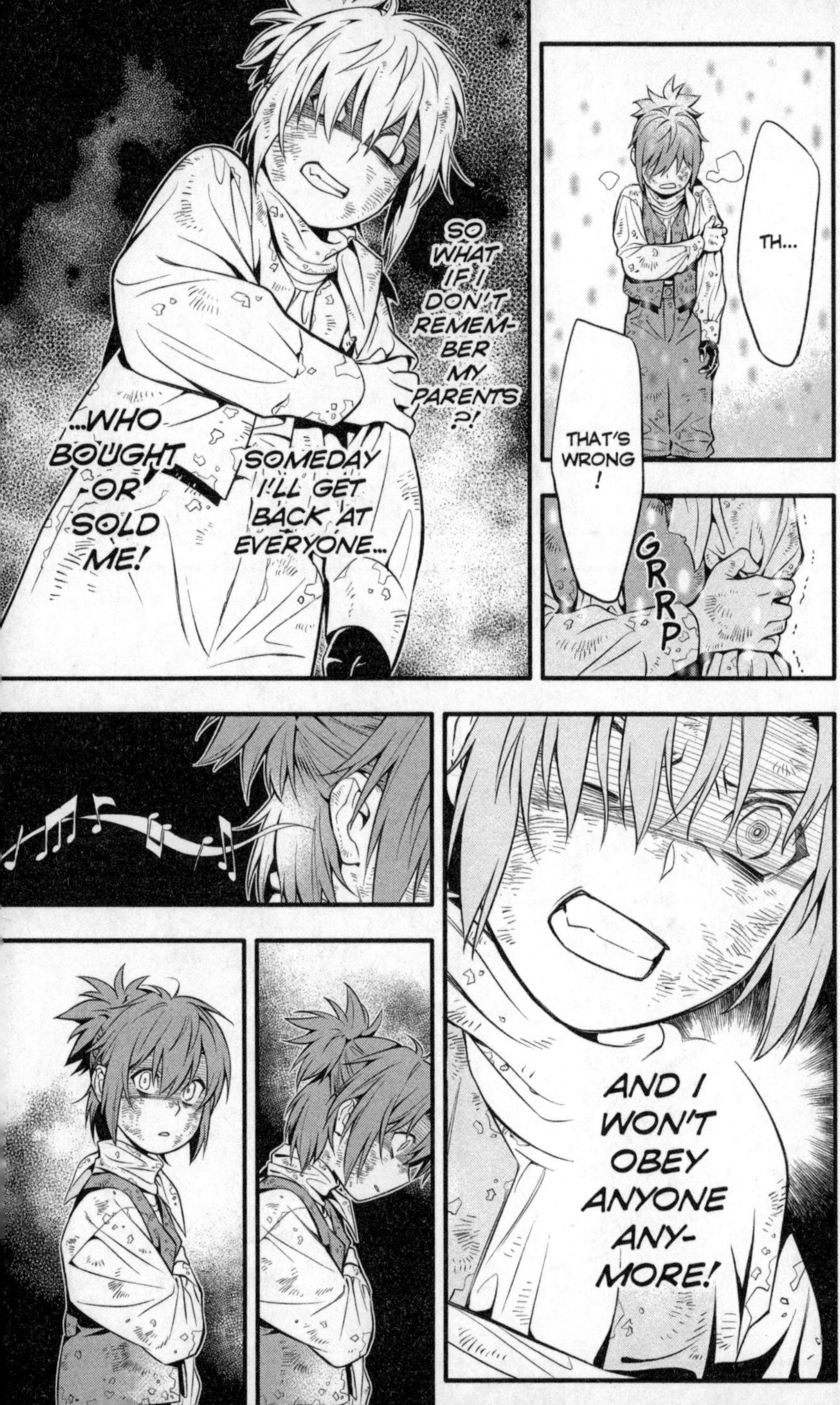
TH...
THAT'S WRONG!
GRRP
SO WHAT IF I DON'T REMEMBER MY PARENTS?!
SOMEDAY I'LL GET BACK AT EVERYONE...
...WHO BOUGHT OR SOLD ME!
AND I WON'T OBEY ANYONE ANYMORE!

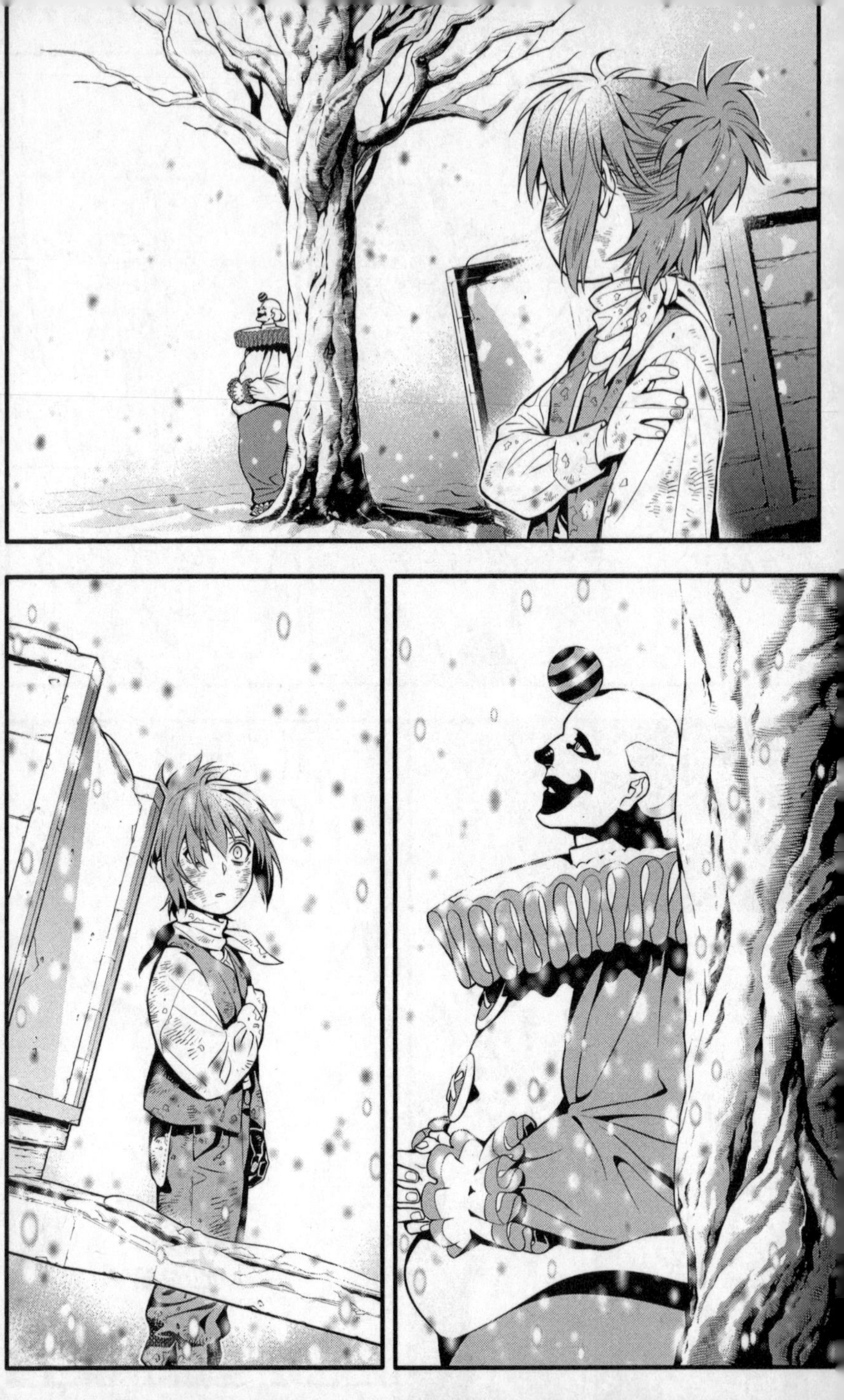

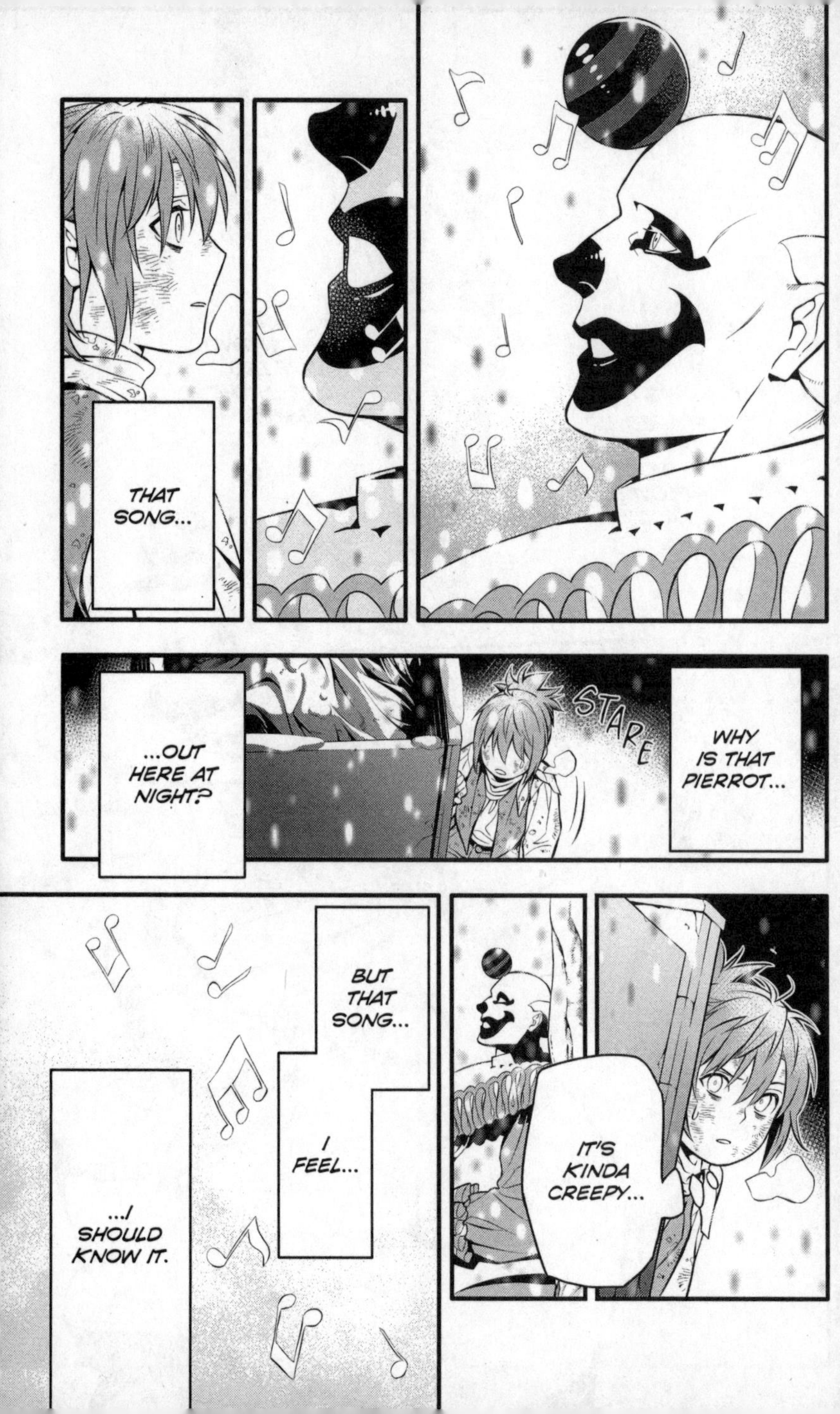
THAT SONG...
WHY IS THAT PIERROT...
STARE
...OUT HERE AT NIGHT?
IT'S KINDA CREEPY...
BUT THAT SONG...
I FEEL...
...I SHOULD KNOW IT.

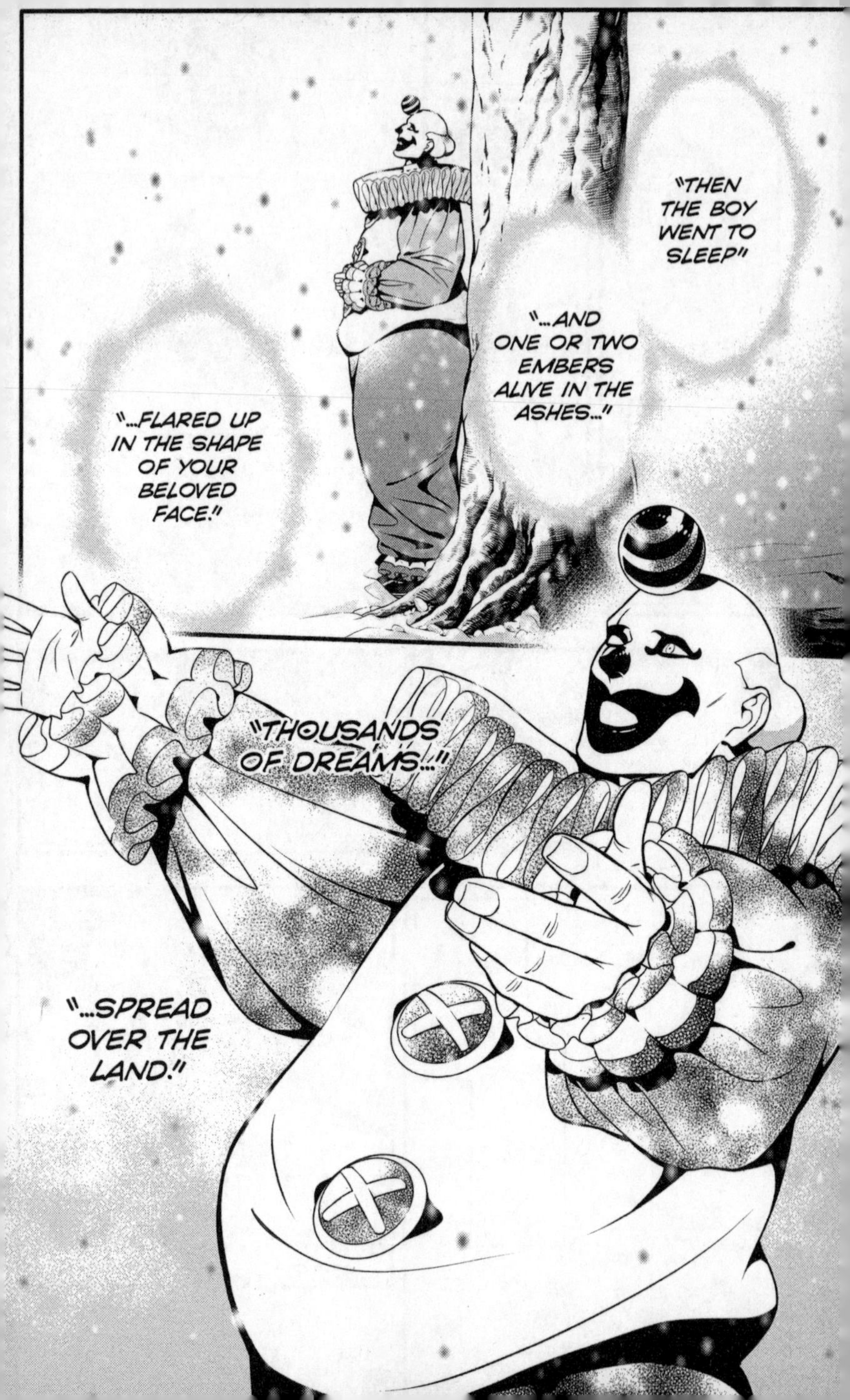
"THEN THE BOY WENT TO SLEEP"
"...AND ONE OR TWO EMBERS ALIVE IN THE ASHES..."
"...FLARED UP IN THE SHAPE OF YOUR BELOVED FACE."
"THOUSANDS OF DREAMS..."
"...SPREAD OVER THE LAND."

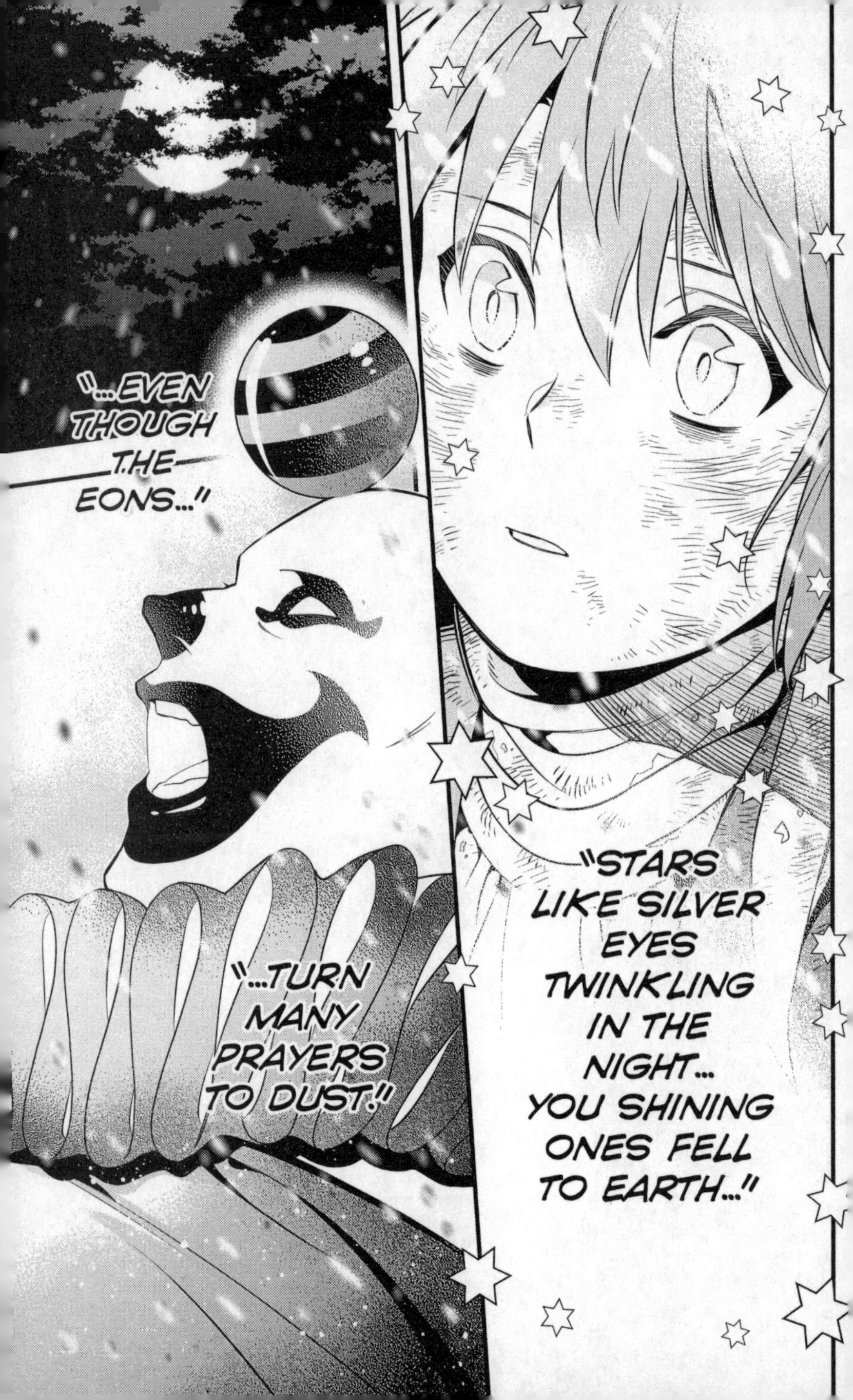
"STARS LIKE SILVER EYES TWINKLING IN THE NIGHT... YOU SHINING ONES FELL TO EARTH..."
"...EVEN THOUGH THE EONS..."
"...TURN MANY PRAYERS TO DUST!"

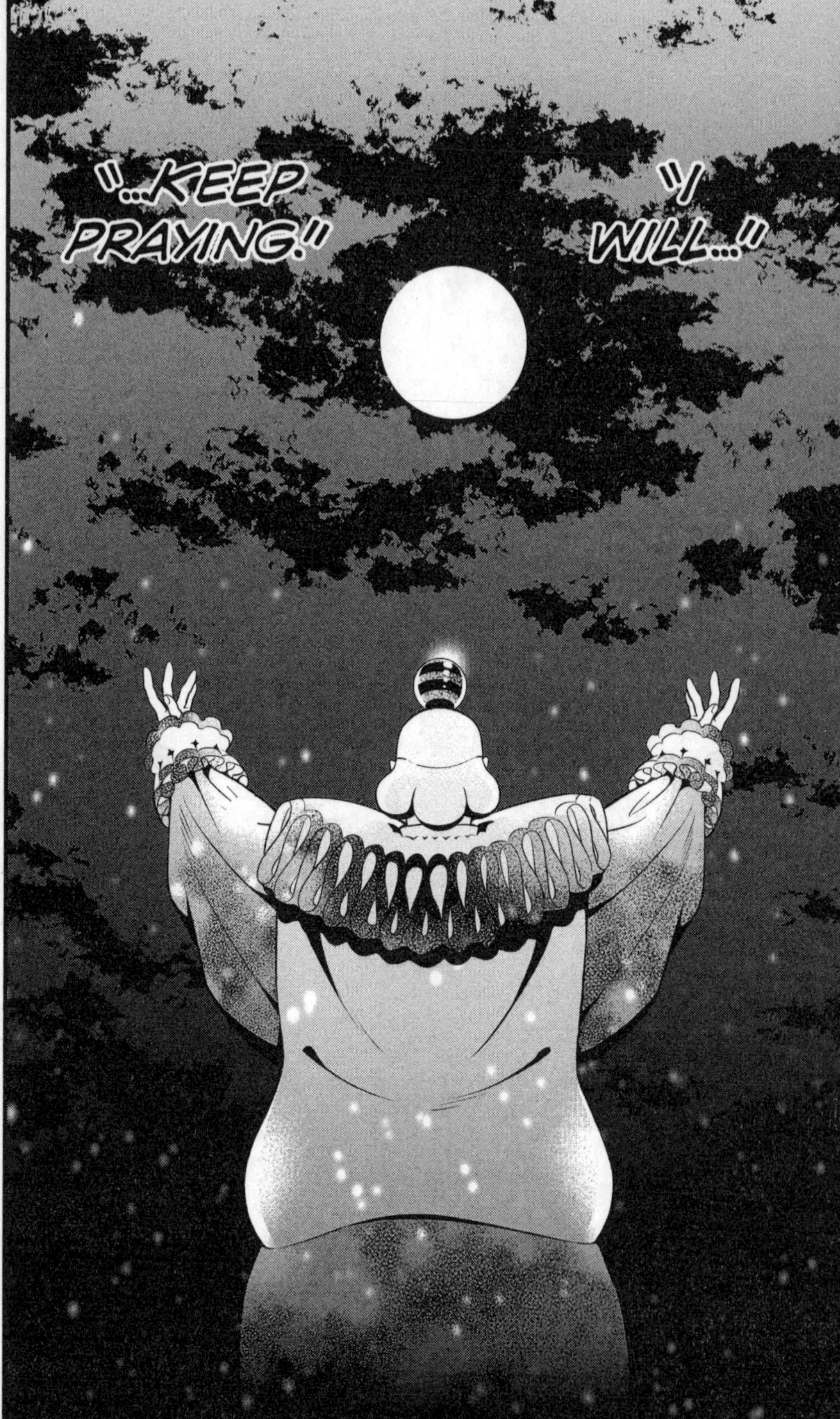
"I WILL..."
"...KEEP PRAYING."

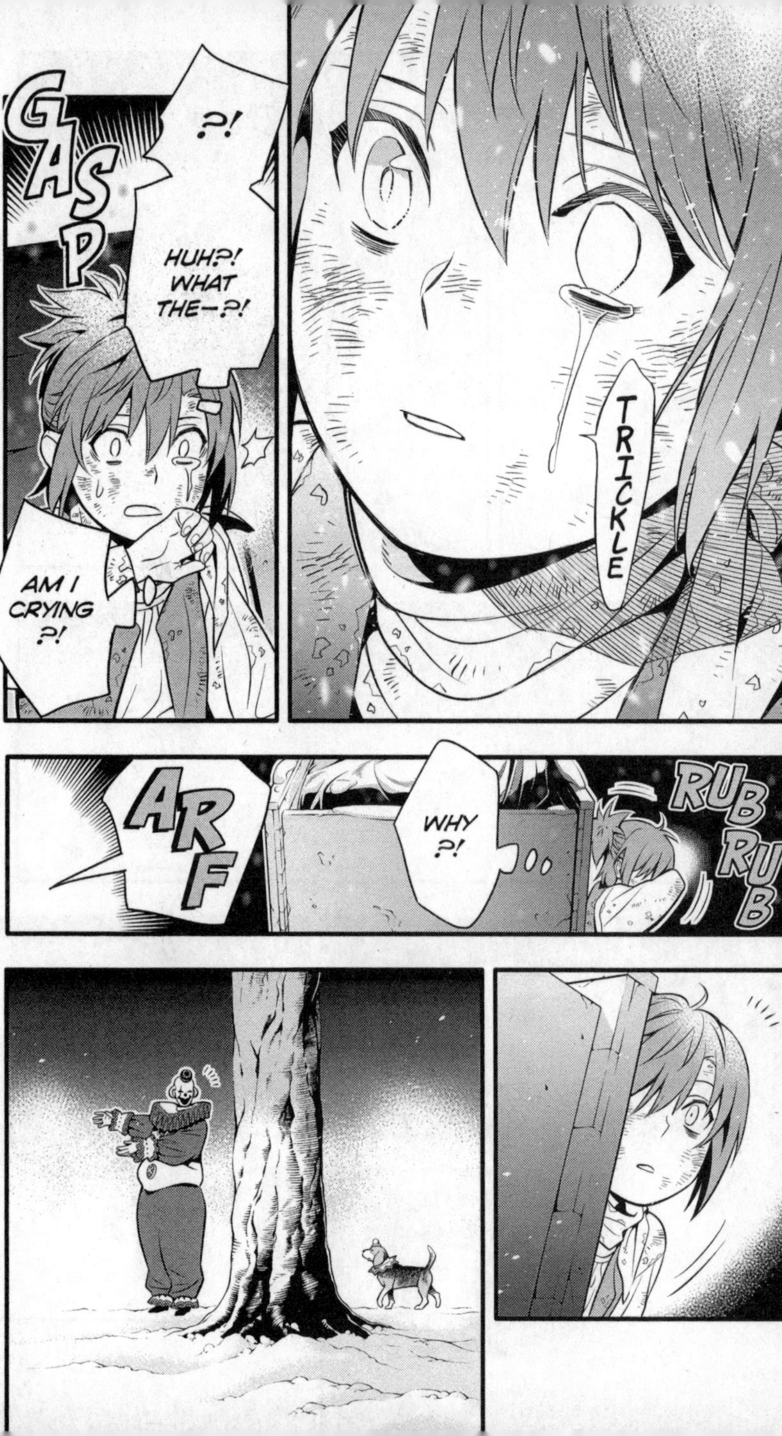
TRICKLE
?!
GASP
HUH?! WHAT THE—?!
AM I CRYING ?!
RUB RUB
WHY ?!
ARF

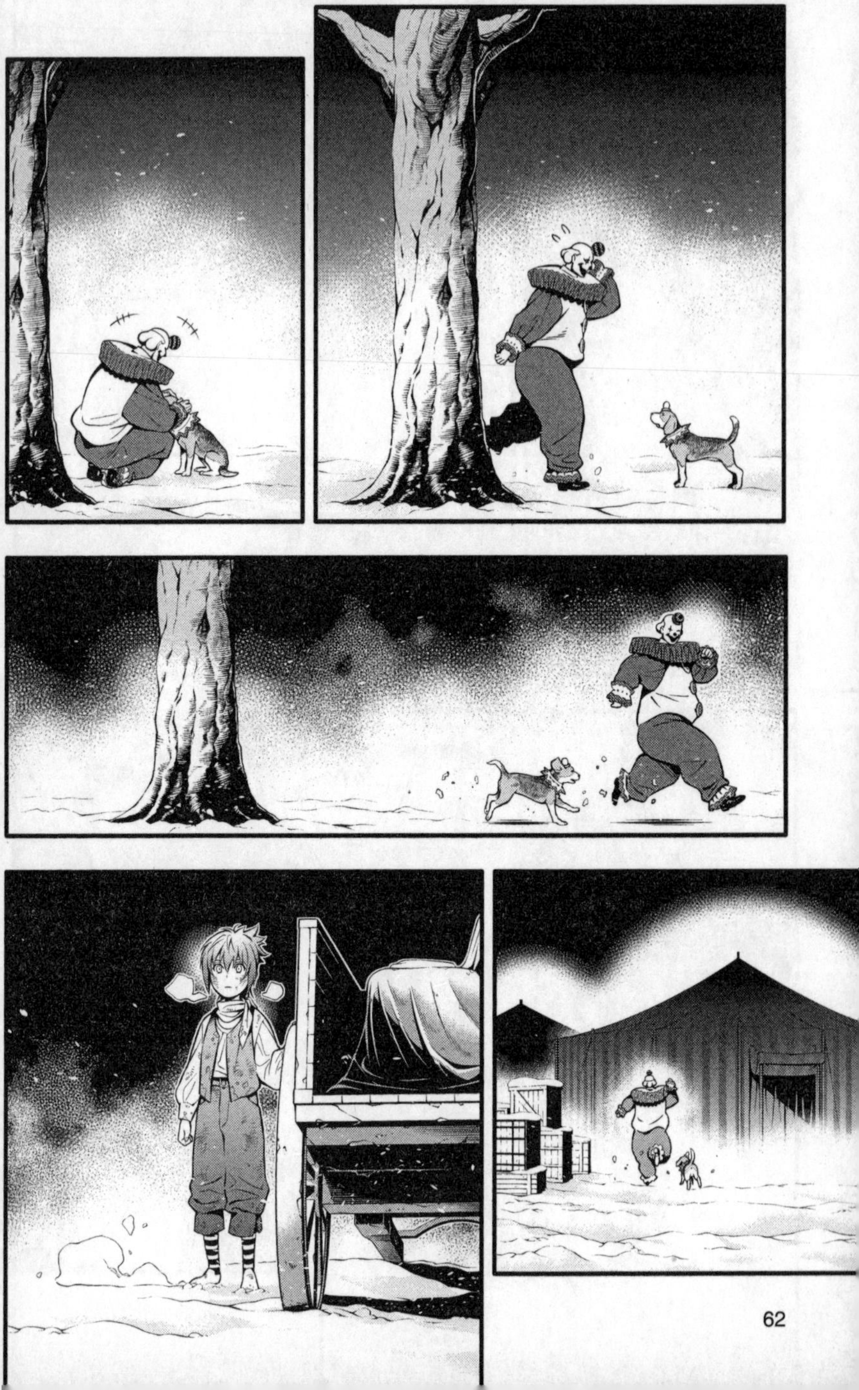

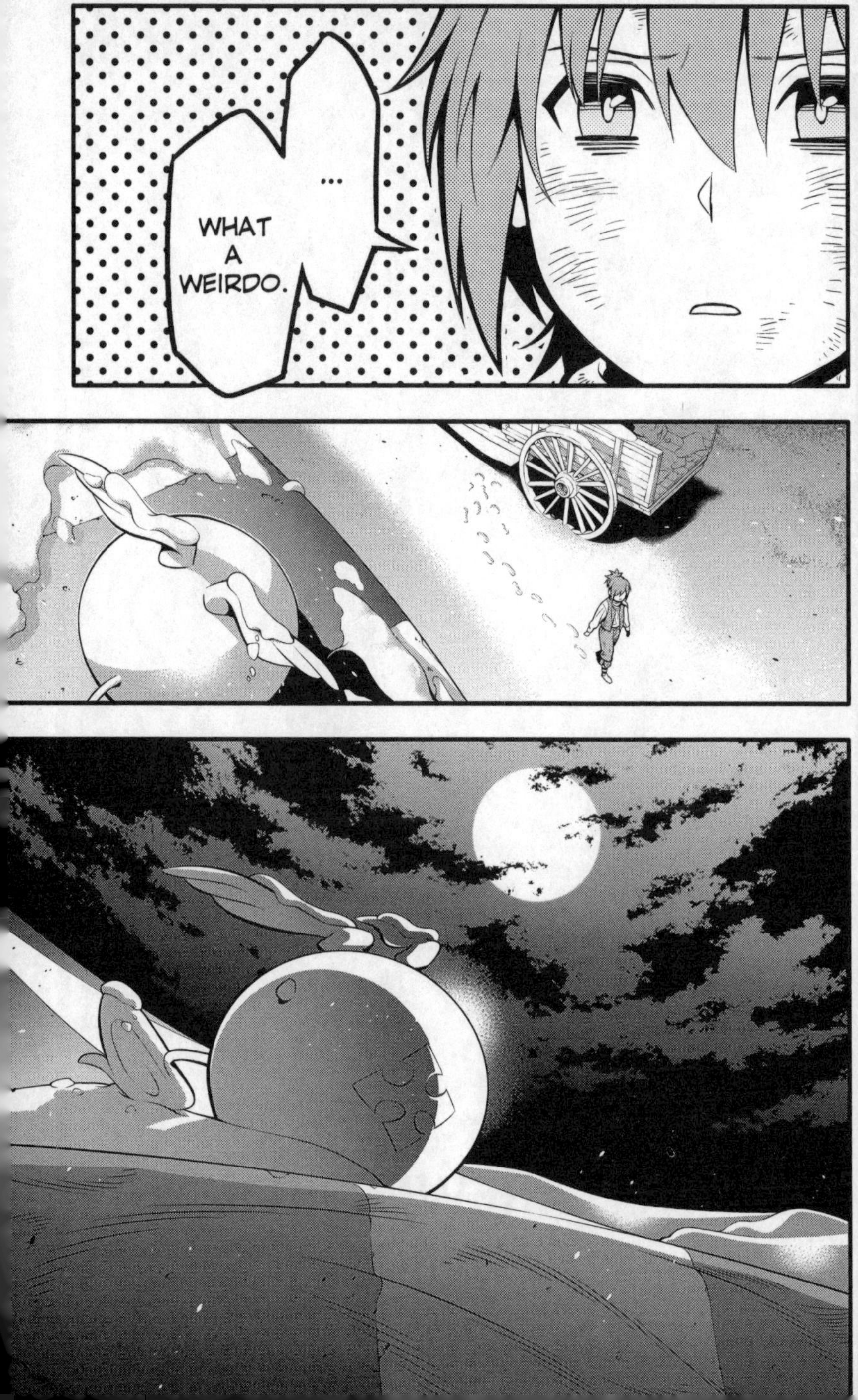
...
WHAT A WEIRDO.

233RD NIGHT
SAYING FAREWELL TO A.W.: THE WAY OF THE THREE

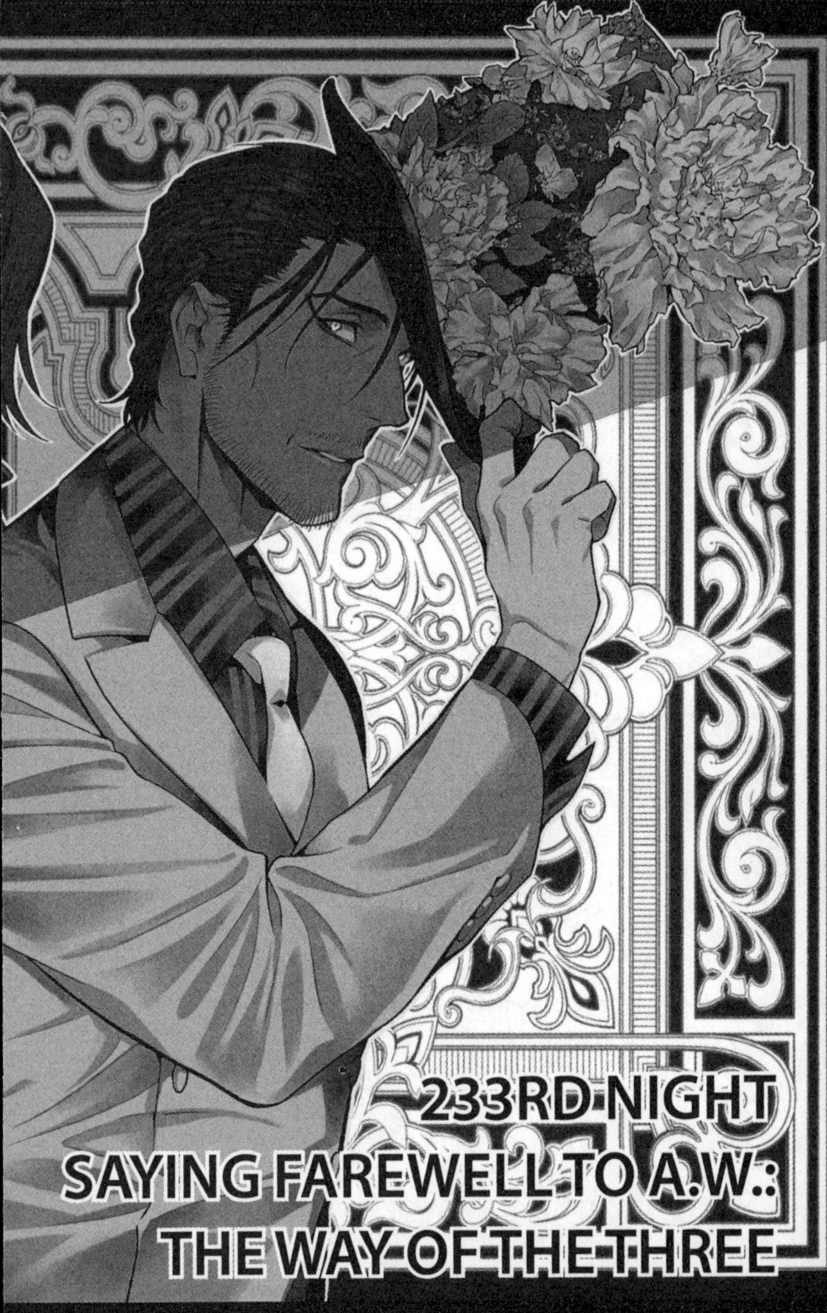

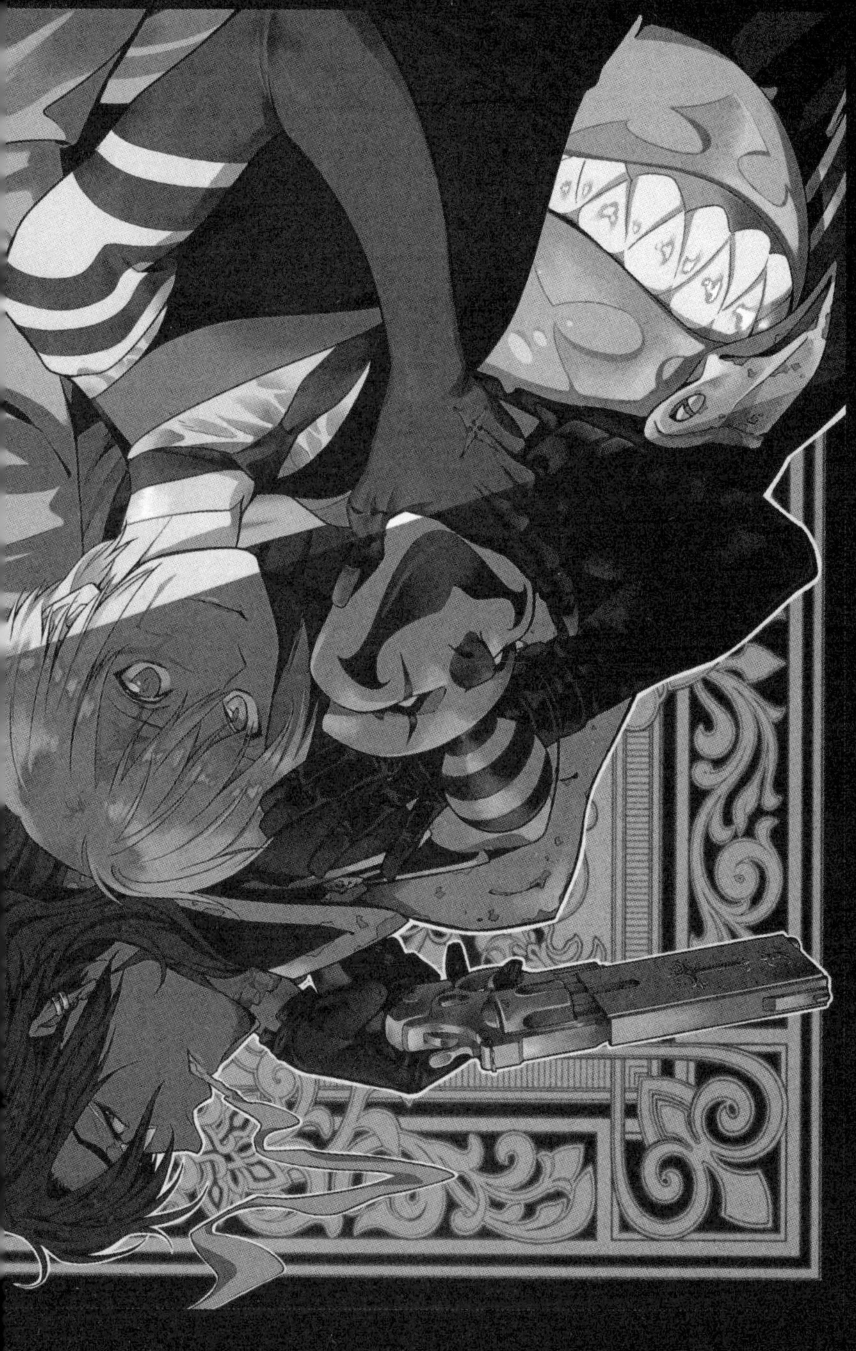

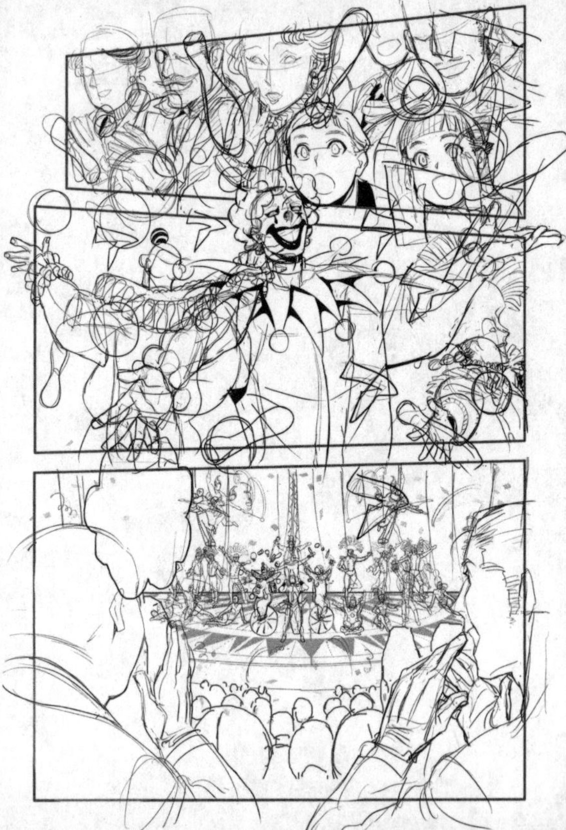

The 232nd Night Rough Layout

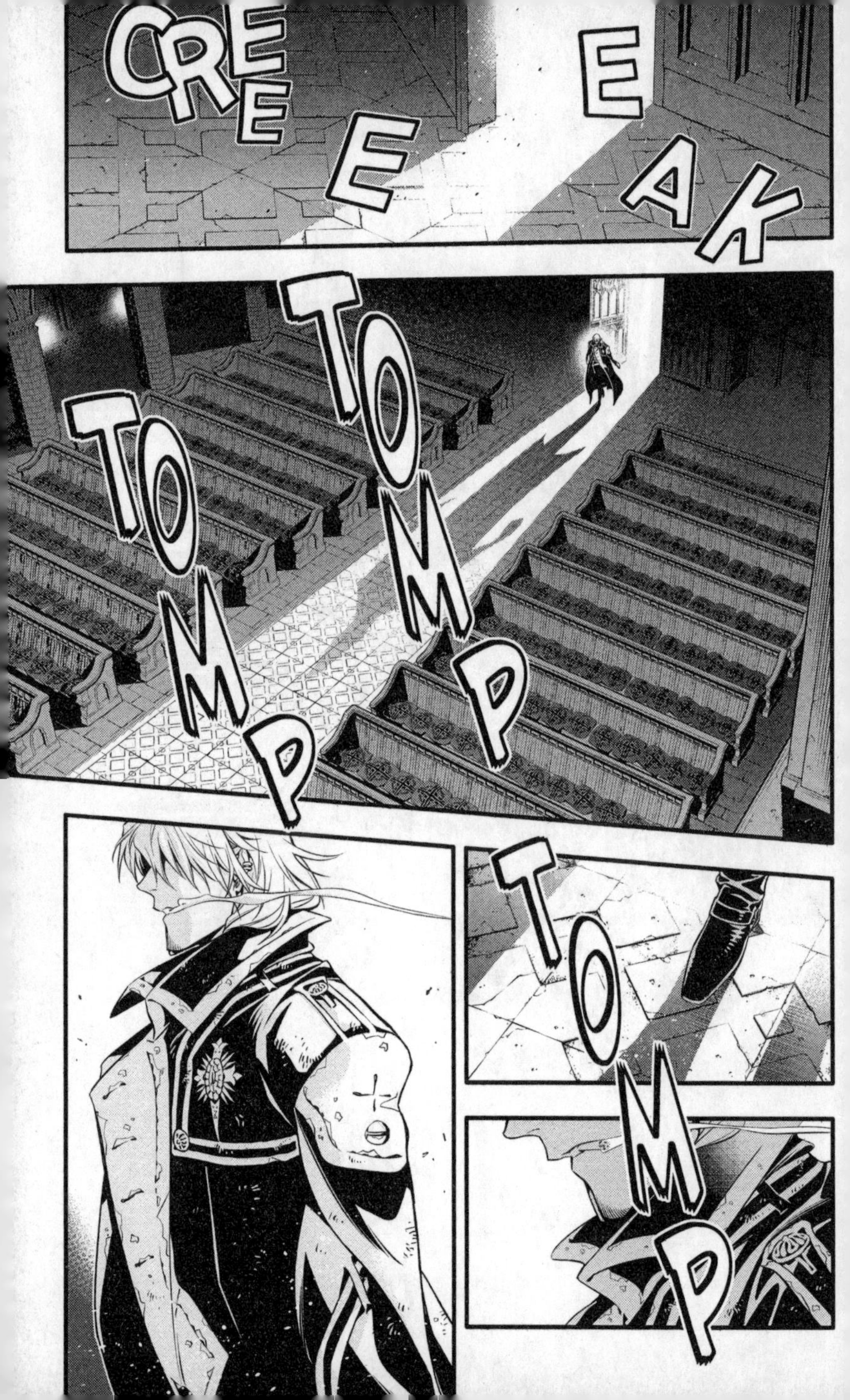
CREEEAK
TOMP
TOMP
TOMP

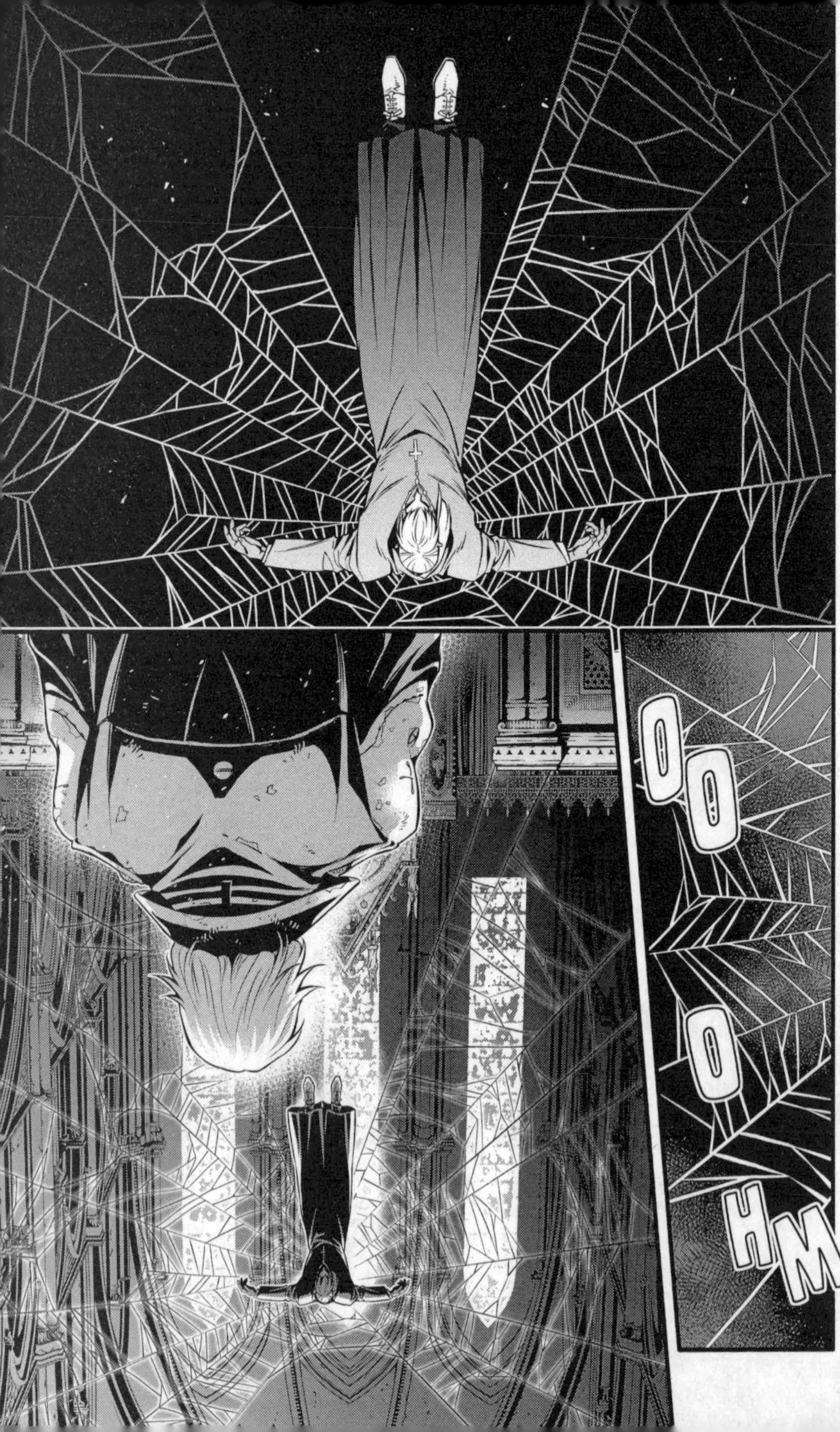
OOOOHM

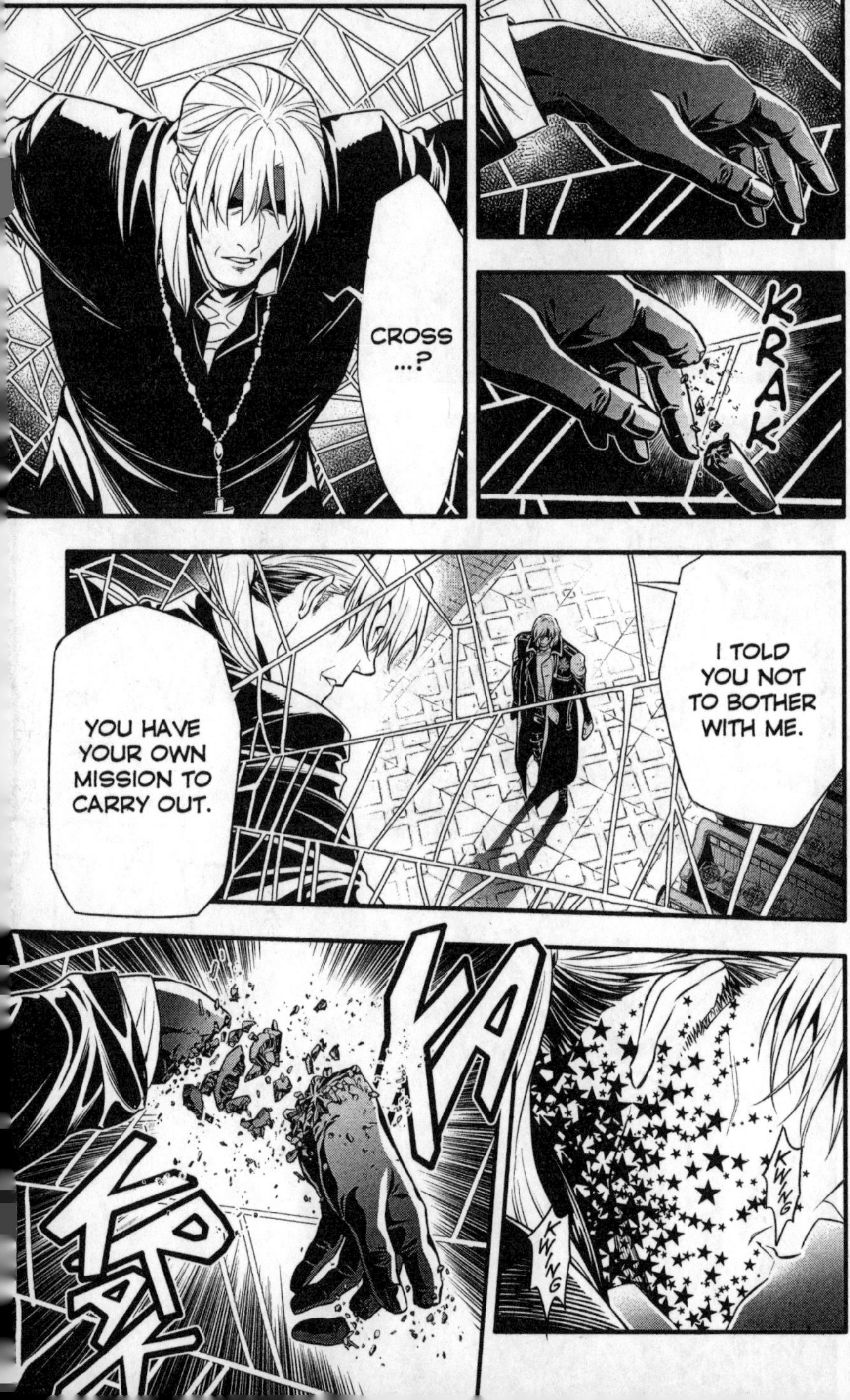
KRAK
CROSS
...?
I TOLD
YOU NOT
TO BOTHER
WITH ME.
YOU HAVE
YOUR OWN
MISSION TO
CARRY OUT.
KWING
KWING
KAKRAK

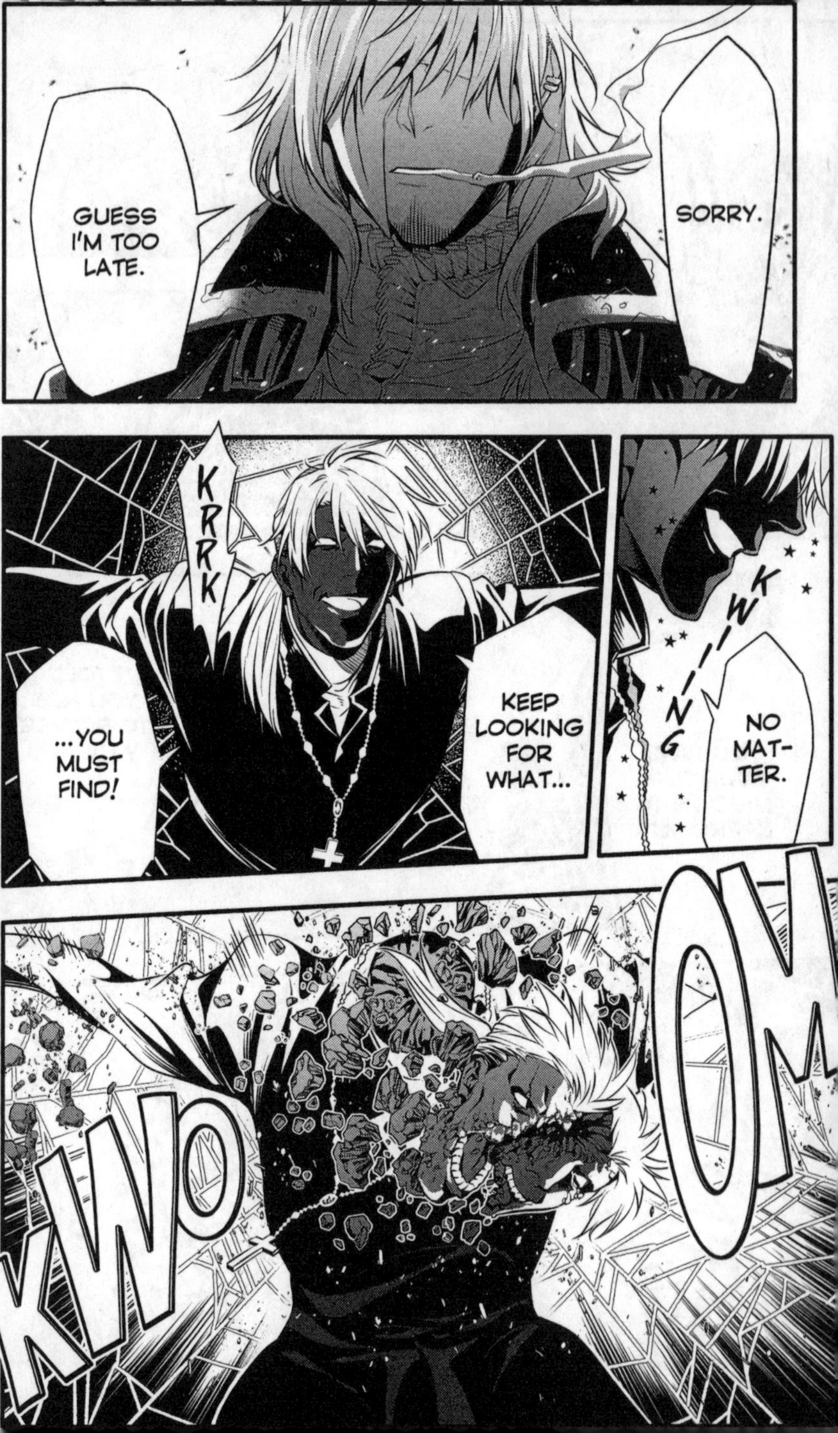
SORRY.
GUESS I'M TOO LATE.
KWIIING
NO MAT-TER.
KEEP LOOKING FOR WHAT...
KRRK
...YOU MUST FIND!
KWOOM

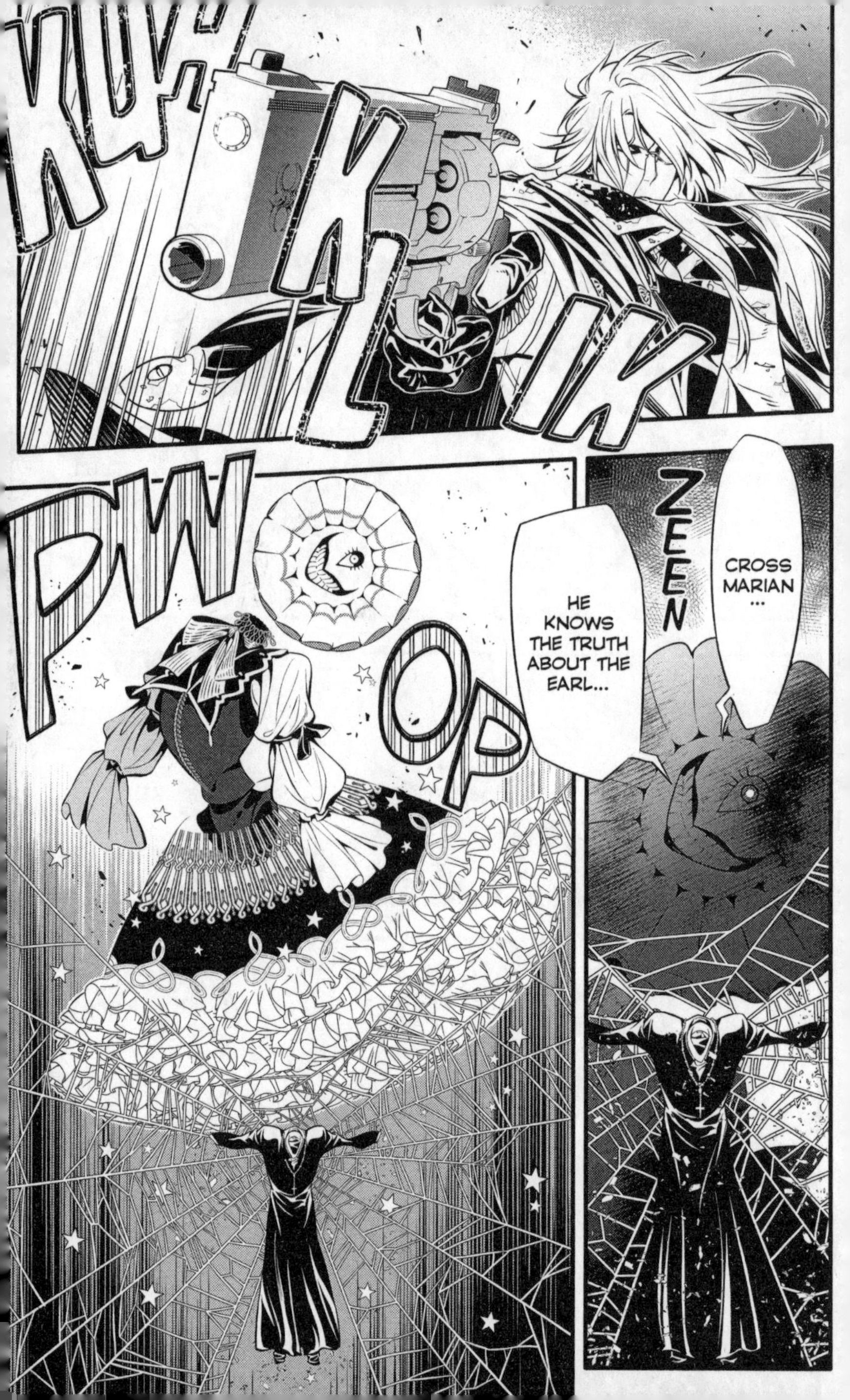
KLIK
KLIK
ZEEN
CROSS MARIAN...
HE KNOWS THE TRUTH ABOUT THE EARL...
PWOP

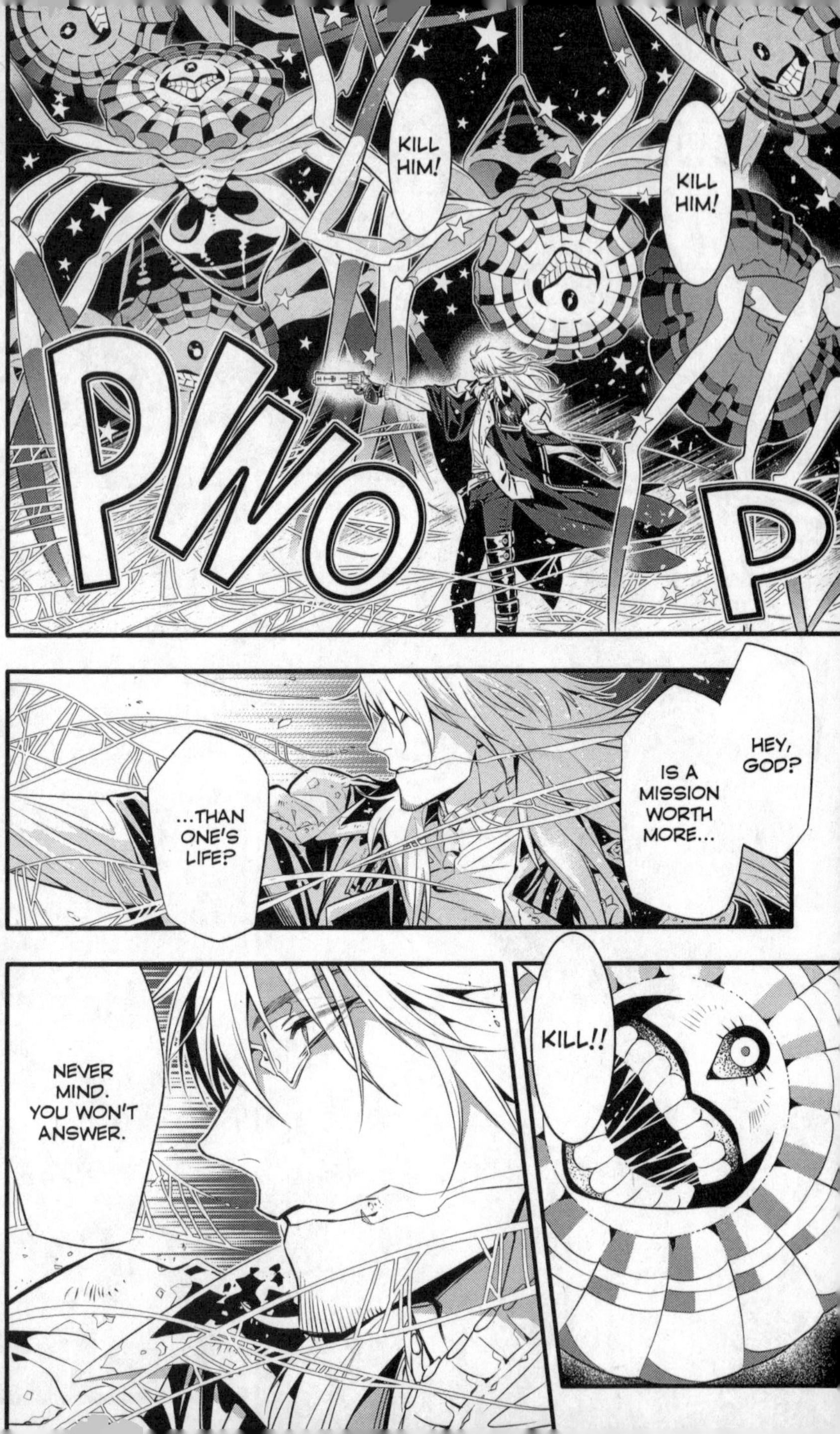
KILL HIM!
KILL HIM!
PWOP
HEY, GOD?
IS A MISSION WORTH MORE...
...THAN ONE'S LIFE?
KILL!!
NEVER MIND. YOU WON'T ANSWER.

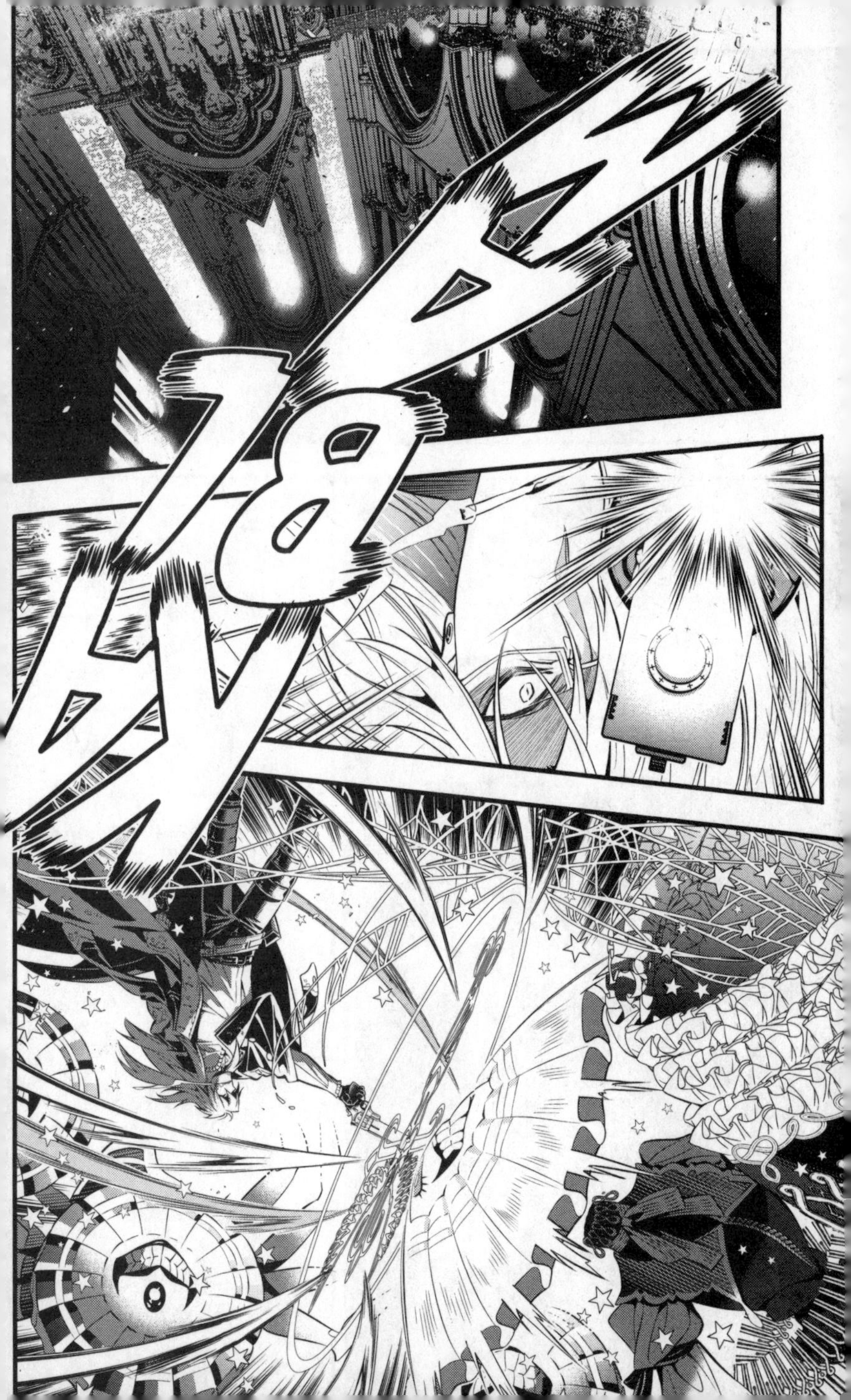
KABLAM

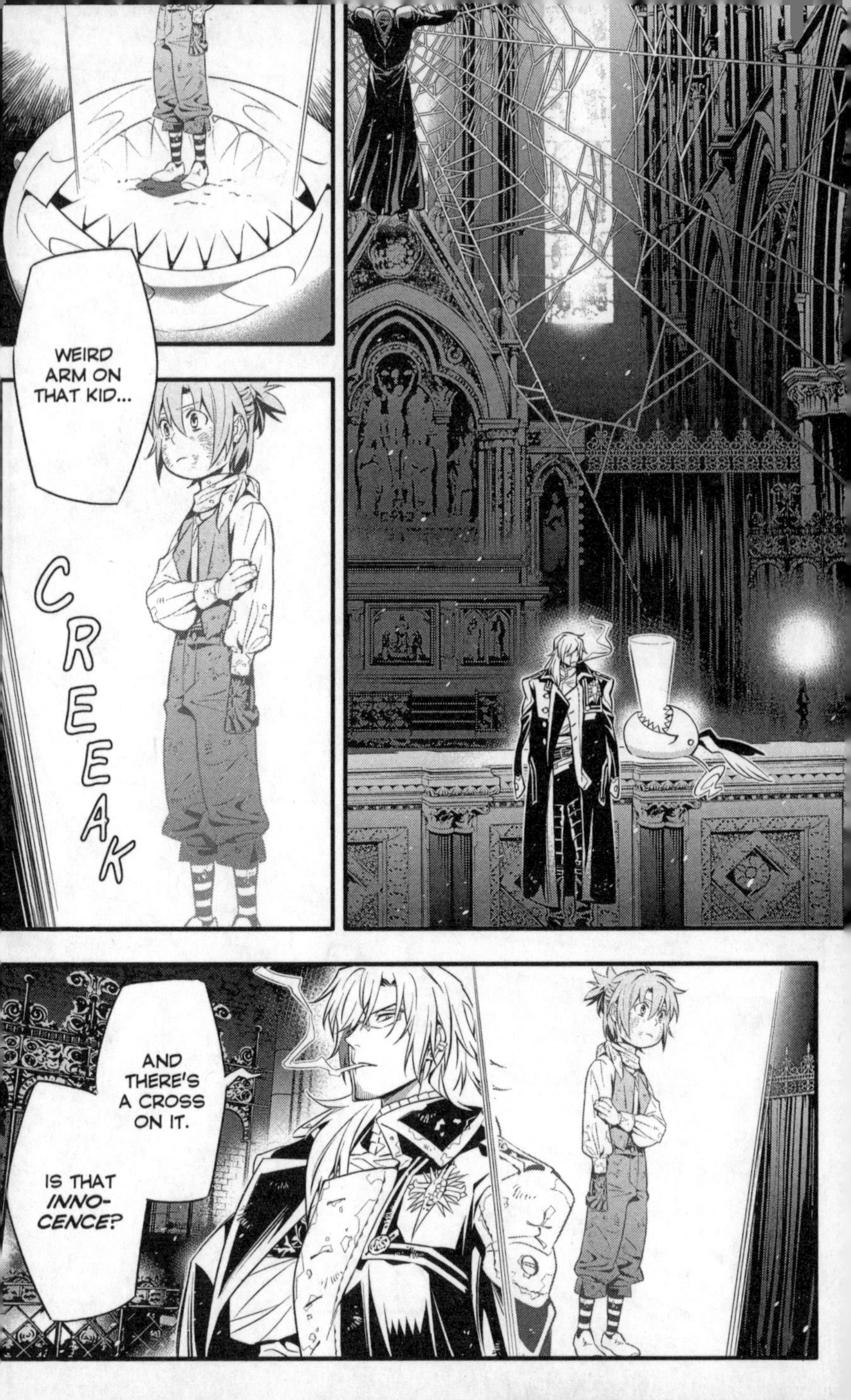
WEIRD ARM ON THAT KID...
CREEAK
AND THERE'S A CROSS ON IT.
IS THAT *INNO-CENCE?*

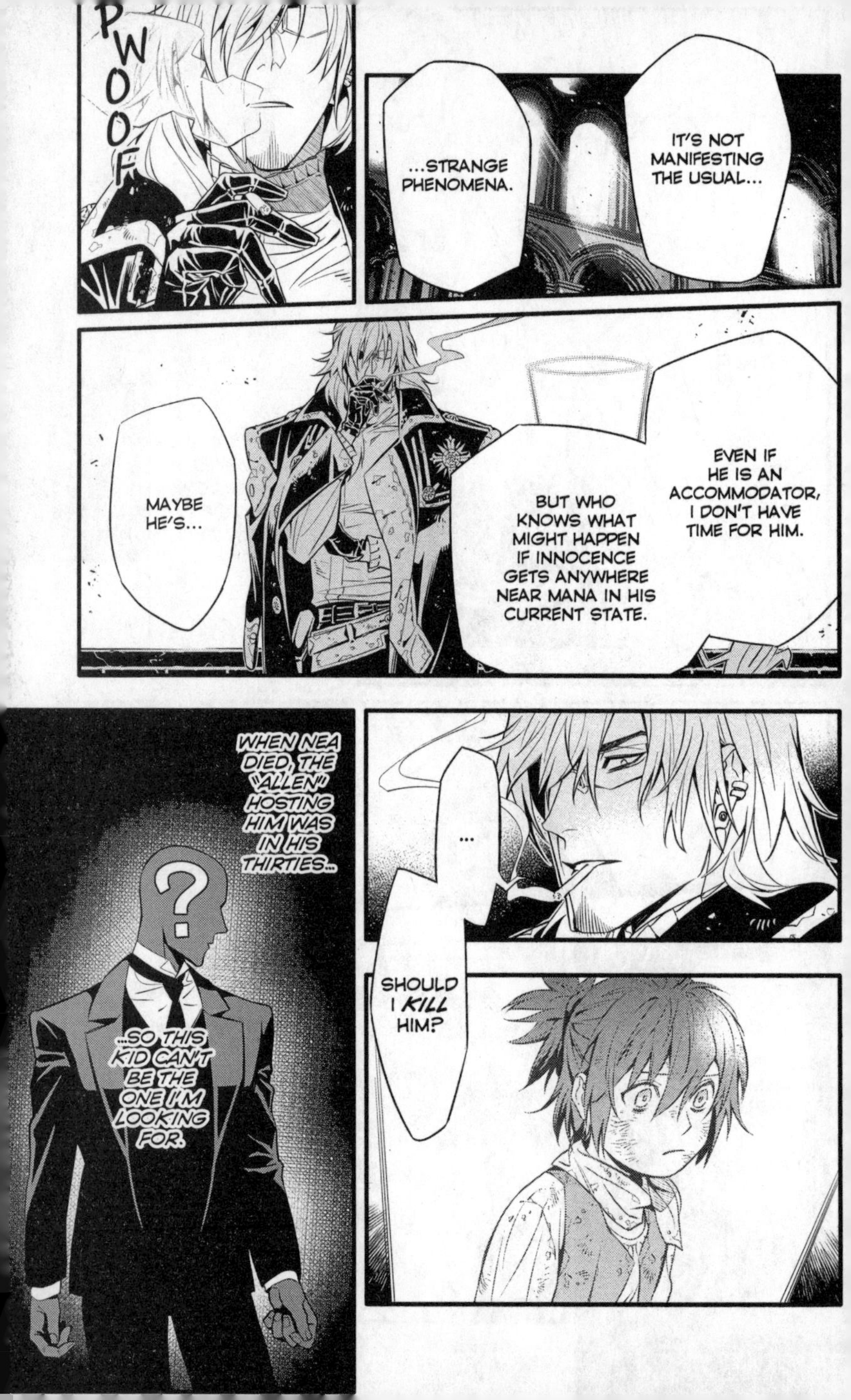
IT'S NOT MANIFESTING THE USUAL...
...STRANGE PHENOMENA.
PWOOF
EVEN IF HE IS AN ACCOMMODATOR, I DON'T HAVE TIME FOR HIM.
BUT WHO KNOWS WHAT MIGHT HAPPEN IF INNOCENCE GETS ANYWHERE NEAR MANA IN HIS CURRENT STATE.
MAYBE HE'S...
...
SHOULD I KILL HIM?
WHEN NEA DIED, THE "ALLEN" HOSTING HIM WAS IN HIS THIRTIES...
...SO THIS KID CAN'T BE THE ONE I'M LOOKING FOR.

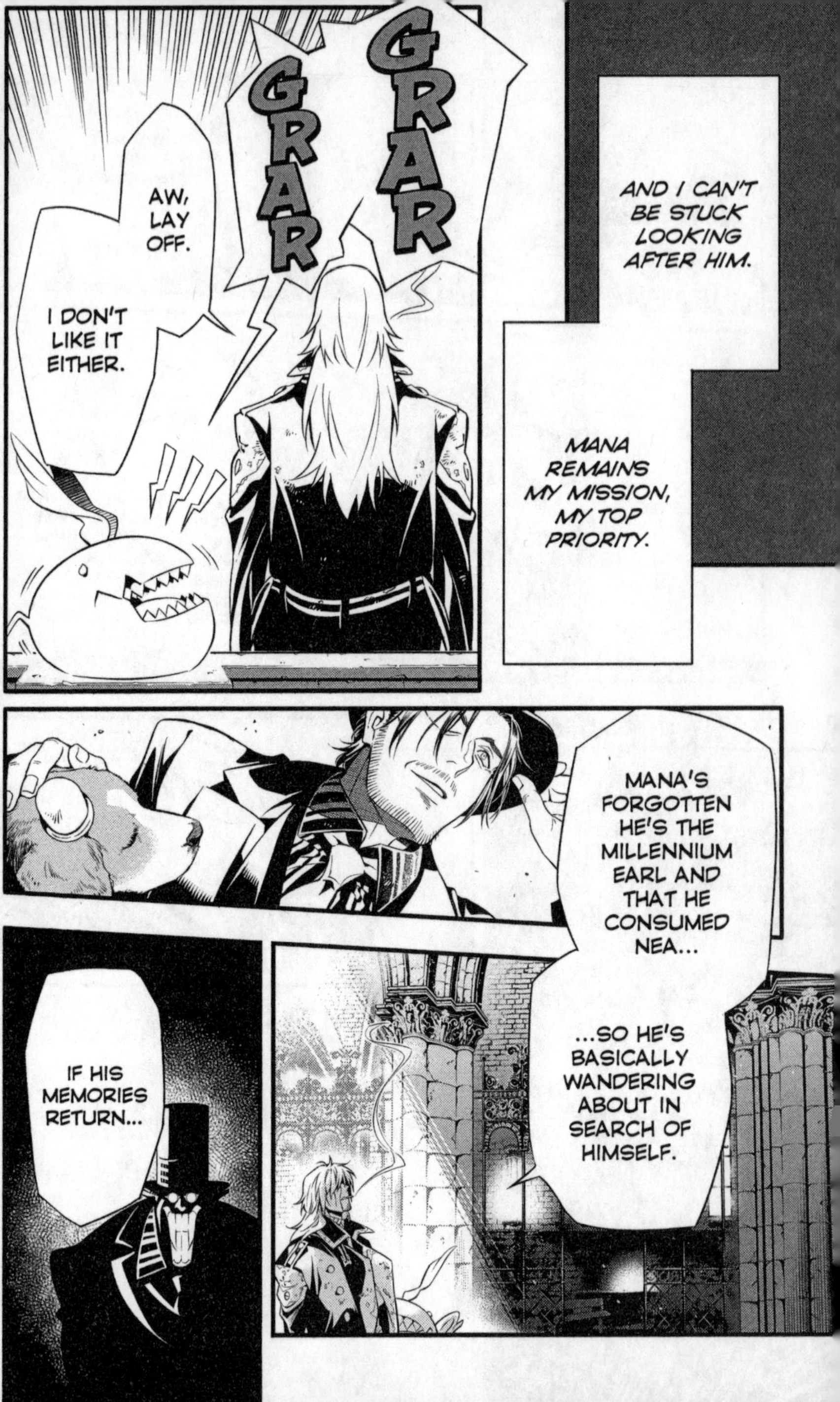
AND I CAN'T BE STUCK LOOKING AFTER HIM.
MANA REMAINS MY MISSION, MY TOP PRIORITY.
GRAR
GRAR
AW, LAY OFF.
I DON'T LIKE IT EITHER.
MANA'S FORGOTTEN HE'S THE MILLENNIUM EARL AND THAT HE CONSUMED NEA...
...SO HE'S BASICALLY WANDERING ABOUT IN SEARCH OF HIMSELF.
IF HIS MEMORIES RETURN...

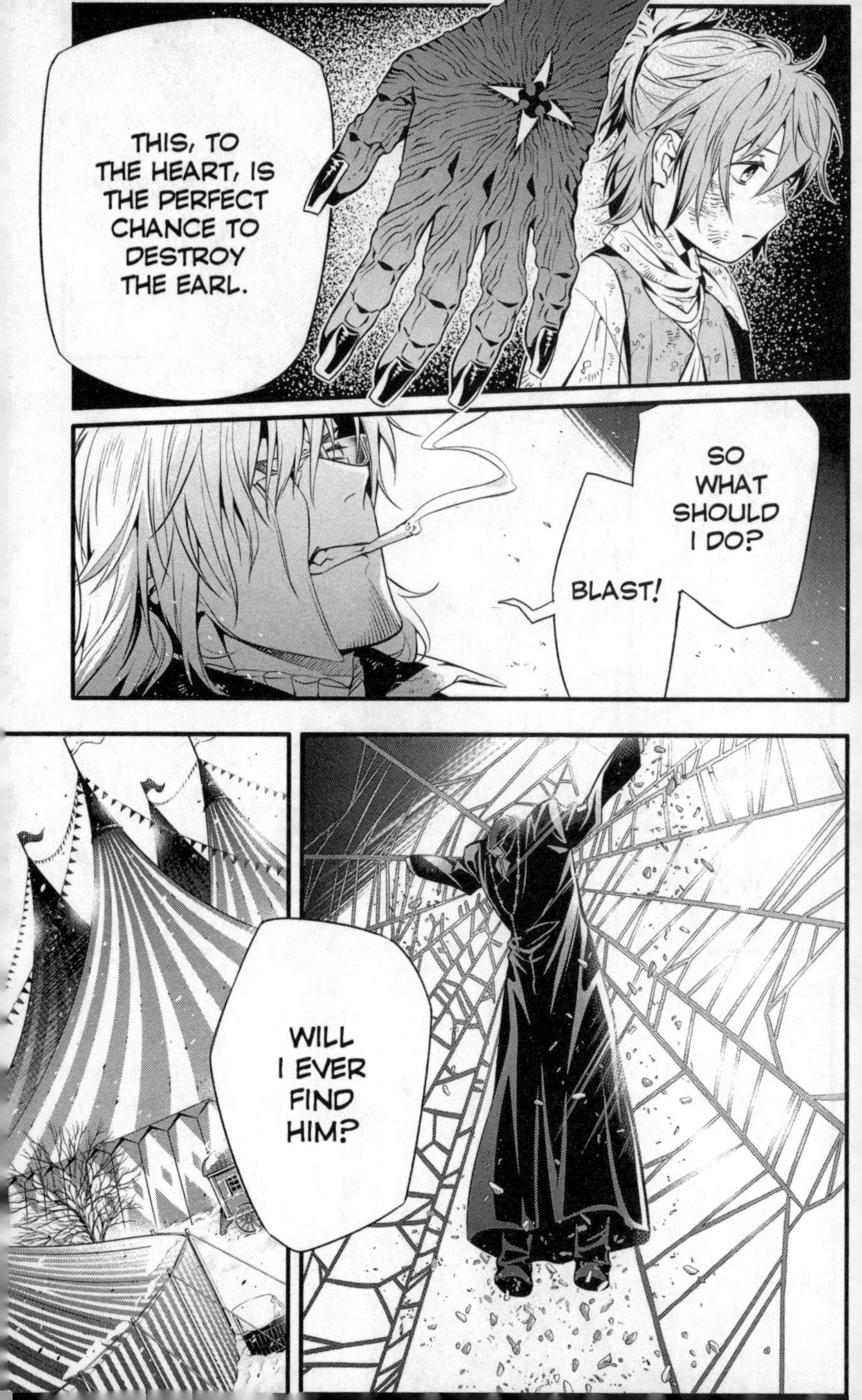
THIS, TO THE HEART, IS THE PERFECT CHANCE TO DESTROY THE EARL.
SO WHAT SHOULD I DO?
BLAST!
WILL I EVER FIND HIM?

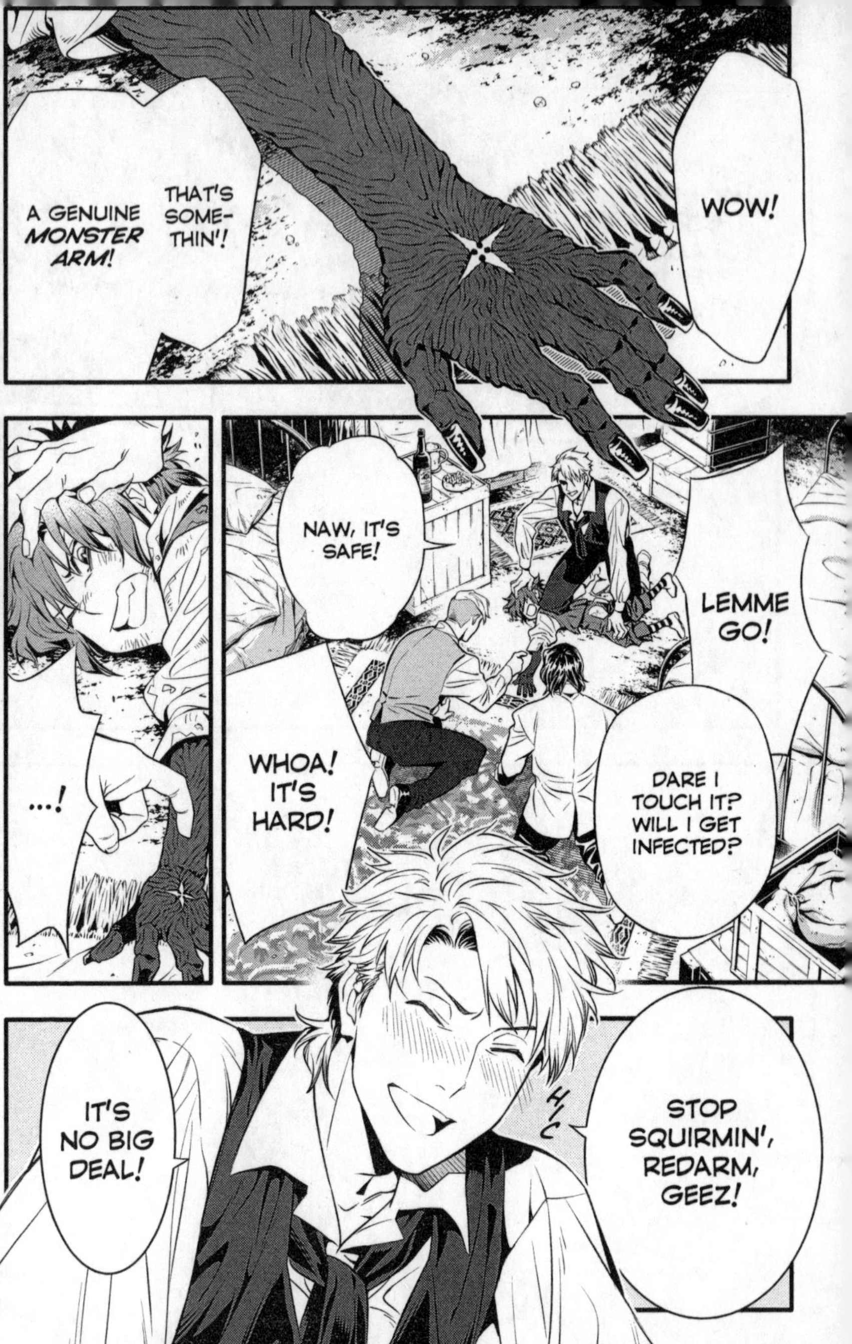
WOW!
THAT'S SOME-THIN'!
A GENUINE *MONSTER ARM!*
LEMME GO!
DARE I TOUCH IT? WILL I GET INFECTED?
WHOA! IT'S HARD!
NAW, IT'S SAFE!
...!
STOP SQUIRMIN', REDARM, GEEZ!
HIC
IT'S NO BIG DEAL!

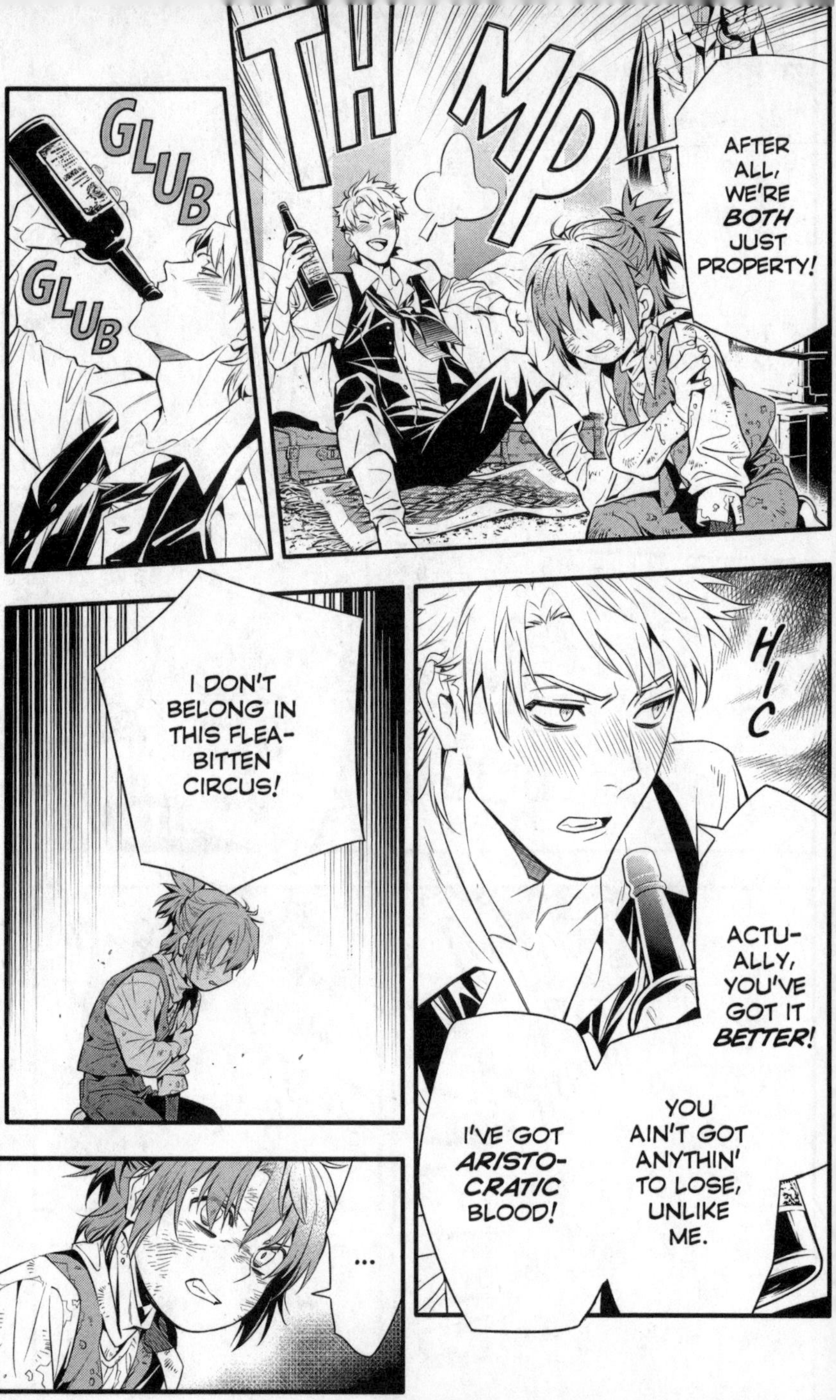
AFTER ALL, WE'RE *BOTH* JUST PROPERTY!
THMP
GLUB GLUB
HIC
ACTU-ALLY, YOU'VE GOT IT *BETTER*!
YOU AIN'T GOT ANYTHIN' TO LOSE, UNLIKE ME.
I'VE GOT *ARISTO-CRATIC* BLOOD!
I DON'T BELONG IN THIS FLEA-BITTEN CIRCUS!
...

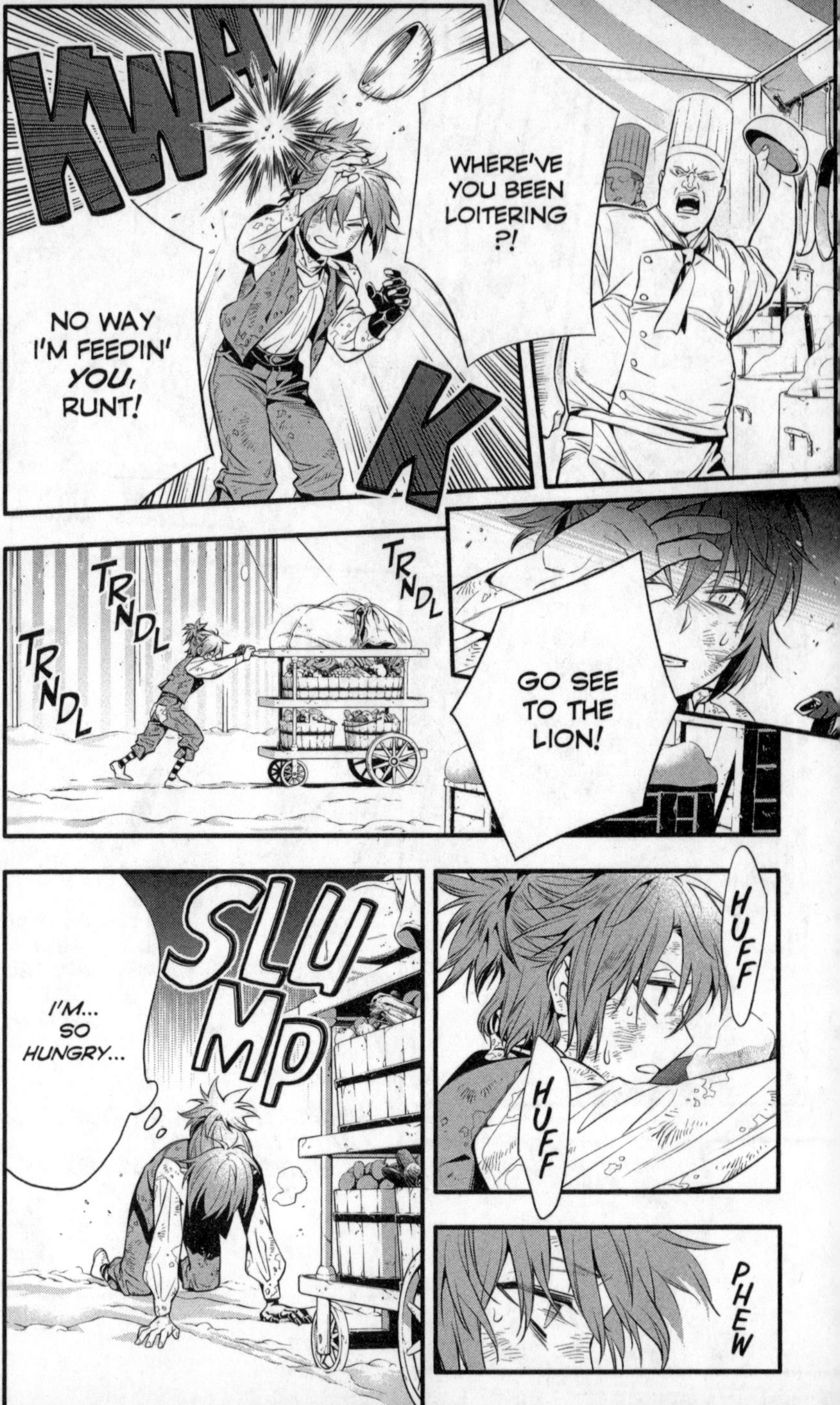
WHERE'VE YOU BEEN LOITERING ?!
KWAK
NO WAY I'M FEEDIN' YOU, RUNT!
GO SEE TO THE LION!
TRNDL
TRNDL
TRNDL
HUFF
HUFF
PHEW
SLUMP
I'M... SO HUNGRY...

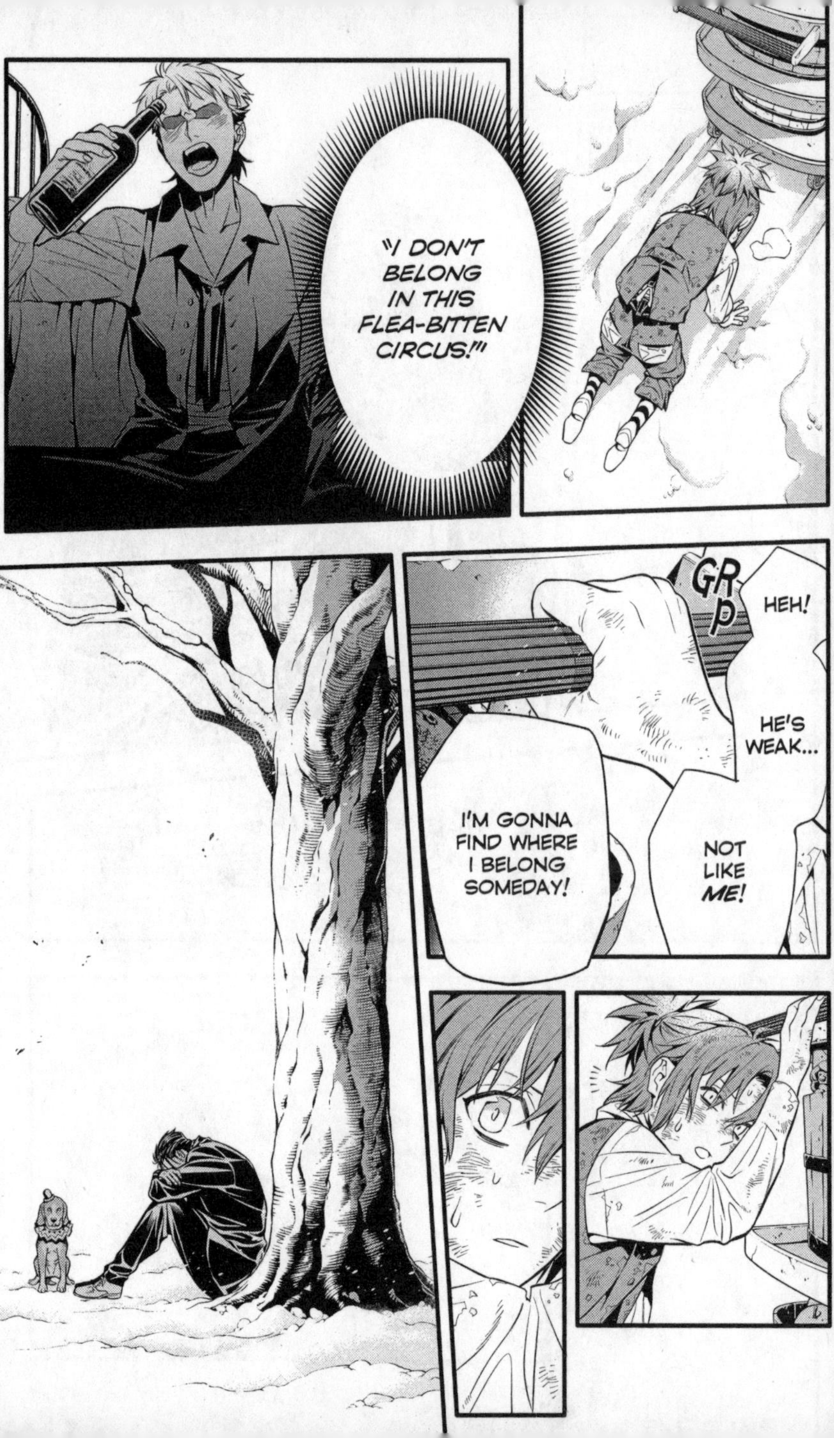
"I DON'T BELONG IN THIS FLEA-BITTEN CIRCUS!"
GRP
HEH!
HE'S WEAK...
NOT LIKE ME!
I'M GONNA FIND WHERE I BELONG SOMEDAY!

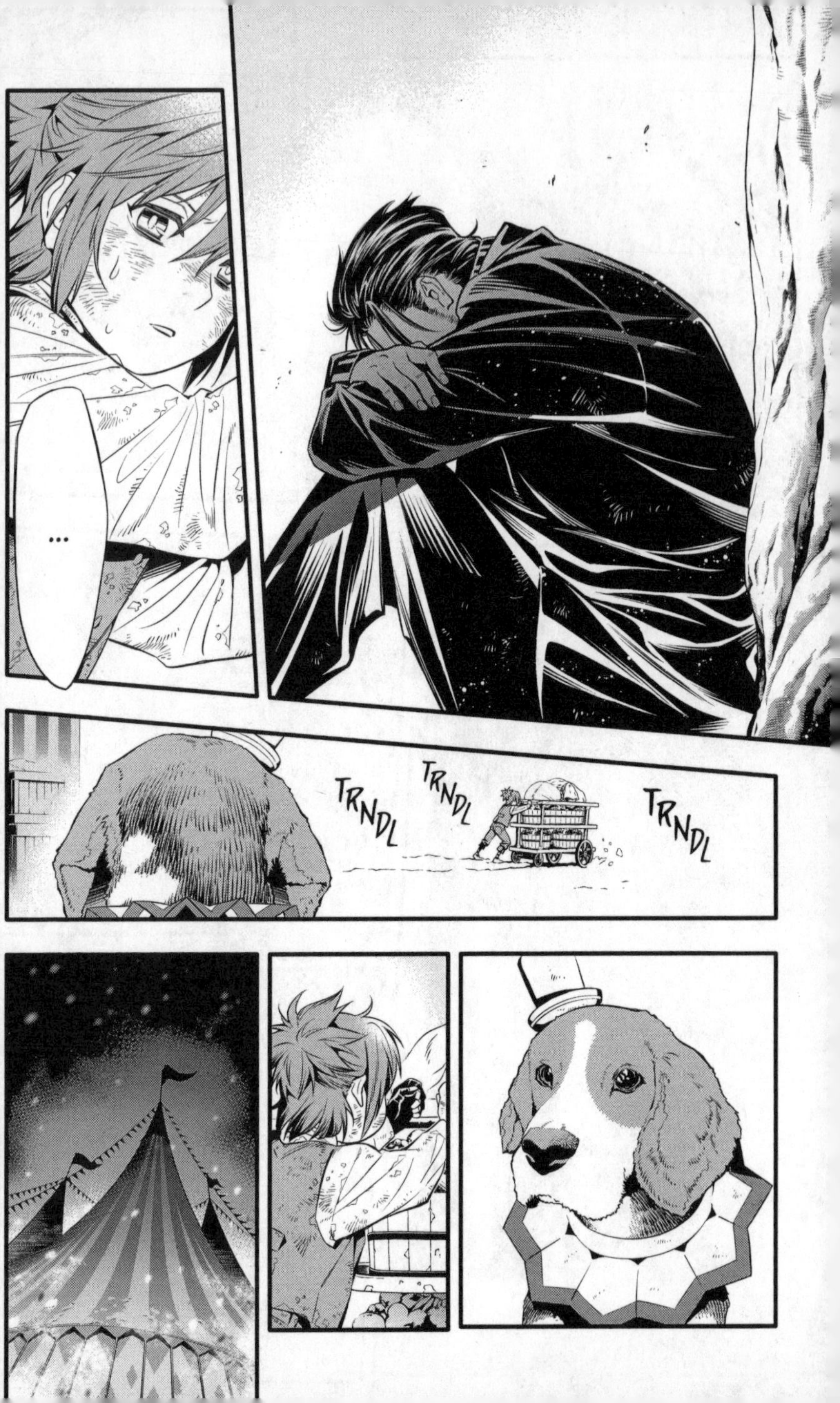
...
TRNDL
TRNDL
TRNDL

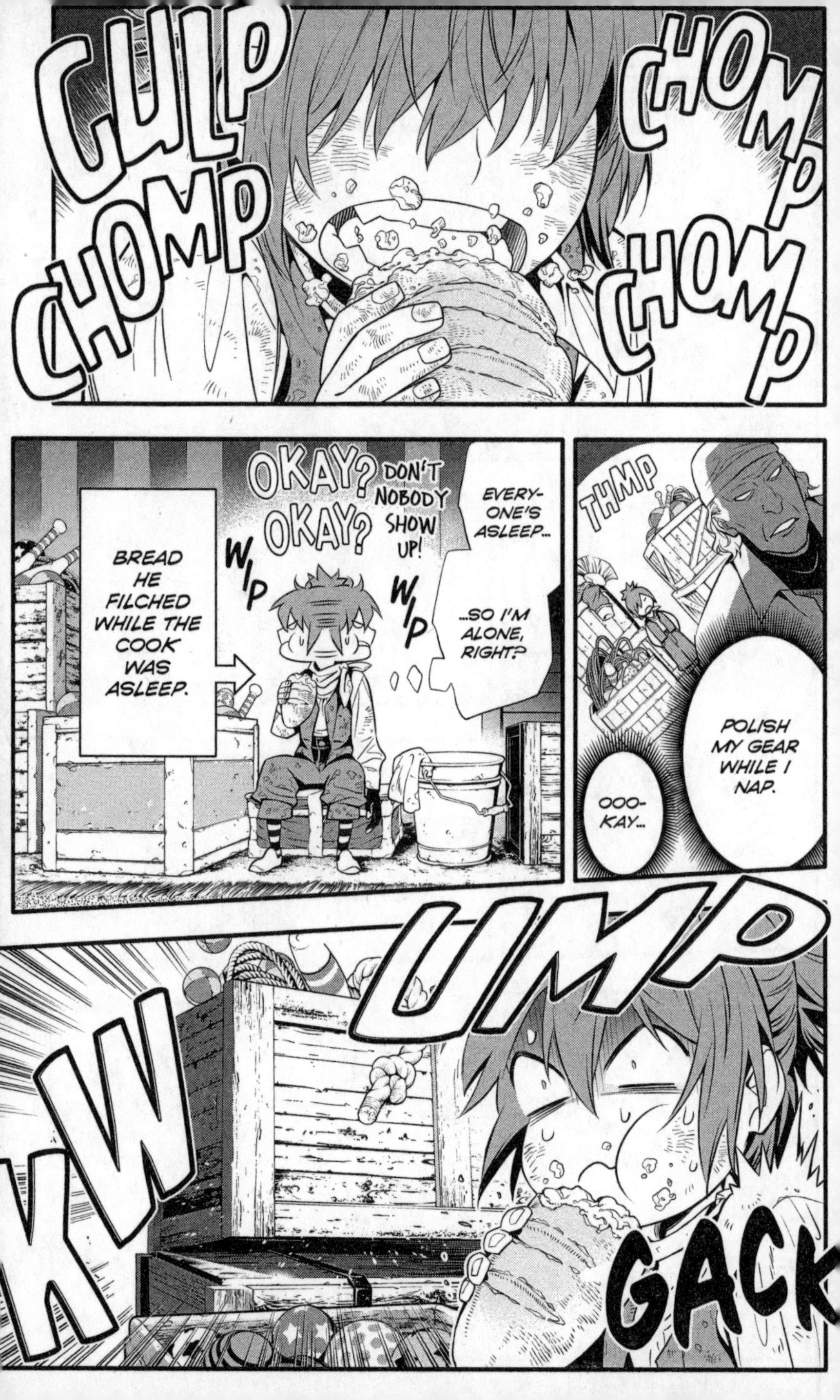
CHOMP
CHOMP
GULP
CHOMP
THMP
POLISH MY GEAR WHILE I NAP.
OOO-KAY...
EVERY-ONE'S ASLEEP...
...SO I'M ALONE, RIGHT?
OKAY? OKAY? DON'T NOBODY SHOW UP!
WIP
WIP
BREAD HE FILCHED WHILE THE COOK WAS ASLEEP.
KWUMP
GACK

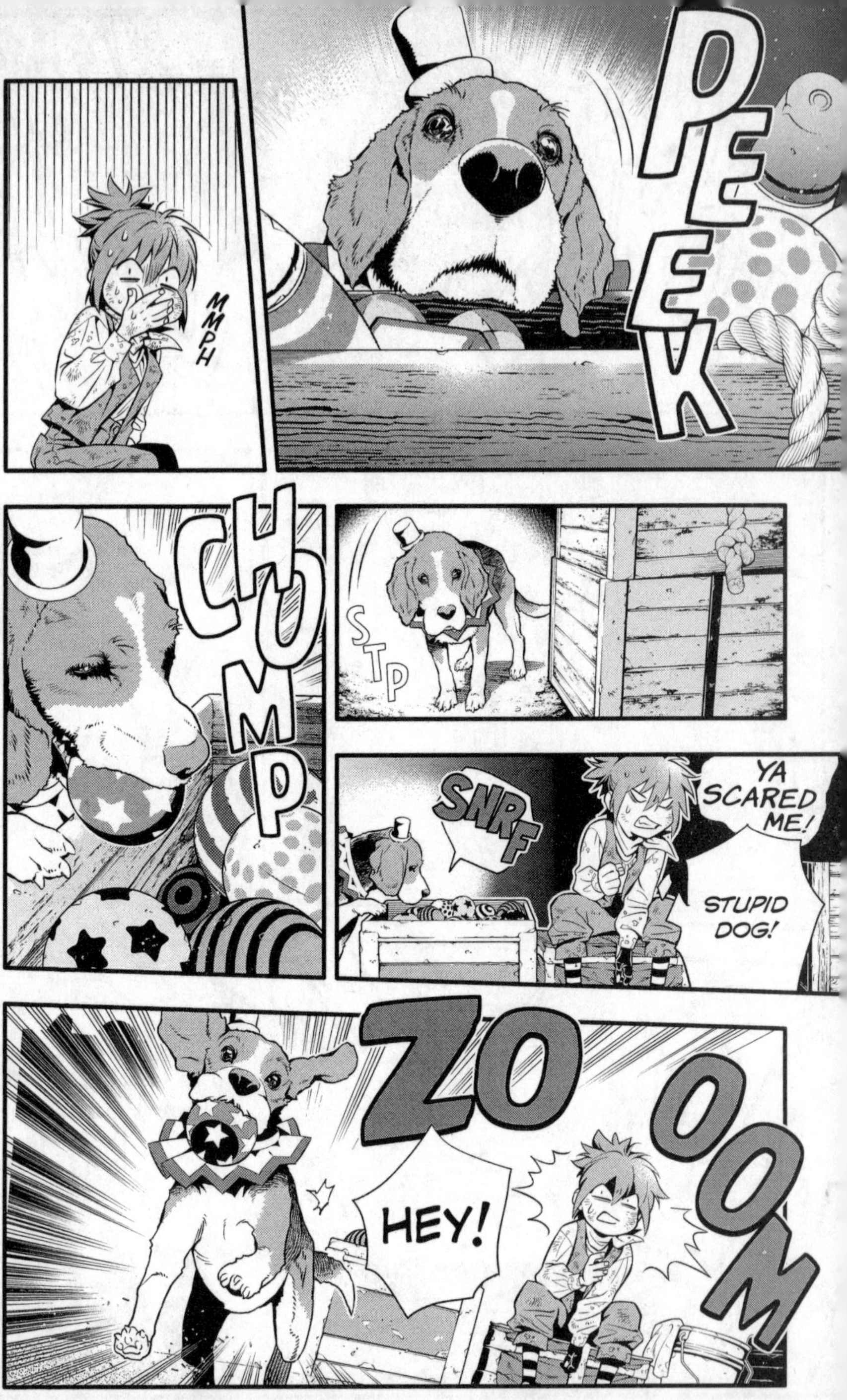
PEEK
MMPH
STP
YA SCARED ME!
STUPID DOG!
SNRF
CHOMP
ZOOOM
HEY!

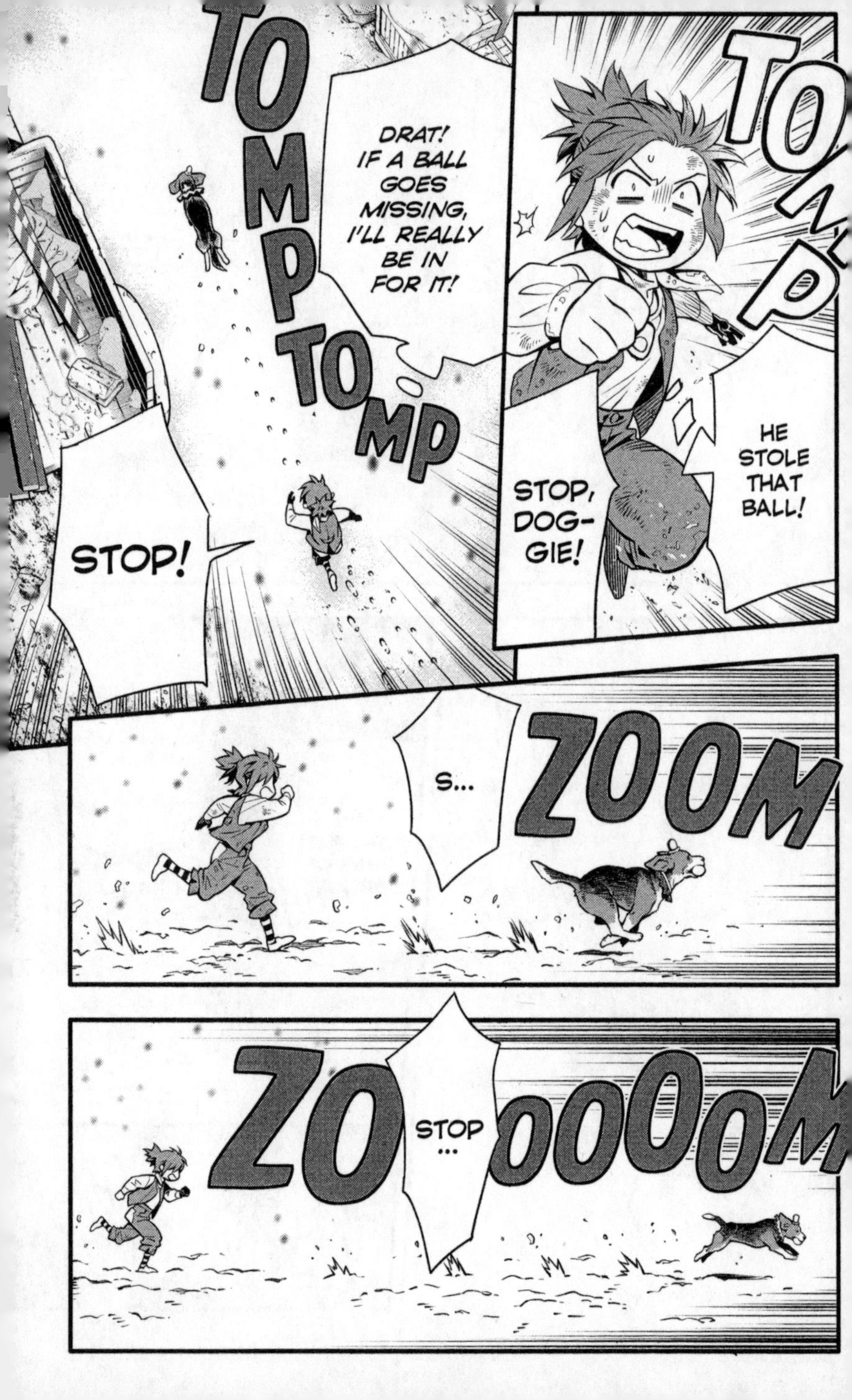
TOMP
HE STOLE THAT BALL!
STOP, DOGGIE!
TOMP TOMP TOMP
DRAT! IF A BALL GOES MISSING, I'LL REALLY BE IN FOR IT!
STOP!
ZOOM
S...
ZOOOOOM
STOP...

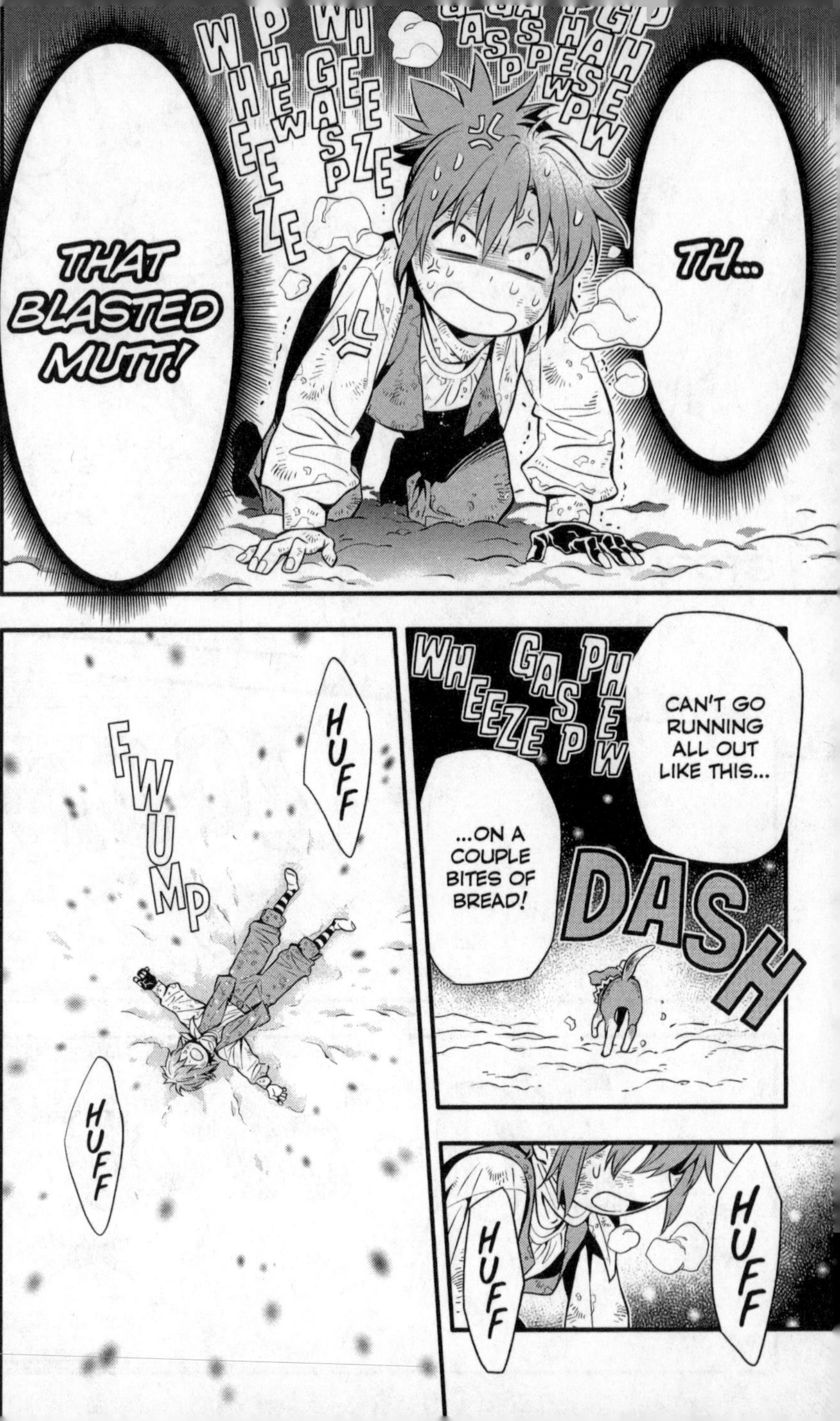
GASP GASP PHEW PHEW
WHEEZE WHEEZE
WHEEZE
TH...
THAT BLASTED MUTT!
PHEW
GASP
WHEEZE
CAN'T GO RUNNING ALL OUT LIKE THIS...
...ON A COUPLE BITES OF BREAD!
DASH
HUFF
HUFF
FWUMP
HUFF
HUFF

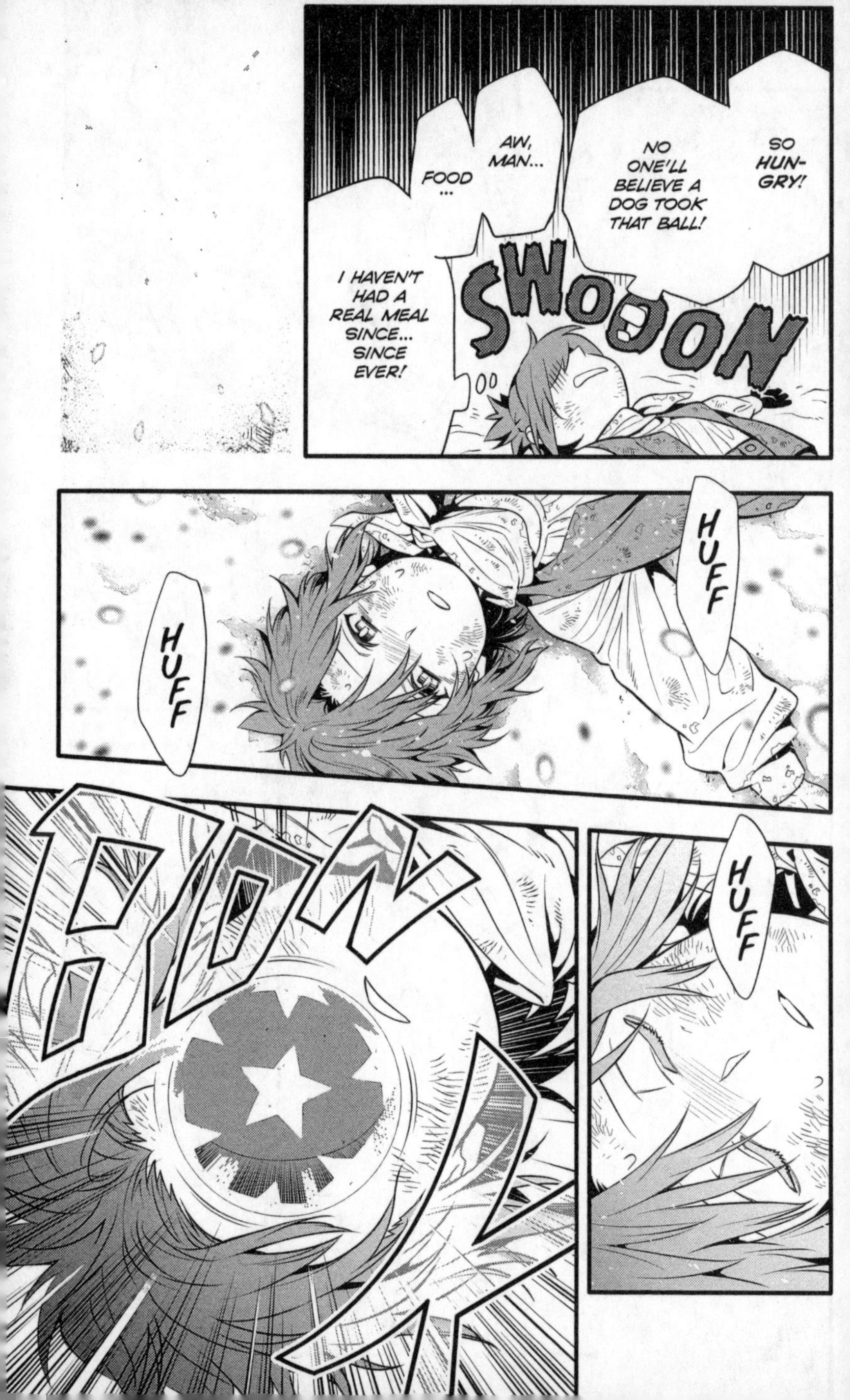
SO HUNGRY!
NO ONE'LL BELIEVE A DOG TOOK THAT BALL!
AW, MAN...
FOOD...
SWOOON
I HAVEN'T HAD A REAL MEAL SINCE... SINCE EVER!
HUFF
HUFF
HUFF
BOM

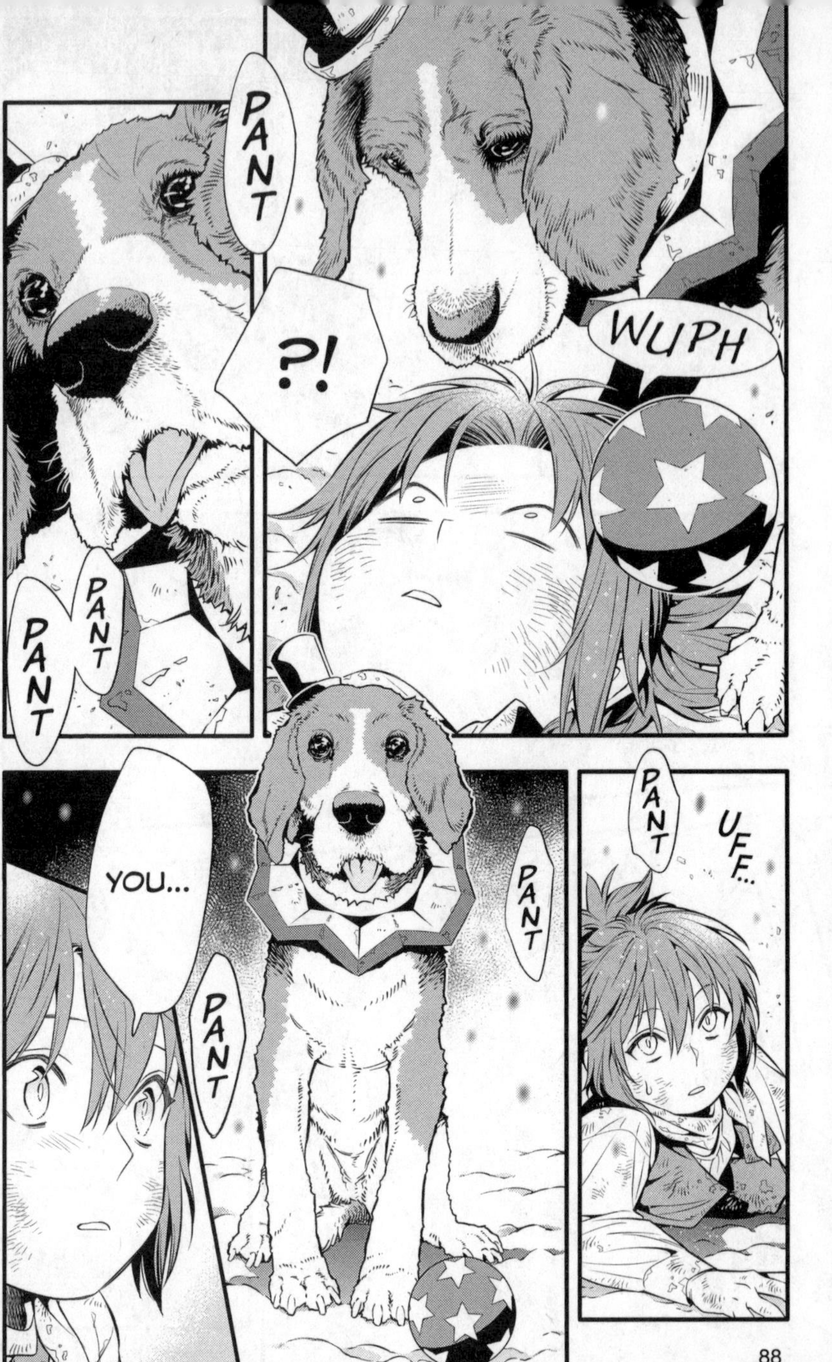
WUPH
PANT
?!
PANT
PANT
PANT
UFF...
PANT
PANT
YOU...

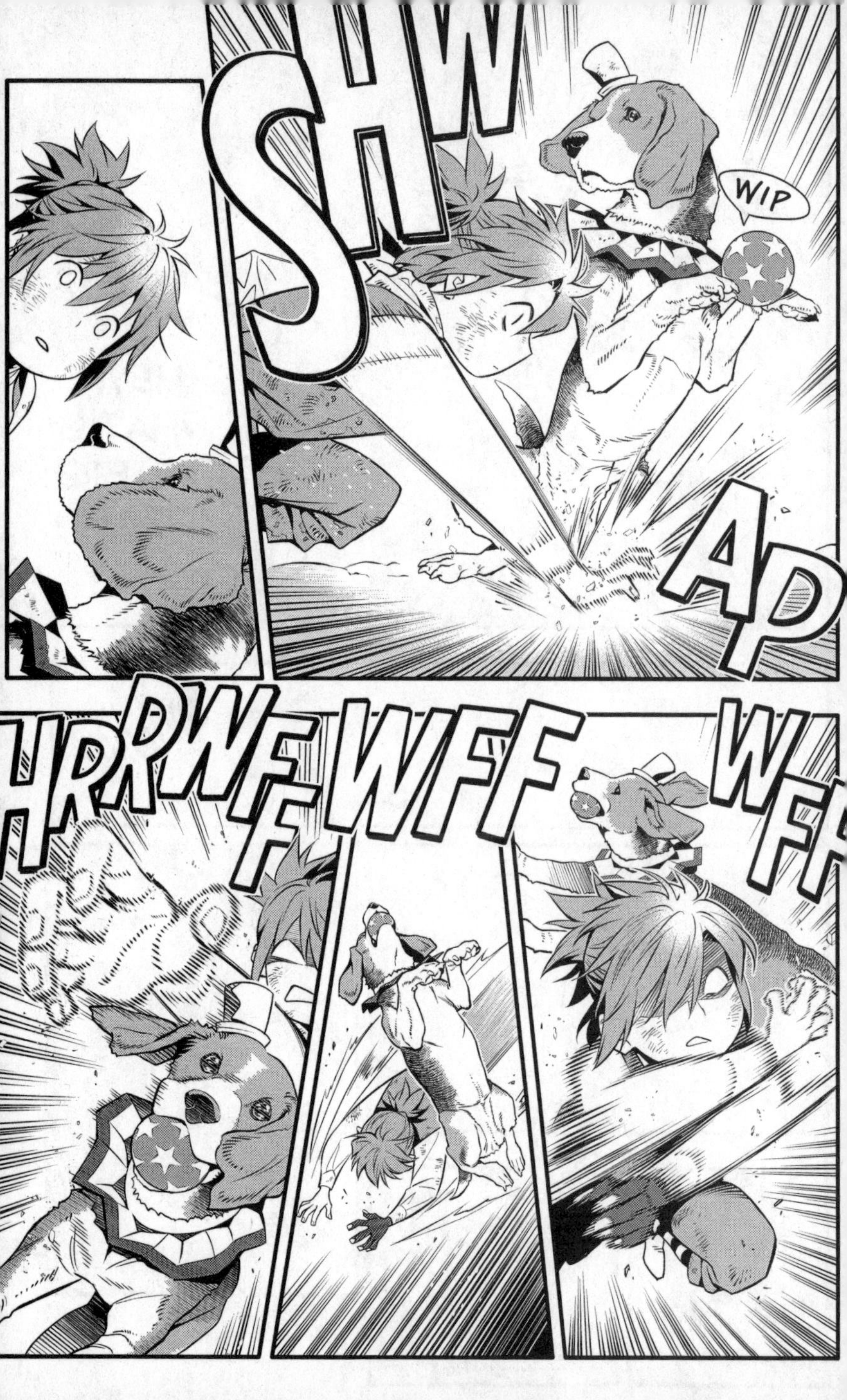
WIP
SHWAP
WFF
WFF
HRRWFF
Bu......

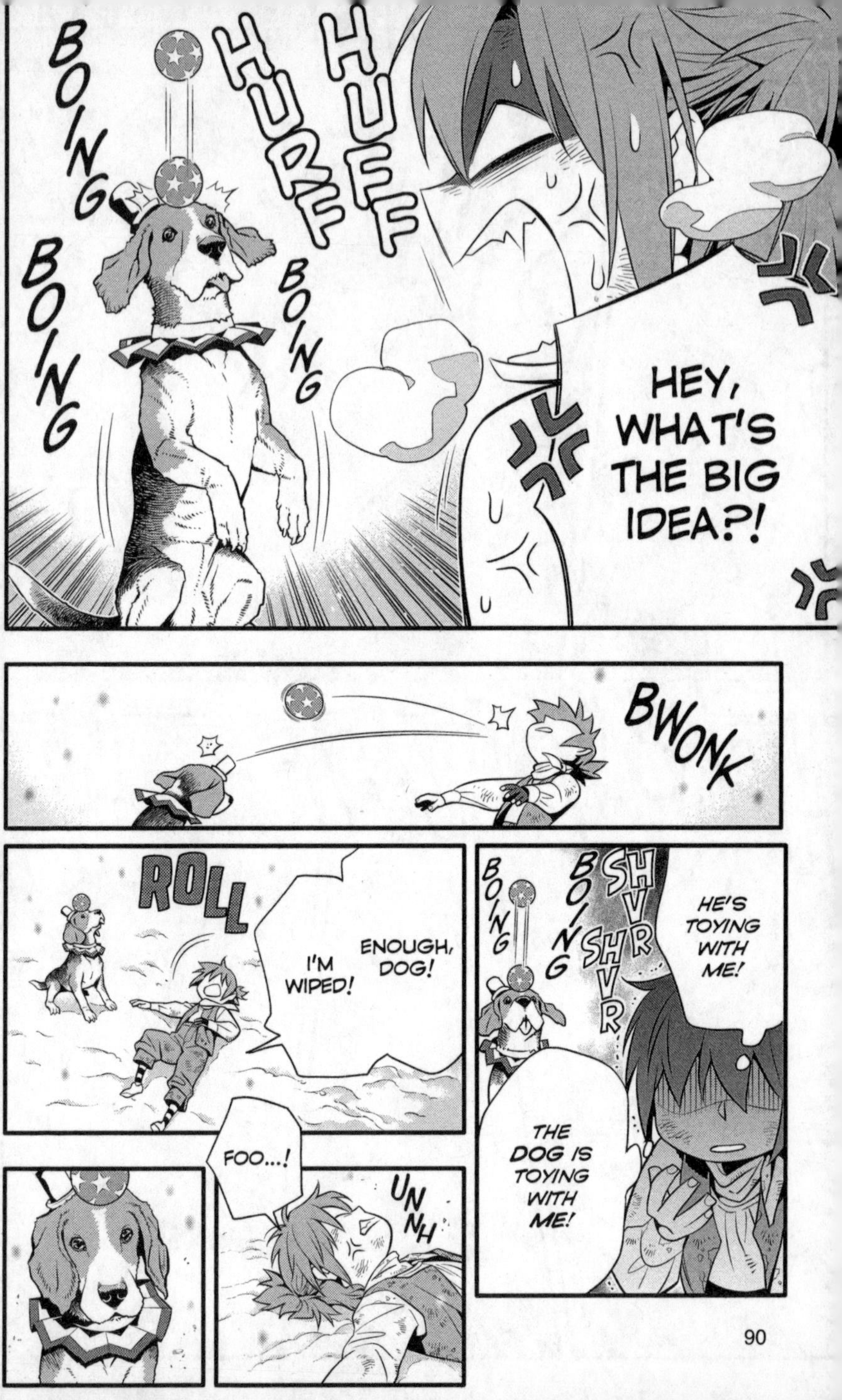
HEY, WHAT'S THE BIG IDEA?!
HUFF HUFF
BOING
BOING BOING
BWONK
HE'S TOYING WITH ME!
SHVR SHVR
BOING BOING
THE DOG IS TOYING WITH ME!
ENOUGH, DOG!
I'M WIPED!
ROLL
UNNH
FOO...!

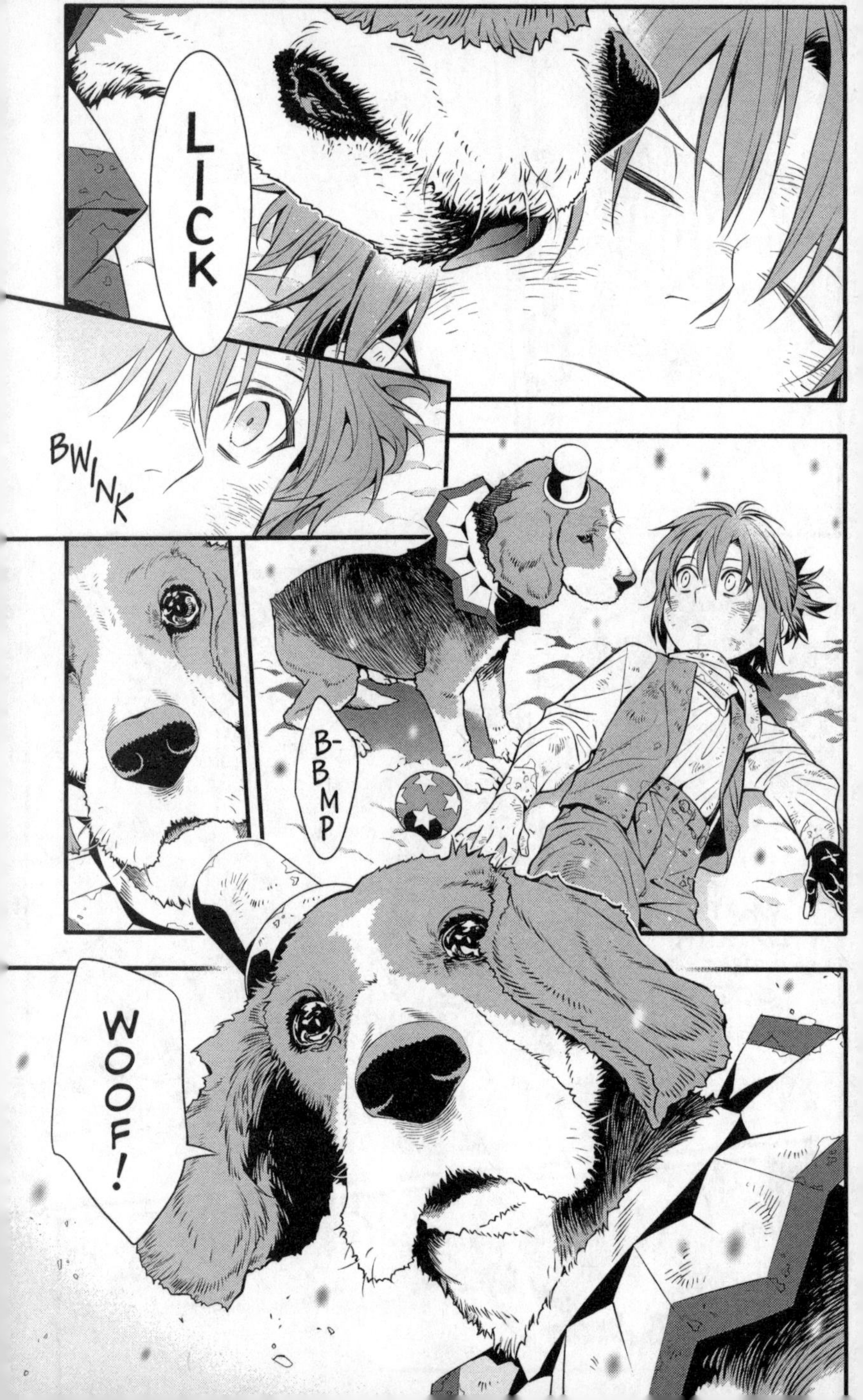
LICK
BWINK
B-BBMP
WOOF!

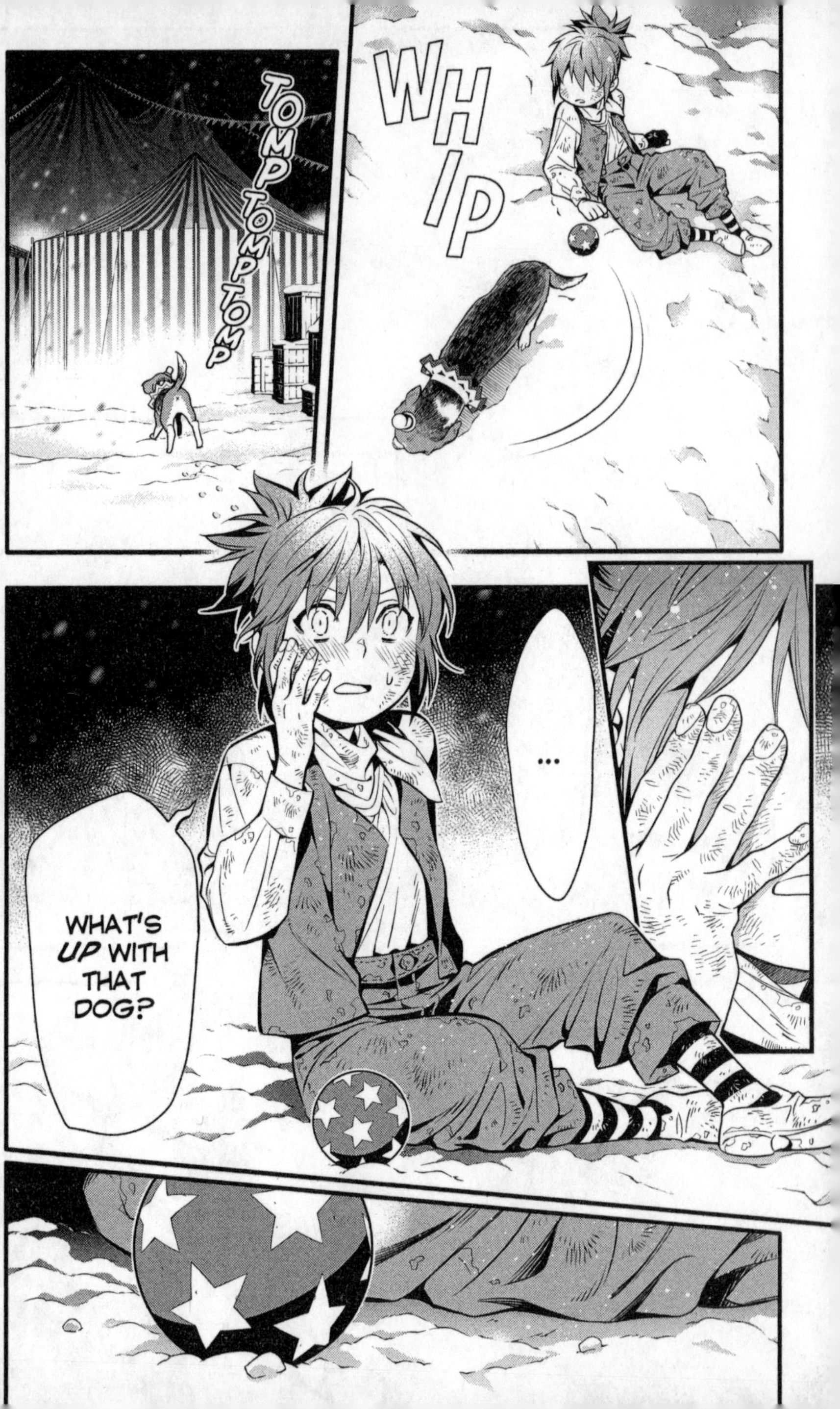
WHIP
TOMP TOMP TOMP
...
WHAT'S *UP* WITH THAT DOG?

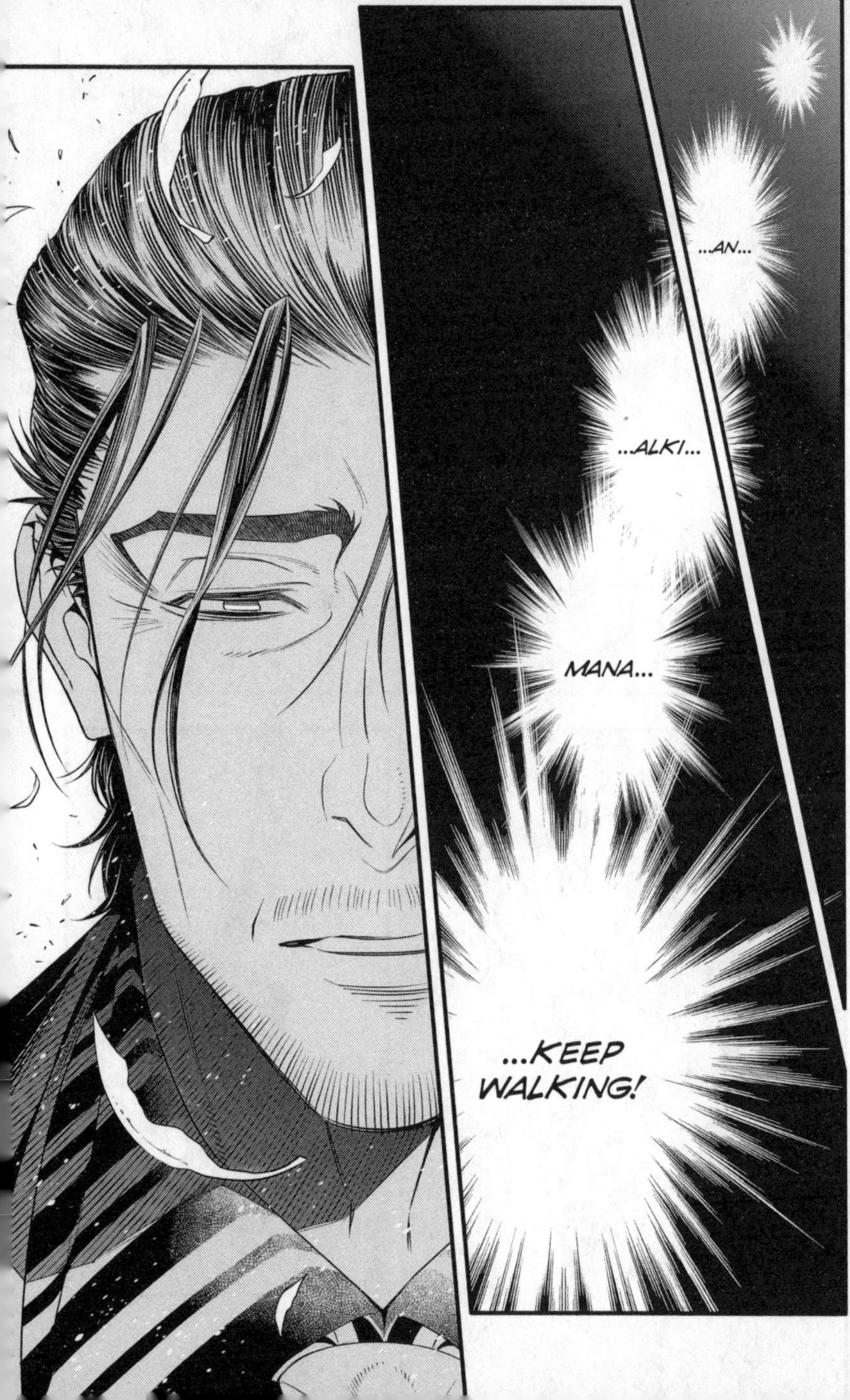
...AN...
...ALKI...
MANA...
...KEEP WALKING!

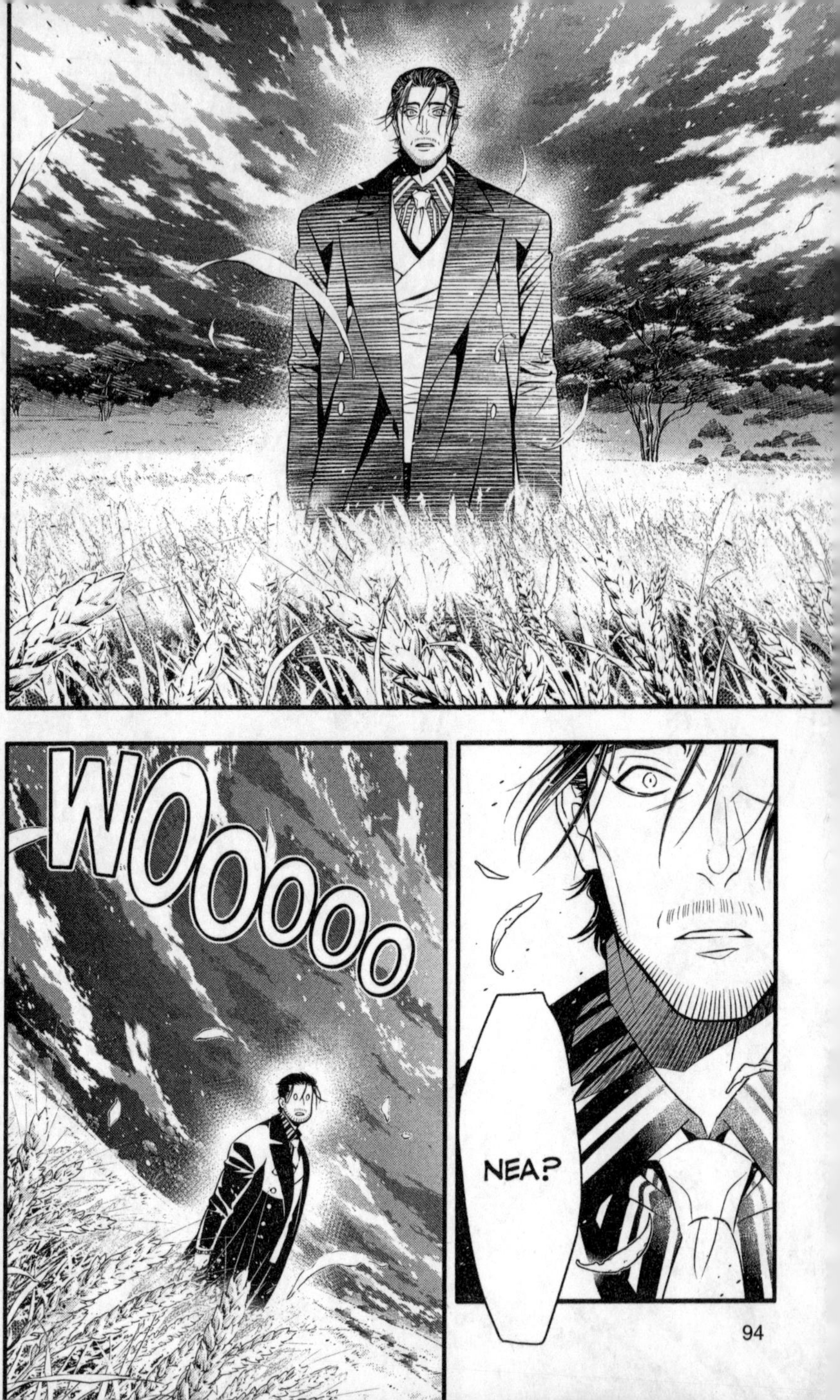
NEA?
WOOOOOO

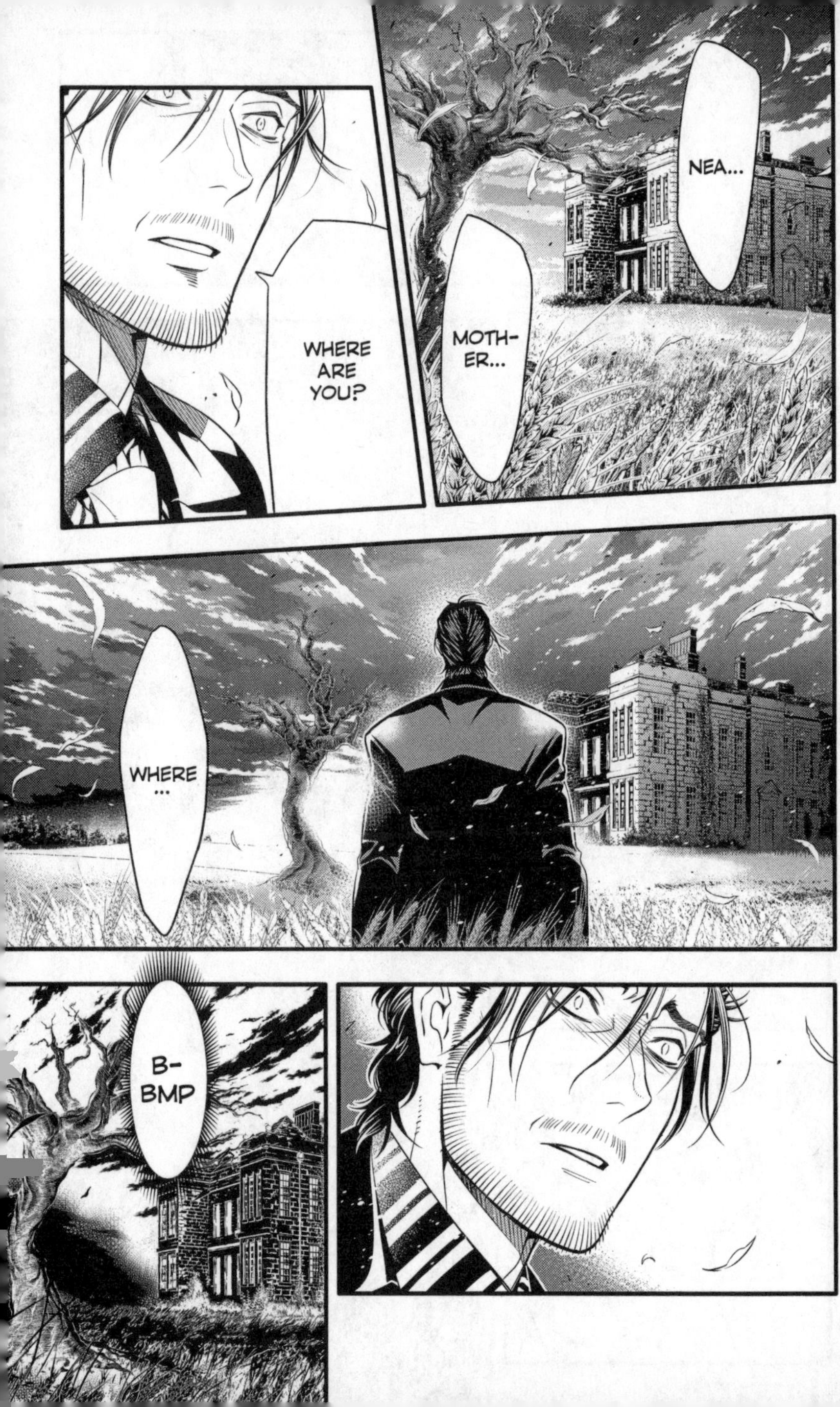
NEA...
MOTH-
ER...
WHERE
ARE
YOU?
WHERE
...
B-
BMP

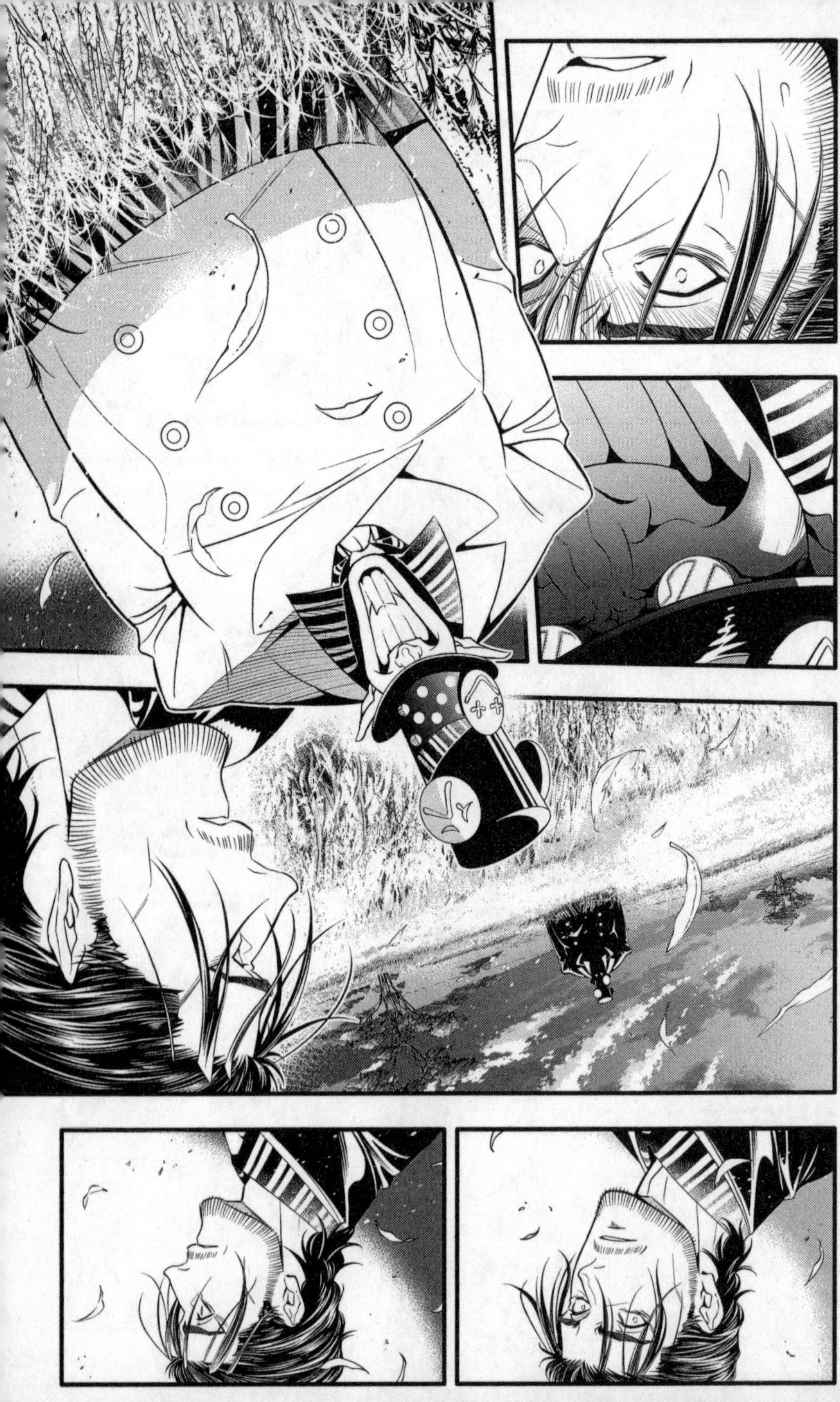

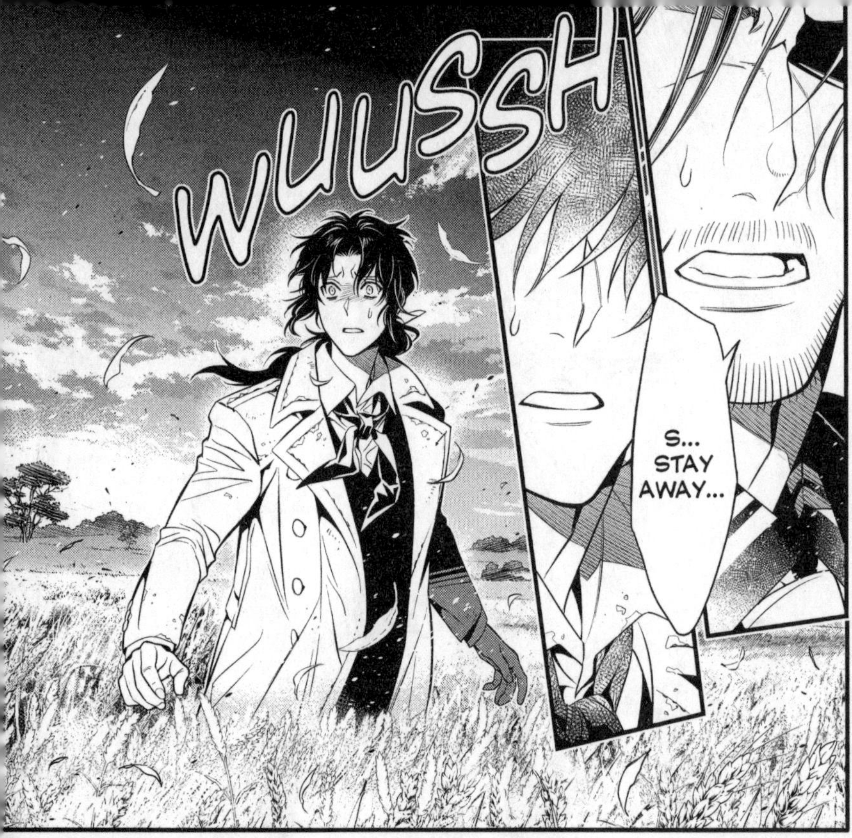
S... STAY AWAY...
WUUSSH
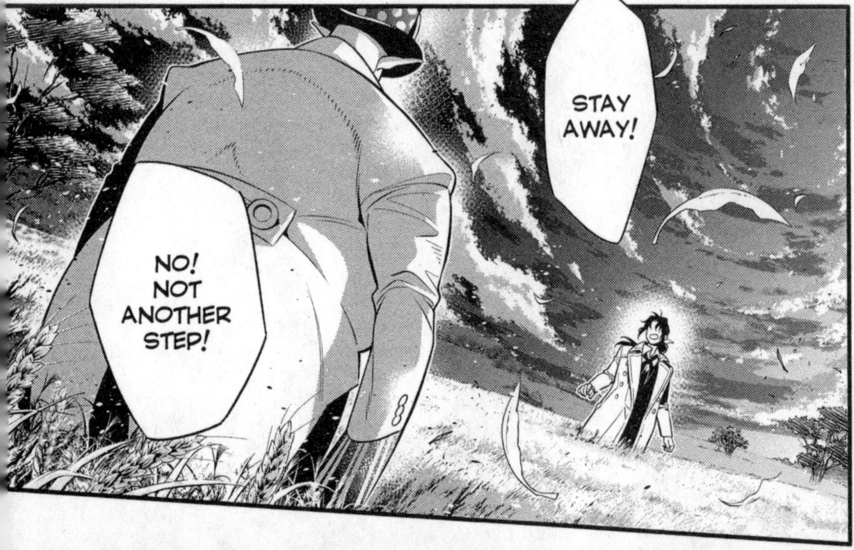
STAY AWAY!
NO! NOT ANOTHER STEP!

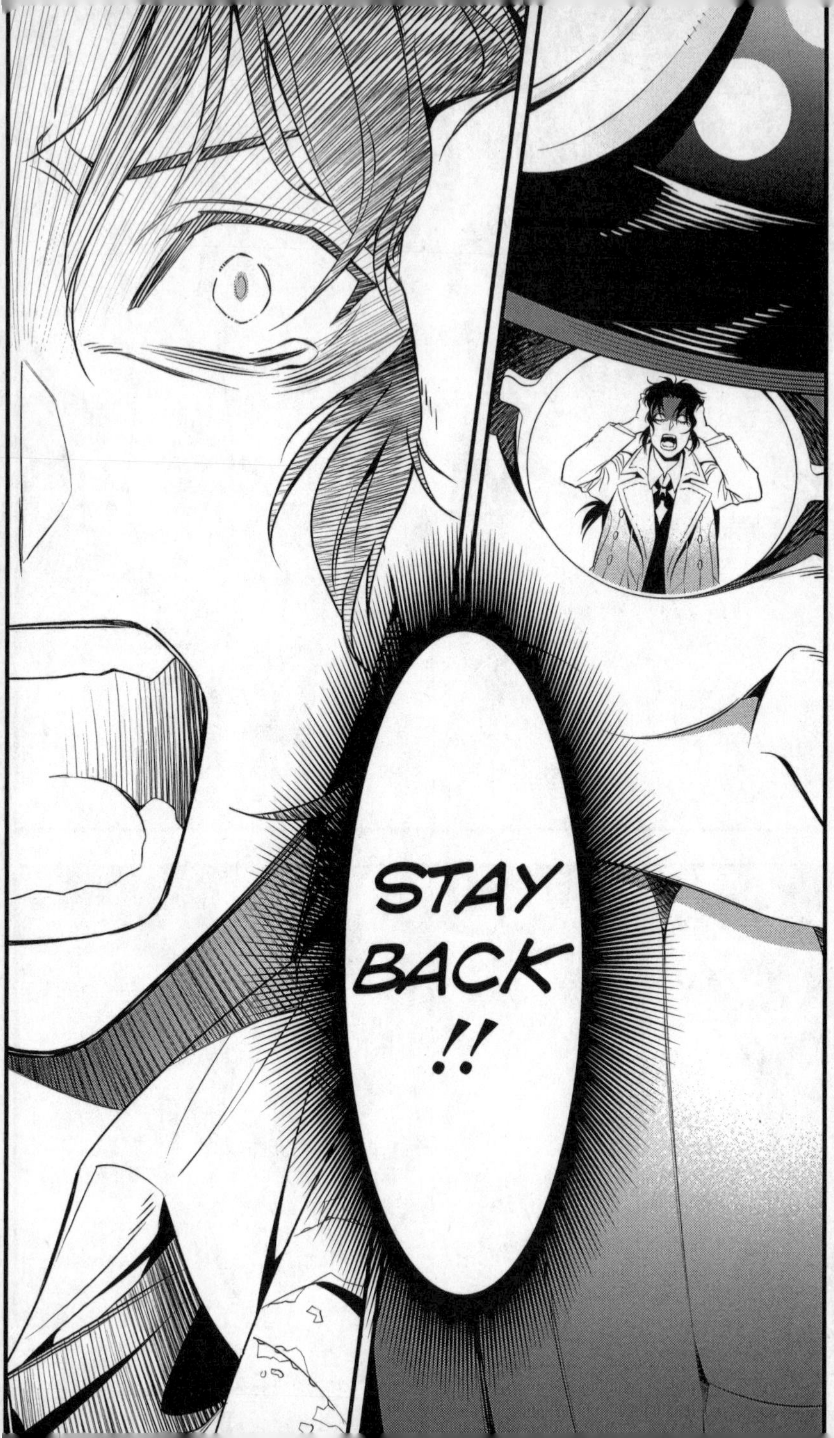
STAY BACK!!

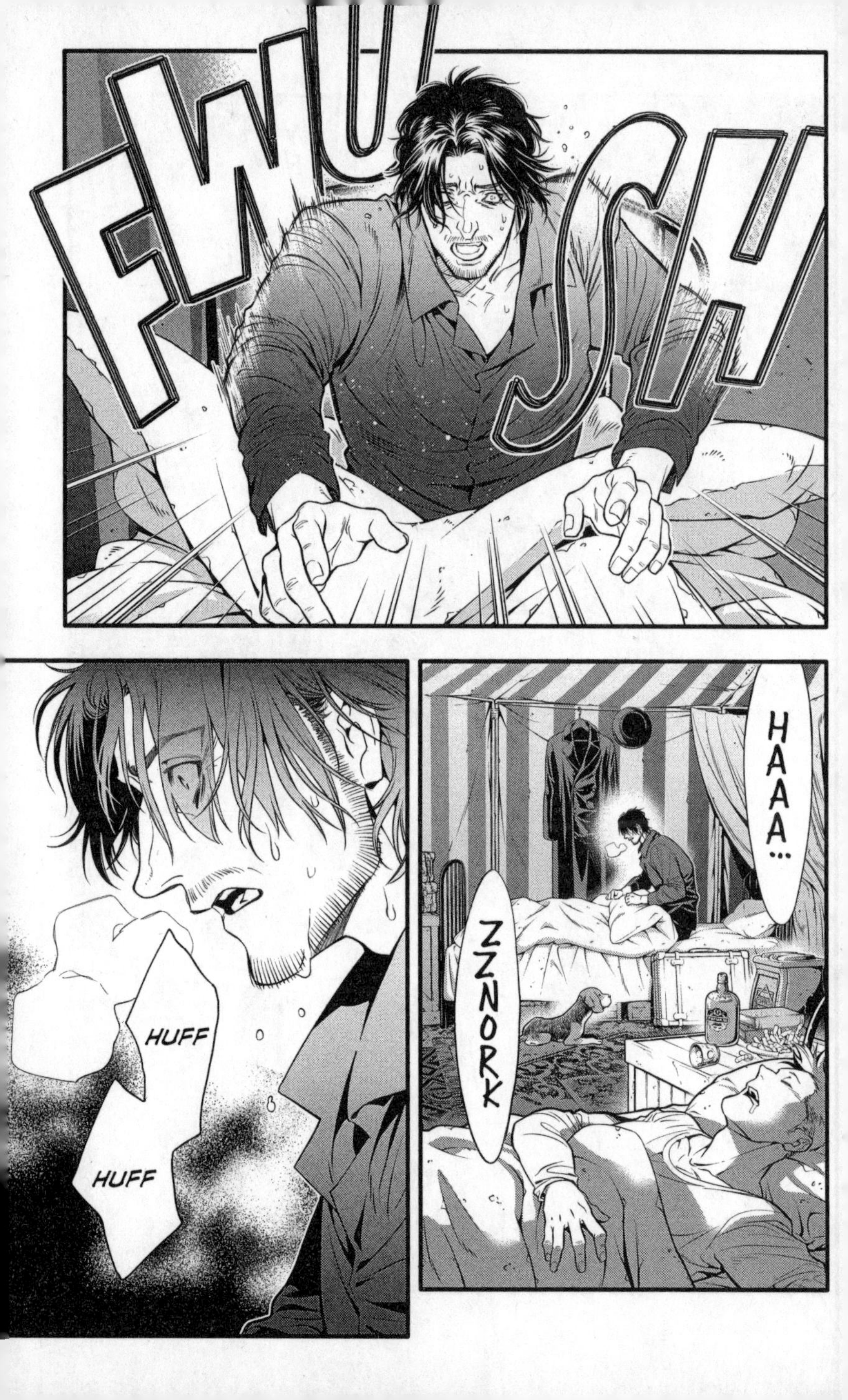
FWUUSCH
HAAA...
ZZNORK
HUFF
HUFF

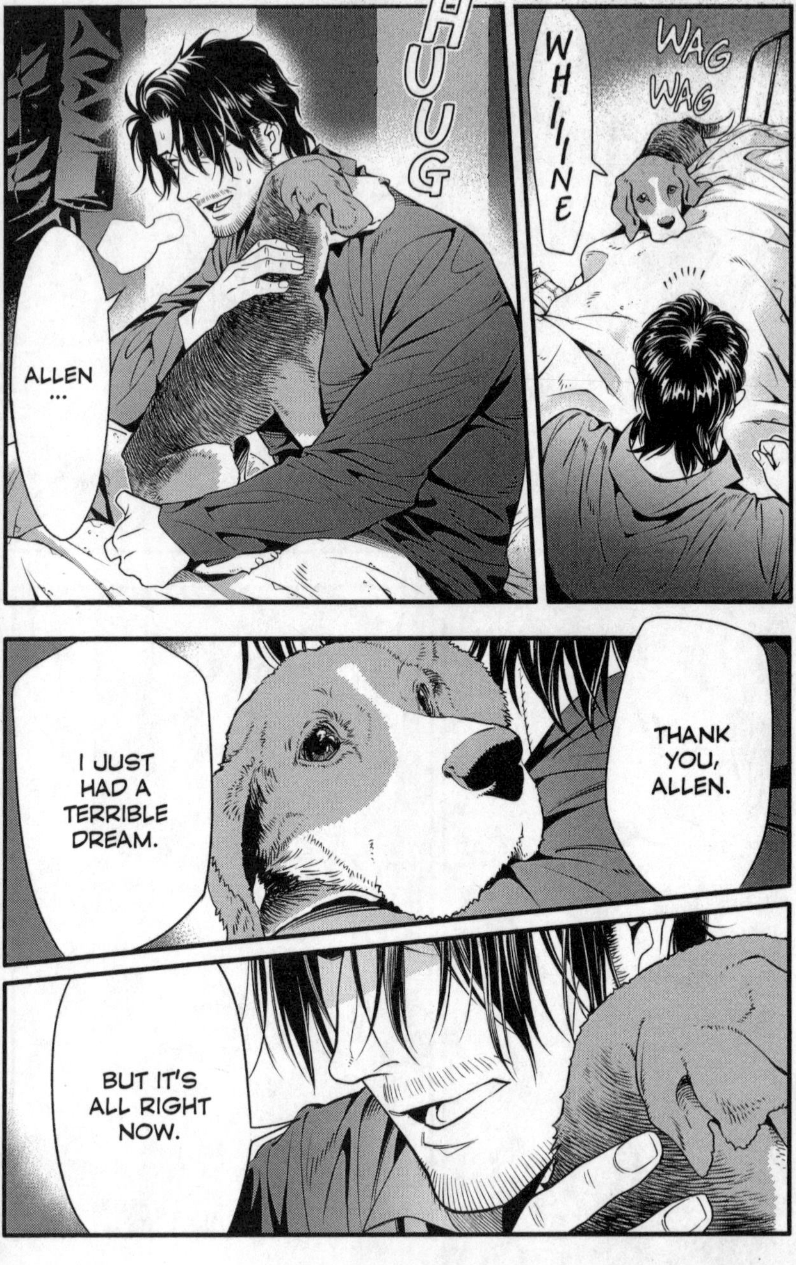
WAG WAG
WHIIIINE
HUUG
ALLEN ...
THANK YOU, ALLEN.
I JUST HAD A TERRIBLE DREAM.
BUT IT'S ALL RIGHT NOW.

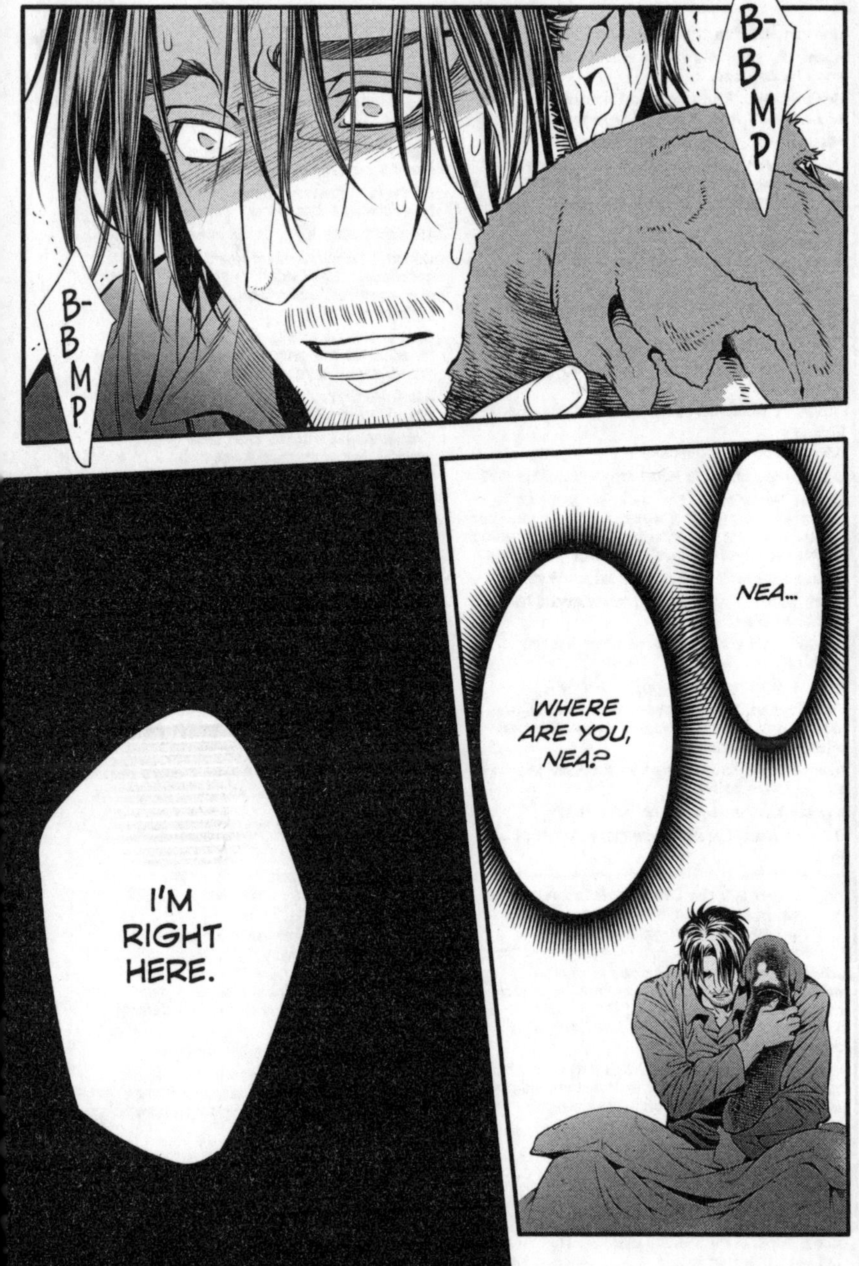
B-BBMP
B-BBMP
NEA...
WHERE ARE YOU, NEA?
I'M RIGHT HERE.

READ THIS WAY

Johnny: Huh? Is that true, Allen?

Allen: Uh, yeah. He wears a mask, but apparently he can see.

Johnny: Oh... I just assumed he couldn't. So why does he wear a mask? *(eyes shining)*

Allen: Uh-oh, Johnny's interested...

Johnny: Heh! General Cross can use magic, so the Science Section is quite interested in him. Always wondered what may be hiding under that mask.

Cross: Sorry, but I don't show what's under my mask even to women who catch my eye.

Allen: I've never seen him without it. Isn't it stuffy wearing that? Doesn't it get stinky? *(SNIFF SNIFF)*

Cross: Don't sniff it, dummy!

Tiedoll: Don't be snotty. Tell us why you wear it. Maybe it's just to look cool, eh?

Cross: It would be easier for me if that were true.

Allen: What do you mean?

Johnny: So there *is* some mystery behind it?!

Cross: Never mind. The question is about Bookman Jr., right? A member of that clan can get by with just one eye, because their physical abilities are well above the average person's.

Johnny: What?! How do you know *that*?!

Allen: Master, what do you know about the Bookman Clan?

Cross: I know a little about their founder. Now back off.

Allen & Johnny: Intriguing!

Tiedoll: Hmm... Maybe those physical abilities explain why even Yu couldn't defeat Bookman when they've sparred.

Allen: Huh? I know Bookman is tough, but Lavi always loses to Kanda.

Kanda: That's because he doesn't try.

Johnny: Man, I wish I knew more about all of this!

Q Johnny left the Order to follow Allen. He was in charge of making Order uniforms, so who took over for him?

Johnny: I wasn't the only one in charge of making uniforms. We draw on knowledge from various fields to make them. But I guess I was often in charge of design. I bet Cash is in charge of that now.

Allen: Come to think of it, there was another question like this one. Does the scrunchie you always wear match the one Cash wears?

Johnny: Uh...yeah. (blushes) She gave it to me.

Allen: *Ohhh...* (speculating)

Tiedoll: Isn't that sweet, Yu?

Kanda: Hunh?!

Cross: He left a woman to chase after my stupid pupil. Well, the Science Section always was big on suffering...

Q Krory is a count, so he must be cultured. Can he play a musical instrument? The piano and violin would suit him.

Allen: He can play both the piano and violin. And he's a good singer.

Johnny: I often overheard him at the Order talking with Marie about music.

Tiedoll: That's nice. Marie must enjoy that.

Johnny: Someone also asked if Krory is a good cook, but I don't really know. I've only ever seen him order food at the Order's cafeteria.

Cross: His cooking's not bad, but it's not as good as the grub whipped up by his grandfather, Arystar Krory I.

Allen: Huh? You've eaten Krory's cooking?! When? Where?!

Cross: At his castle, that time when his grandfather entrusted Roseanne (a carnivorous flower) to me and I went to deliver her. *(See vol. 5.)*

Allen: Roseanne! Now I remember! Master, did you know she had an Innocence? That flower turned Krory into an Accommodator.

Cross: You cretin, who do you think I am?! Of course I knew!

Allen: And you used your friendship with Krory's grandfather to borrow money from Krory!

Cross: Eh? I don't remember that.

Allen: Well, you did!

Cross: Really? Then you'd better pay it back.

Tiedoll: Marian, you are the worst.

Allen: Krory is a great friend. I can't believe this dolt of a master would take advantage of him!

Johnny: E-easy now, Allen, calm down! *(sweating)*

Cross: Hey, the question is whether Krory's a good cook, and I'm answering it! But you wanna criticize me?!

Johnny: Oh dear, oh dear, oh dear... *(sweating profusely)* Um, there was another question about Krory! Someone wanted to know what Kanda and Krory think of each other since they rarely interact. Answer that, Kanda!

Kanda: Why? I don't think about him.

Johnny: But when Jiji was talking about which was sharper and tougher, Krory's fangs or Mugen, it seemed like you had something to say.

Kanda: W-well, I didn't!

Johnny: But when it came up how Krory stopped Lavi's hammer with his fangs, you kept glancing over!

Continued on page 184...

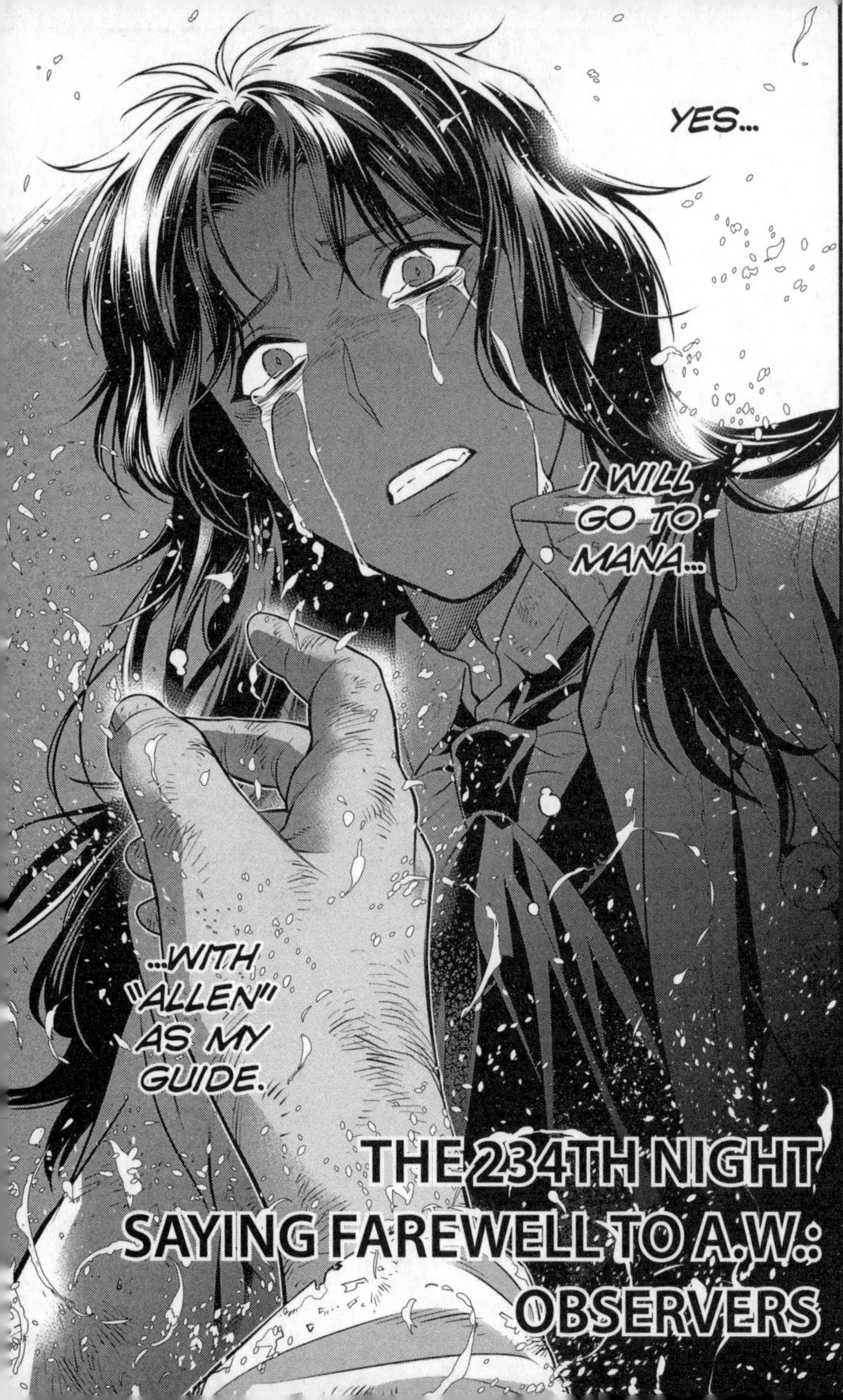
YES...
I WILL GO TO MANA...
...WITH "ALLEN" AS MY GUIDE.
THE 234TH NIGHT
SAYING FAREWELL TO A.W.: OBSERVERS

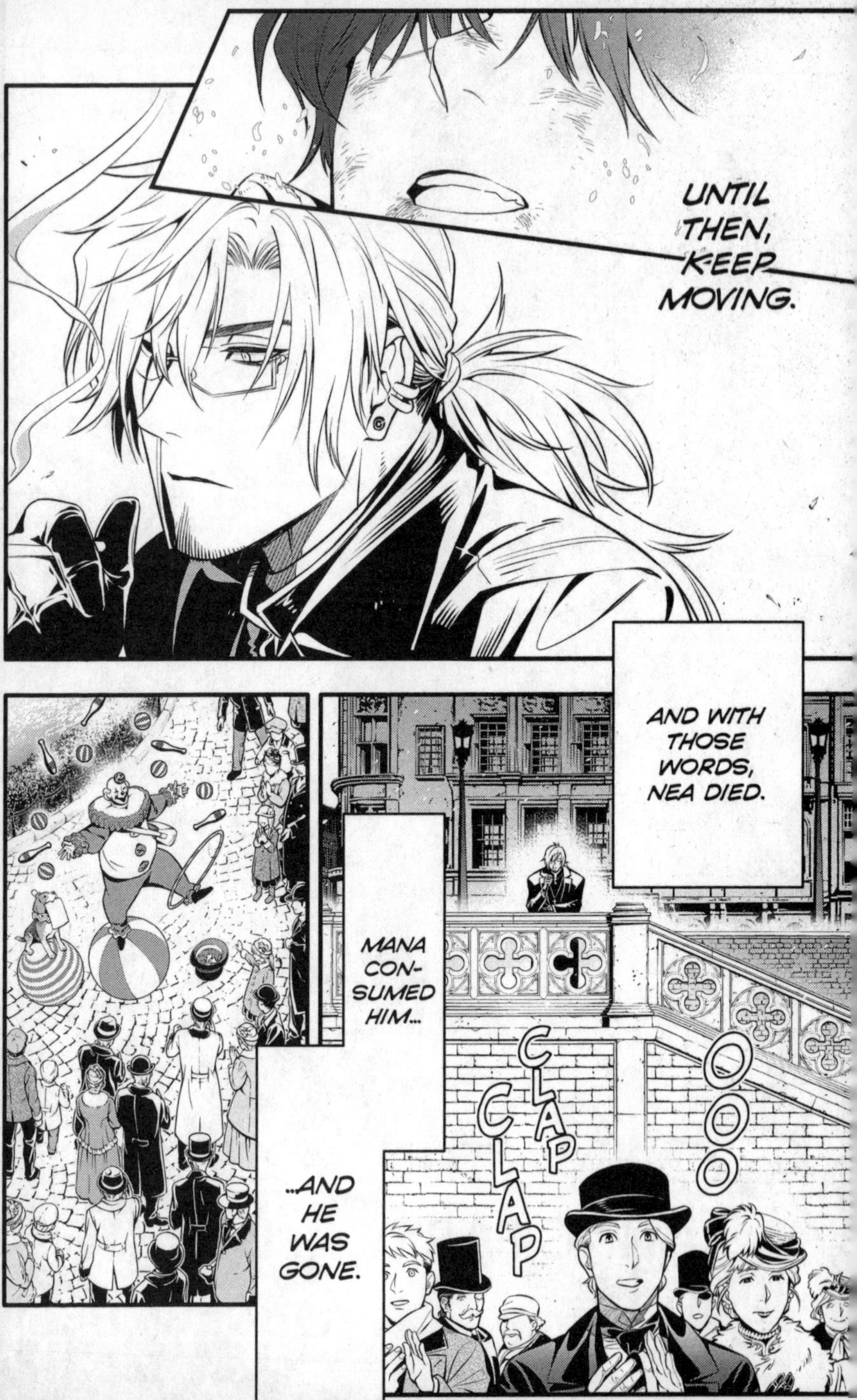
UNTIL THEN, KEEP MOVING.
AND WITH THOSE WORDS, NEA DIED.
MANA CON-SUMED HIM...
OOO
CLAP CLAP
...AND HE WAS GONE.

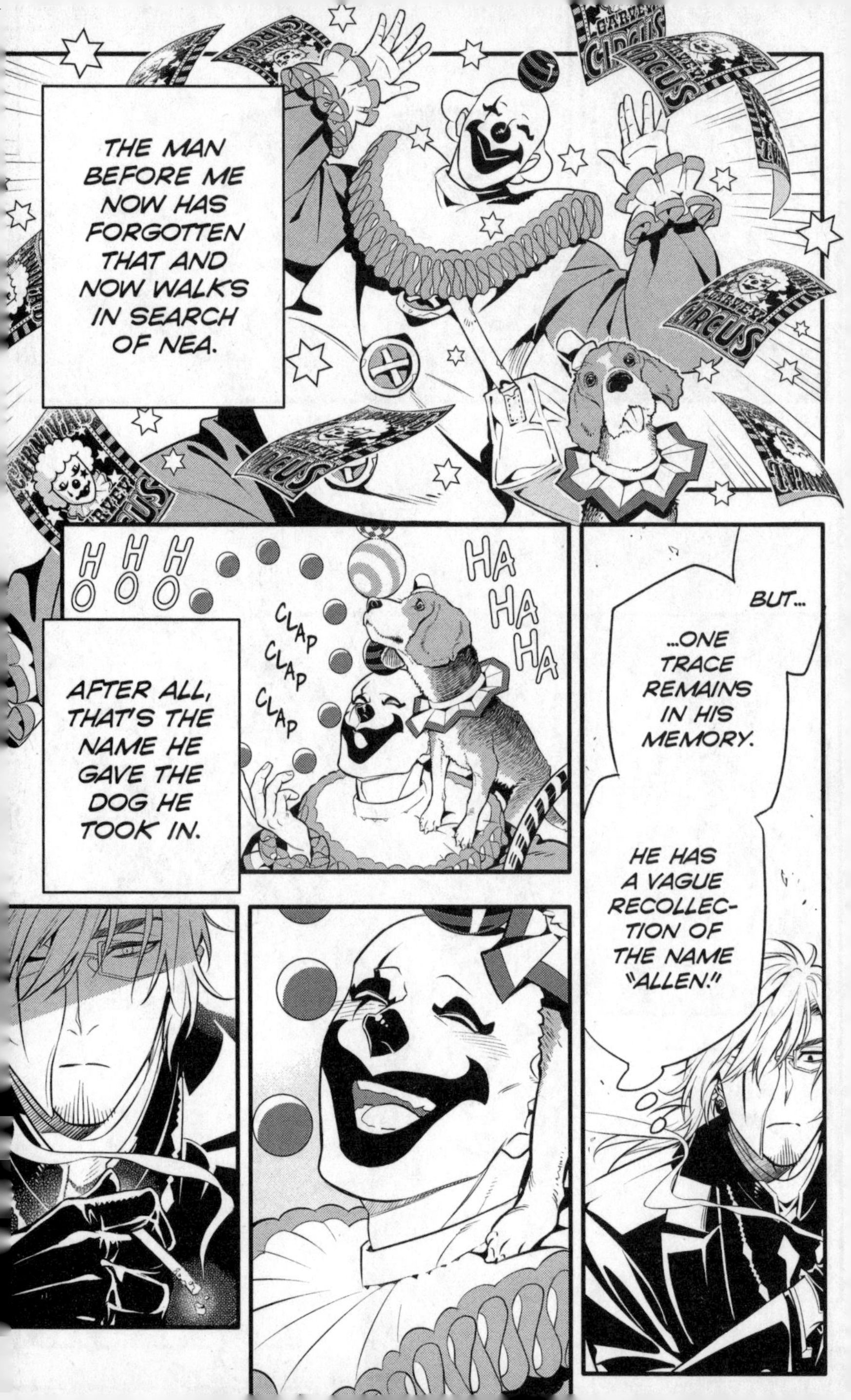
THE MAN BEFORE ME NOW HAS FORGOTTEN THAT AND NOW WALKS IN SEARCH OF NEA.
BUT...
...ONE TRACE REMAINS IN HIS MEMORY.
HE HAS A VAGUE RECOLLECTION OF THE NAME "ALLEN."
HA HA HA
HO HO HO
CLAP CLAP CLAP
AFTER ALL, THAT'S THE NAME HE GAVE THE DOG HE TOOK IN.

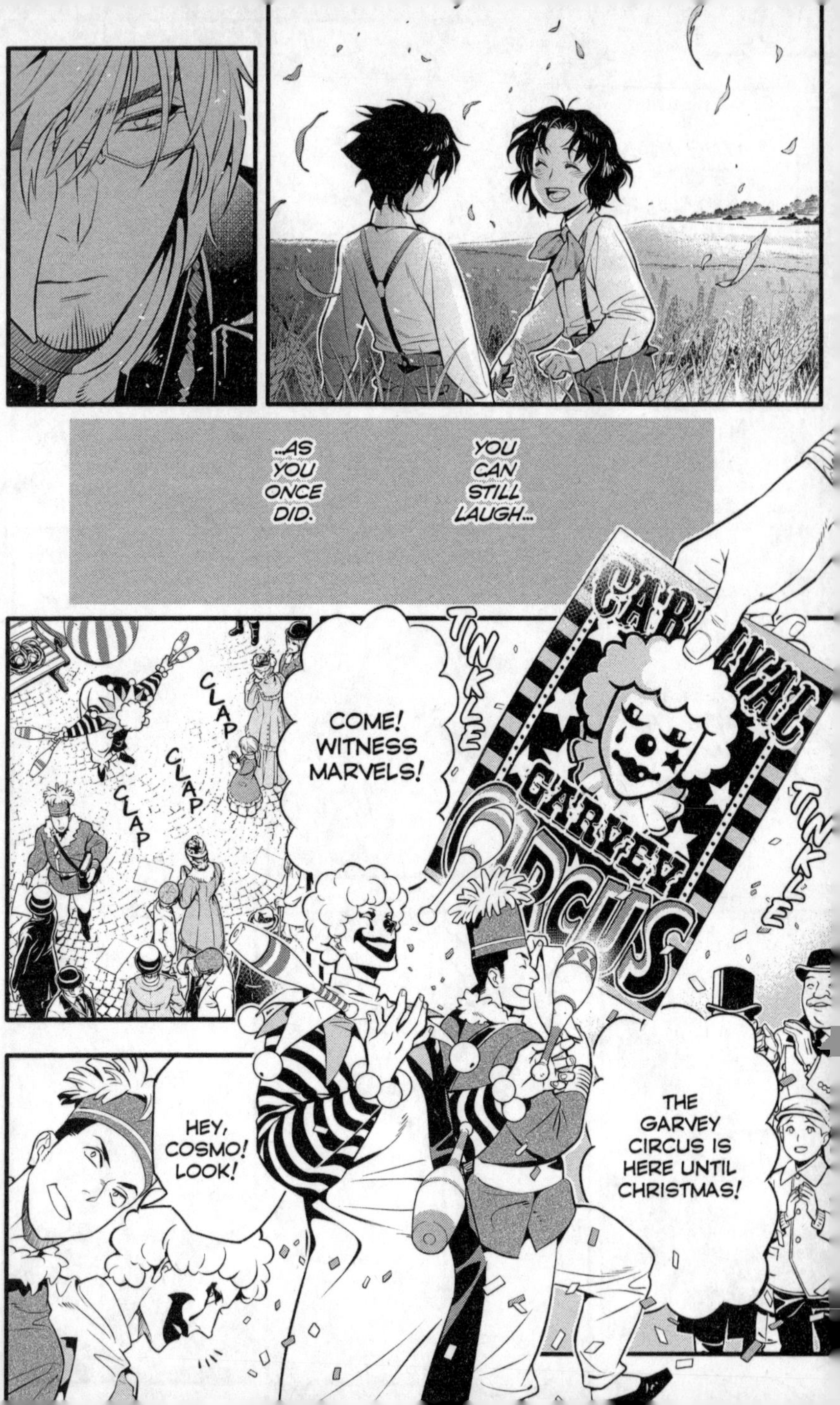
YOU CAN STILL LAUGH...
...AS YOU ONCE DID.
TINKLE
TINKLE
COME! WITNESS MARVELS!
CARNIVAL
GARVEY CIRCUS
CLAP
CLAP
CLAP
THE GARVEY CIRCUS IS HERE UNTIL CHRISTMAS!
HEY, COSMO! LOOK!

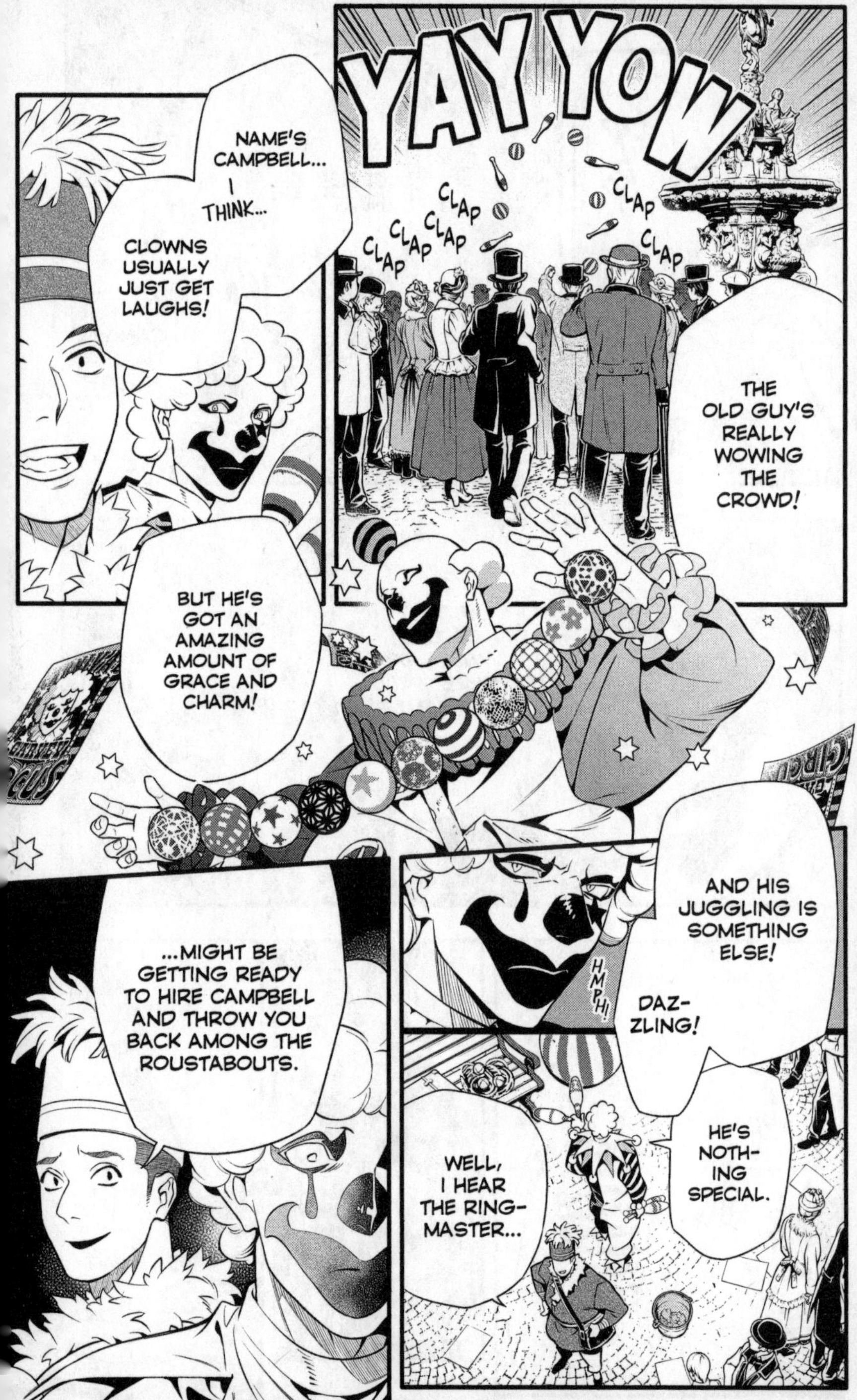
YAY YOW
CLAP CLAP CLAP CLAP CLAP CLAP
THE OLD GUY'S REALLY WOWING THE CROWD!
NAME'S CAMPBELL... I THINK...
CLOWNS USUALLY JUST GET LAUGHS!
BUT HE'S GOT AN AMAZING AMOUNT OF GRACE AND CHARM!
AND HIS JUGGLING IS SOMETHING ELSE!
HMPH!
DAZ-ZLING!
HE'S NOTH-ING SPECIAL.
WELL, I HEAR THE RING-MASTER...
...MIGHT BE GETTING READY TO HIRE CAMPBELL AND THROW YOU BACK AMONG THE ROUSTABOUTS.

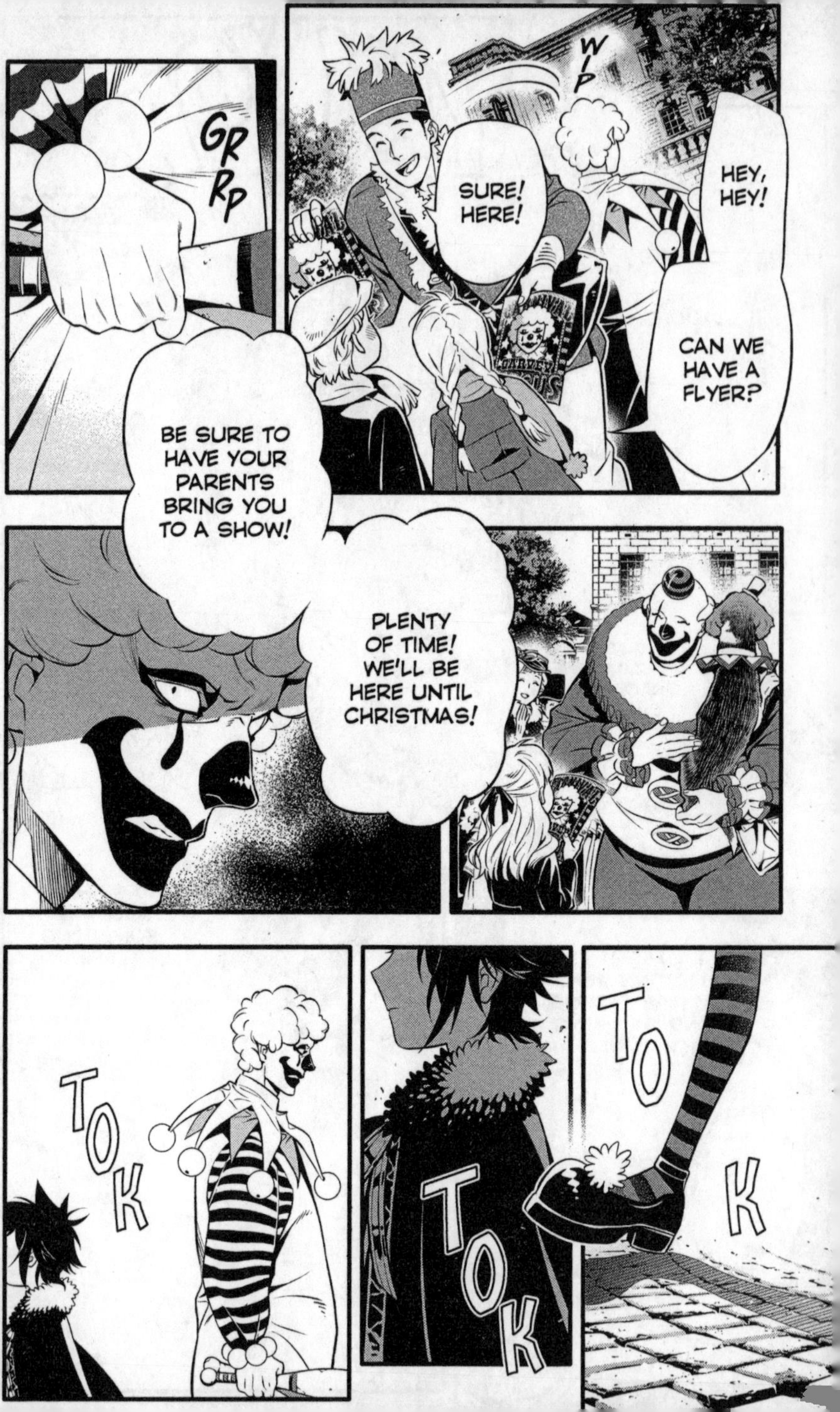
HEY, HEY!
CAN WE HAVE A FLYER?
WIP
SURE! HERE!
GRRP
BE SURE TO HAVE YOUR PARENTS BRING YOU TO A SHOW!
PLENTY OF TIME! WE'LL BE HERE UNTIL CHRISTMAS!
TOK
TOK
TOK

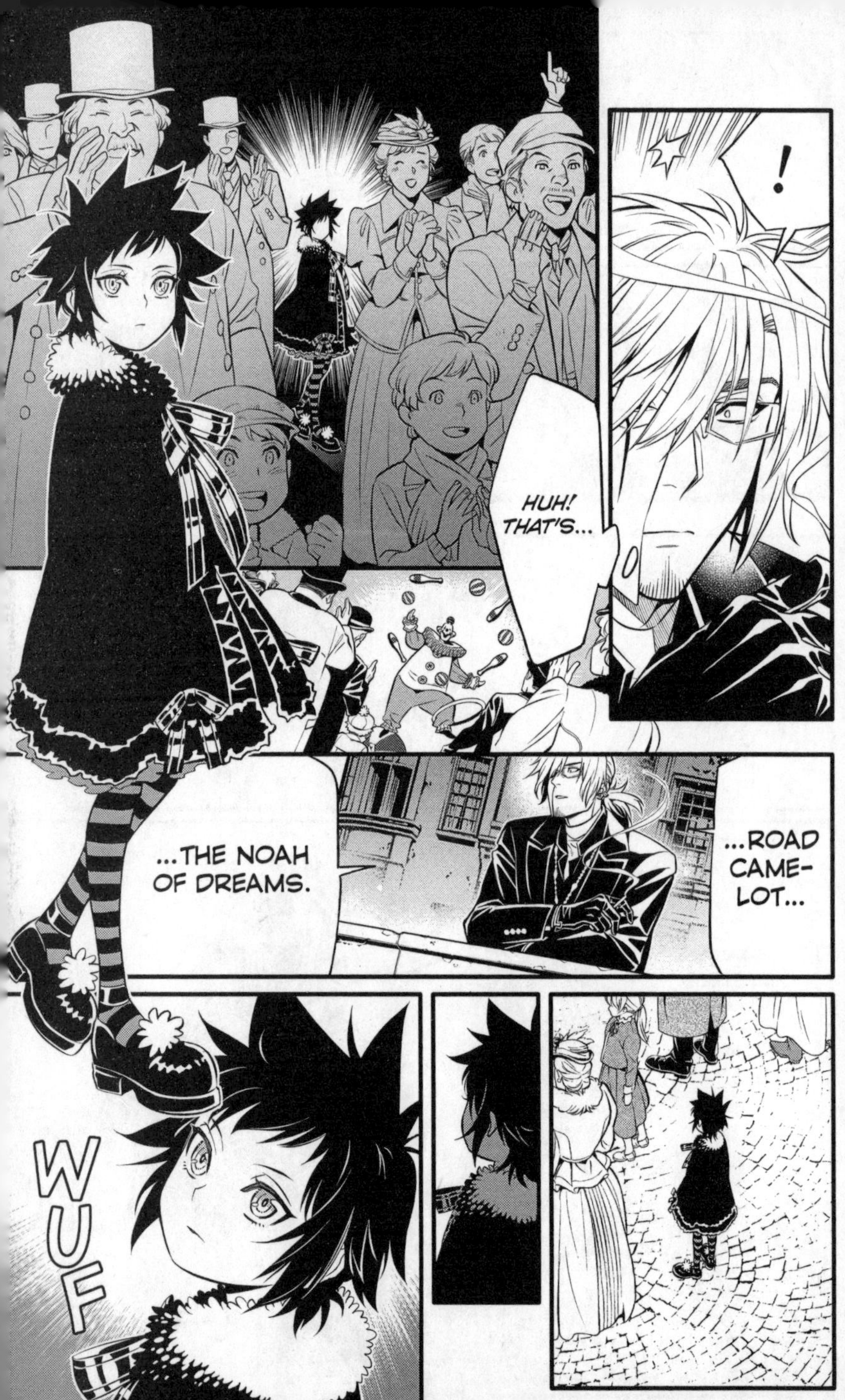
!
HUH! THAT'S...
...ROAD CAME-LOT...
...THE NOAH OF DREAMS.
WUF

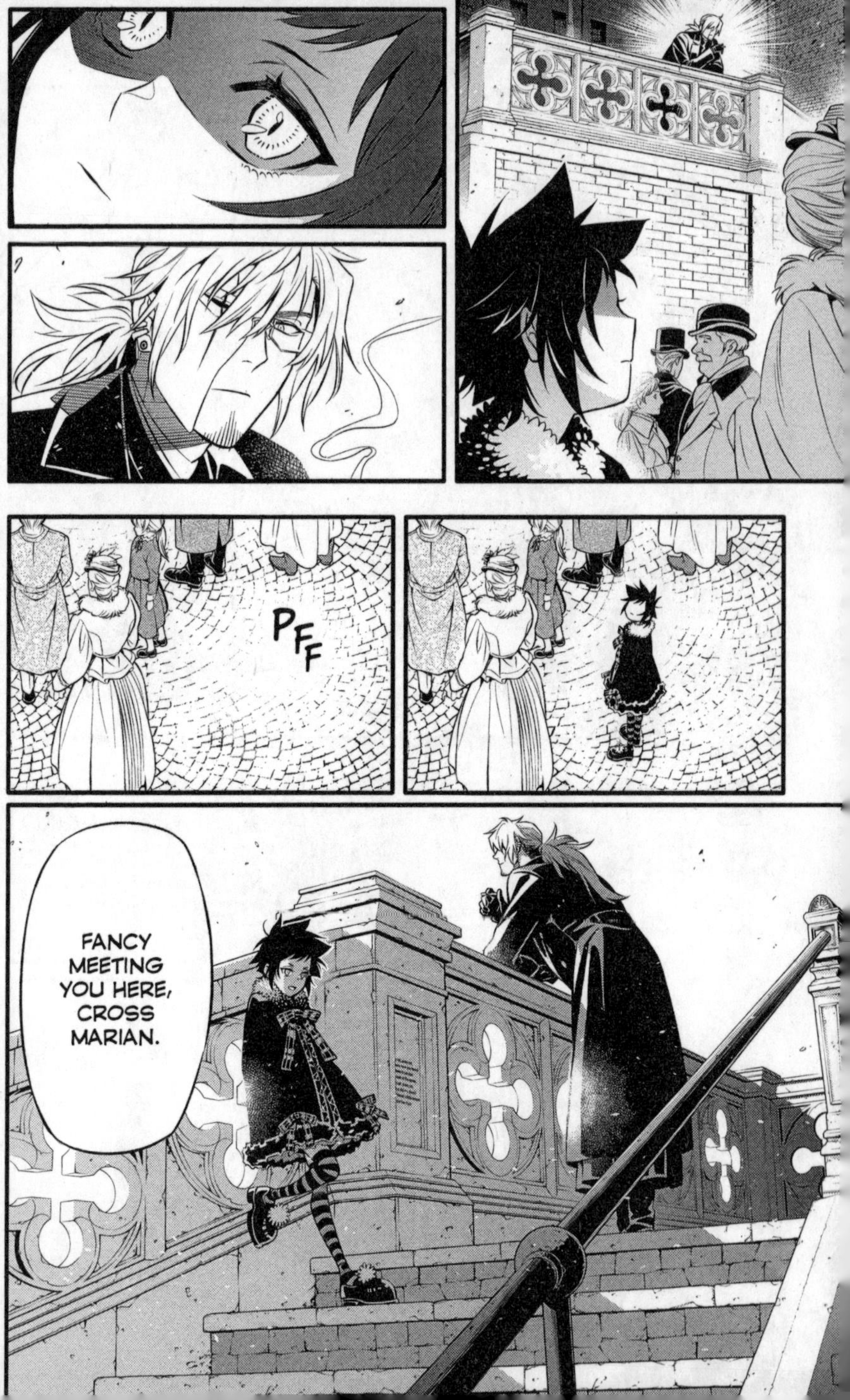
PFF
FANCY MEETING YOU HERE, CROSS MARIAN.

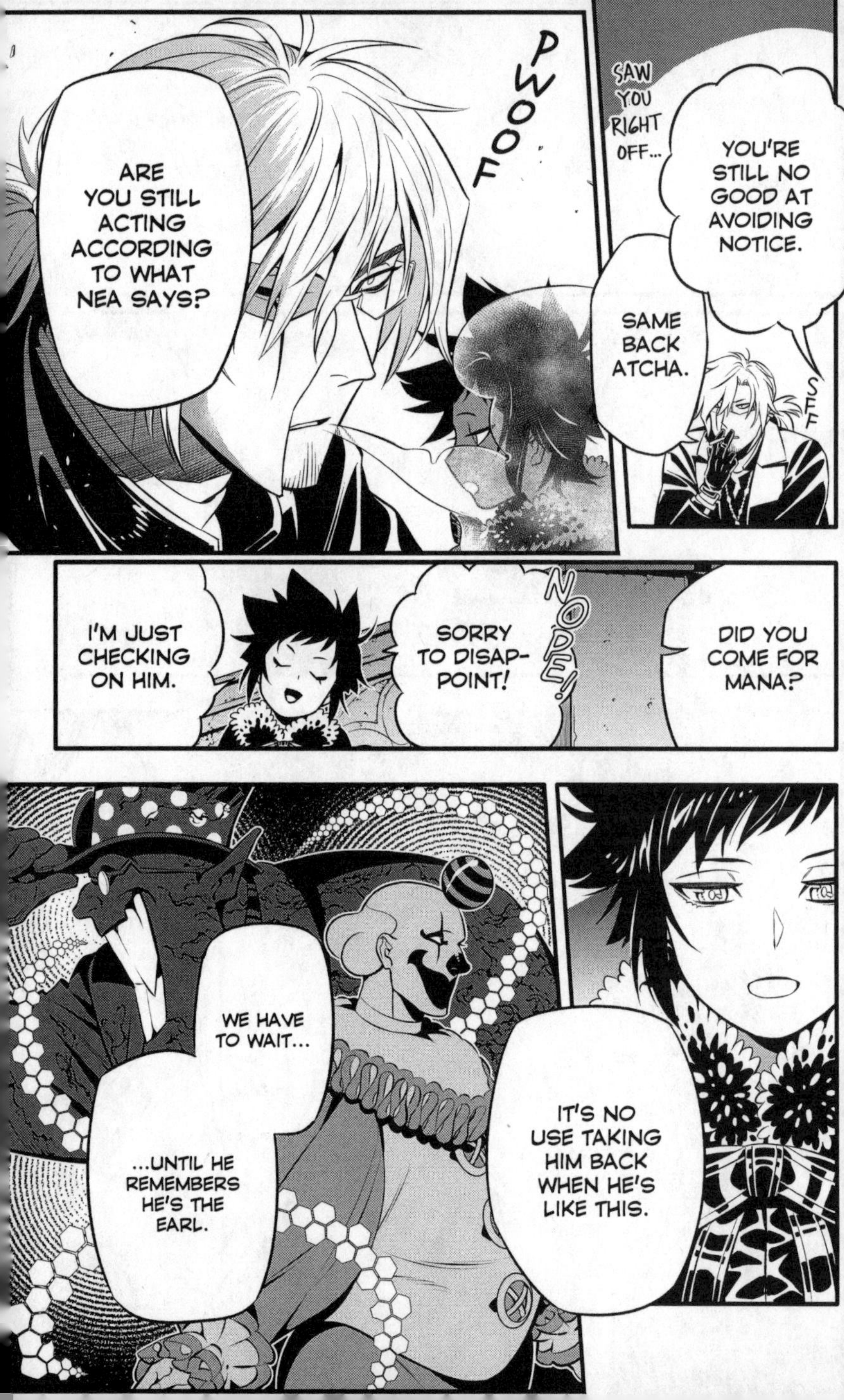
SAW YOU RIGHT OFF...
YOU'RE STILL NO GOOD AT AVOIDING NOTICE.
SFF
SAME BACK ATCHA.
PWOOF
ARE YOU STILL ACTING ACCORDING TO WHAT NEA SAYS?
DID YOU COME FOR MANA?
NOPE!
SORRY TO DISAP-POINT!
I'M JUST CHECKING ON HIM.
IT'S NO USE TAKING HIM BACK WHEN HE'S LIKE THIS.
WE HAVE TO WAIT...
...UNTIL HE REMEMBERS HE'S THE EARL.

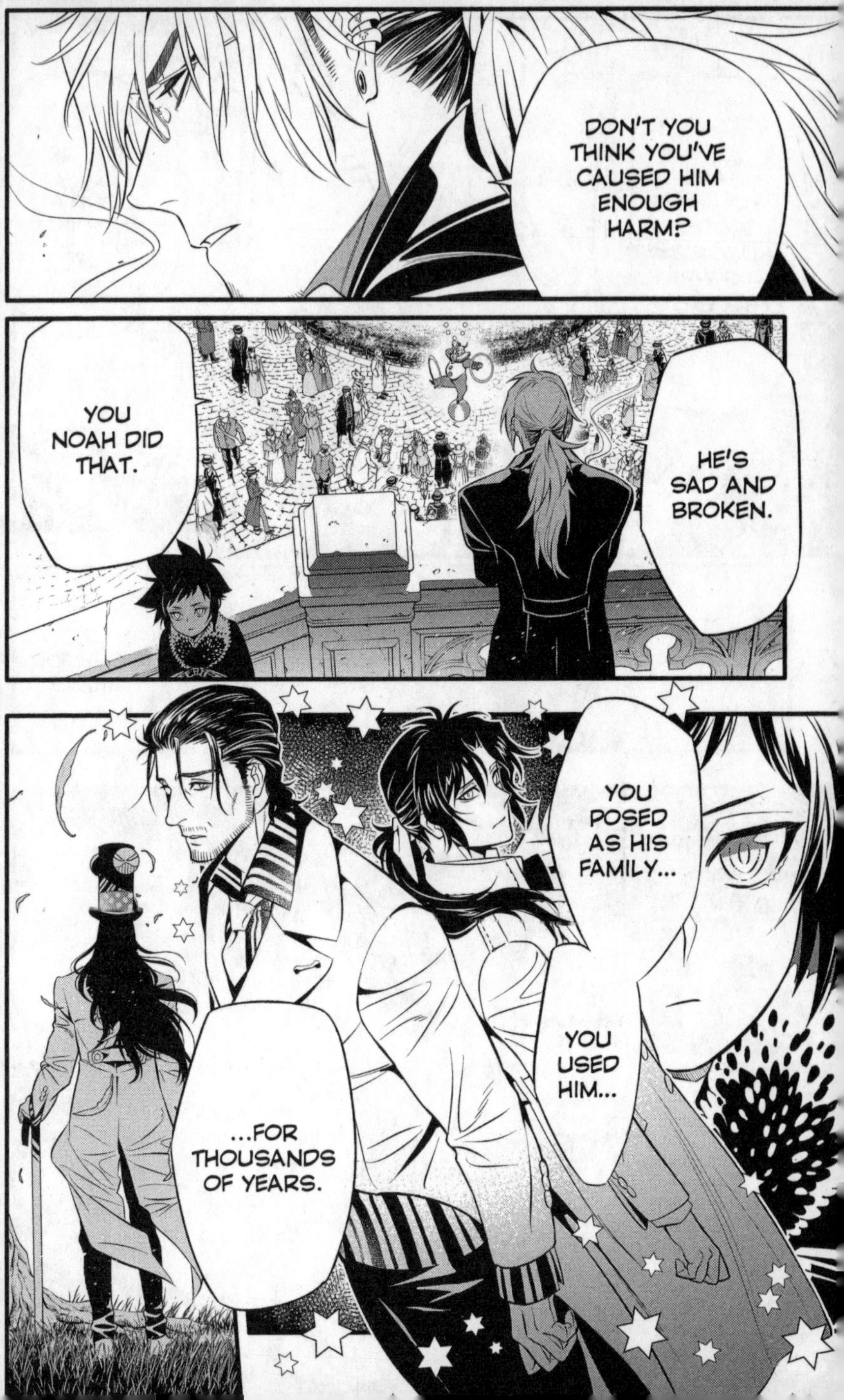
DON'T YOU THINK YOU'VE CAUSED HIM ENOUGH HARM?
HE'S SAD AND BROKEN.
YOU NOAH DID THAT.
YOU POSED AS HIS FAMILY...
YOU USED HIM...
...FOR THOUSANDS OF YEARS.

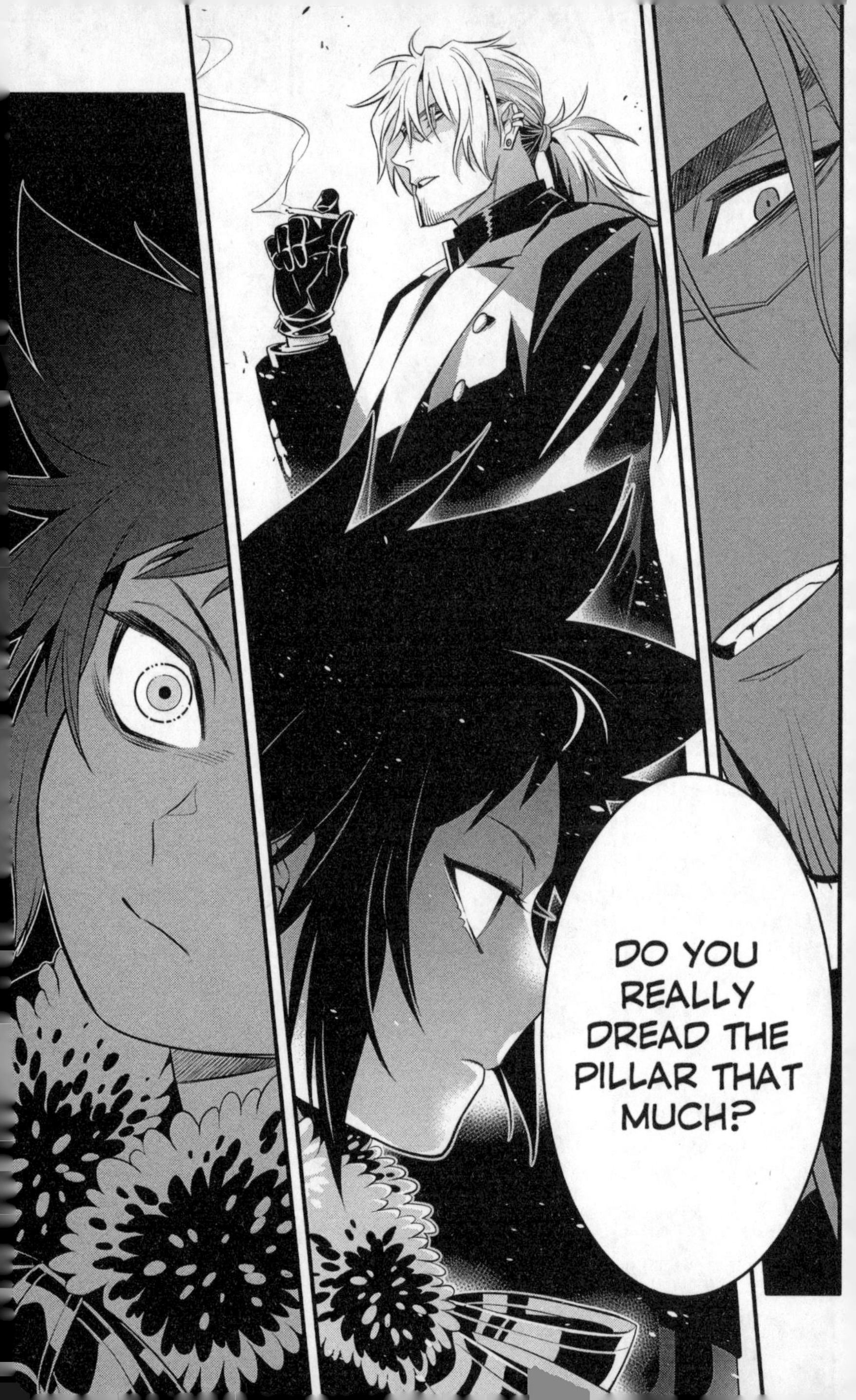
DO YOU REALLY DREAD THE PILLAR THAT MUCH?

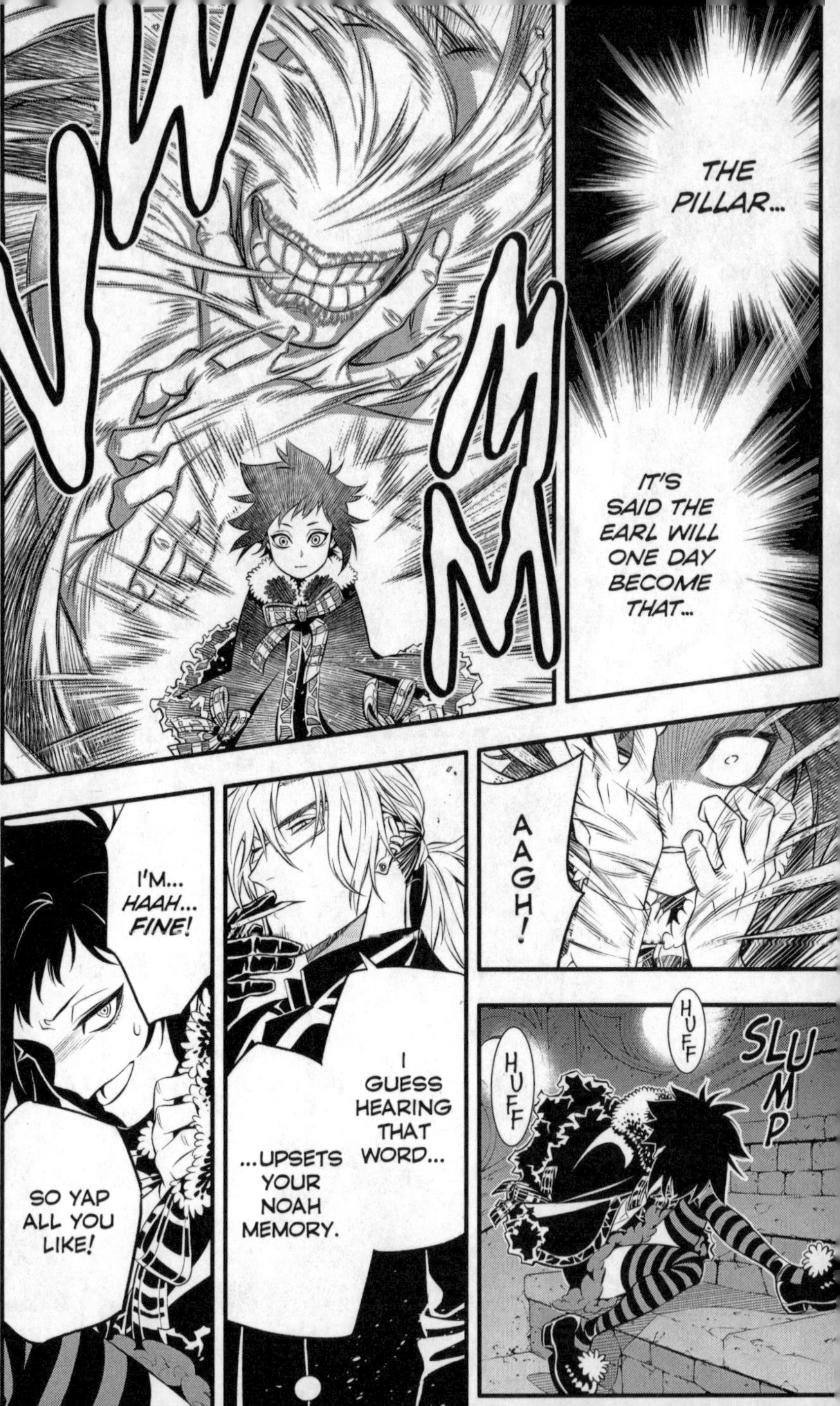
THE PILLAR...
IT'S SAID THE EARL WILL ONE DAY BECOME THAT...
AAGH!
SLUMP
HUFF
HUFF
I GUESS HEARING THAT WORD...
...UPSETS YOUR NOAH MEMORY.
I'M... HAAH... FINE!
SO YAP ALL YOU LIKE!

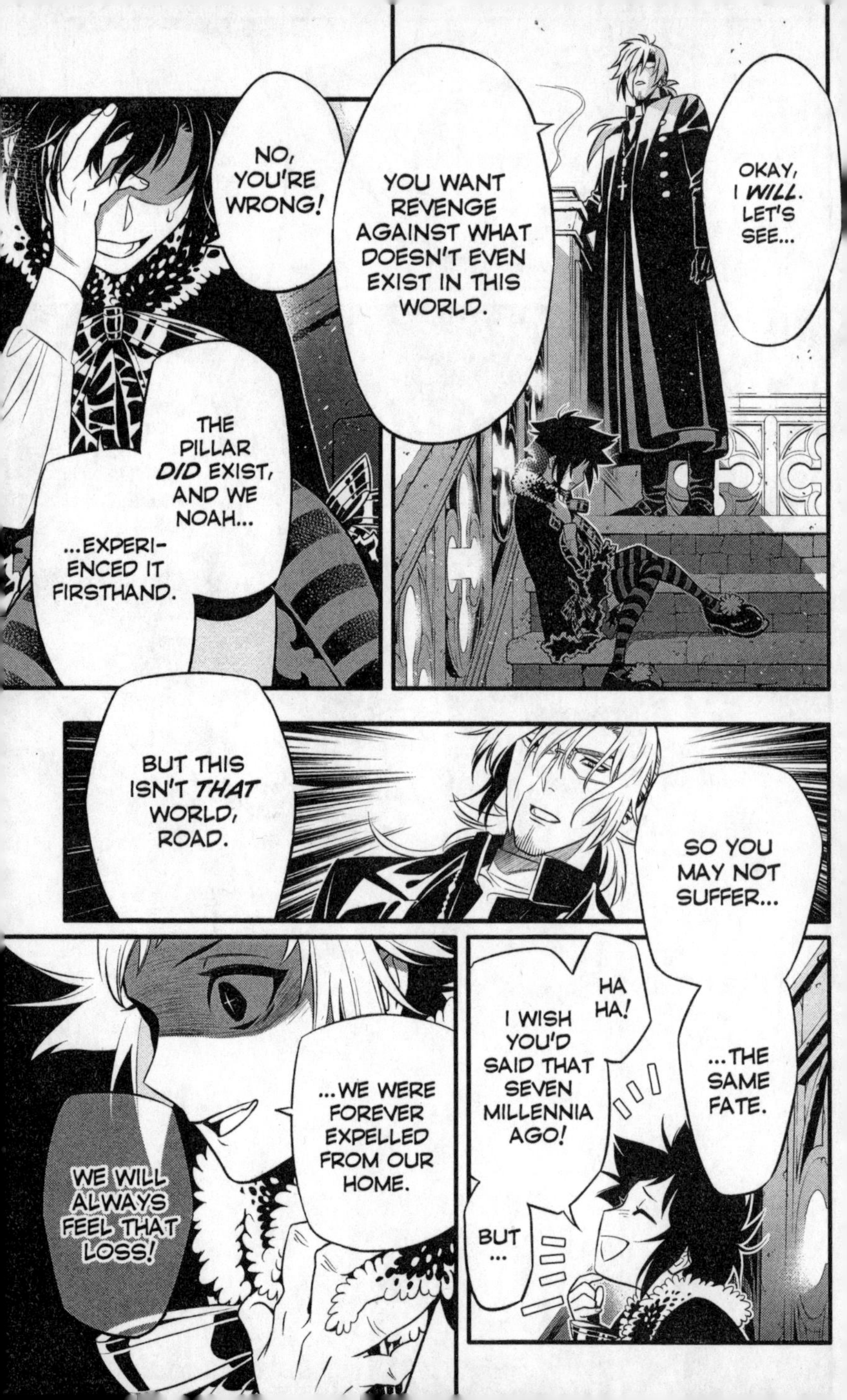
OKAY, I *WILL*. LET'S SEE...
YOU WANT REVENGE AGAINST WHAT DOESN'T EVEN EXIST IN THIS WORLD.
NO, YOU'RE WRONG!
THE PILLAR *DID* EXIST, AND WE NOAH...
...EXPERI-ENCED IT FIRSTHAND.
BUT THIS ISN'T *THAT* WORLD, ROAD.
SO YOU MAY NOT SUFFER...
...THE SAME FATE.
HA HA!
I WISH YOU'D SAID THAT SEVEN MILLENNIA AGO!
BUT ...
...WE WERE FOREVER EXPELLED FROM OUR HOME.
WE WILL ALWAYS FEEL THAT LOSS!

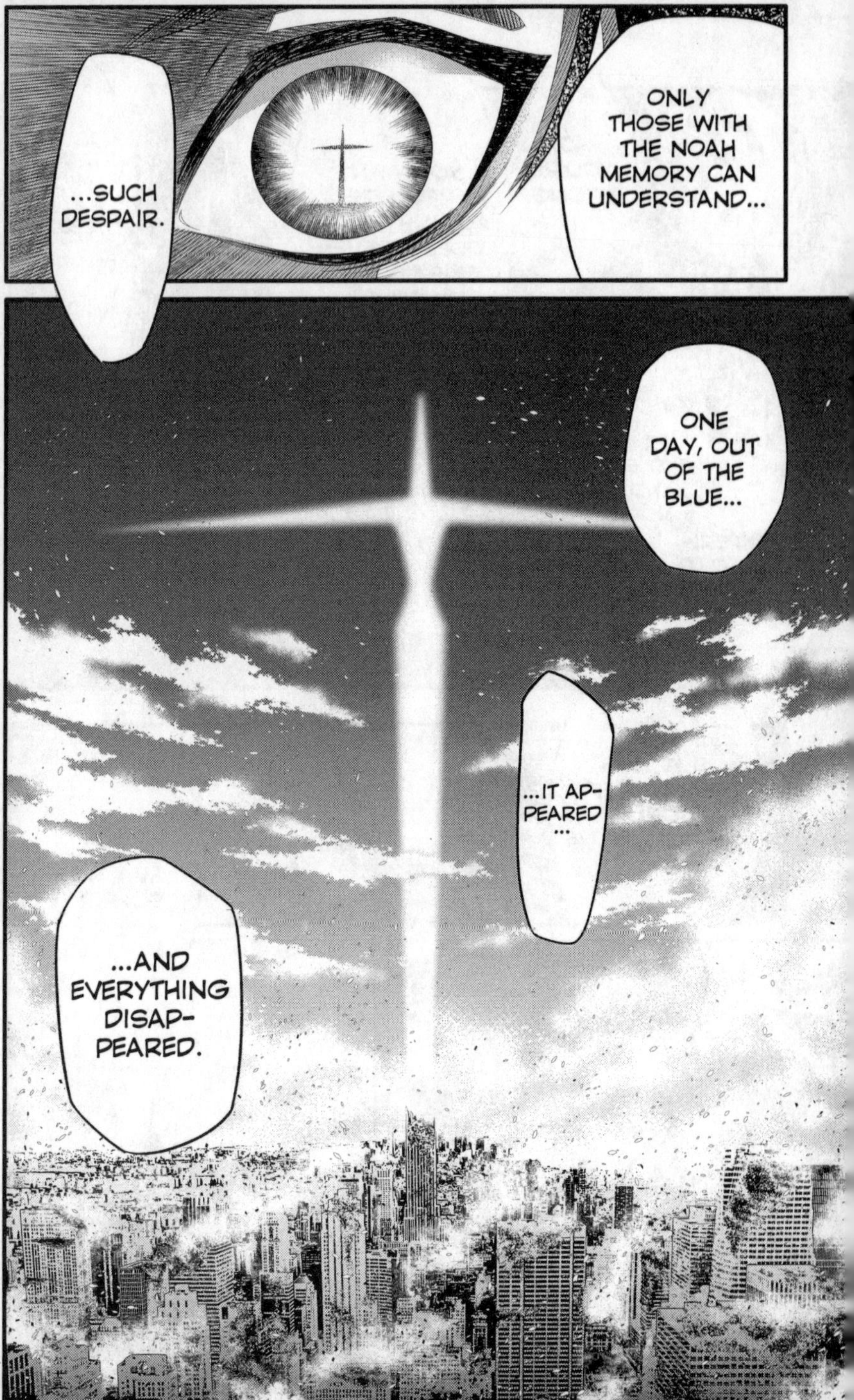
ONLY THOSE WITH THE NOAH MEMORY CAN UNDERSTAND...
...SUCH DESPAIR.
ONE DAY, OUT OF THE BLUE...
...IT AP-PEARED...
...AND EVERYTHING DISAP-PEARED.

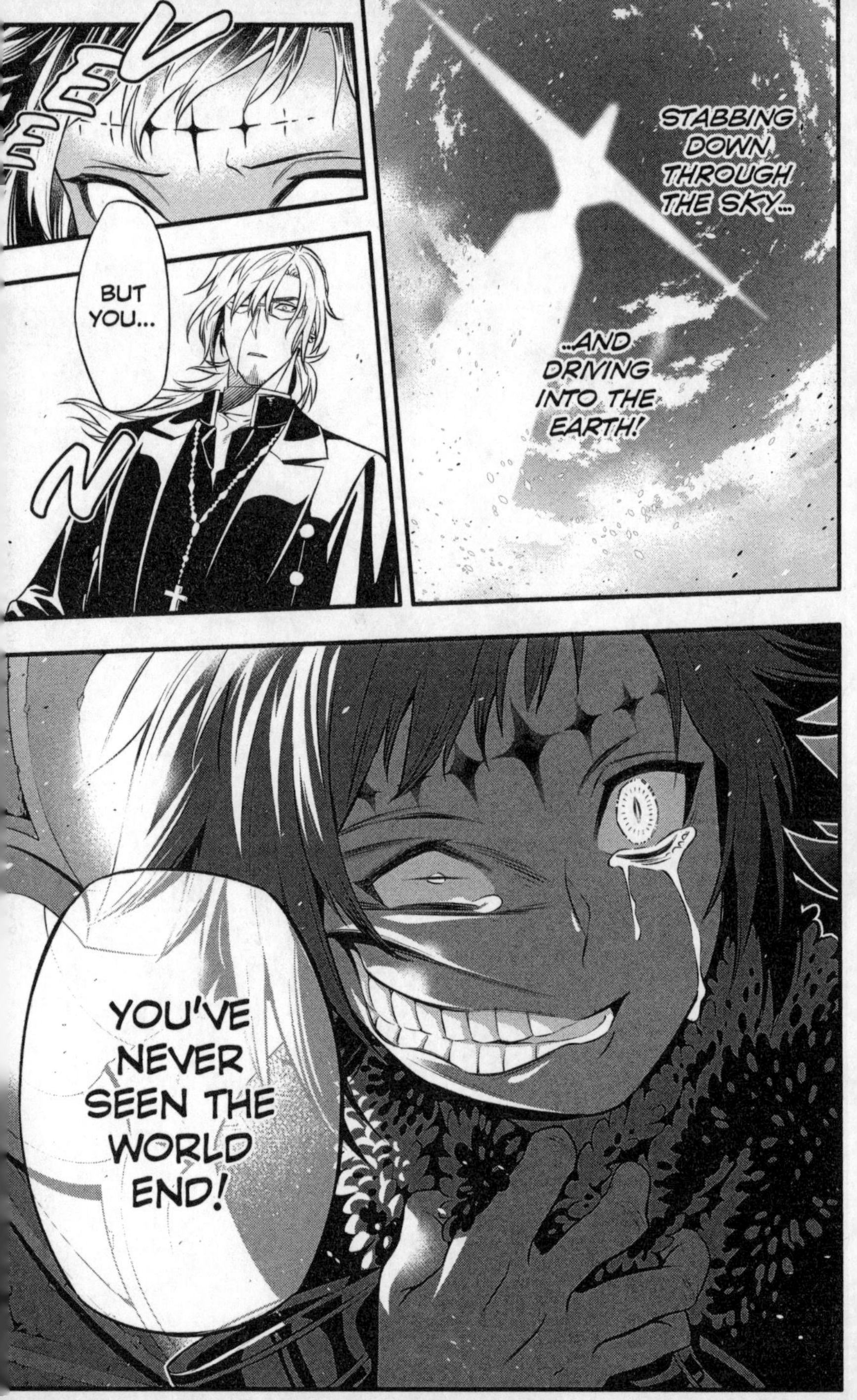
STABBING DOWN THROUGH THE SKY...
...AND DRIVING INTO THE EARTH!
EEEVVVE
BUT YOU...
NN
YOU'VE NEVER SEEN THE WORLD END!

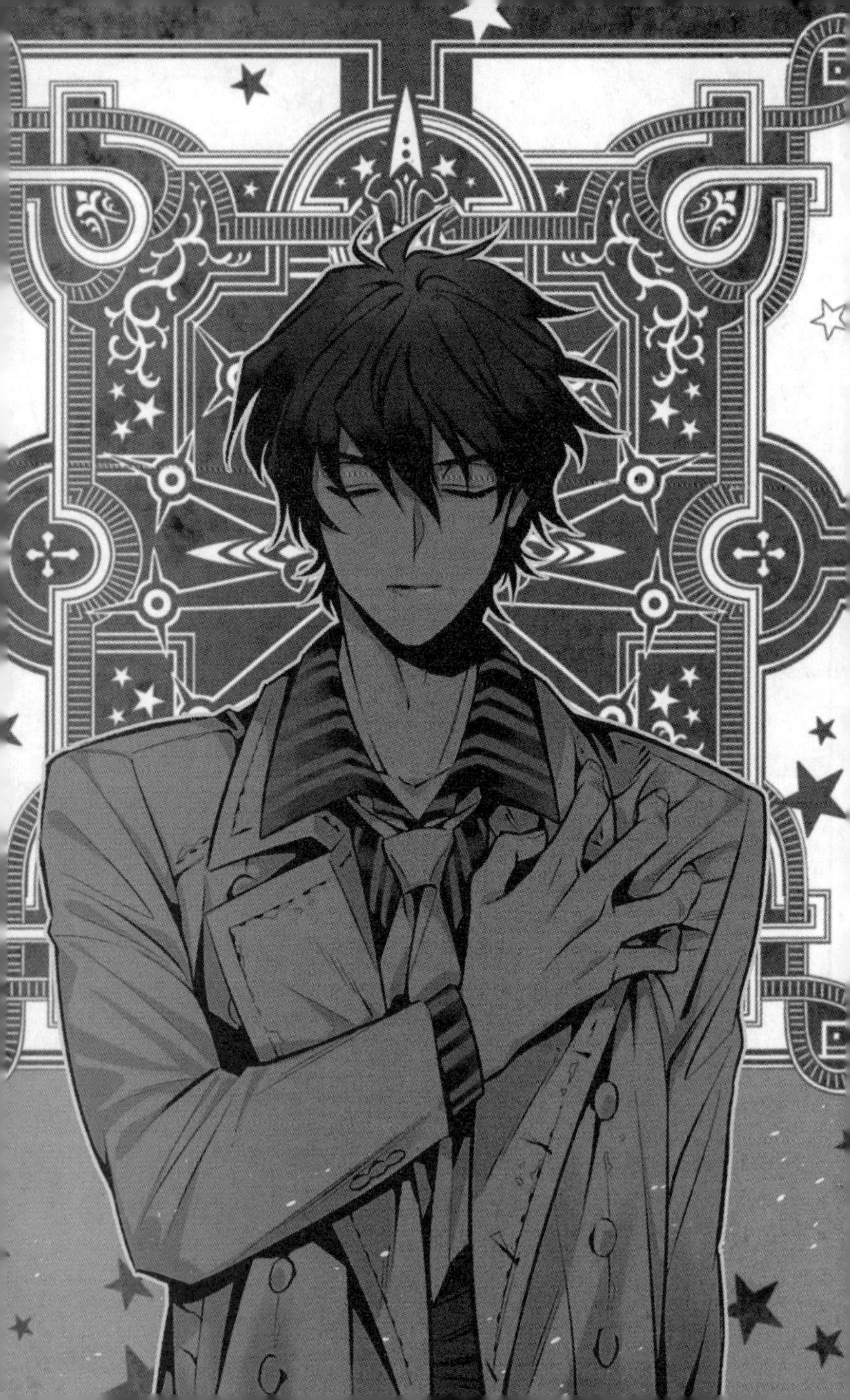

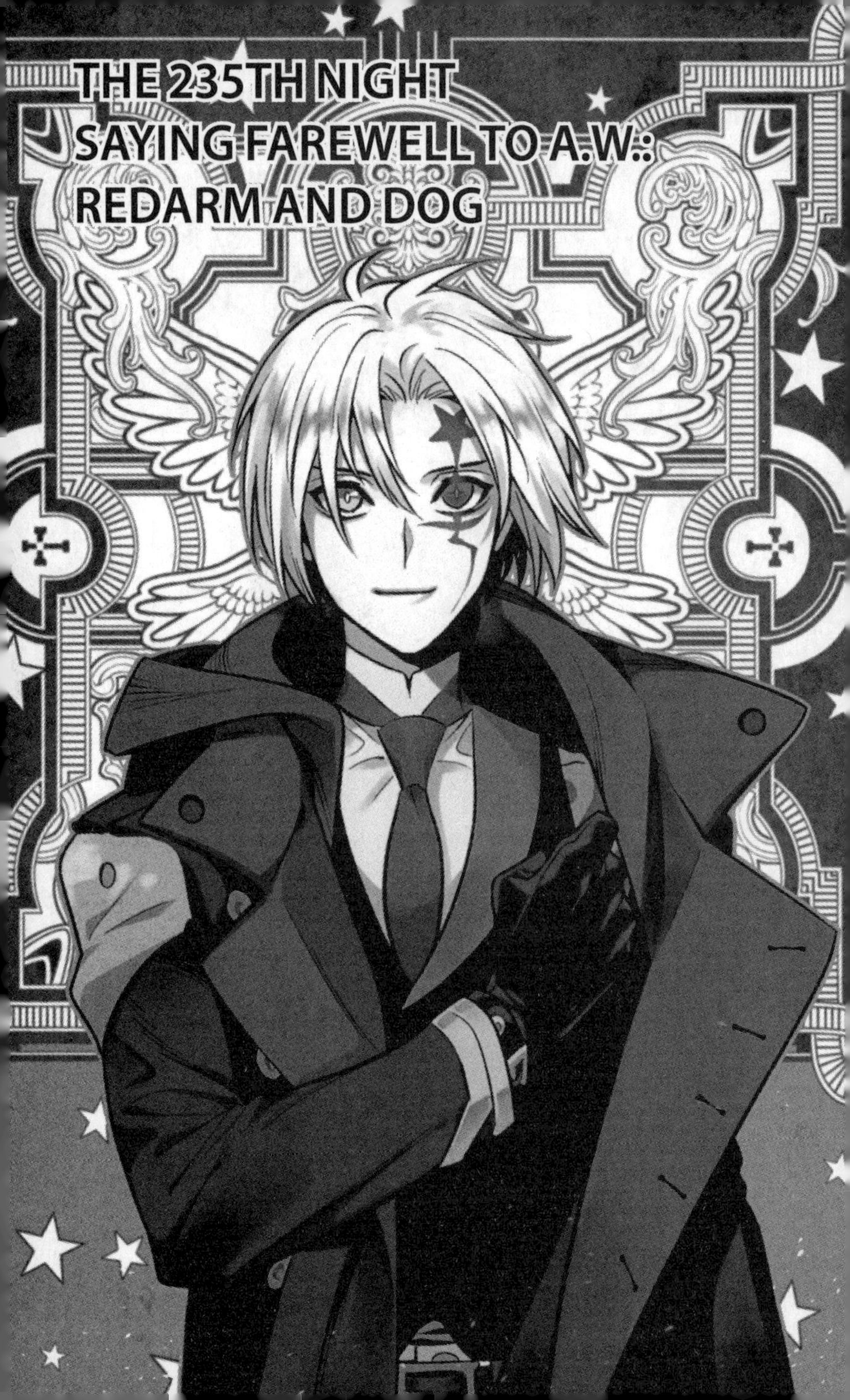
THE 235TH NIGHT
SAYING FAREWELL TO A.W.:
REDARM AND DOG

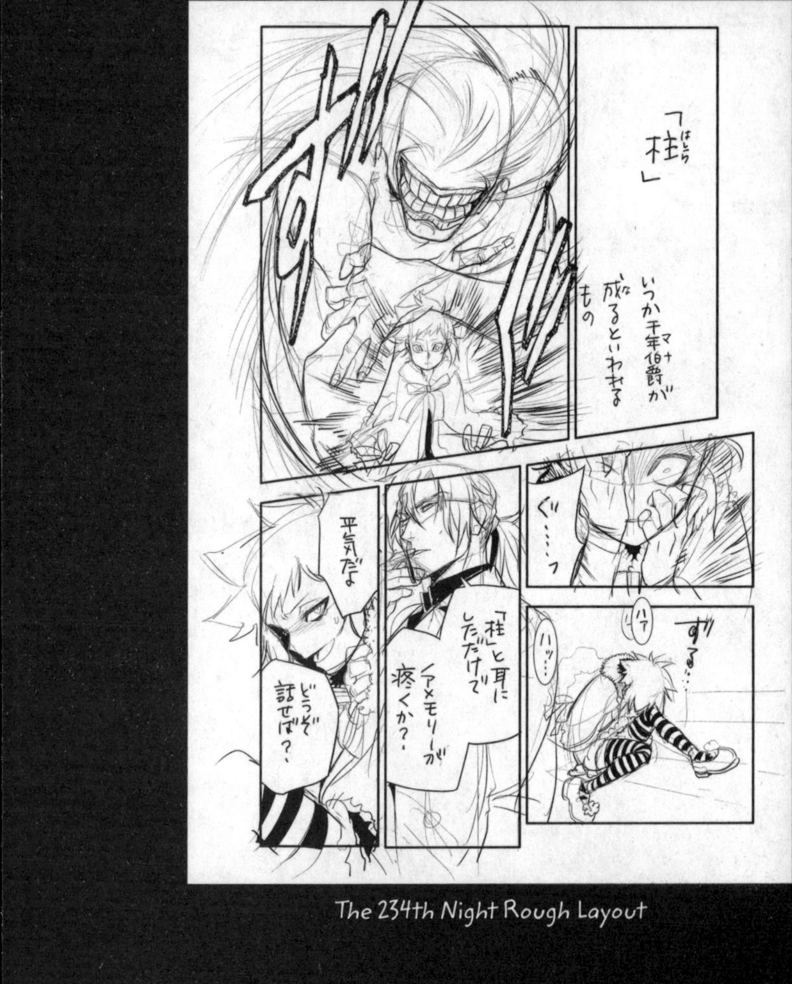
「柱」
いつか千年伯爵が成るといわれるもの
ぐ…っ
ずる…
ハァ
ハッ…
「柱」と耳にしただけでメモリーが疼くか?
平気だよ
どうぞ話せば?

The 234th Night Rough Layout

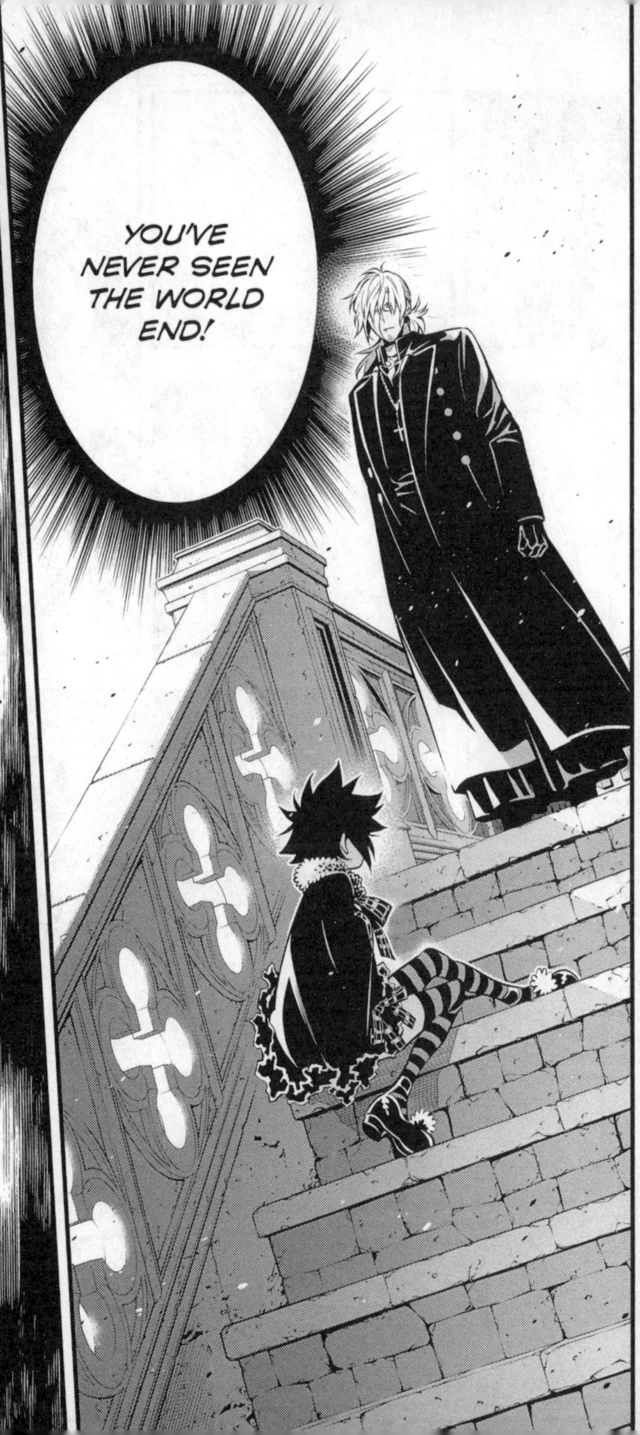
YOU'VE NEVER SEEN THE WORLD END!
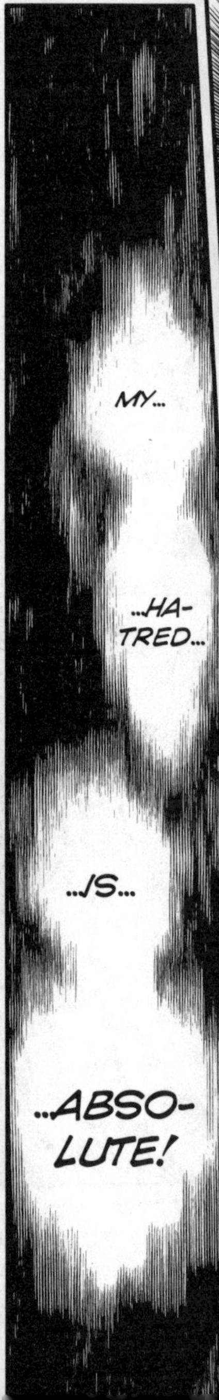
MY...
...HA-TRED...
...IS...
...ABSO-LUTE!

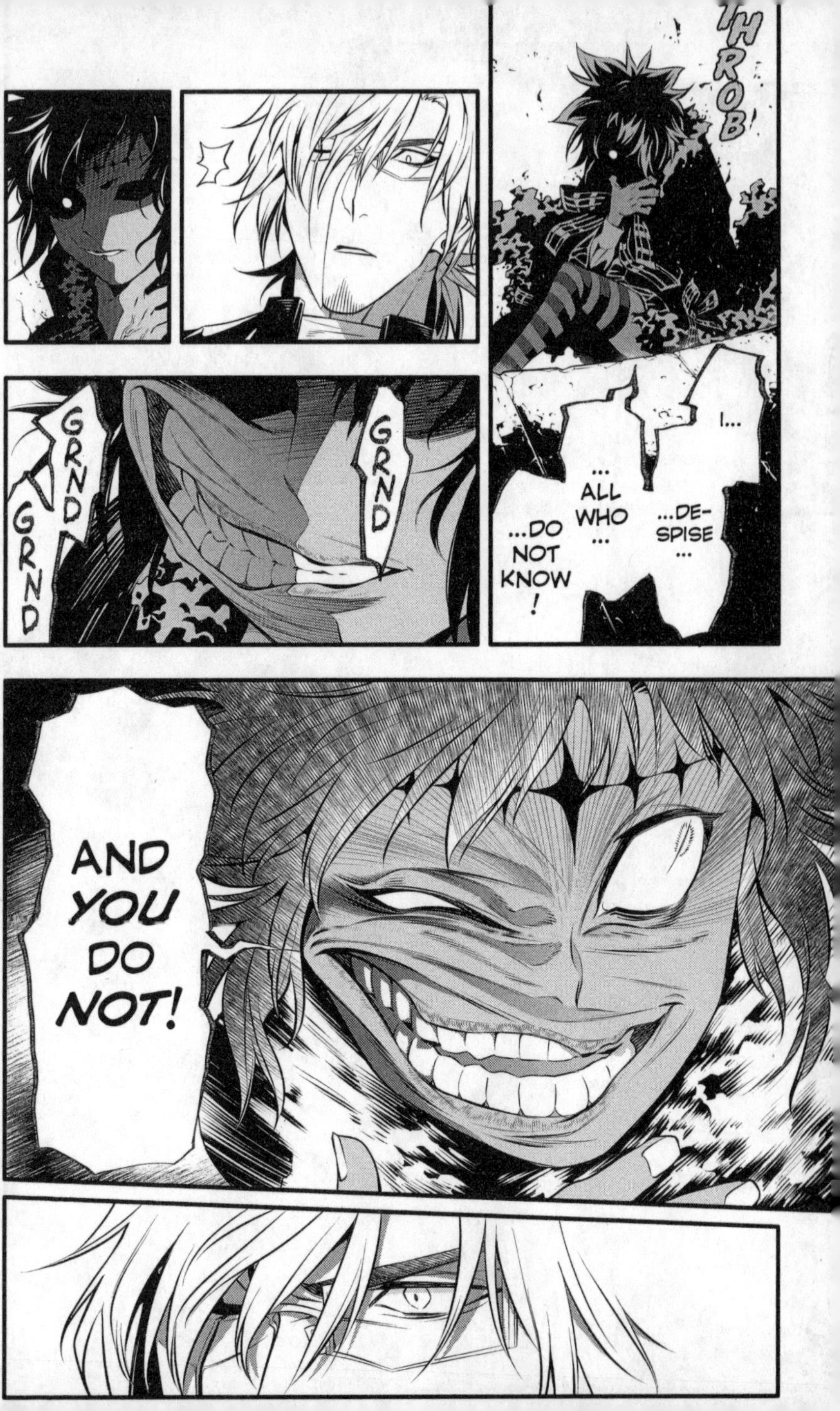
THROB
I...
...DE-SPISE...
...ALL WHO...
...DO NOT KNOW!
GRND
GRND GRND
AND YOU DO NOT!

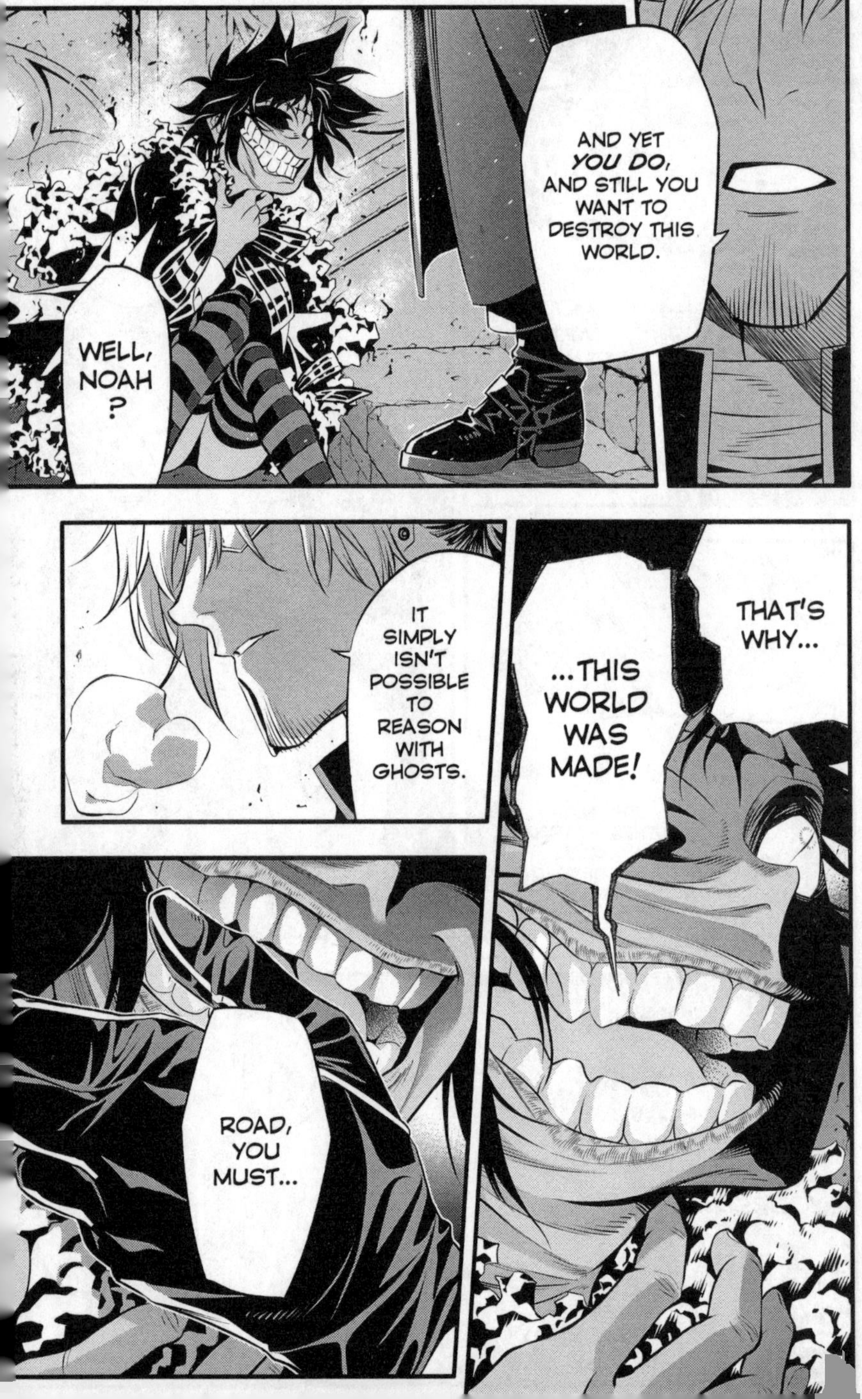
AND YET *YOU DO*, AND STILL YOU WANT TO DESTROY THIS WORLD.
WELL, NOAH ?
THAT'S WHY...
...THIS WORLD WAS MADE!
IT SIMPLY ISN'T POSSIBLE TO REASON WITH GHOSTS.
ROAD, YOU MUST...

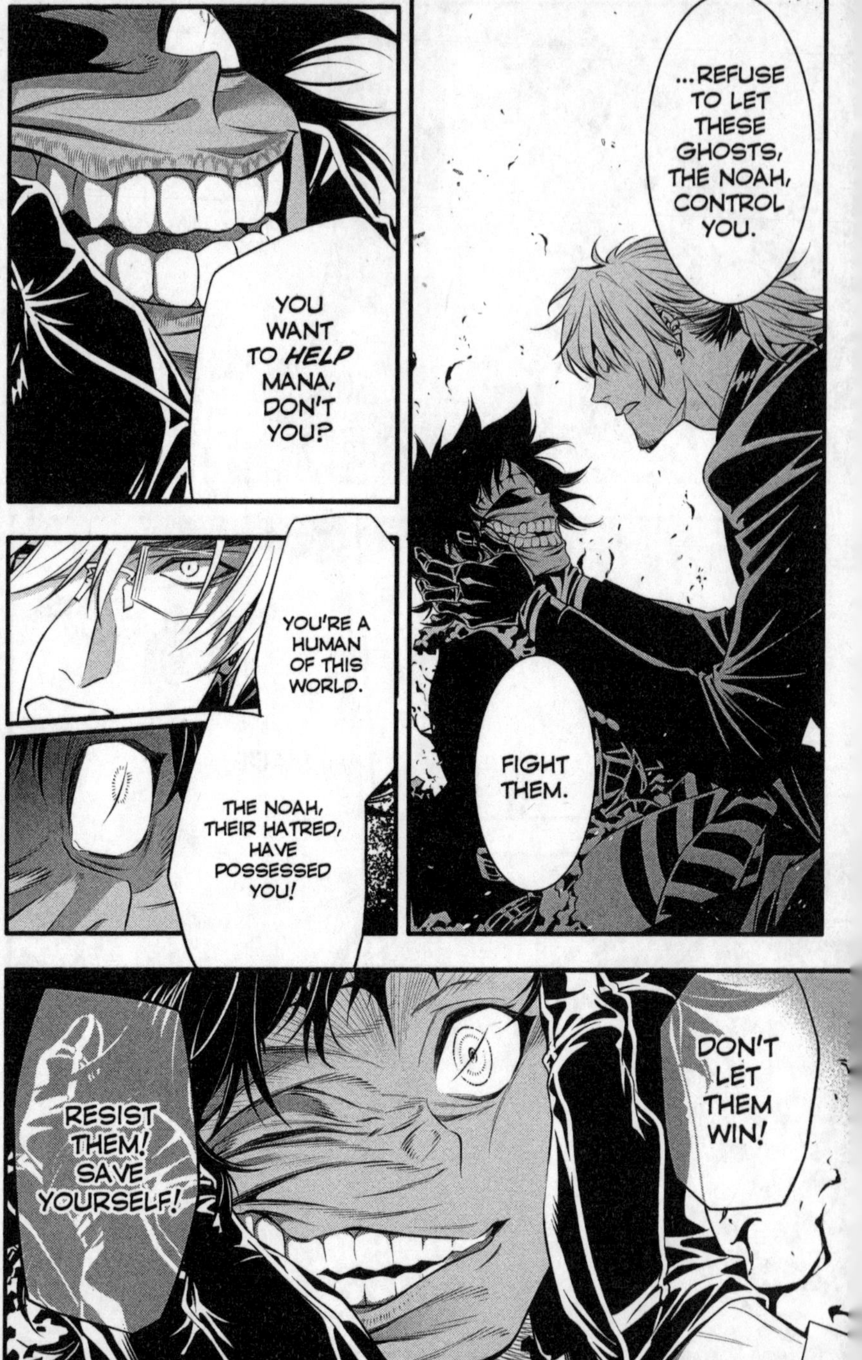
...REFUSE TO LET THESE GHOSTS, THE NOAH, CONTROL YOU.
FIGHT THEM.
YOU WANT TO *HELP* MANA, DON'T YOU?
YOU'RE A HUMAN OF THIS WORLD.
THE NOAH, THEIR HATRED, HAVE POSSESSED YOU!
DON'T LET THEM WIN!
RESIST THEM! SAVE YOURSELF!

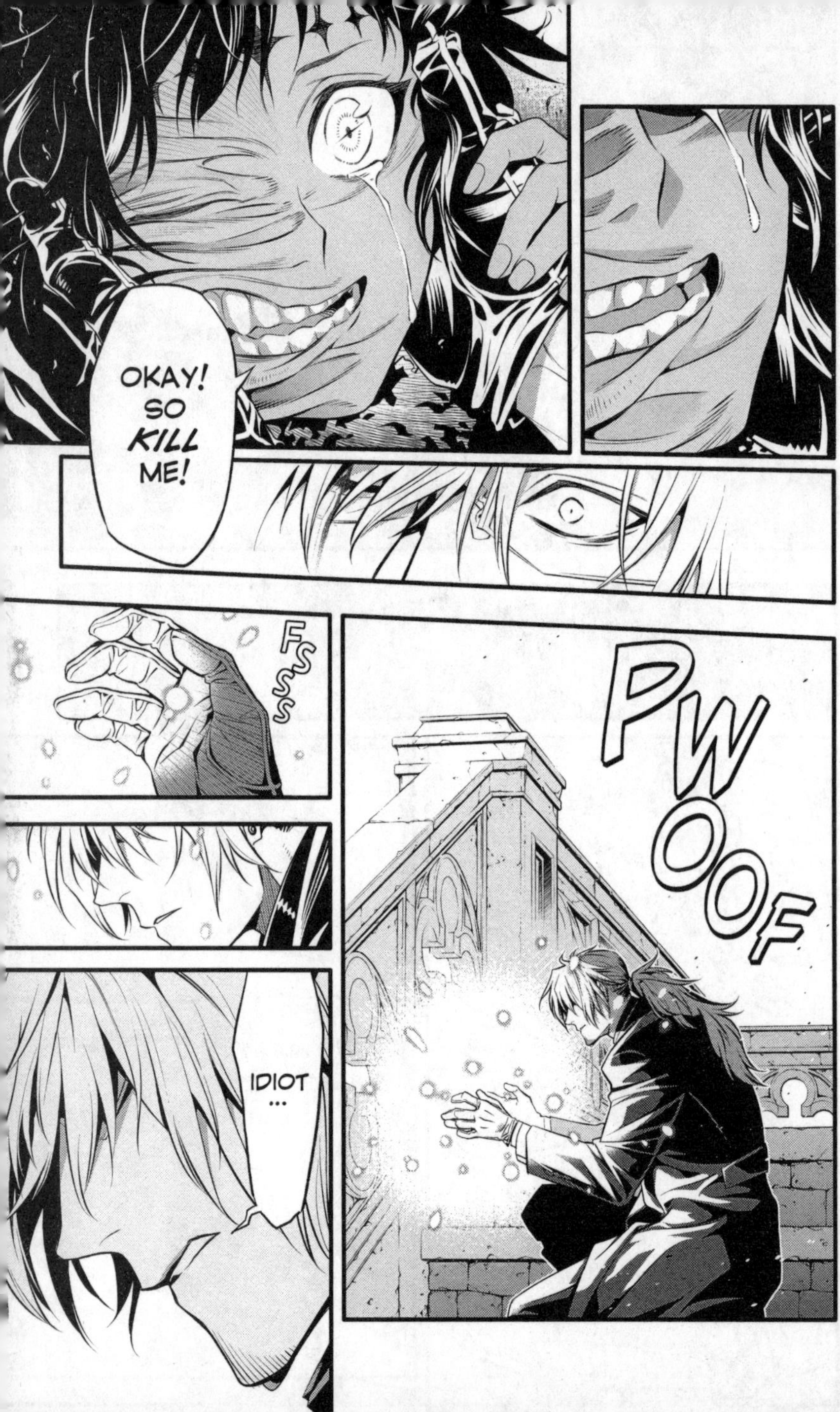
OKAY! SO KILL ME!
PWOOF
FSSS
IDIOT...

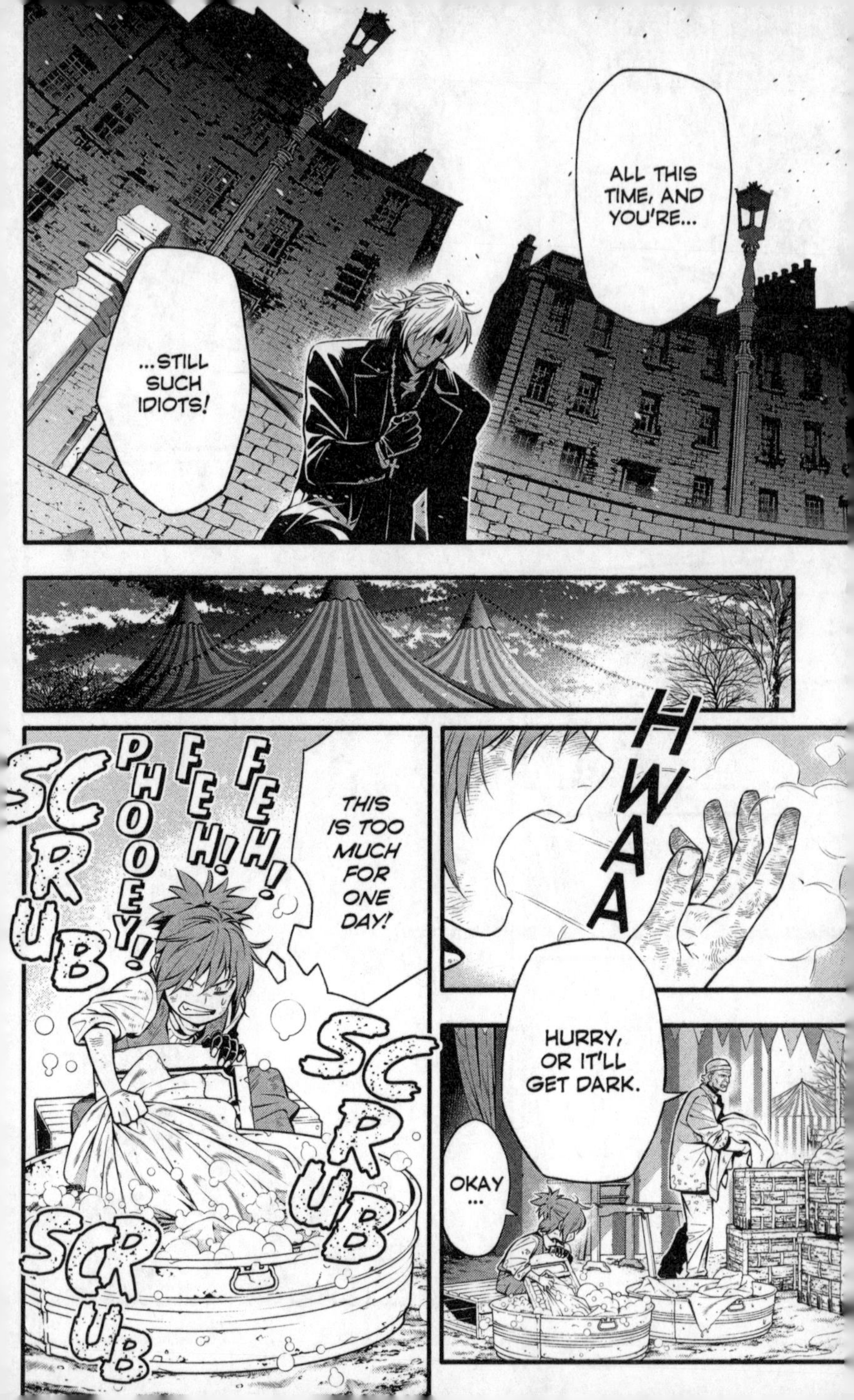
ALL THIS TIME, AND YOU'RE...
...STILL SUCH IDIOTS!
HWAA
HURRY, OR IT'LL GET DARK.
OKAY...
THIS IS TOO MUCH FOR ONE DAY!
FEEH!
FEEH!
PHOOEY!
SCRUB
SCRUB
SCRUB

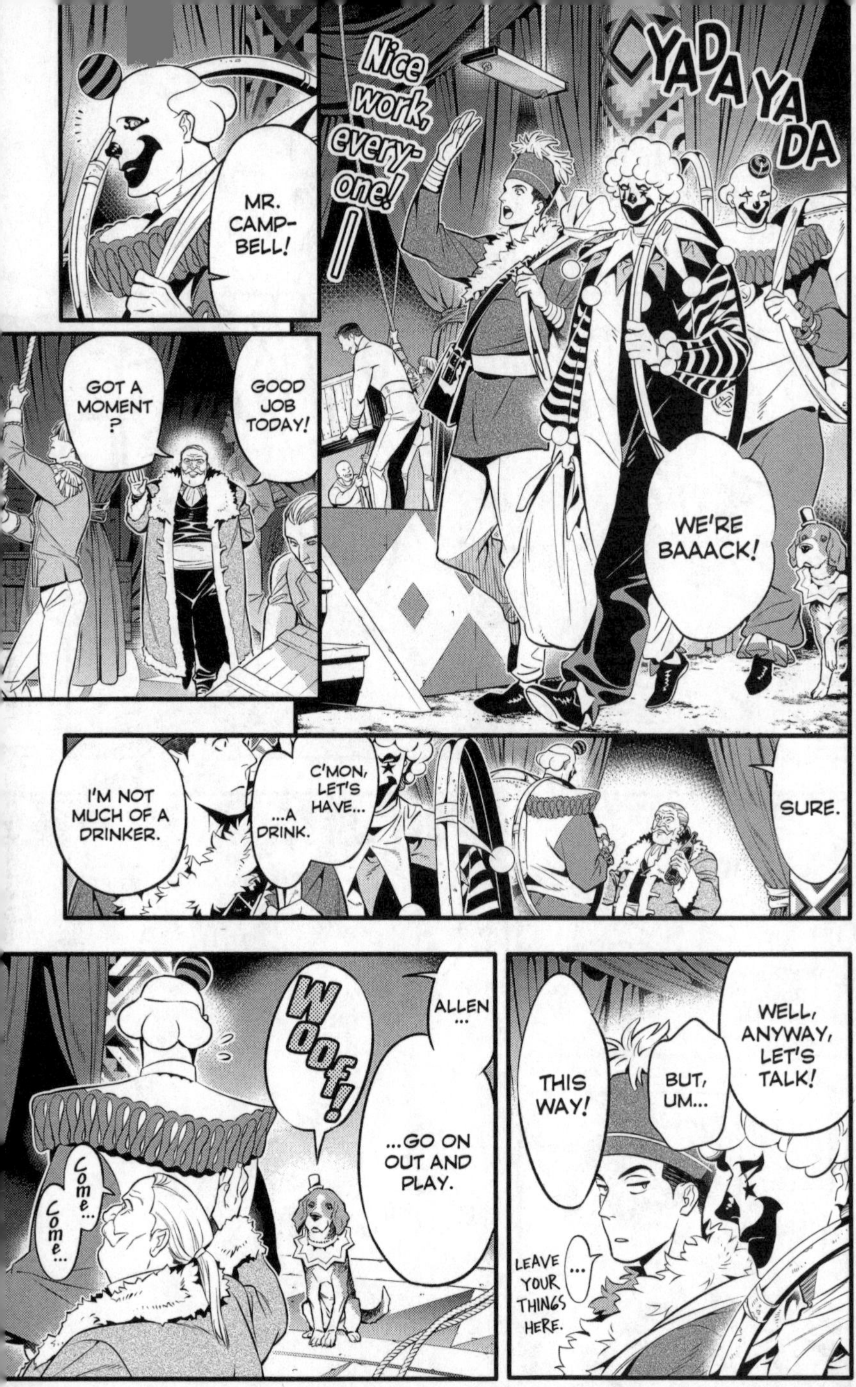
YA DA YA DA
Nice work, every-one!
WE'RE BAAACK!
MR. CAMP-BELL!
GOOD JOB TODAY!
GOT A MOMENT?
SURE.
C'MON, LET'S HAVE...
...A DRINK.
I'M NOT MUCH OF A DRINKER.
WELL, ANYWAY, LET'S TALK!
BUT, UM...
THIS WAY!
...
LEAVE YOUR THINGS HERE.
ALLEN...
...GO ON OUT AND PLAY.
WOOF!
Come... Come...

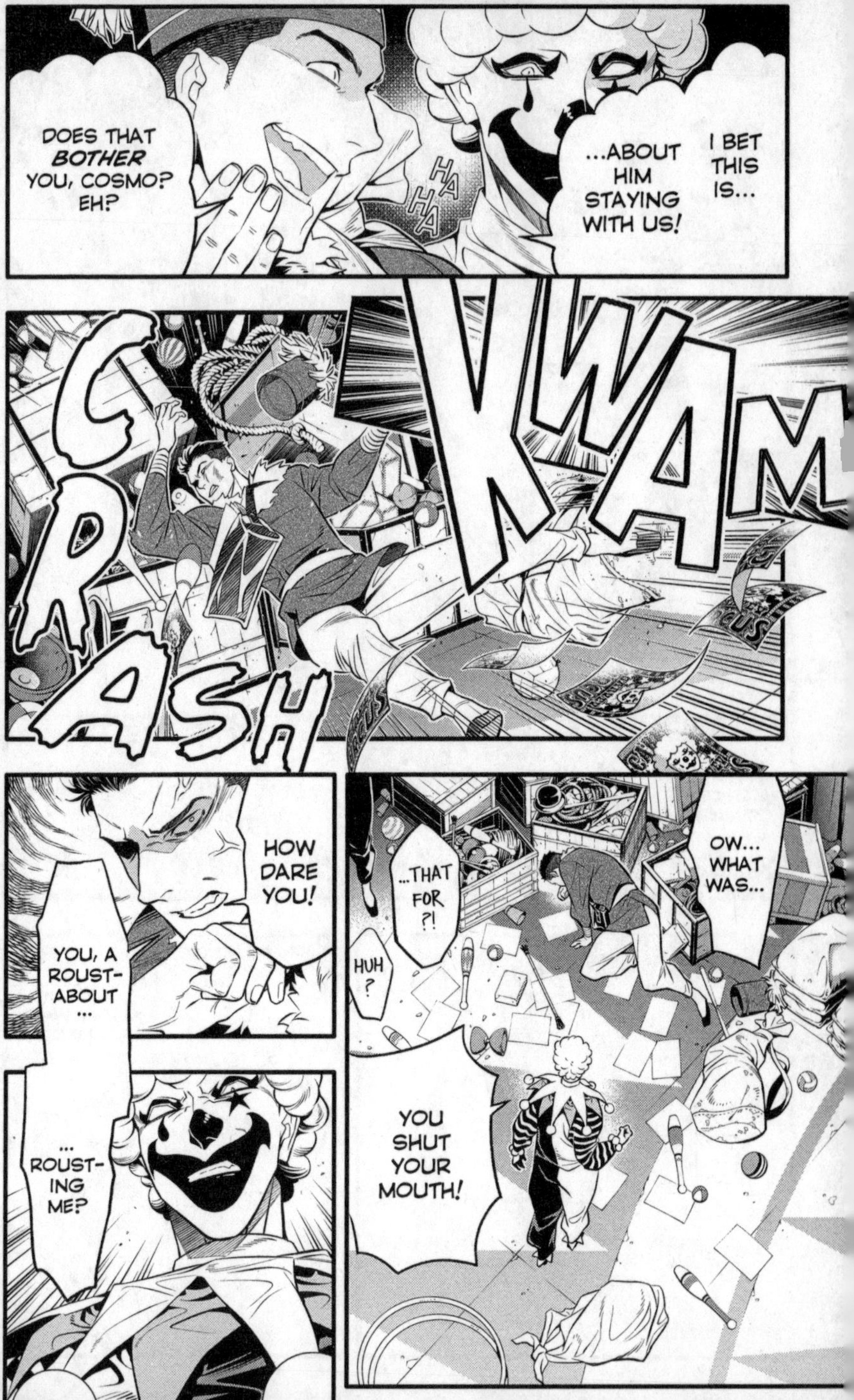
I BET THIS IS...
...ABOUT HIM STAYING WITH US!
HA HA
DOES THAT *BOTHER* YOU, COSMO? EH?
KWAM
CRASH
OW... WHAT WAS...
...THAT FOR ?!
HUH ?
YOU SHUT YOUR MOUTH!
HOW DARE YOU!
YOU, A ROUST-ABOUT ...
... ROUST-ING ME?

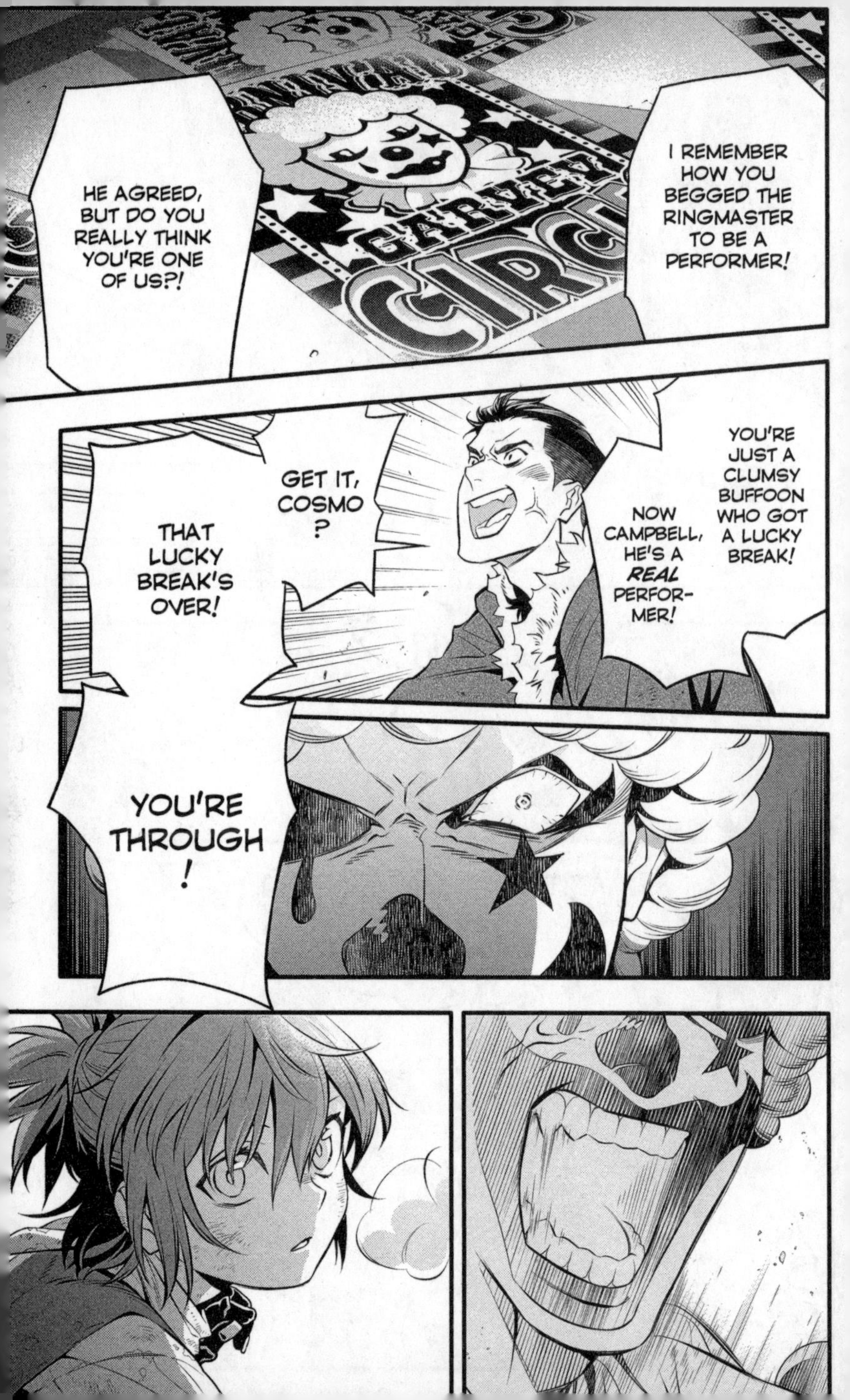
I REMEMBER HOW YOU BEGGED THE RINGMASTER TO BE A PERFORMER!
HE AGREED, BUT DO YOU REALLY THINK YOU'RE ONE OF US?!
YOU'RE JUST A CLUMSY BUFFOON WHO GOT A LUCKY BREAK!
NOW CAMPBELL, HE'S A *REAL* PERFORMER!
GET IT, COSMO?
THAT LUCKY BREAK'S OVER!
YOU'RE THROUGH!

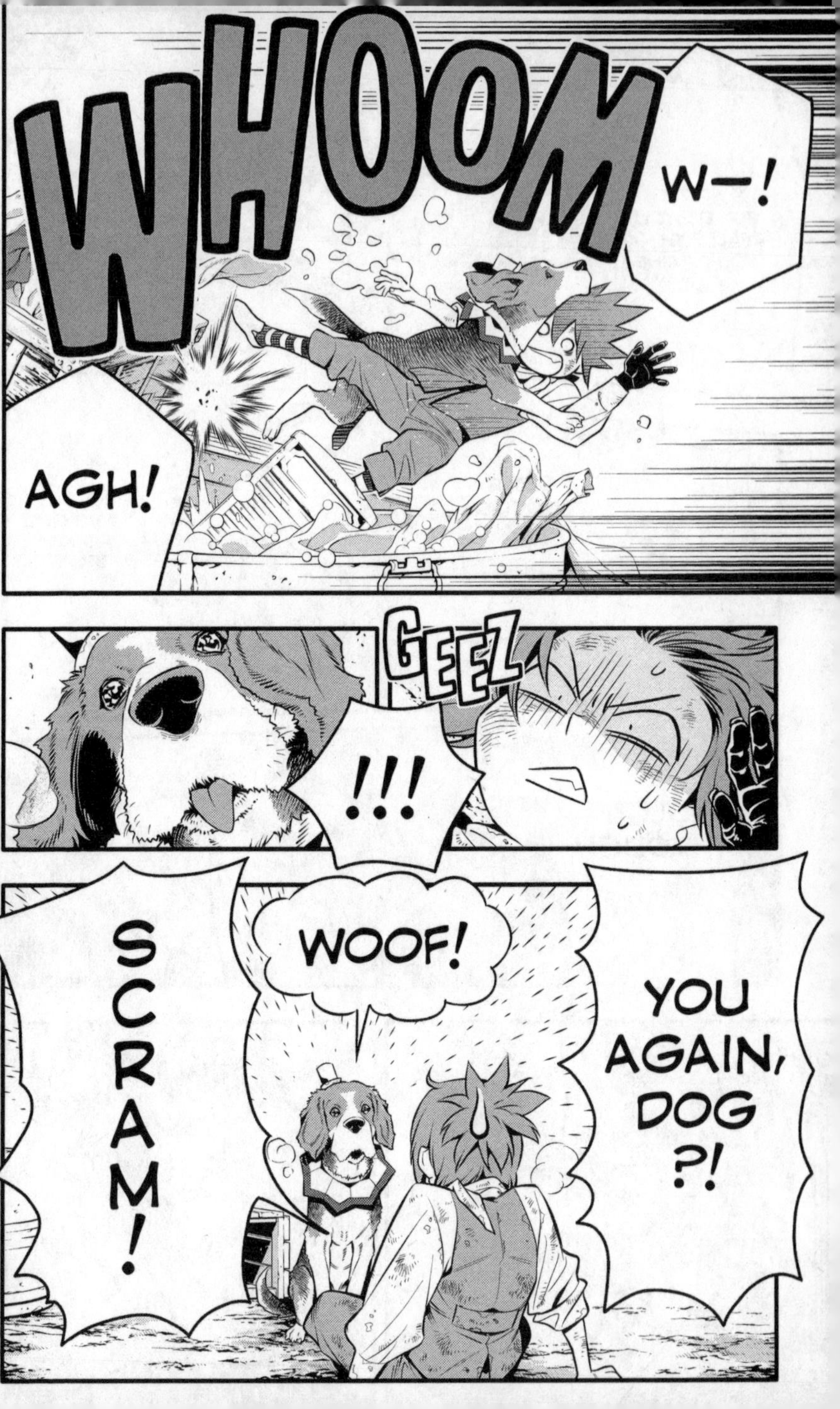
W—!
WHOOM
AGH!
GEEZ
!!!
YOU AGAIN, DOG?!
WOOF!
SCRAM!

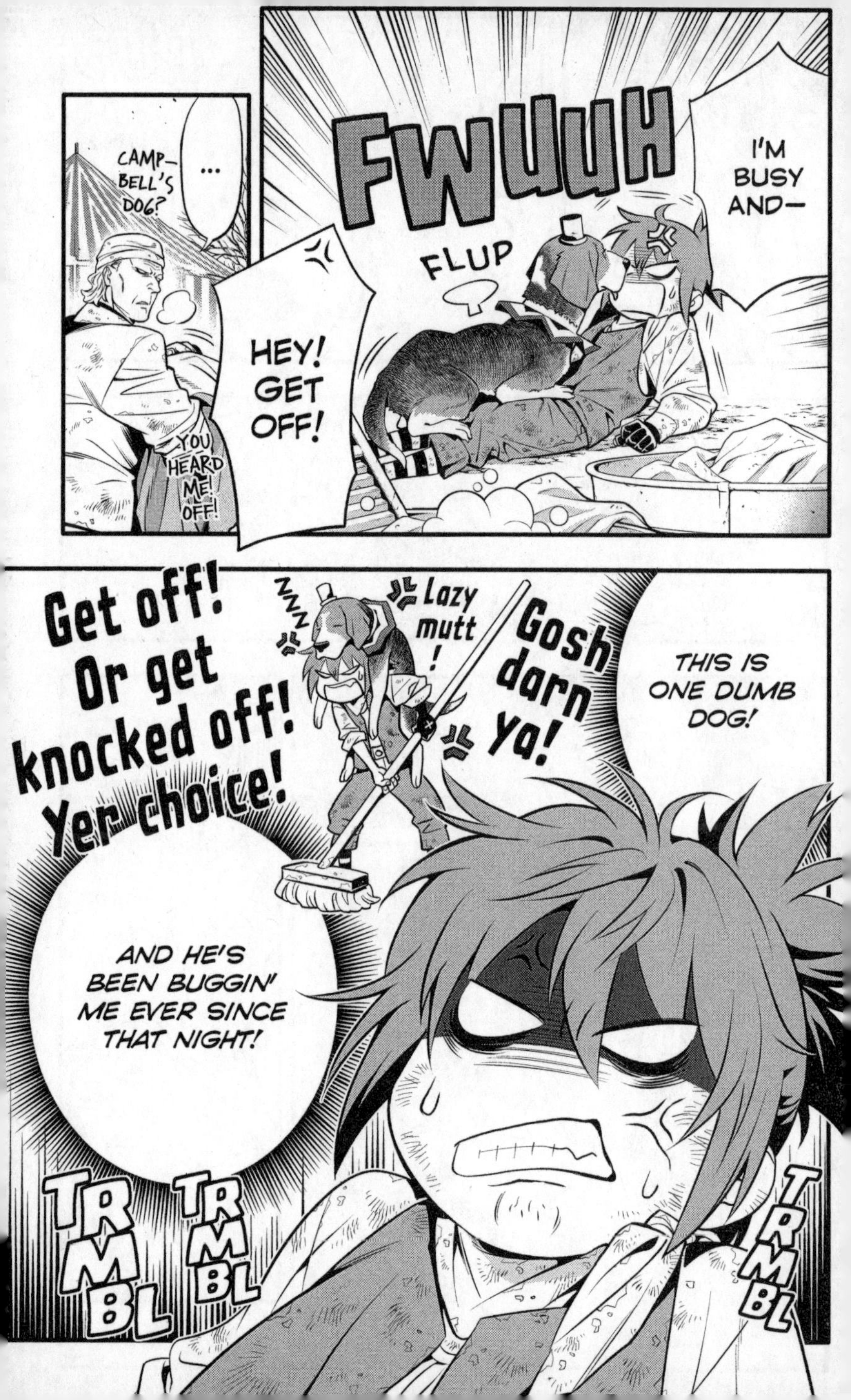
I'M BUSY AND—
FWUUUH
FLUP
HEY! GET OFF!
...
CAMP-BELL'S DOG?
YOU HEARD ME! OFF!
THIS IS ONE DUMB DOG!
Gosh darn ya!
Lazy mutt!
ZZZ
Get off! Or get knocked off! Yer choice!
AND HE'S BEEN BUGGIN' ME EVER SINCE THAT NIGHT!
TRMBL
TRMBL
TRMBL

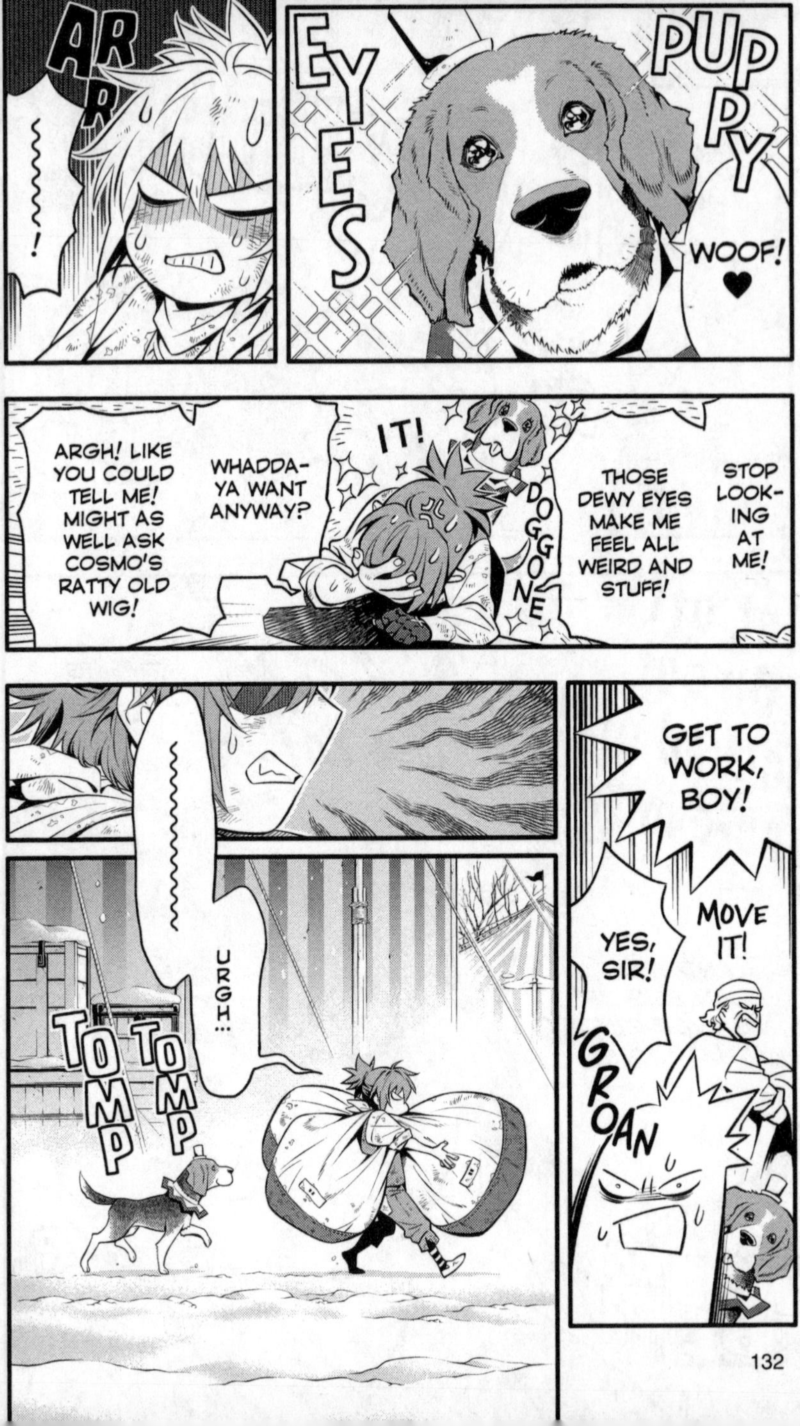
PUPPY
EYES
WOOF! ♥
ARR
~~~~~!
STOP LOOKING AT ME!
THOSE DEWY EYES MAKE ME FEEL ALL WEIRD AND STUFF!
DOGGONE
IT!
WHADDAYA WANT ANYWAY?
ARGH! LIKE YOU COULD TELL ME! MIGHT AS WELL ASK COSMO'S RATTY OLD WIG!
GET TO WORK, BOY!
MOVE IT!
YES, SIR!
GROAN
~~~~~~
URGH...
TOMP
TOMP

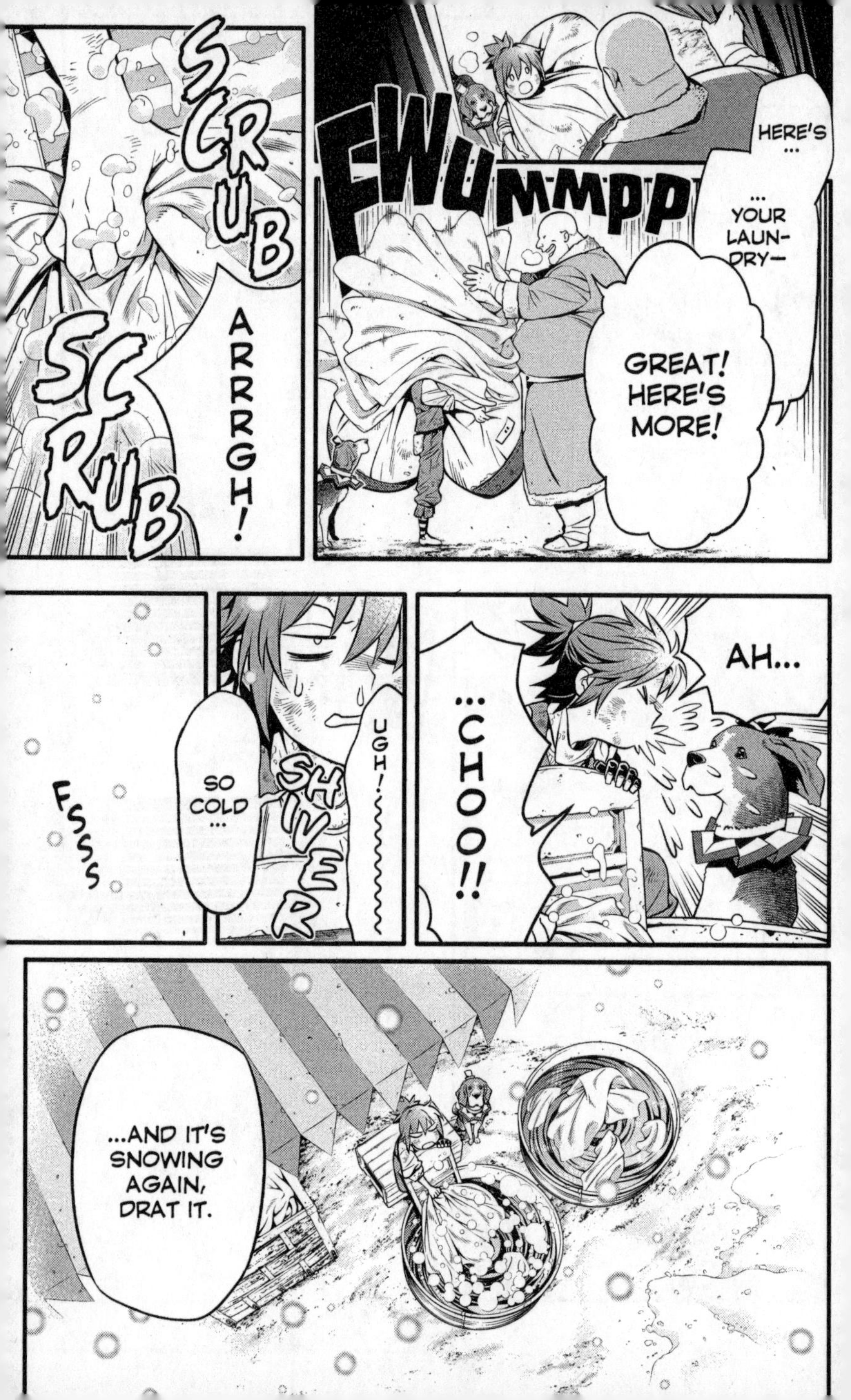
HERE'S ...
... YOUR LAUN-DRY—
FWUMMPP
GREAT! HERE'S MORE!
SCRUB
SCRUB
ARRRGH!
AH...
...CHOO!!
UGH!
SHIVER
SO COLD ...
FSSS
...AND IT'S SNOWING AGAIN, DRAT IT.

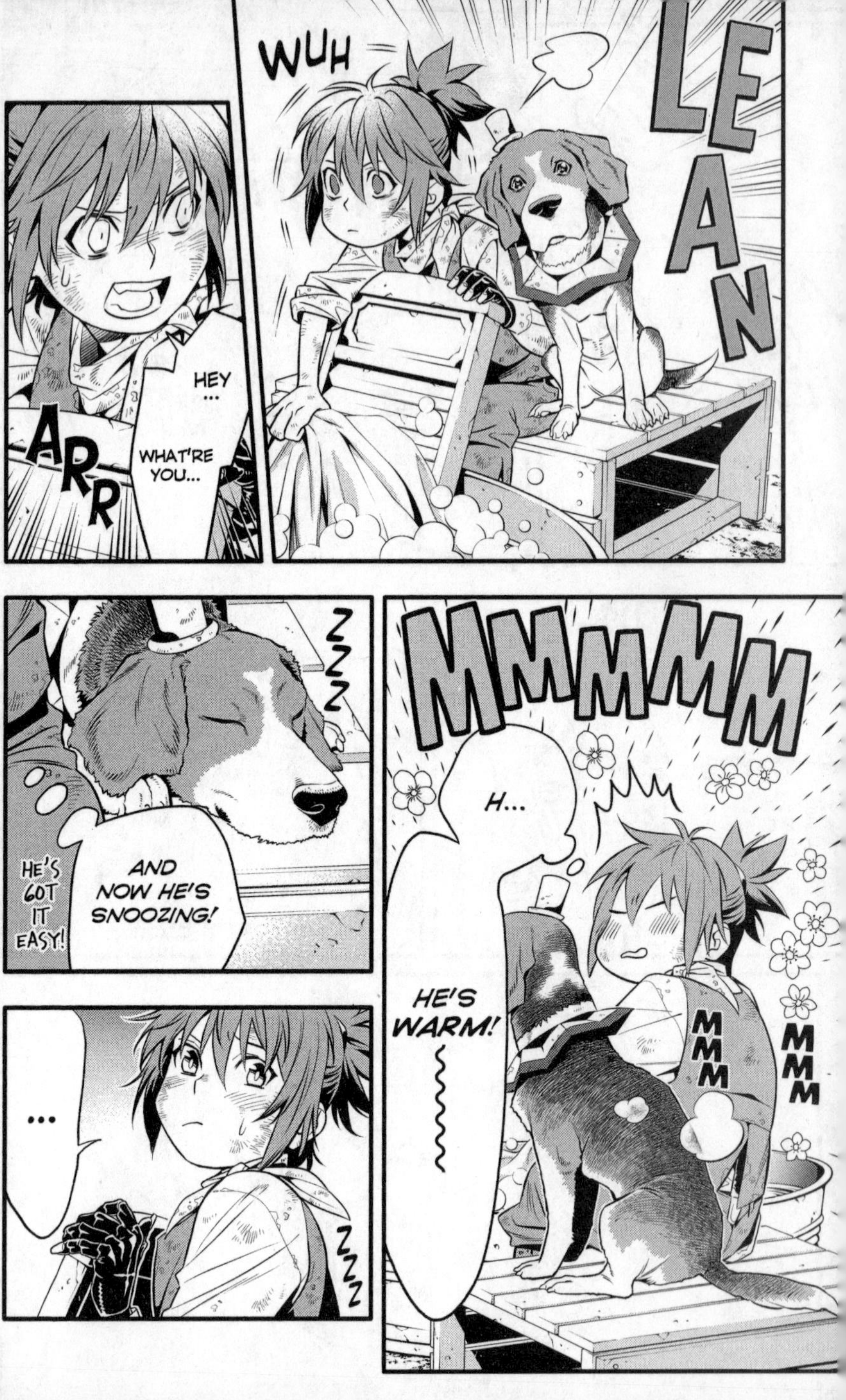
LEAN
WUH
HEY ... WHAT'RE YOU...
ARR
MMMMMM
H...
HE'S WARM!
MMM
MMM
ZZZ
AND NOW HE'S SNOOZING!
HE'S GOT IT EASY!
...
ZZZ

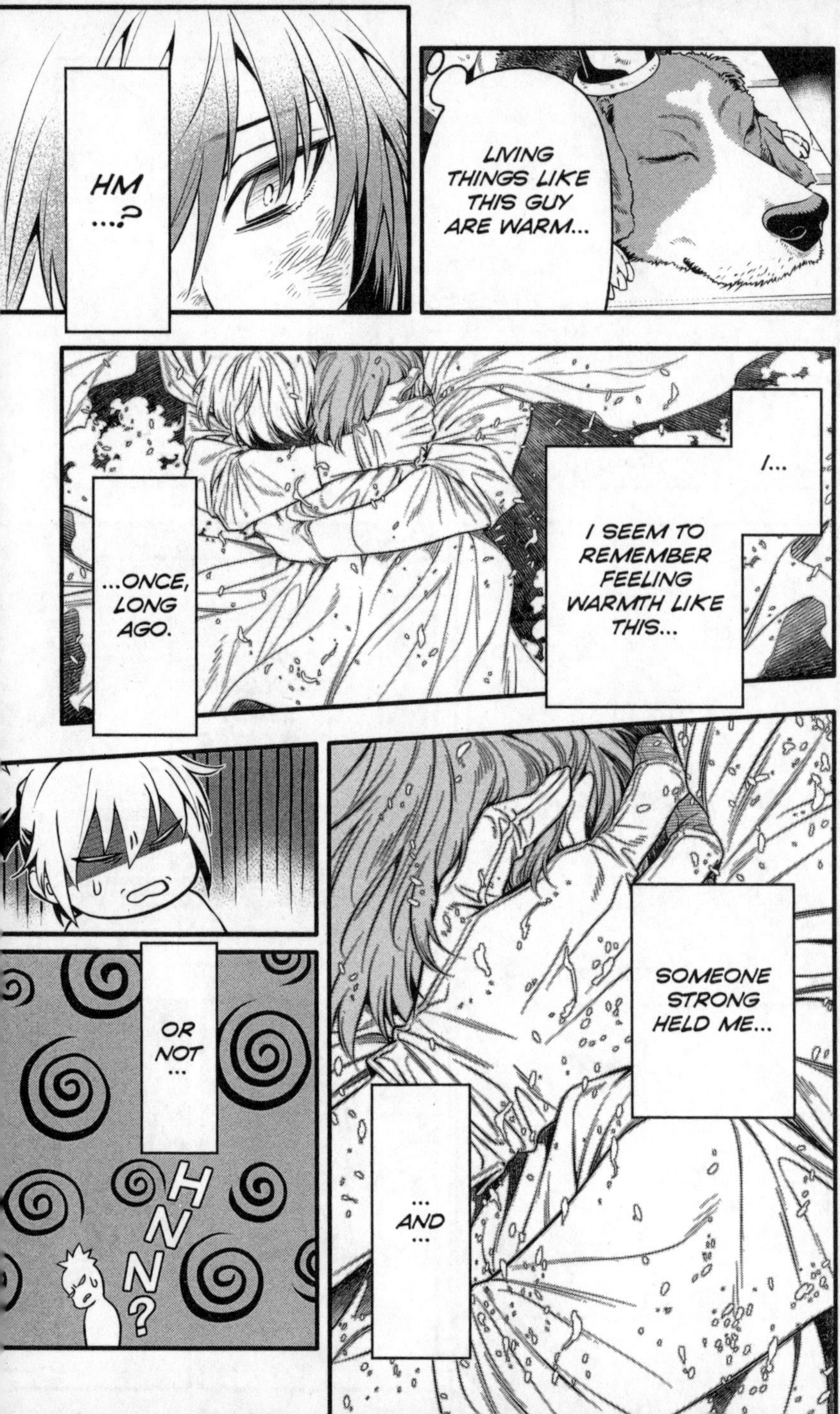
LIVING THINGS LIKE THIS GUY ARE WARM...
HM ...?
I...
I SEEM TO REMEMBER FEELING WARMTH LIKE THIS...
...ONCE, LONG AGO.
SOMEONE STRONG HELD ME...
...AND...
OR NOT...
HNN?

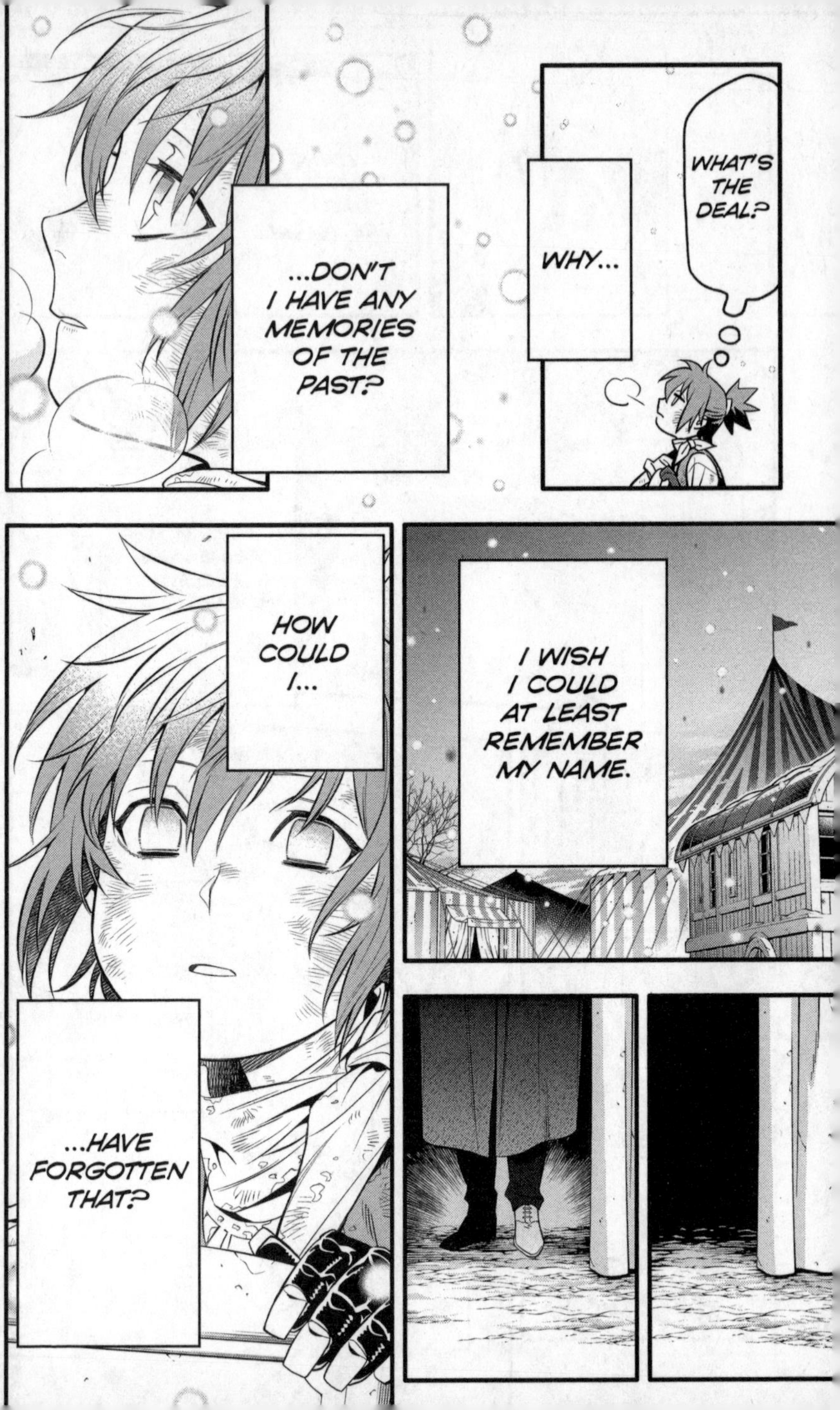
WHAT'S THE DEAL?
WHY...
...DON'T I HAVE ANY MEMORIES OF THE PAST?
I WISH I COULD AT LEAST REMEMBER MY NAME.
HOW COULD I...
...HAVE FORGOTTEN THAT?

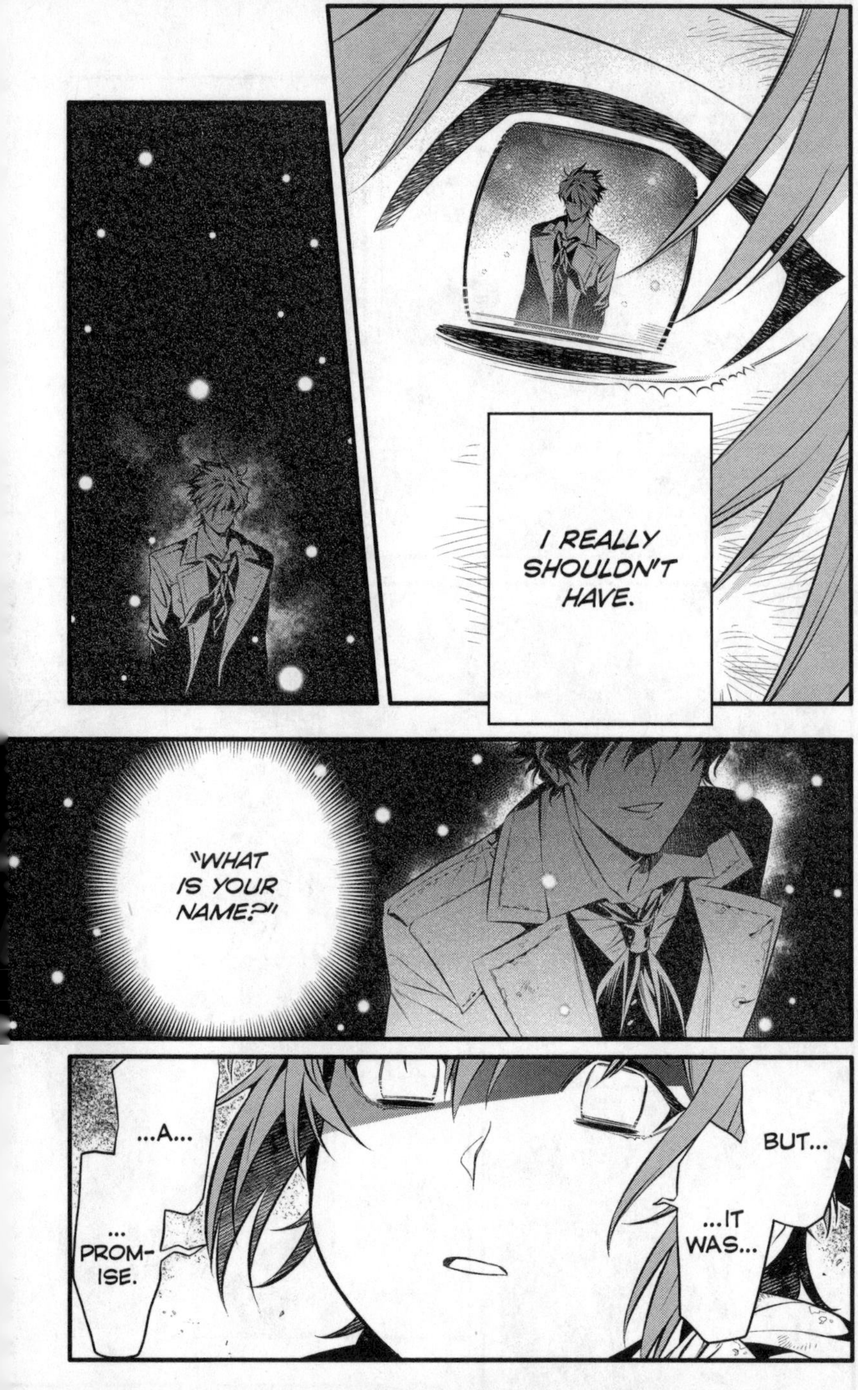
I REALLY SHOULDN'T HAVE.
"WHAT IS YOUR NAME?"
BUT...
...IT WAS...
...A...
... PROM-ISE.

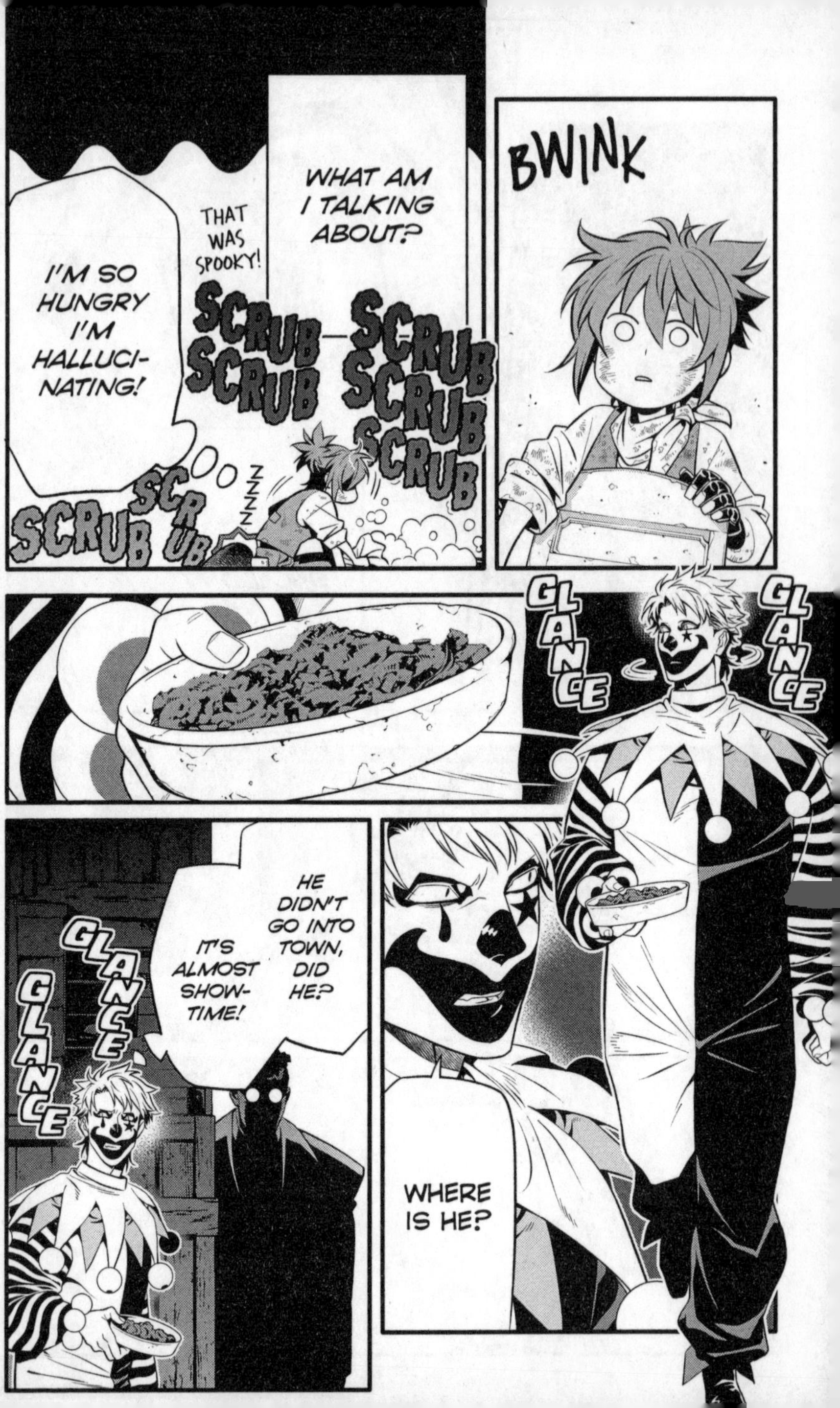
BWINK
WHAT AM I TALKING ABOUT?
SCRUB SCRUB—SCRUB SCRUB SCRUB
THAT WAS SPOOKY!
SCRUB SCRUB
I'M SO HUNGRY I'M HALLUCI-NATING!
SCRUB SCRUB
ZZZZ
GLANCE
GLANCE
HE DIDN'T GO INTO TOWN, DID HE?
WHERE IS HE?
IT'S ALMOST SHOW-TIME!
GLANCE
GLANCE

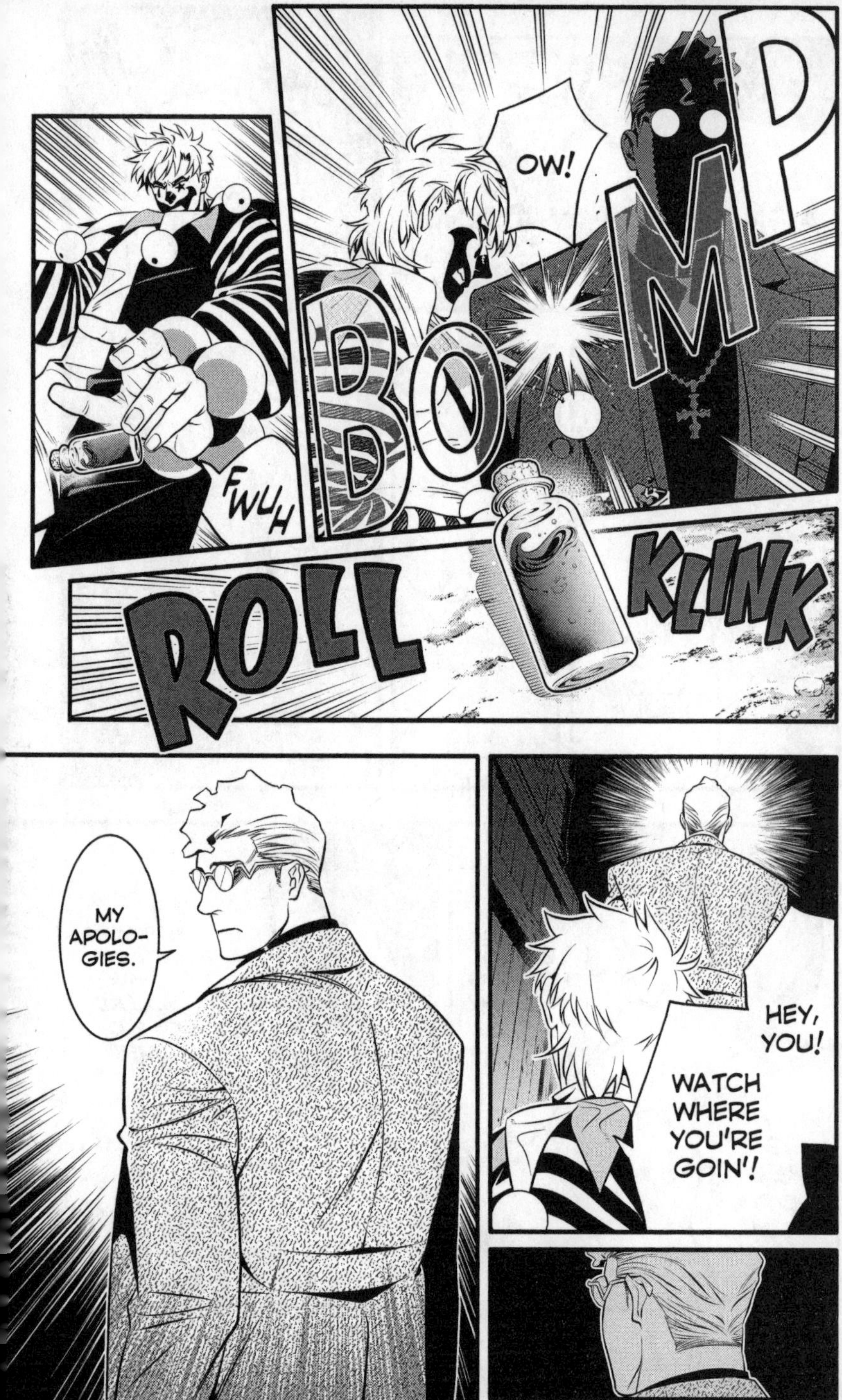
OW!
BOMP
FWUH
KLINK
ROLL
HEY, YOU!
WATCH WHERE YOU'RE GOIN'!
MY APOLO- GIES.

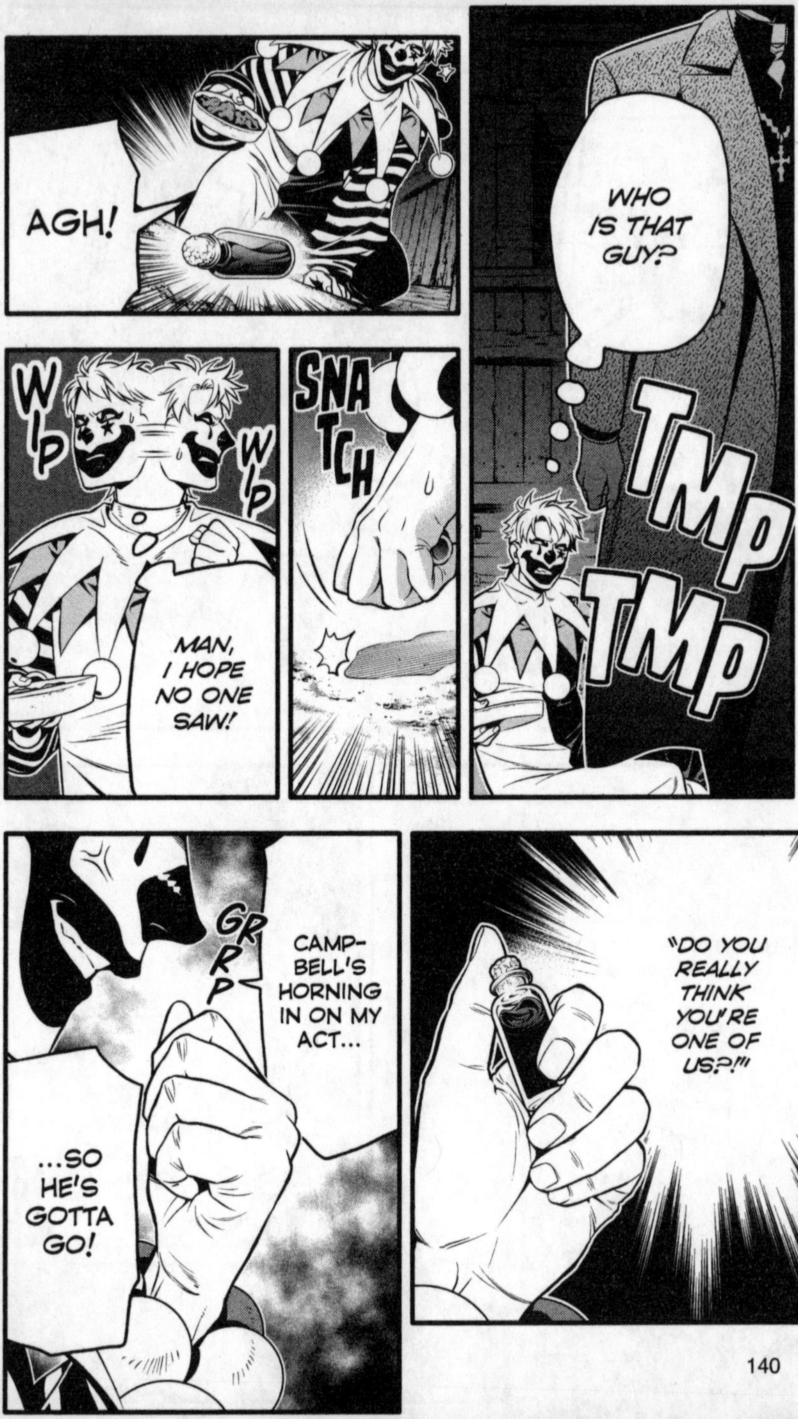
WHO IS THAT GUY?
TMP TMP
AGH!
SNATCH
WIP WIP
MAN, I HOPE NO ONE SAW!
"DO YOU REALLY THINK YOU'RE ONE OF US?!"
GRRP
CAMPBELL'S HORNING IN ON MY ACT...
...SO HE'S GOTTA GO!

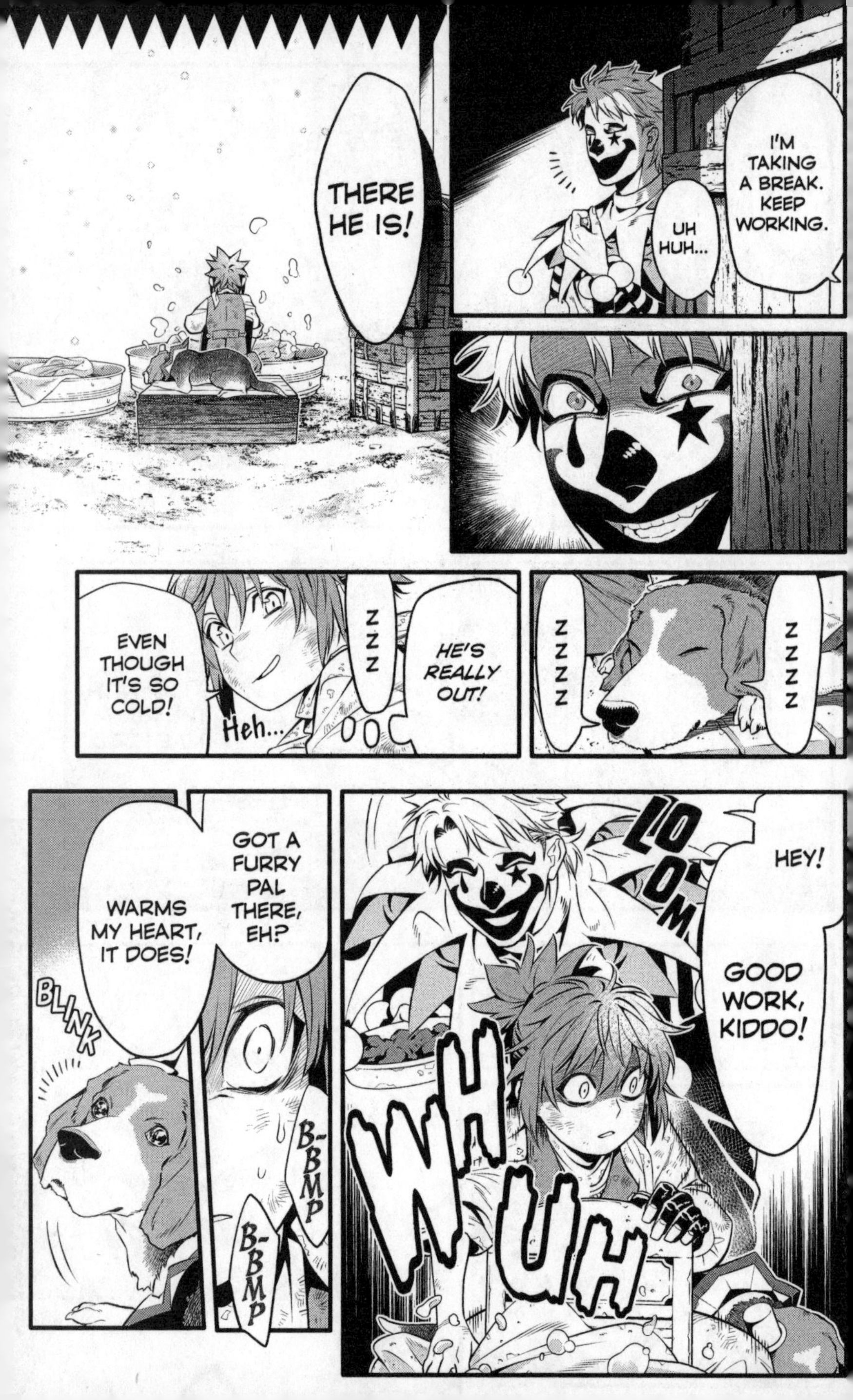
I'M TAKING A BREAK. KEEP WORKING.
UH HUH...
THERE HE IS!
ZZZZ
ZZZZ
HE'S REALLY OUT!
ZZZ
EVEN THOUGH IT'S SO COLD!
Heh...
HEY!
LOOOM
GOOD WORK, KIDDO!
WHUH
GOT A FURRY PAL THERE, EH?
B-BMP
B-BMP
WARMS MY HEART, IT DOES!
BLINK

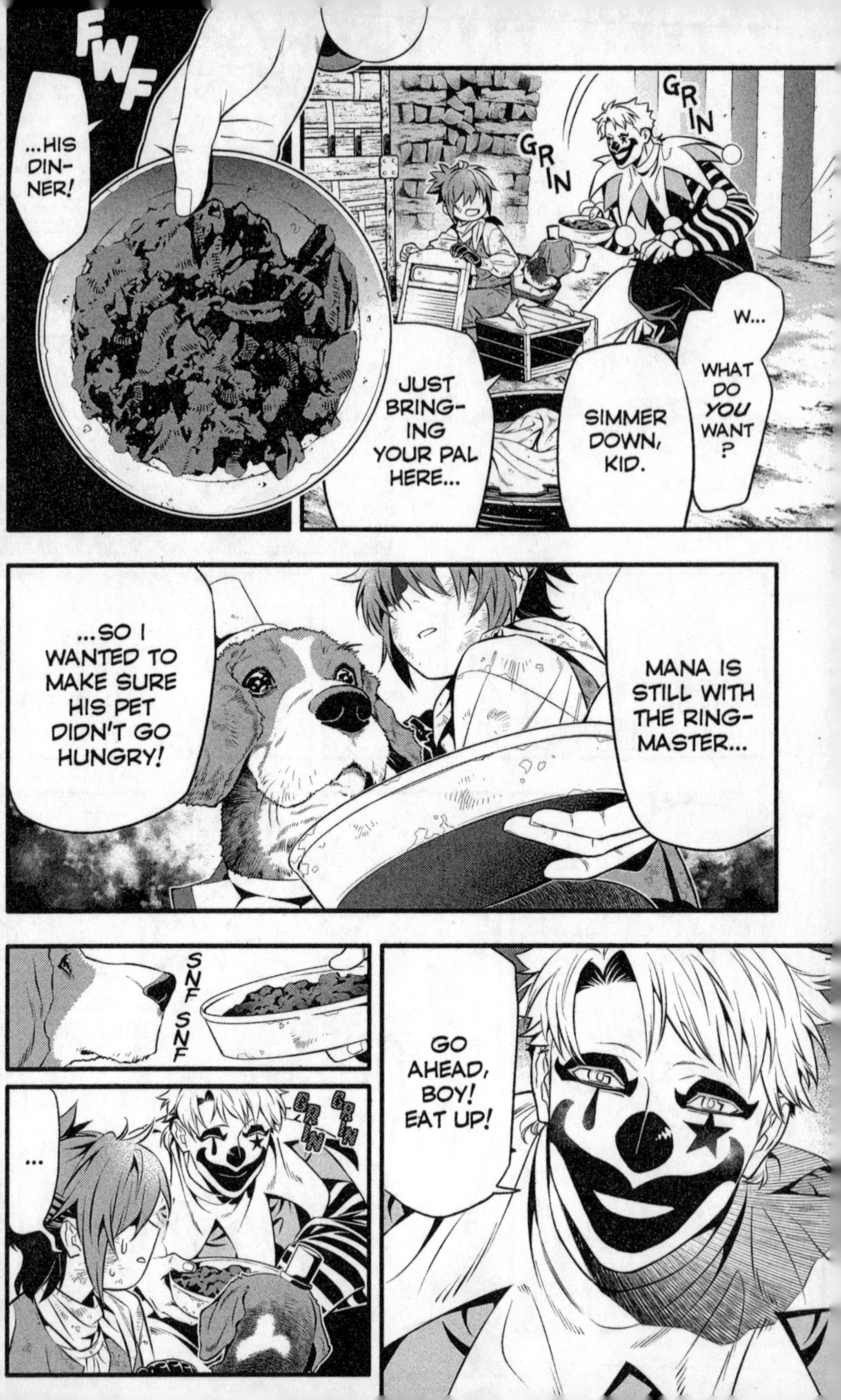
GRIN
GRIN
W...
WHAT DO *YOU* WANT?
SIMMER DOWN, KID.
JUST BRING-ING YOUR PAL HERE...
FWF
...HIS DIN-NER!
MANA IS STILL WITH THE RING-MASTER...
...SO I WANTED TO MAKE SURE HIS PET DIDN'T GO HUNGRY!
GO AHEAD, BOY! EAT UP!
SNF SNF
GRIN
GRIN
...

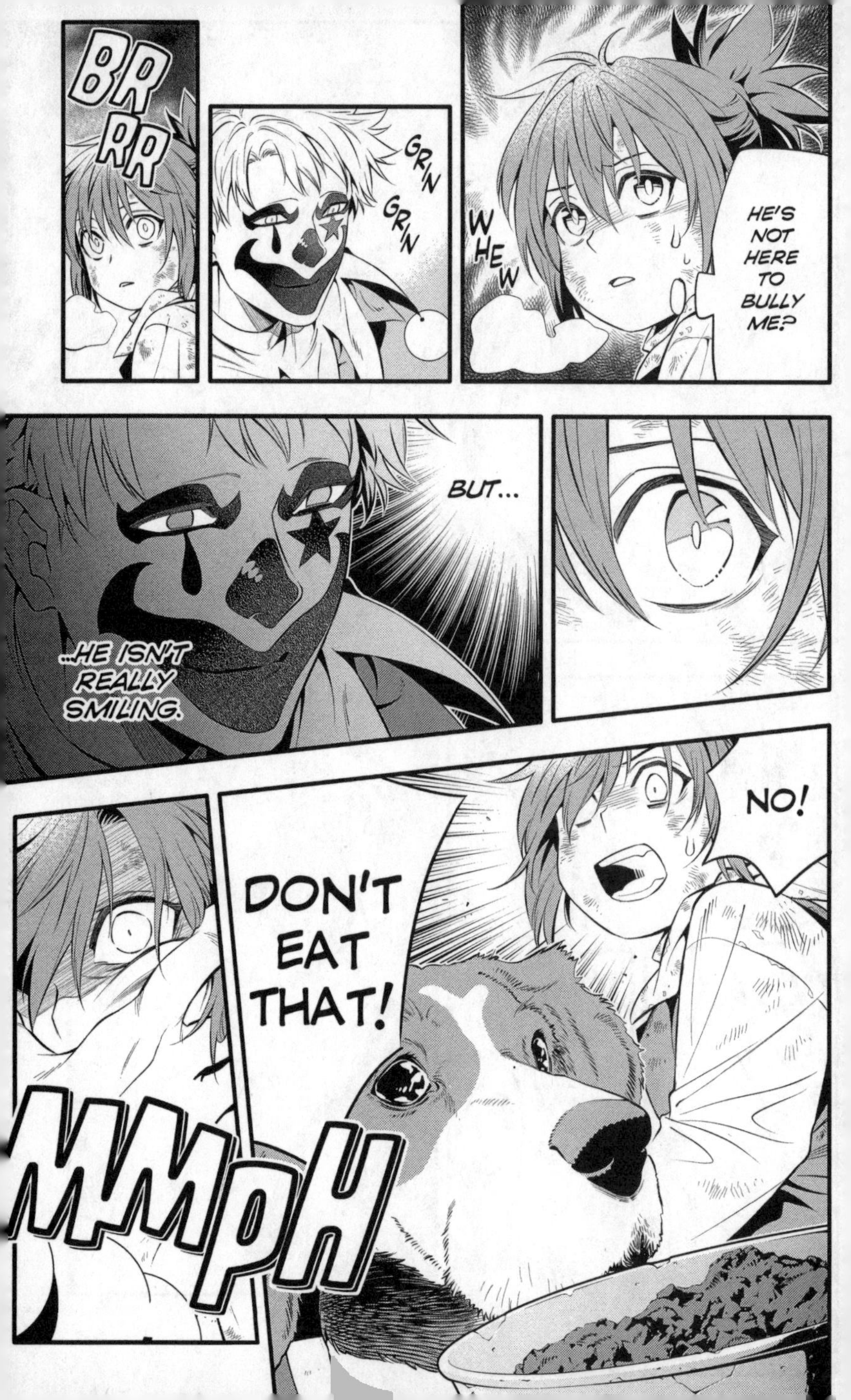
HE'S NOT HERE TO BULLY ME?
WHEW
GRIN GRIN
BRRRR
BUT...
...HE ISN'T REALLY SMILING.
NO!
DON'T EAT THAT!
MMMPH

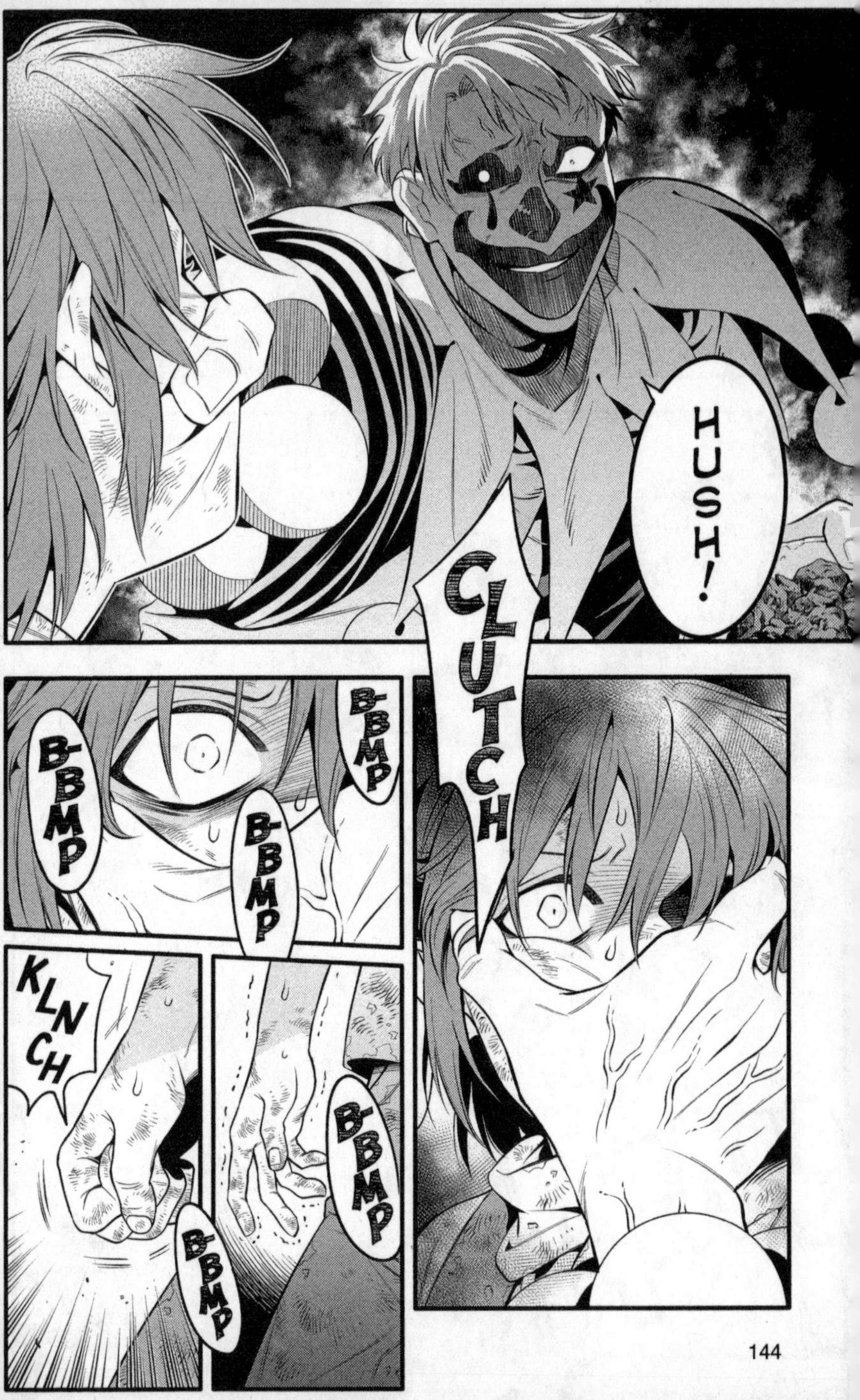
HUSH!
CLUTCH
B-BMP
B-BMP
B-BMP
KLNCH
B-BMP
B-BMP

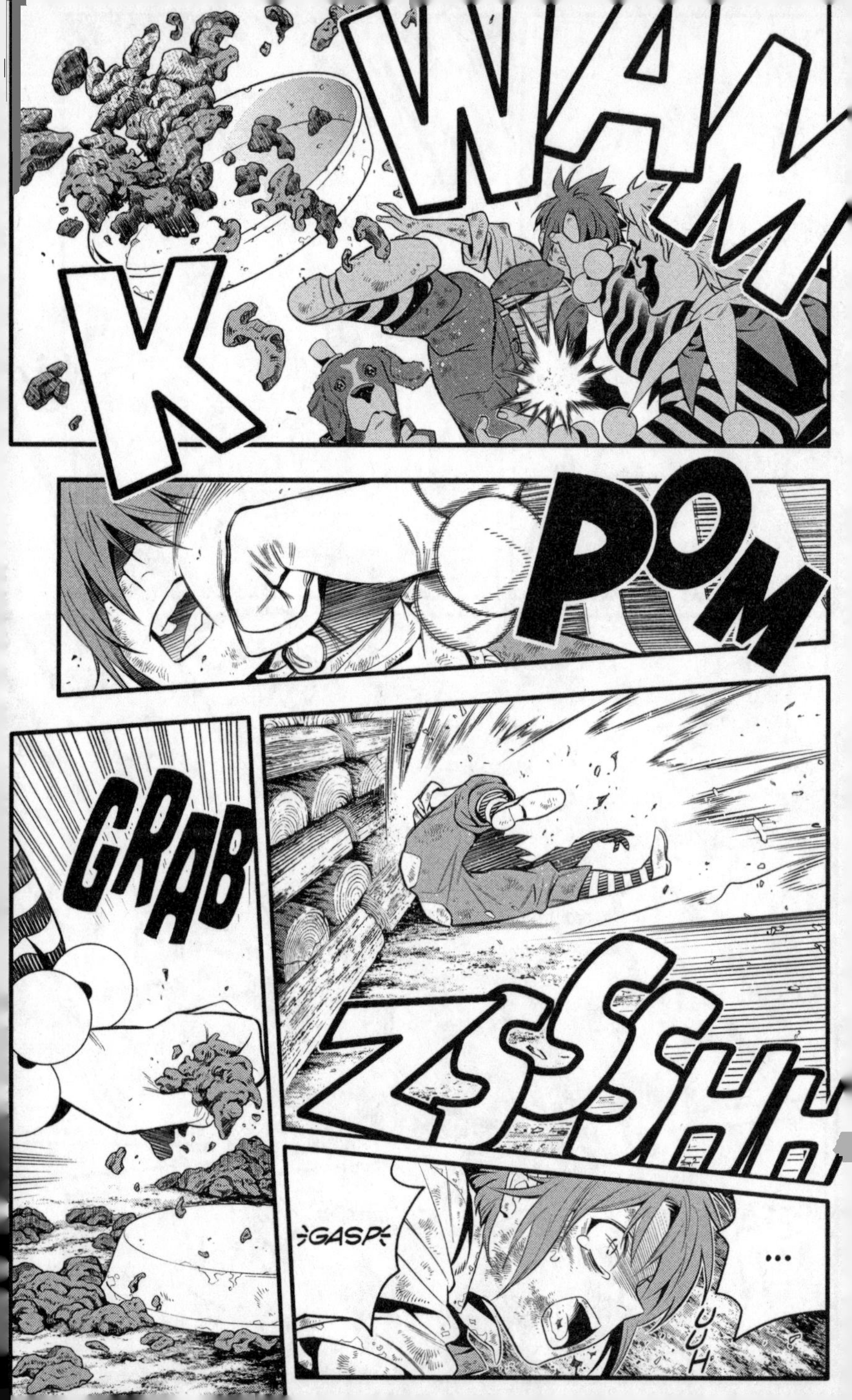
WHAM
K
POM
ZSSHH
...
HUU
GASP
GRAB

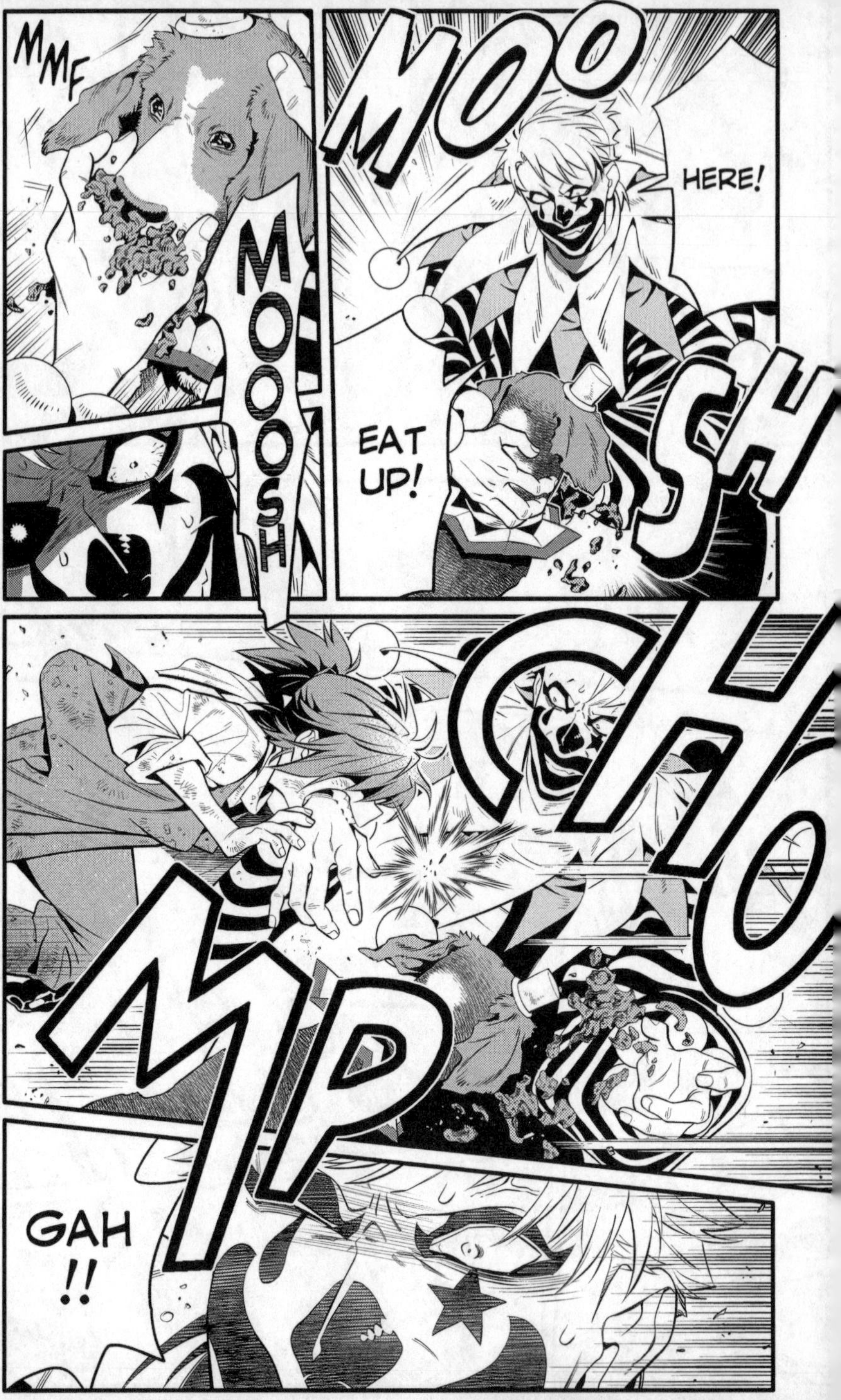
MOO
HERE!
EAT UP!
SH
MMF
MOOOSH
CHOMP
GAH !!

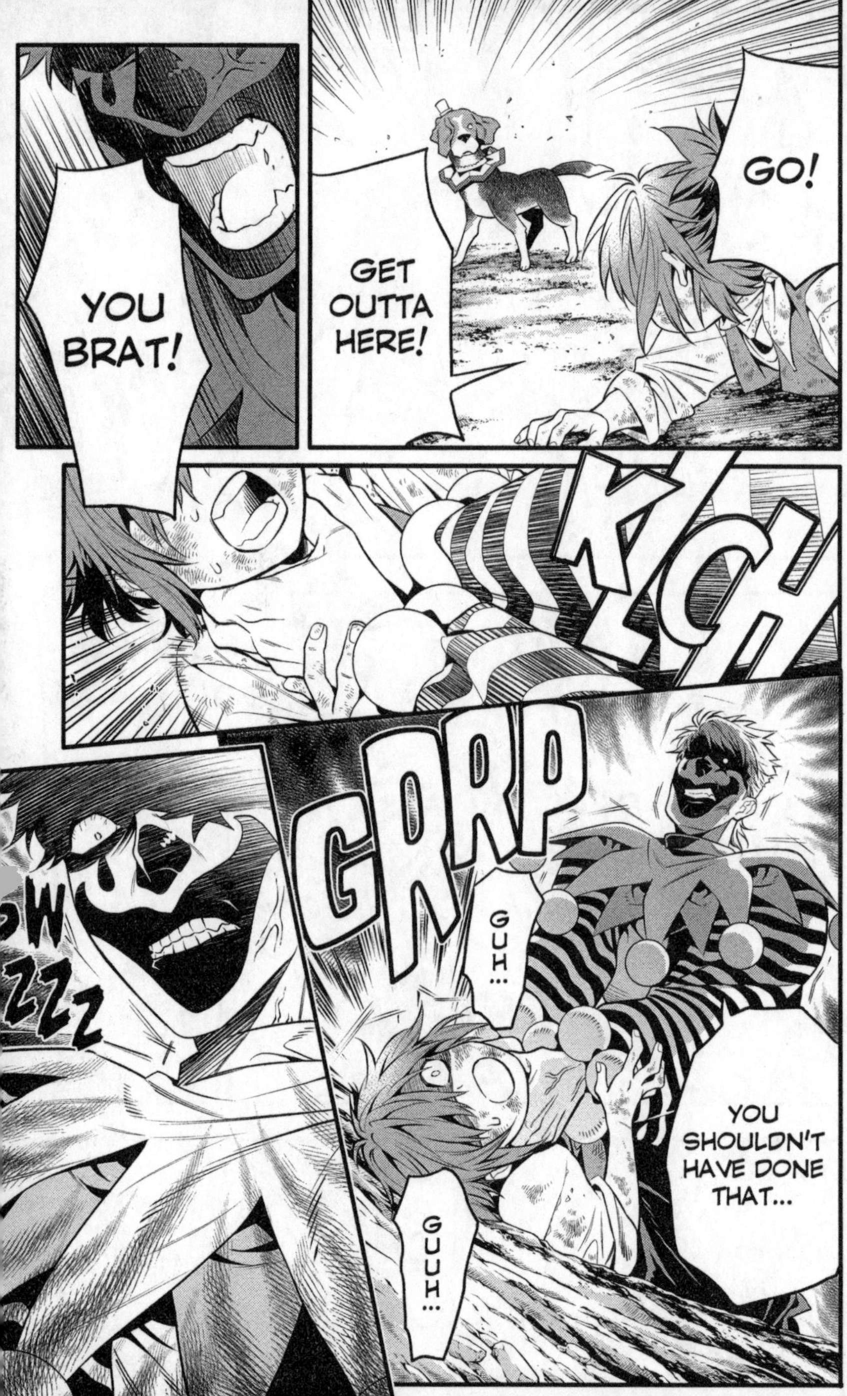
GO!
GET OUTTA HERE!
YOU BRAT!
KCH
GRRP
GUH...
YOU SHOULDN'T HAVE DONE THAT...
GUUH...
WZZZ

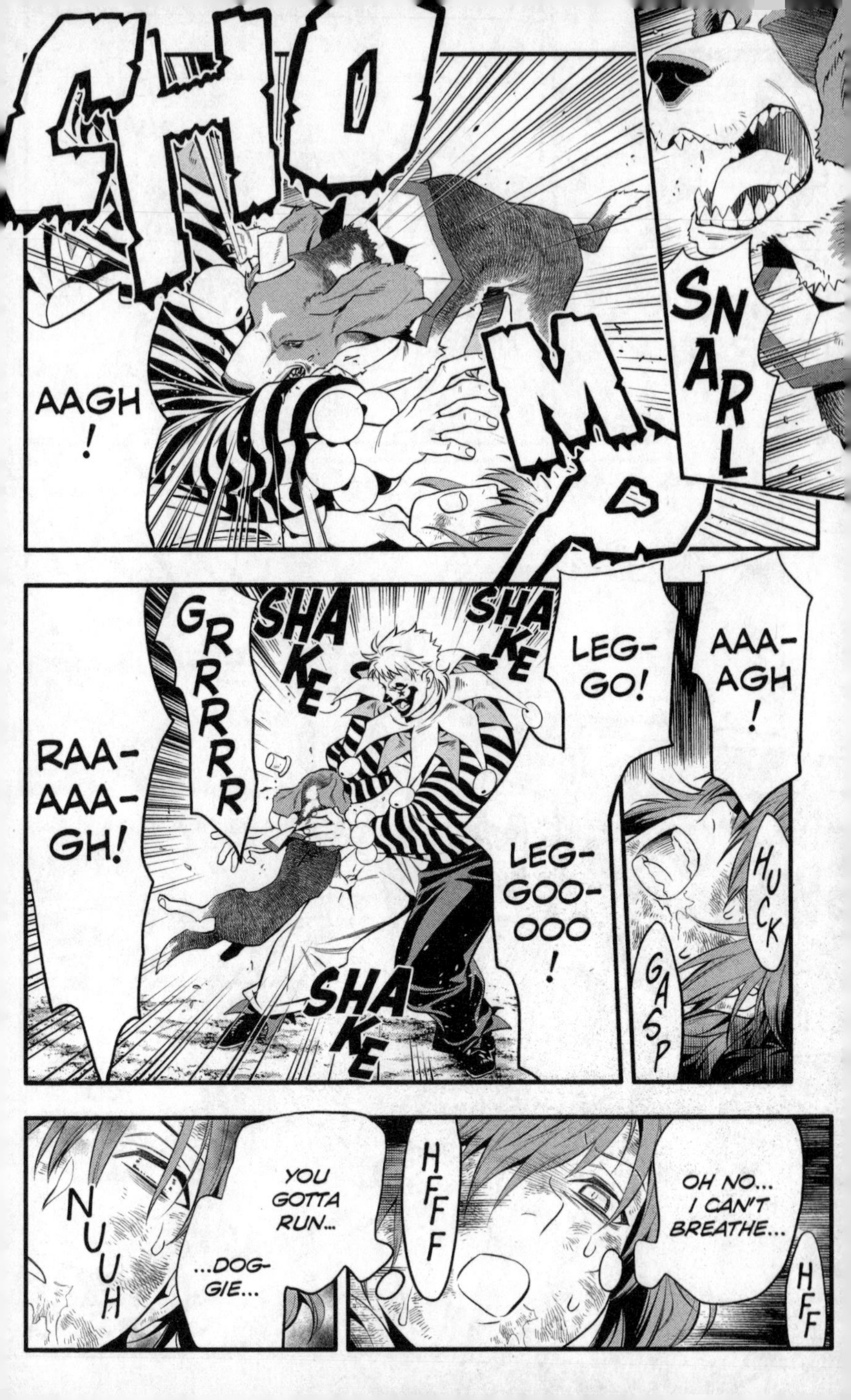
SNARL
CHOMP
AAGH!
AAA-AGH!
HUCK
GASP
LEG-GO!
SHAKE
SHAKE
LEG-GOO-OOO!
GRRRRRR
SHAKE
RAA-AAA-GH!
OH NO... I CAN'T BREATHE...
HFF
HFFF
YOU GOTTA RUN...
...DOG-GIE...
NUUH

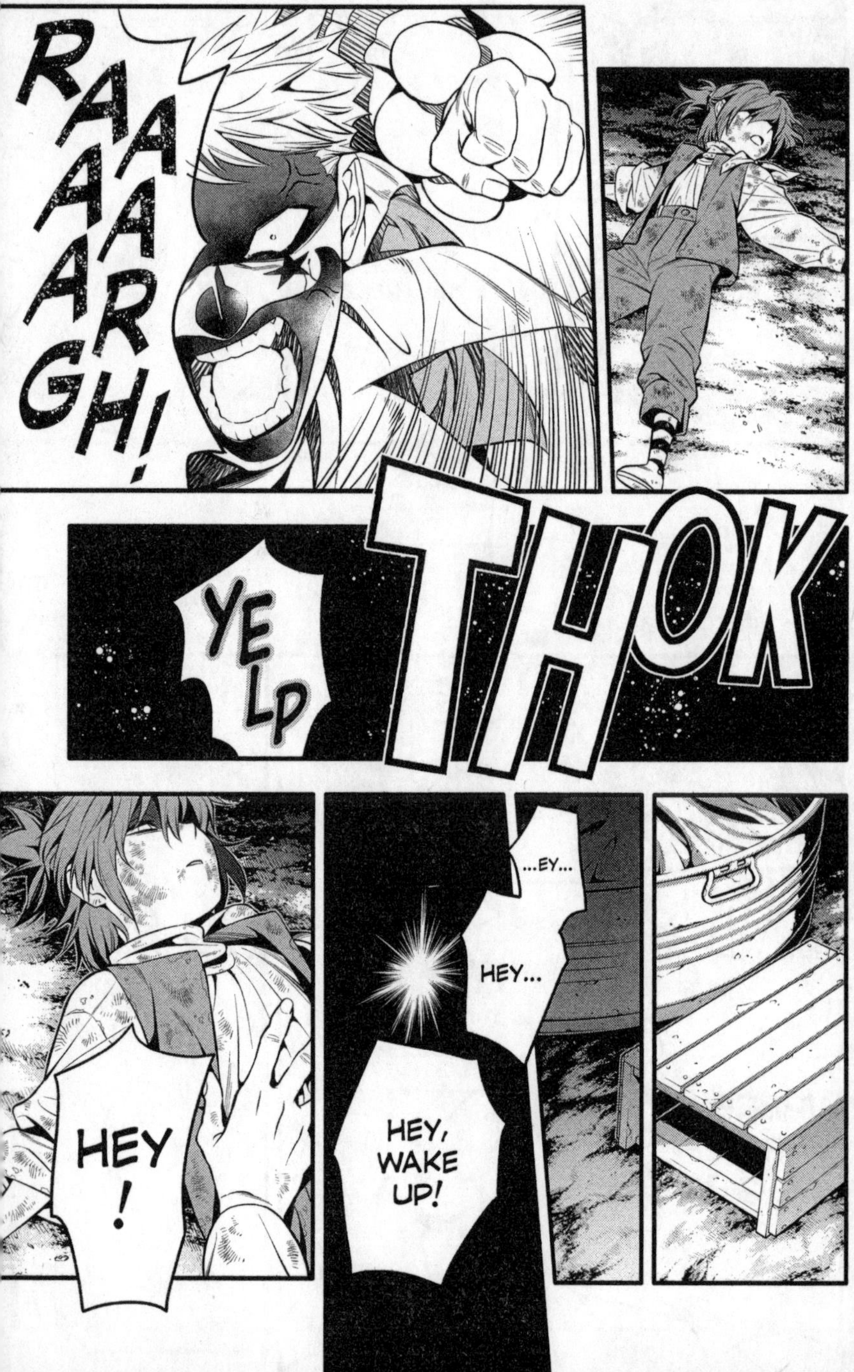
RAAAAARGH!
THOK
YELP
...EY...
HEY...
HEY, WAKE UP!
HEY!

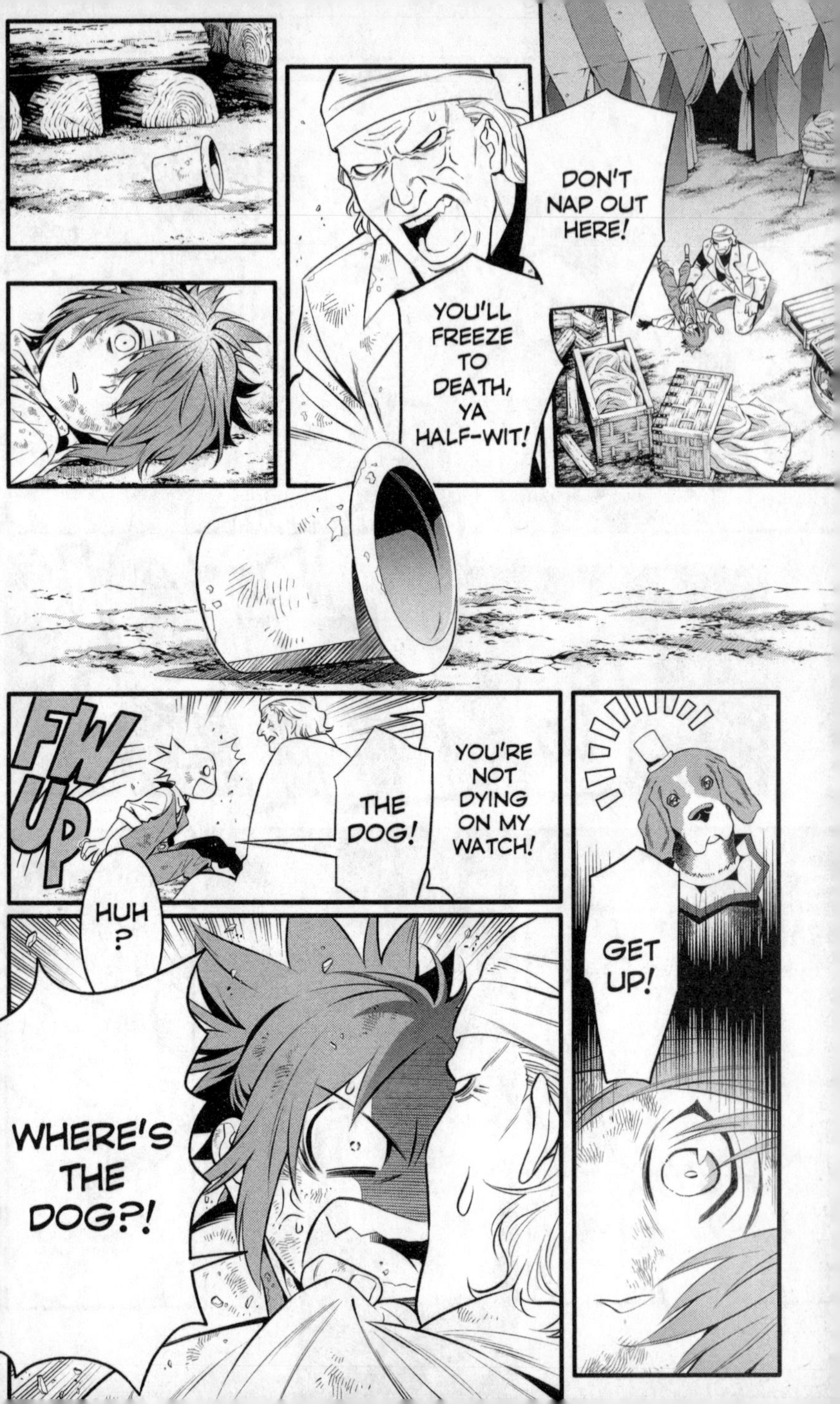
DON'T NAP OUT HERE!
YOU'LL FREEZE TO DEATH, YA HALF-WIT!
GET UP!
YOU'RE NOT DYING ON MY WATCH!
THE DOG!
FWUP
HUH?
WHERE'S THE DOG?!

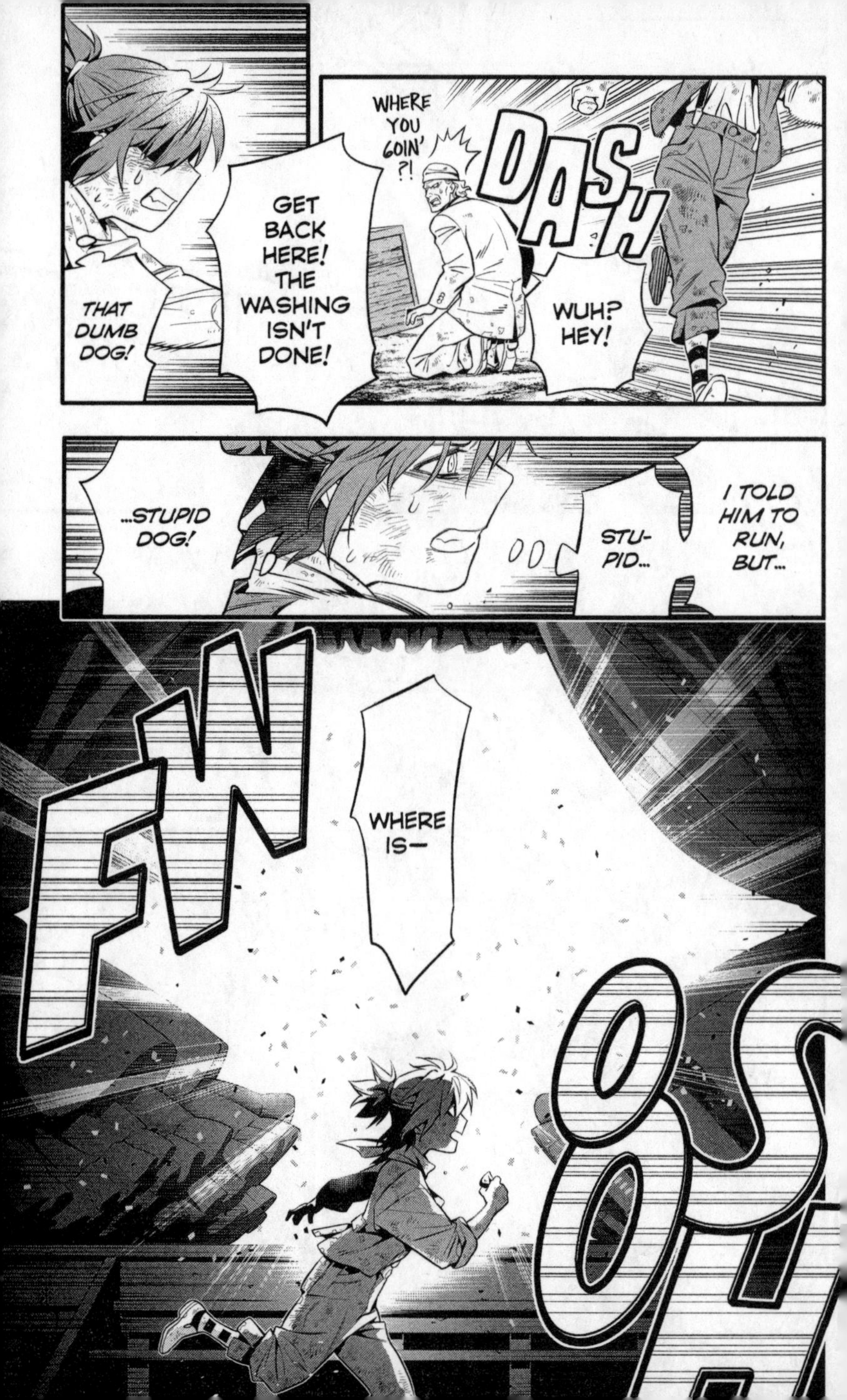
WUH? HEY!
DASH
WHERE YOU GOIN'?!
GET BACK HERE! THE WASHING ISN'T DONE!
THAT DUMB DOG!
I TOLD HIM TO RUN, BUT...
STU-PID...
...STUPID DOG!
WHERE IS—
FWN

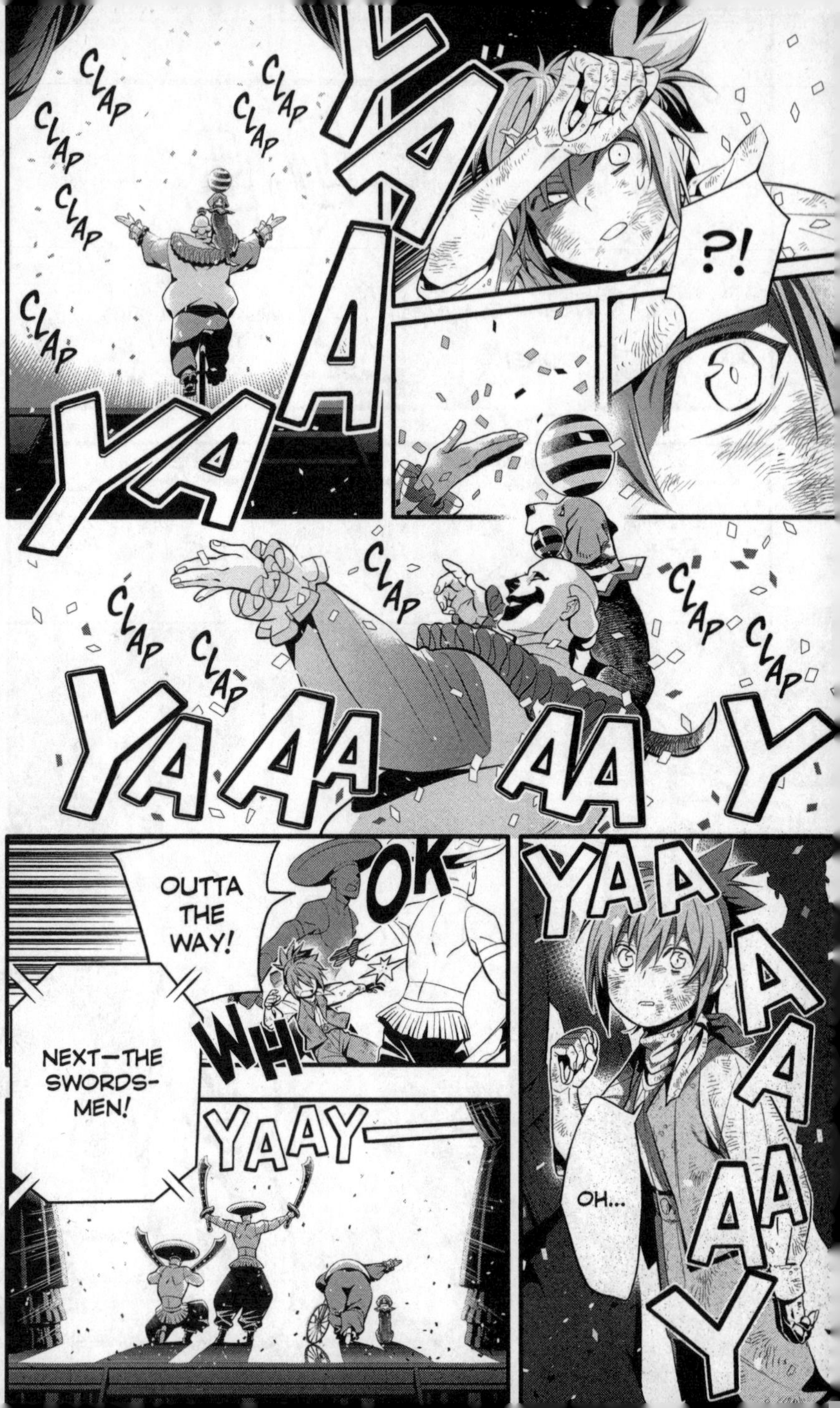
?!
YAAAA
CLAP CLAP CLAP CLAP
CLAP CLAP CLAP
CLAP CLAP CLAP CLAP CLAP
YAAAAAAY
YAAAAAAY
OH...
OK
OUTTA THE WAY!
WH
NEXT—THE SWORDSMEN!
YAAY—

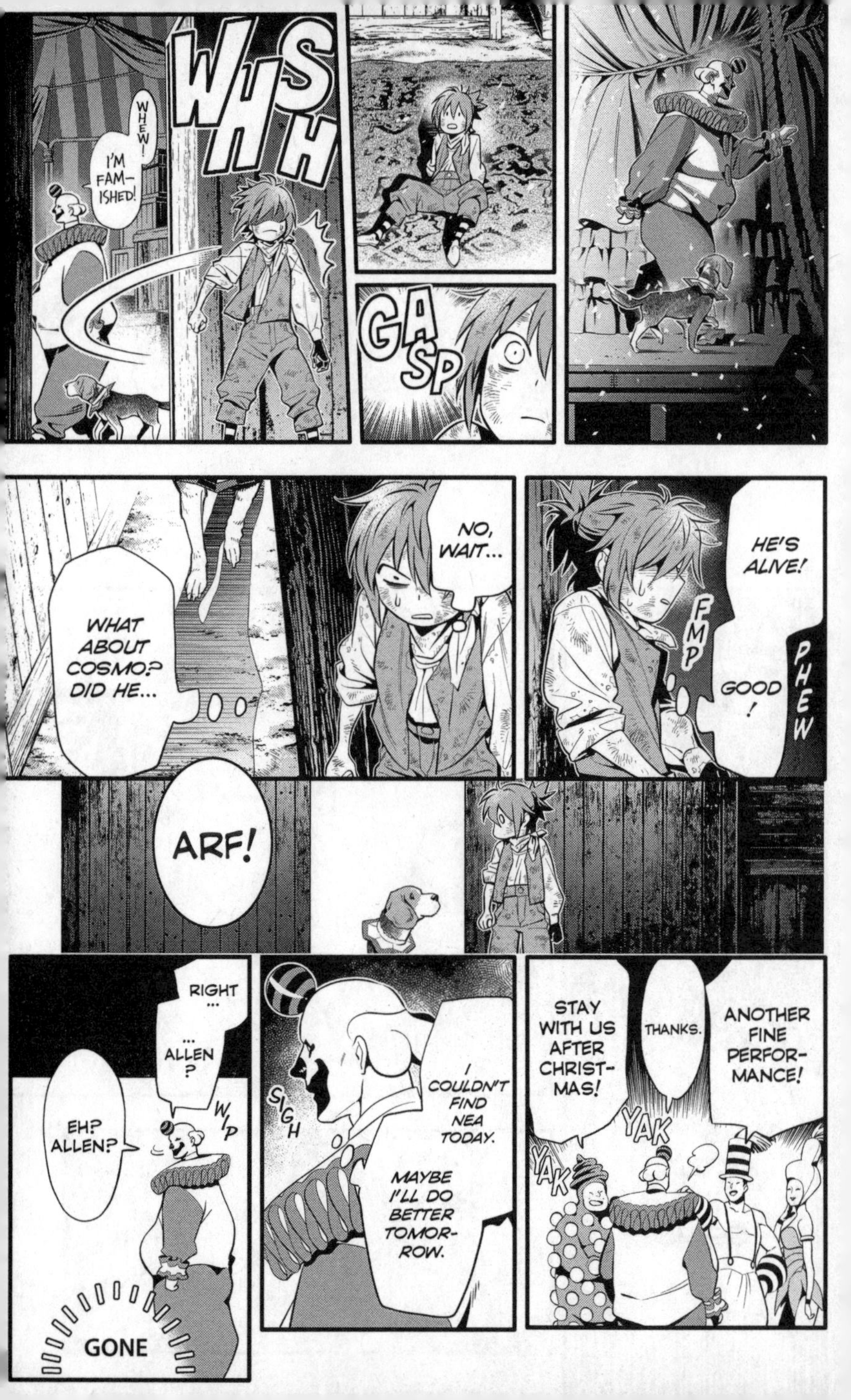
GASP
WHSH
WHEW! I'M FAMISHED!
HE'S ALIVE!
FMP
GOOD!
PHEW
NO, WAIT...
WHAT ABOUT COSMO? DID HE...
ARF!
ANOTHER FINE PERFORMANCE!
THANKS.
STAY WITH US AFTER CHRISTMAS!
YAK
YAK
I COULDN'T FIND NEA TODAY.
SIGH
MAYBE I'LL DO BETTER TOMORROW.
RIGHT...
...ALLEN?
WIP
EH? ALLEN?
GONE

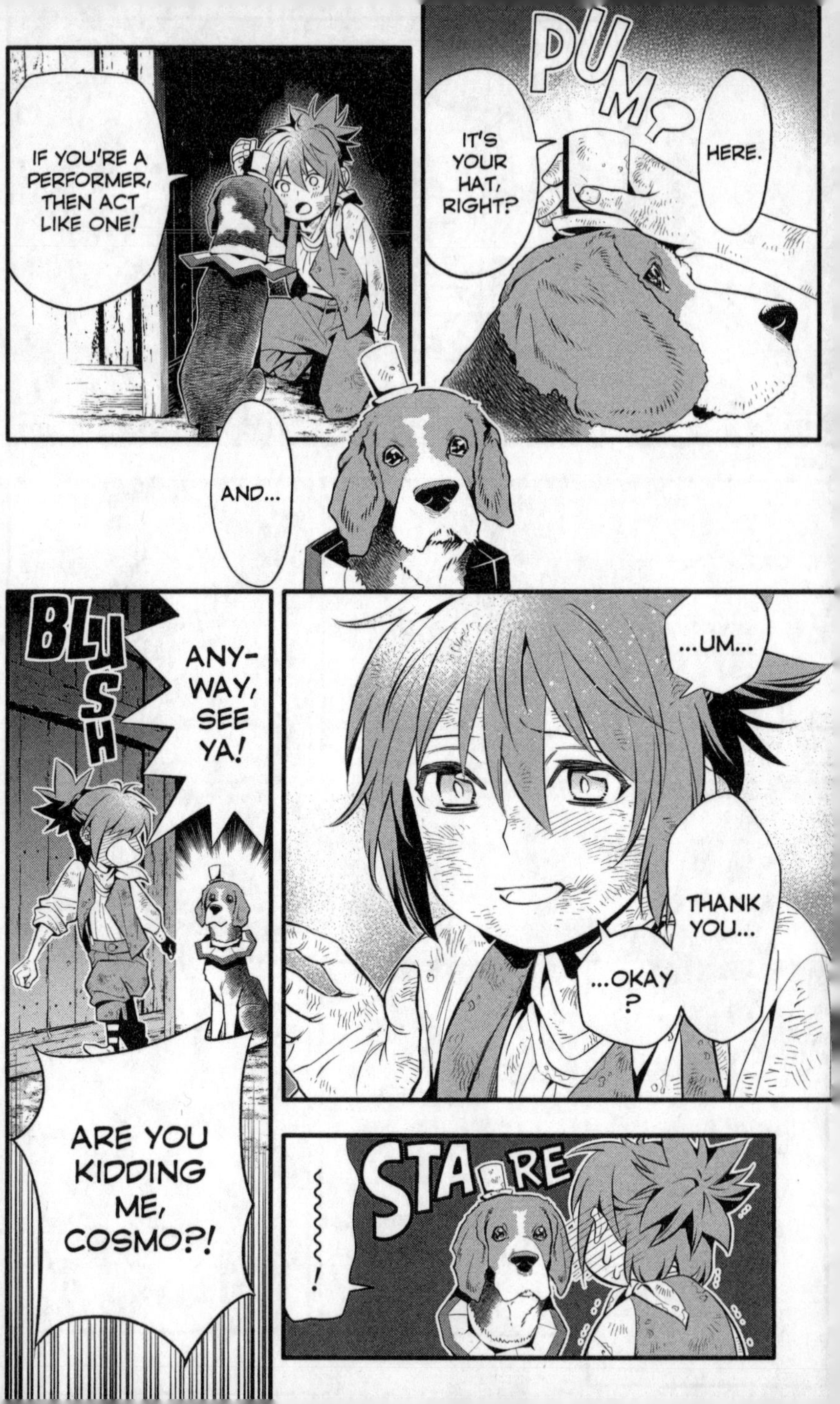
PUMP
HERE.
IT'S YOUR HAT, RIGHT?
IF YOU'RE A PERFORMER, THEN ACT LIKE ONE!
AND...
...UM...
THANK YOU...
...OKAY ?
STARE
!
BLUSH
ANY-WAY, SEE YA!
ARE YOU KIDDING ME, COSMO?!

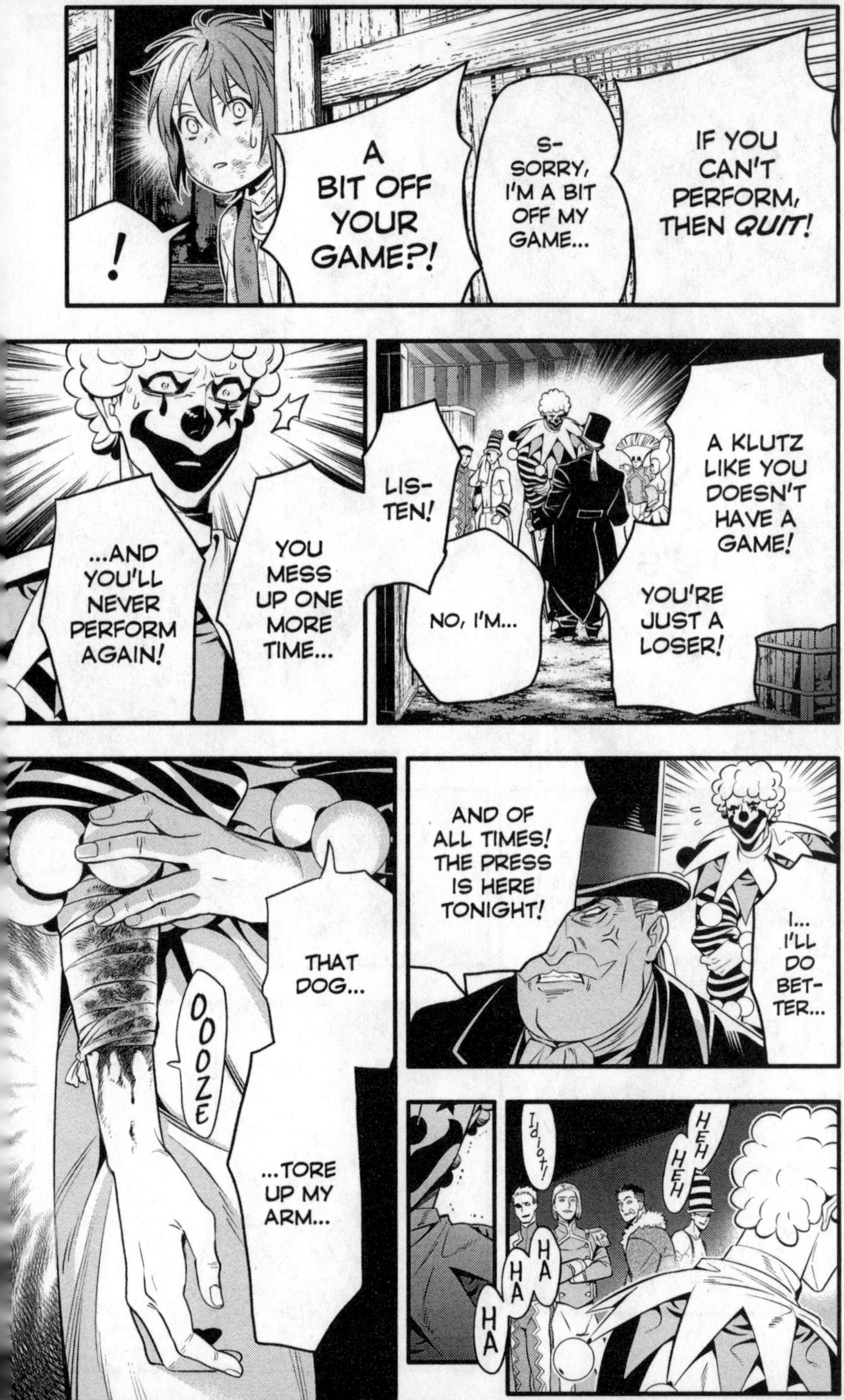
IF YOU CAN'T PERFORM, THEN *QUIT*!
S-SORRY, I'M A BIT OFF MY GAME...
A BIT OFF YOUR GAME?!
!
A KLUTZ LIKE YOU DOESN'T HAVE A GAME!
YOU'RE JUST A LOSER!
NO, I'M...
LIS-TEN!
YOU MESS UP ONE MORE TIME...
...AND YOU'LL NEVER PERFORM AGAIN!
AND OF ALL TIMES! THE PRESS IS HERE TONIGHT!
I... I'LL DO BET-TER...
HEH HEH
Idiot!
HA HA HA HA
THAT DOG...
OOOZE
...TORE UP MY ARM...

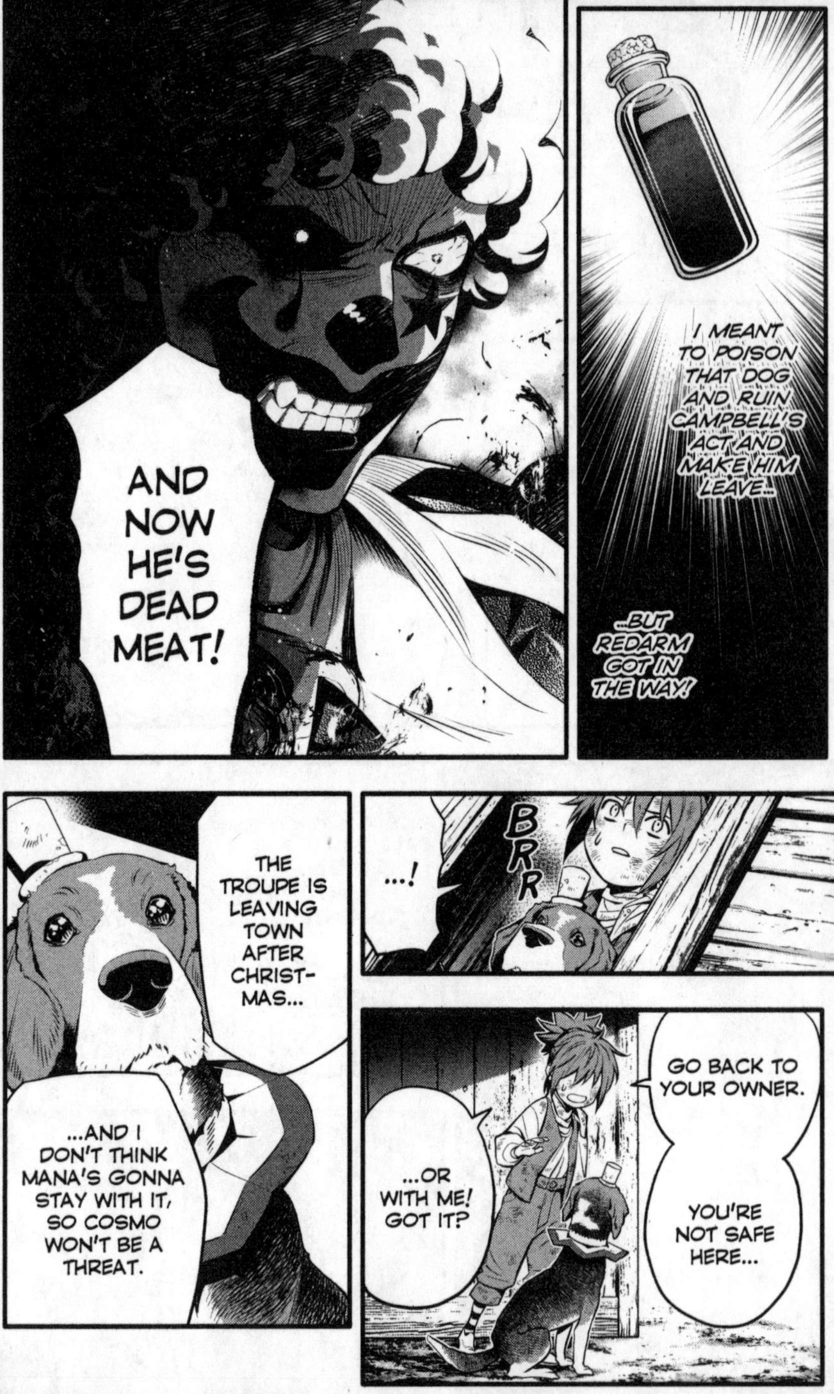
I MEANT TO POISON THAT DOG AND RUIN CAMPBELL'S ACT AND MAKE HIM LEAVE...
...BUT REDARM GOT IN THE WAY!
AND NOW HE'S DEAD MEAT!
BRR
...!
GO BACK TO YOUR OWNER.
YOU'RE NOT SAFE HERE...
...OR WITH ME! GOT IT?
THE TROUPE IS LEAVING TOWN AFTER CHRIST-MAS...
...AND I DON'T THINK MANA'S GONNA STAY WITH IT, SO COSMO WON'T BE A THREAT.

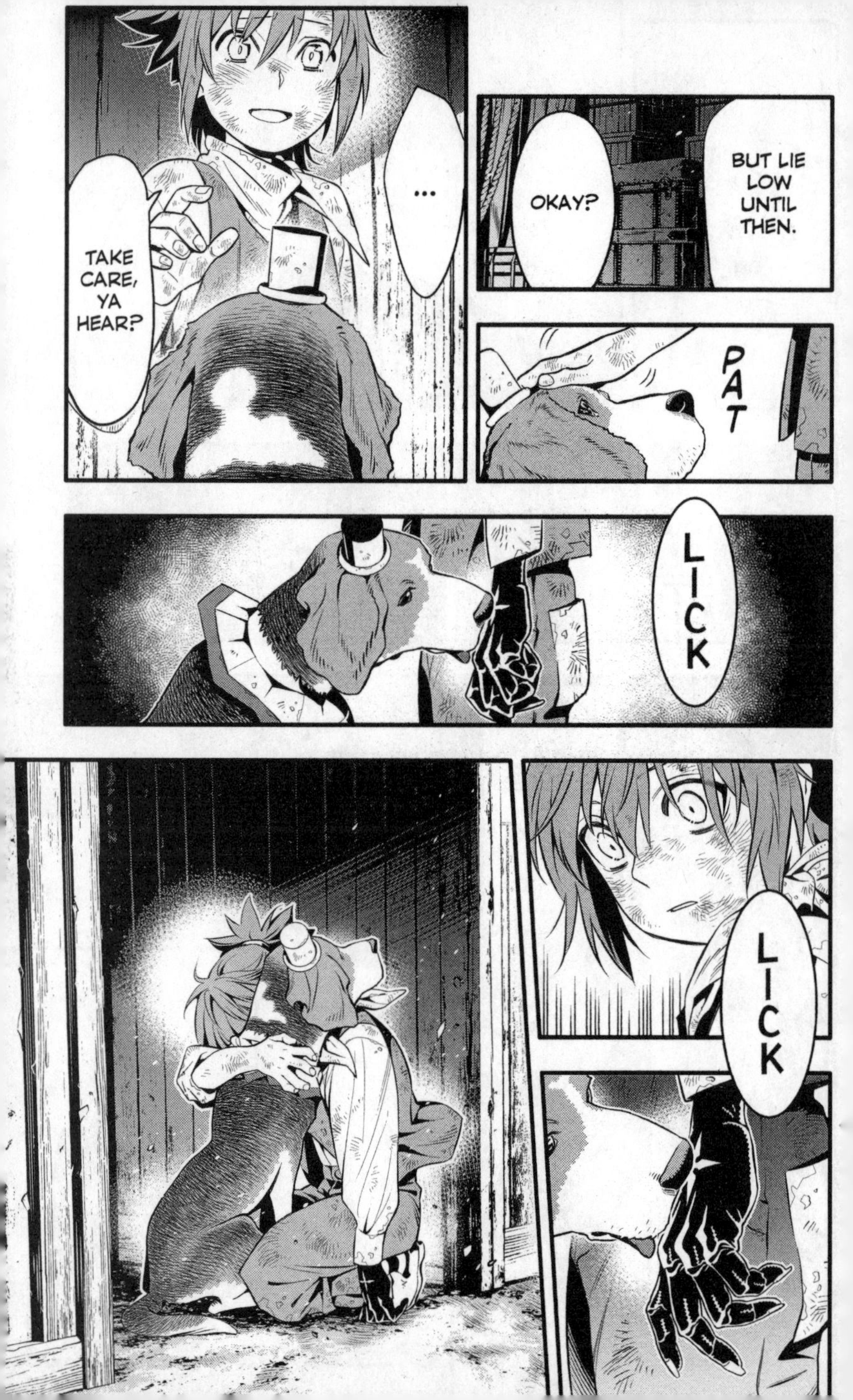
BUT LIE LOW UNTIL THEN.
OKAY?
...
TAKE CARE, YA HEAR?
PAT
LICK
LICK

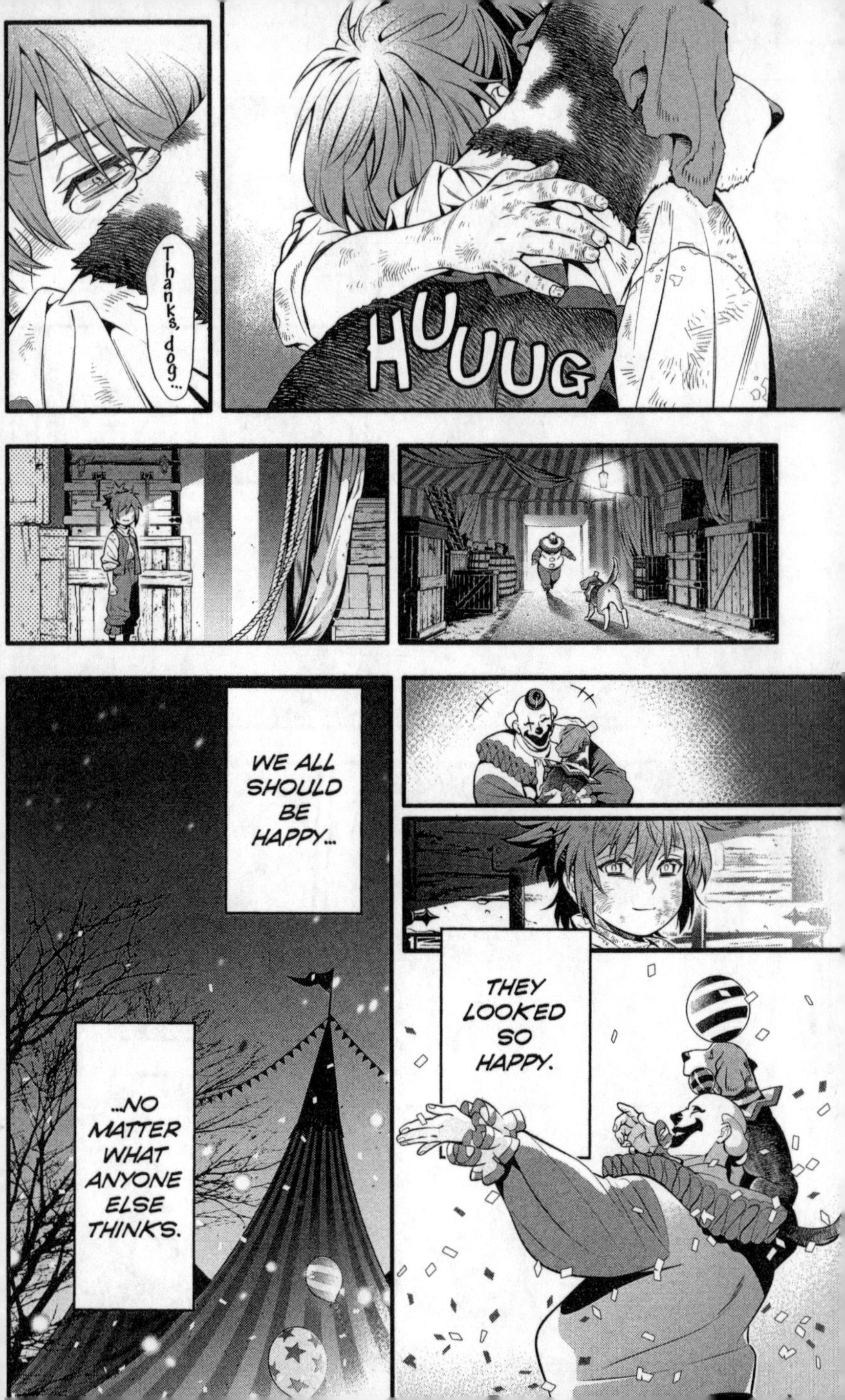
HUUUG
Thanks, dog...
THEY LOOKED SO HAPPY.
WE ALL SHOULD BE HAPPY...
...NO MATTER WHAT ANYONE ELSE THINKS.

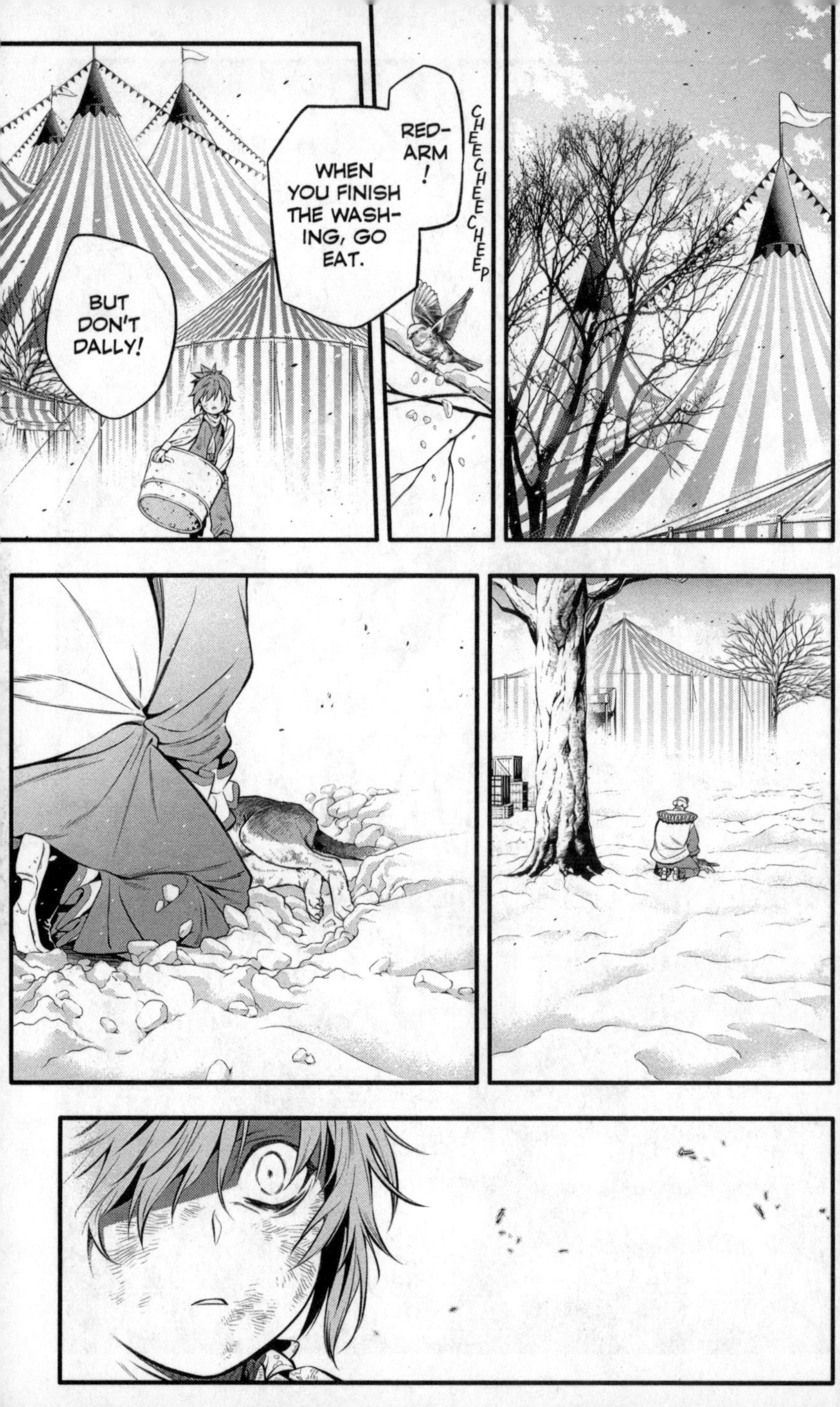
CHEECHEECHEEP
RED-ARM!
WHEN YOU FINISH THE WASHING, GO EAT.
BUT DON'T DALLY!

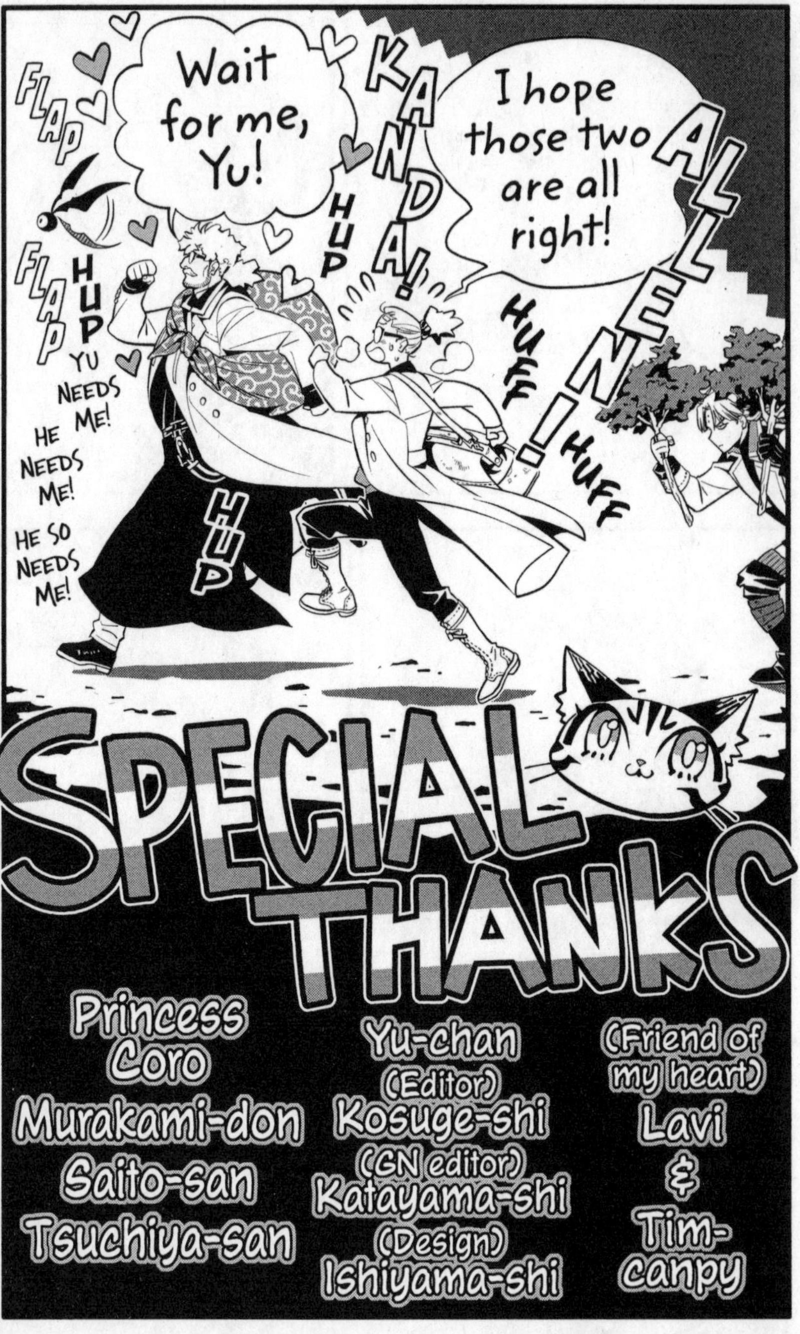
I hope those two are all right!
ALLEN!
HUFF HUFF
KANDA!
HUP
Wait for me, Yu!
FLAP FLAP
HUP HUP
YU NEEDS ME!
HE NEEDS ME!
HE SO NEEDS ME!
HUP
SPECIAL THANKS
Princess Coro
Murakami-don
Saito-san
Tsuchiya-san
Yu-chan
(Editor) Kosuge-shi
(GN editor) Katayama-shi
(Design) Ishiyama-shi
(Friend of my heart) Lavi & Tim-canpy

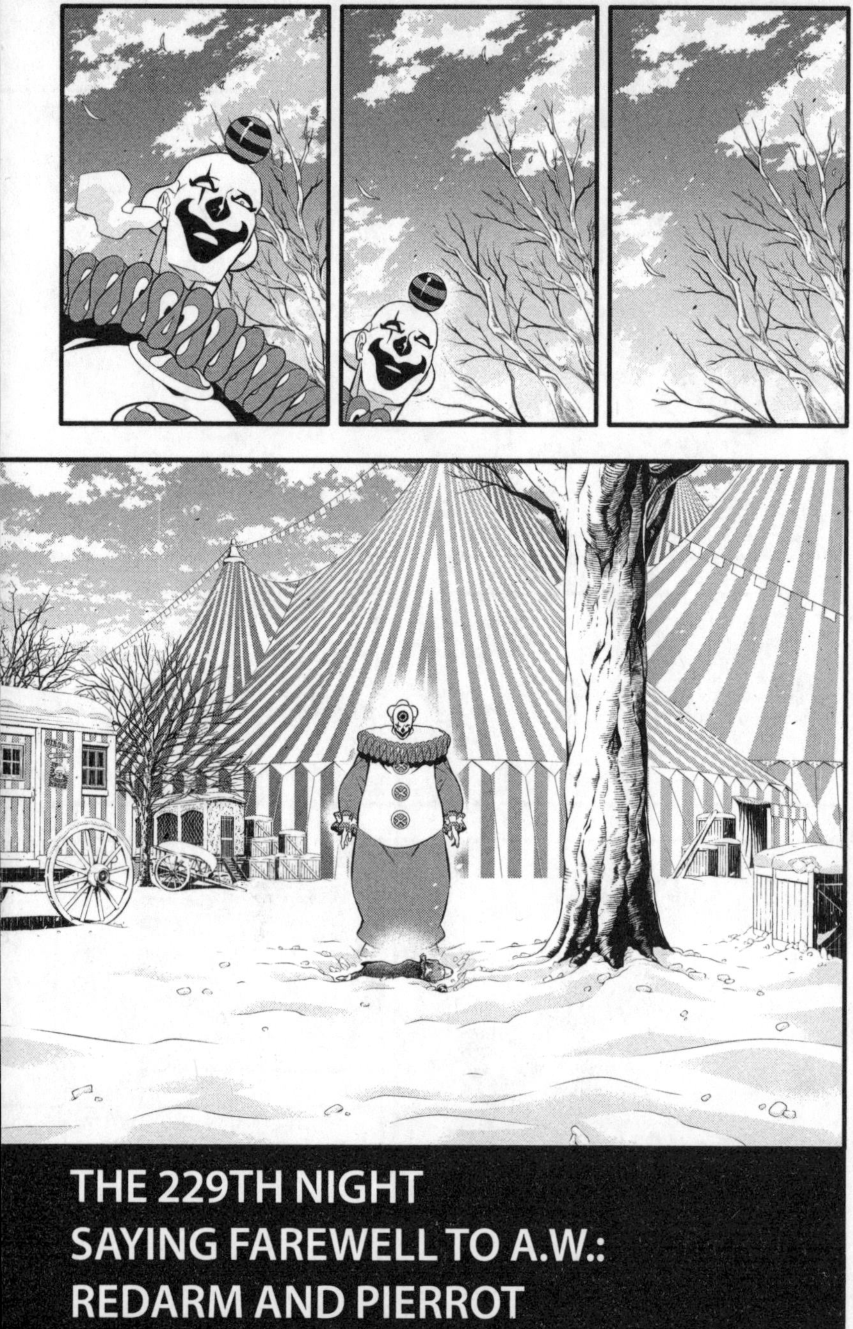

THE 229TH NIGHT
SAYING FAREWELL TO A.W.:
REDARM AND PIERROT

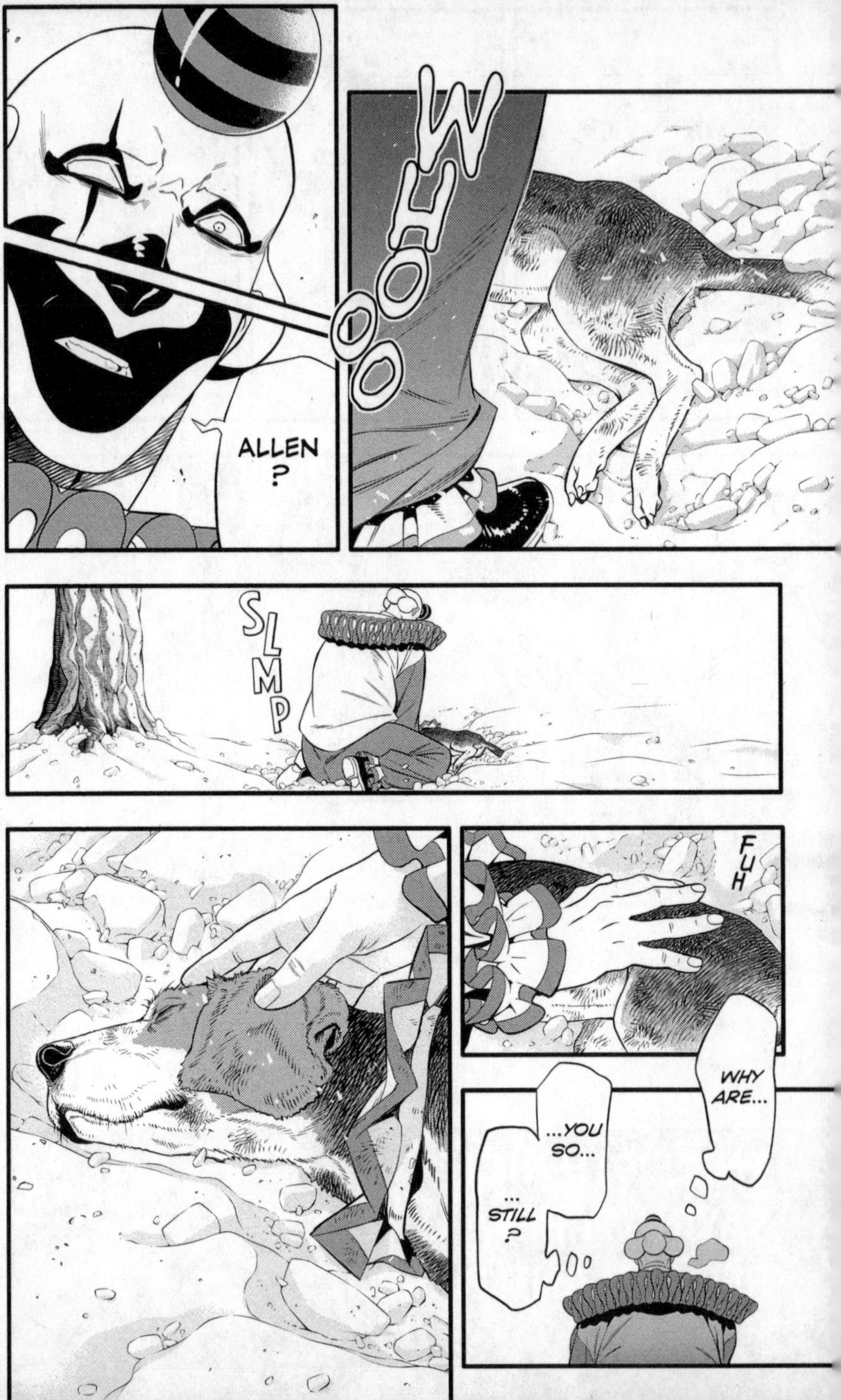
WHOOO
ALLEN?
SLMP
FUH
WHY ARE...
...YOU SO...
...STILL?

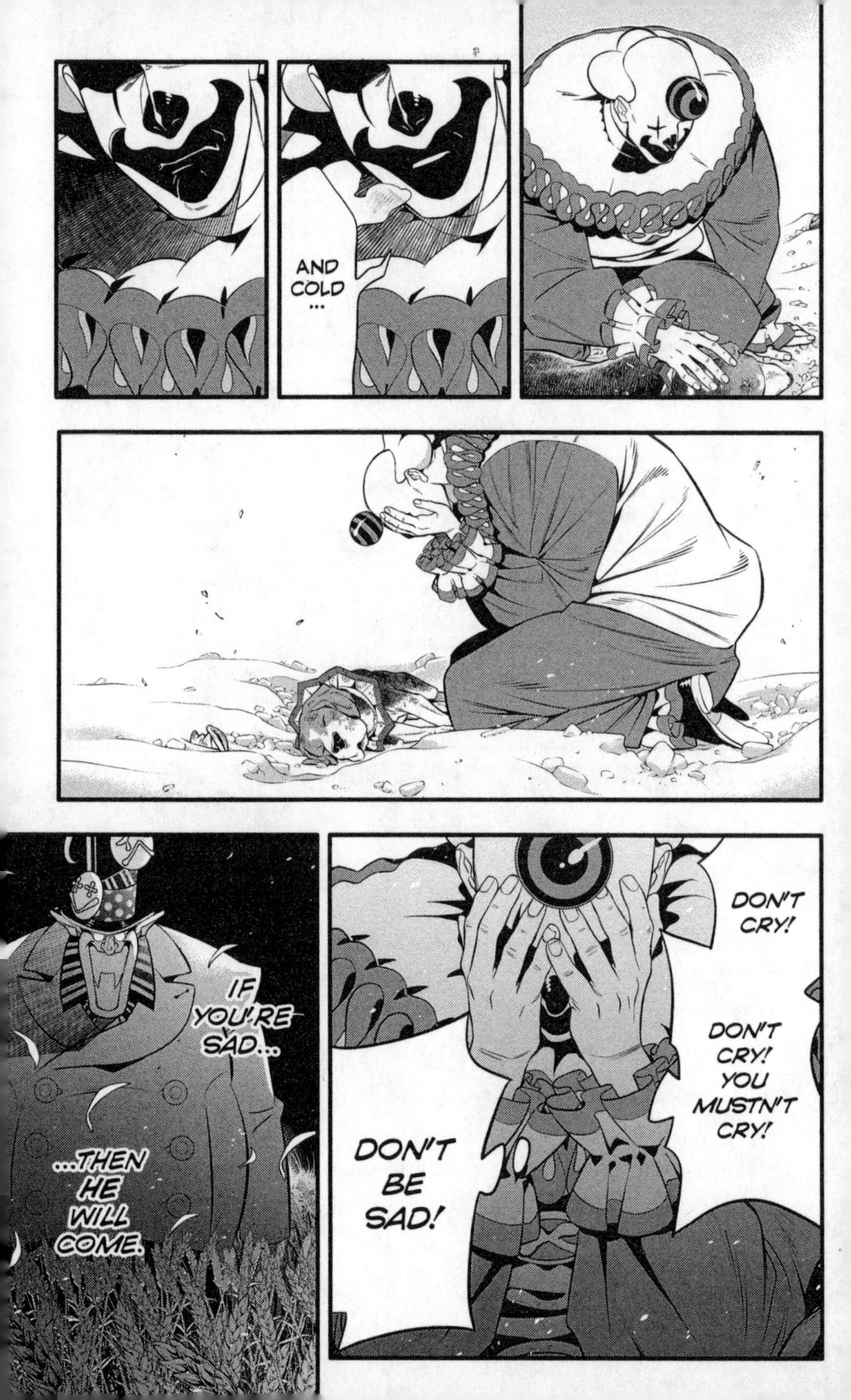
AND COLD ...
DON'T CRY!
DON'T CRY! YOU MUSTN'T CRY!
DON'T BE SAD!
IF YOU'RE SAD...
...THEN HE WILL COME.

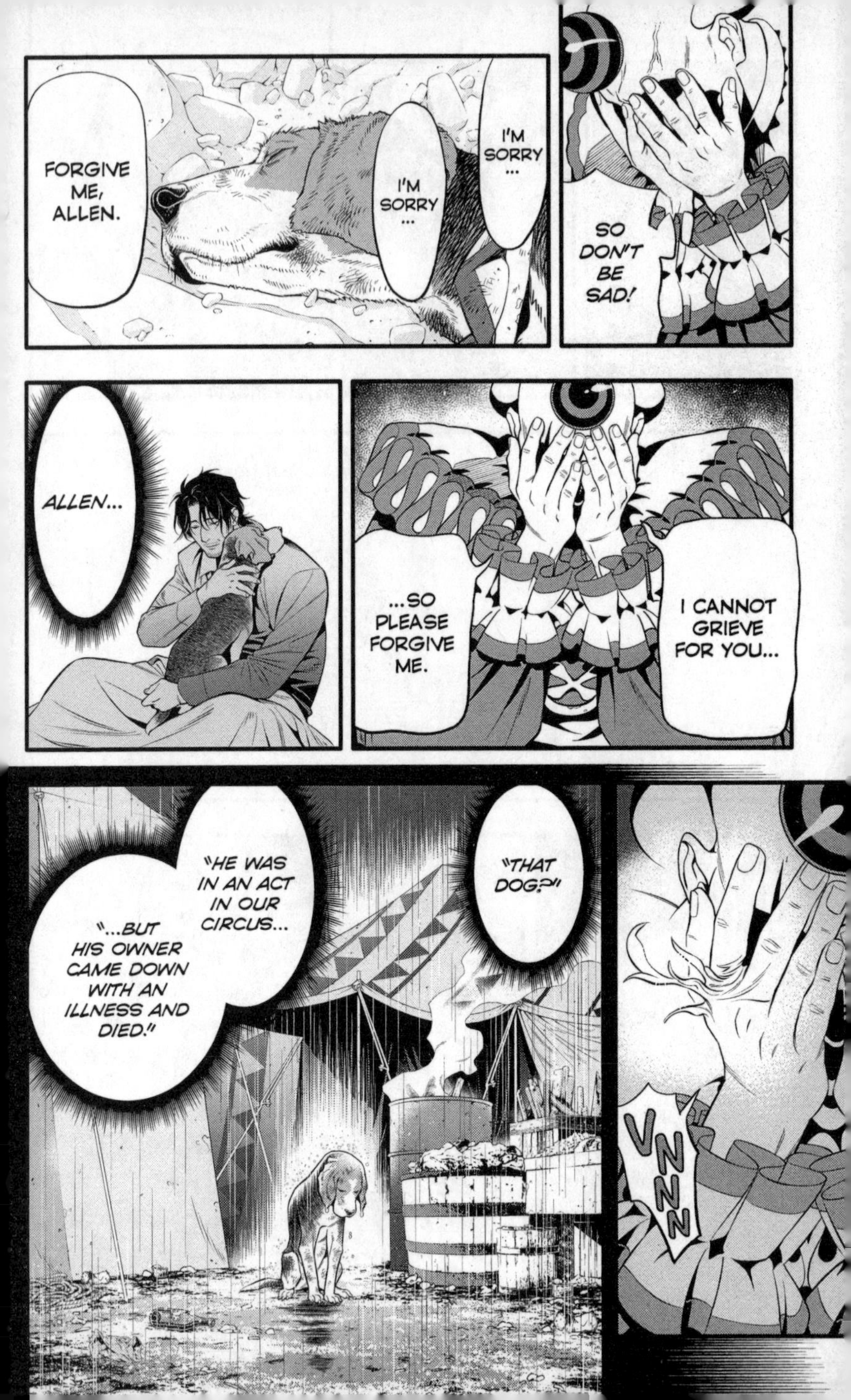
SO DON'T BE SAD!
I'M SORRY...
I'M SORRY...
FORGIVE ME, ALLEN.
I CANNOT GRIEVE FOR YOU...
...SO PLEASE FORGIVE ME.
ALLEN...
VNNN
"THAT DOG?"
"HE WAS IN AN ACT IN OUR CIRCUS...
"...BUT HIS OWNER CAME DOWN WITH AN ILLNESS AND DIED."

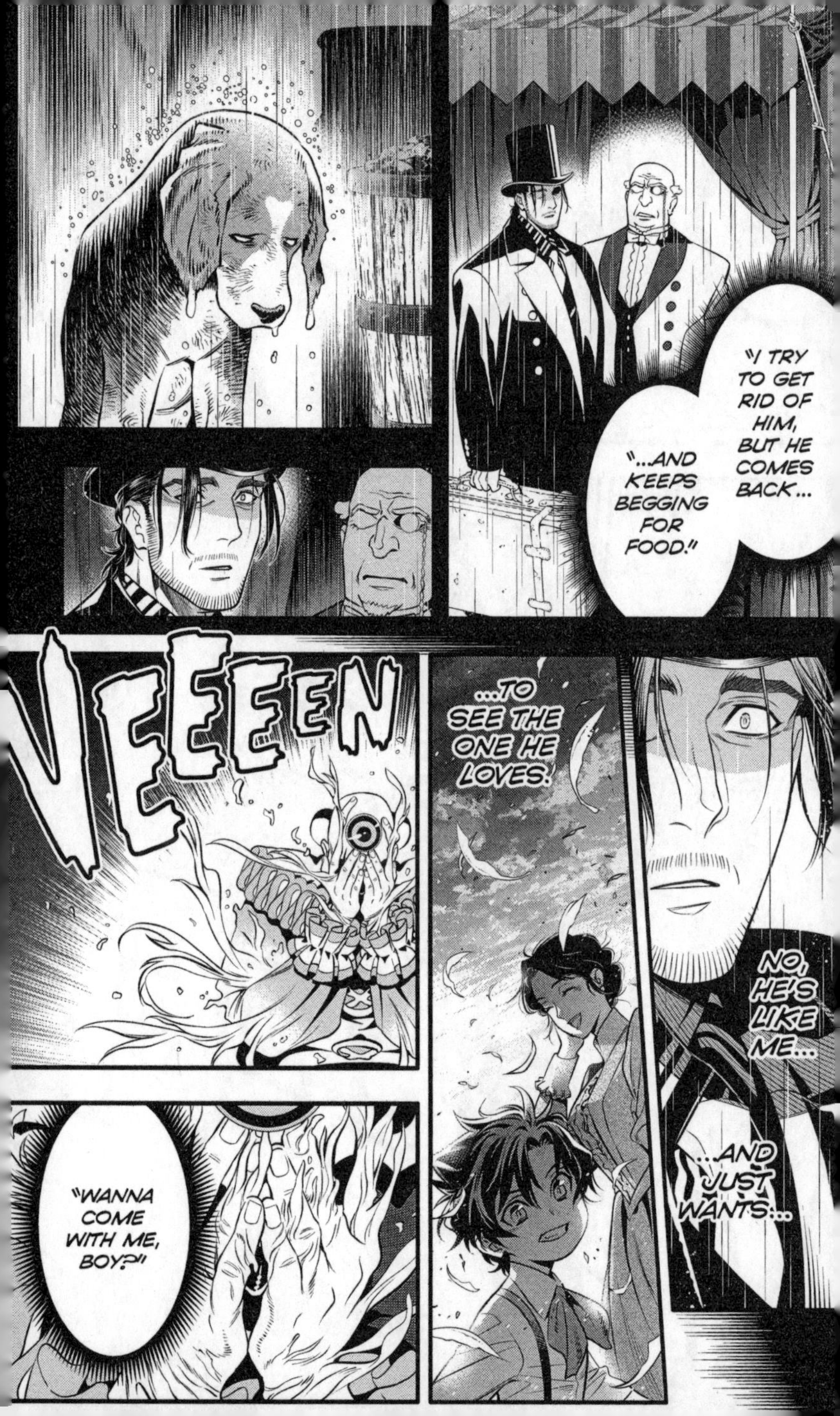
"I TRY TO GET RID OF HIM, BUT HE COMES BACK...
"...AND KEEPS BEGGING FOR FOOD."
NO, HE'S LIKE ME...
...AND JUST WANTS...
...TO SEE THE ONE HE LOVES.
VEEEEN
"WANNA COME WITH ME, BOY?"

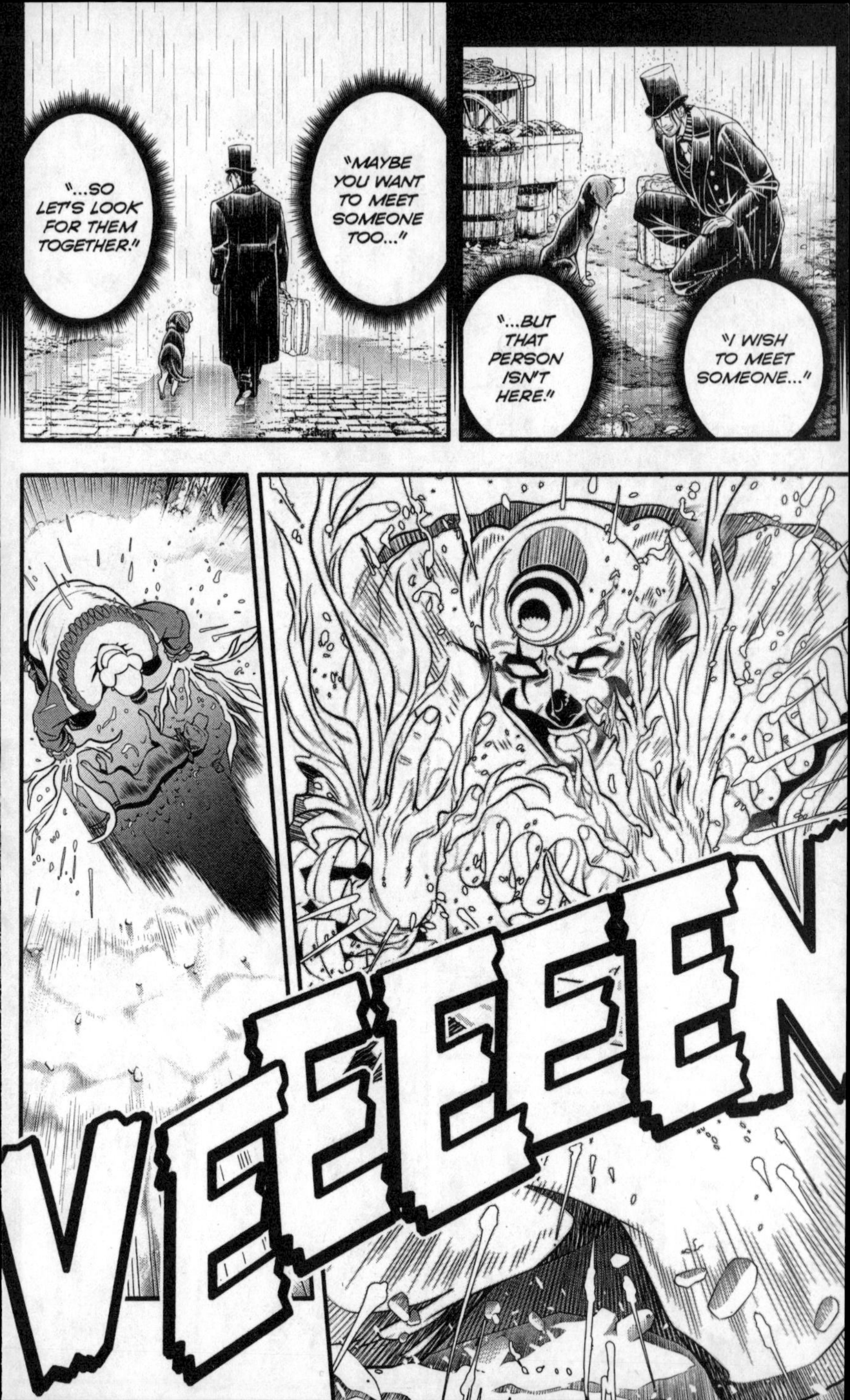
"I WISH TO MEET SOMEONE..."
"...BUT THAT PERSON ISN'T HERE."
"MAYBE YOU WANT TO MEET SOMEONE TOO..."
"...SO LET'S LOOK FOR THEM TOGETHER."
VEEEEN

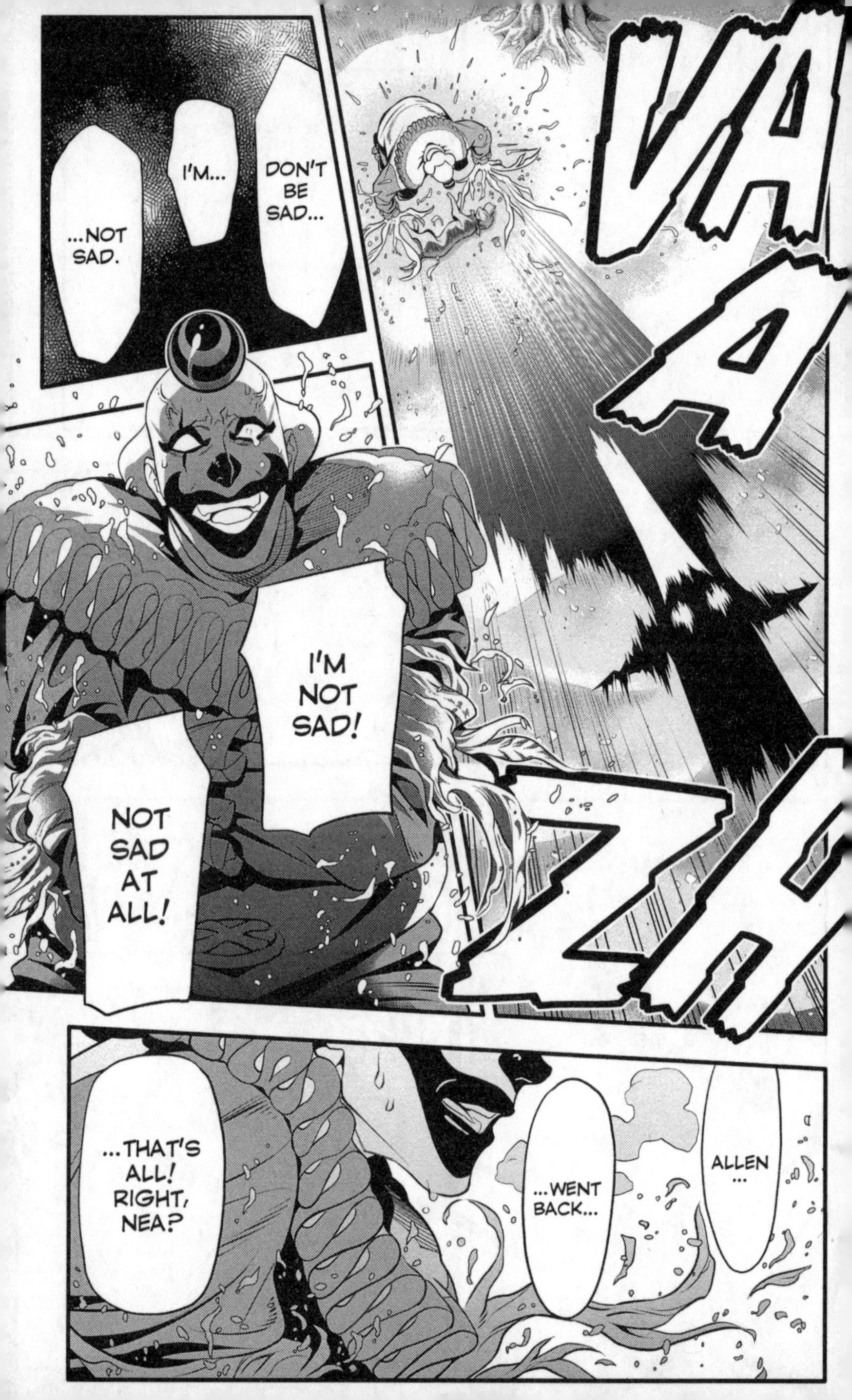
VA
A
ZH
DON'T BE SAD...
I'M...
...NOT SAD.
I'M NOT SAD!
NOT SAD AT ALL!
ALLEN...
...WENT BACK...
...THAT'S ALL! RIGHT, NEA?

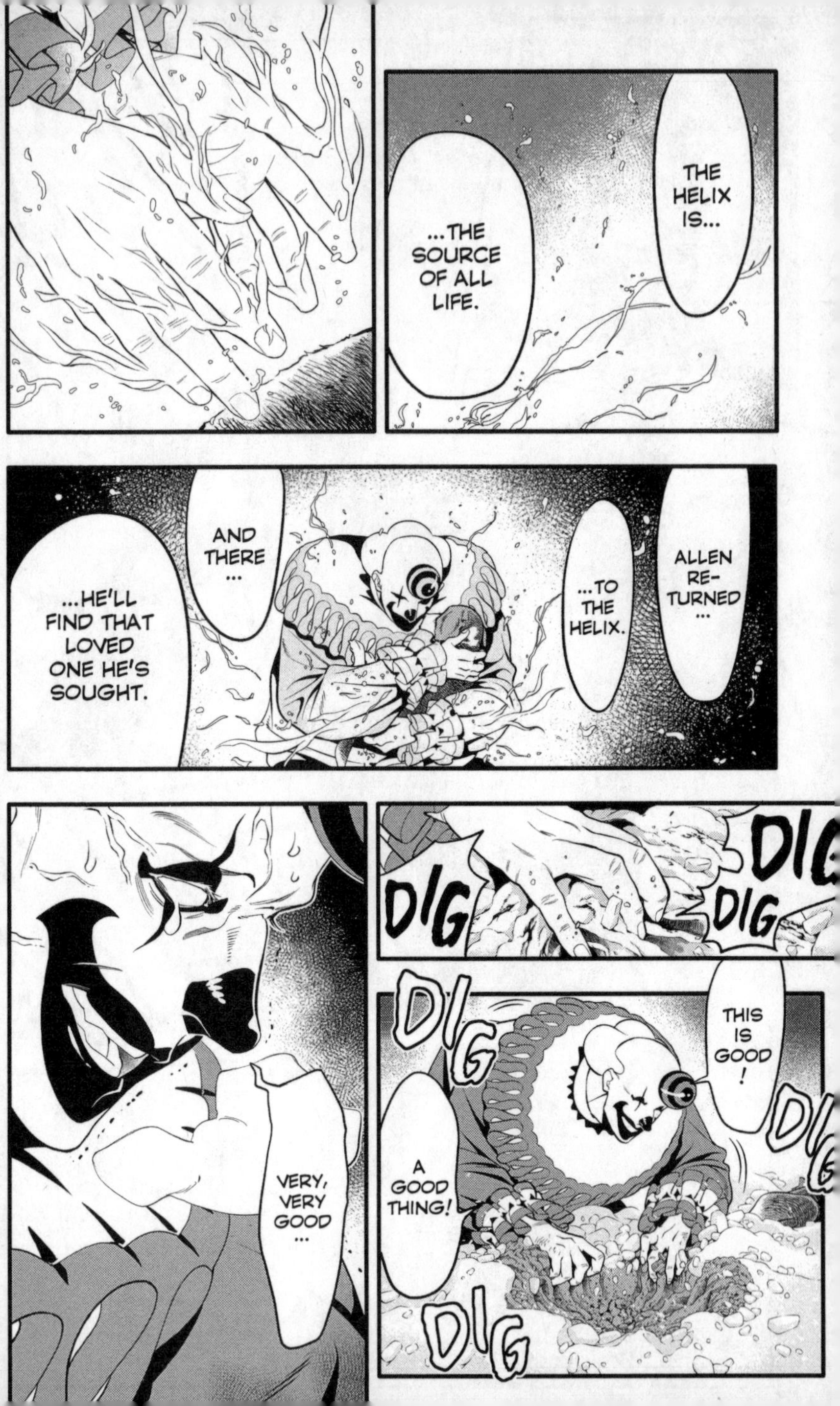
THE HELIX IS...
...THE SOURCE OF ALL LIFE.
ALLEN RE-TURNED ...
...TO THE HELIX.
AND THERE ...
...HE'LL FIND THAT LOVED ONE HE'S SOUGHT.
DIG
DIG
DIG
THIS IS GOOD!
DIG
A GOOD THING!
DIG
DIG
VERY, VERY GOOD ...

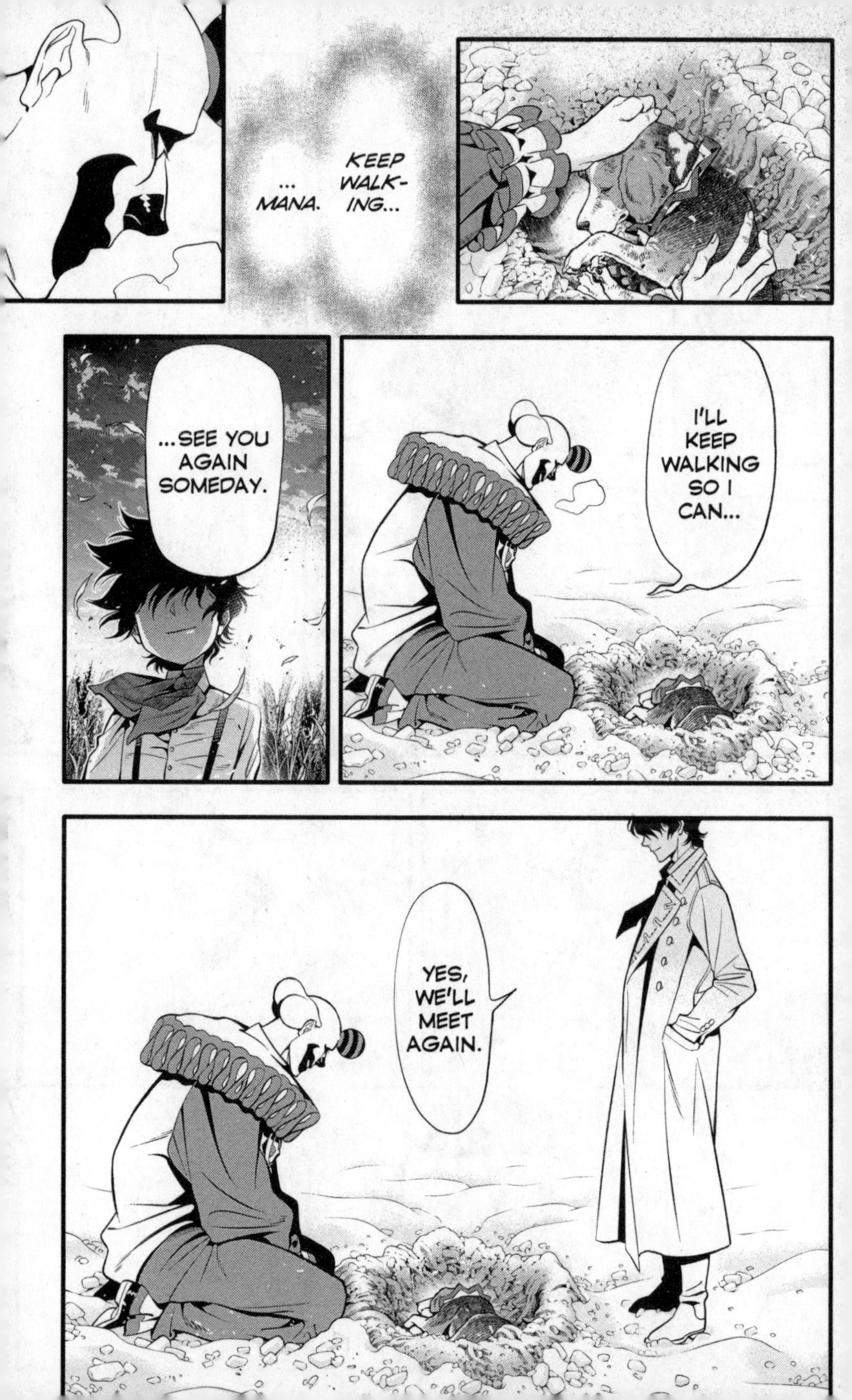
KEEP WALK-ING...
...MANA.
I'LL KEEP WALKING SO I CAN...
...SEE YOU AGAIN SOMEDAY.
YES, WE'LL MEET AGAIN.

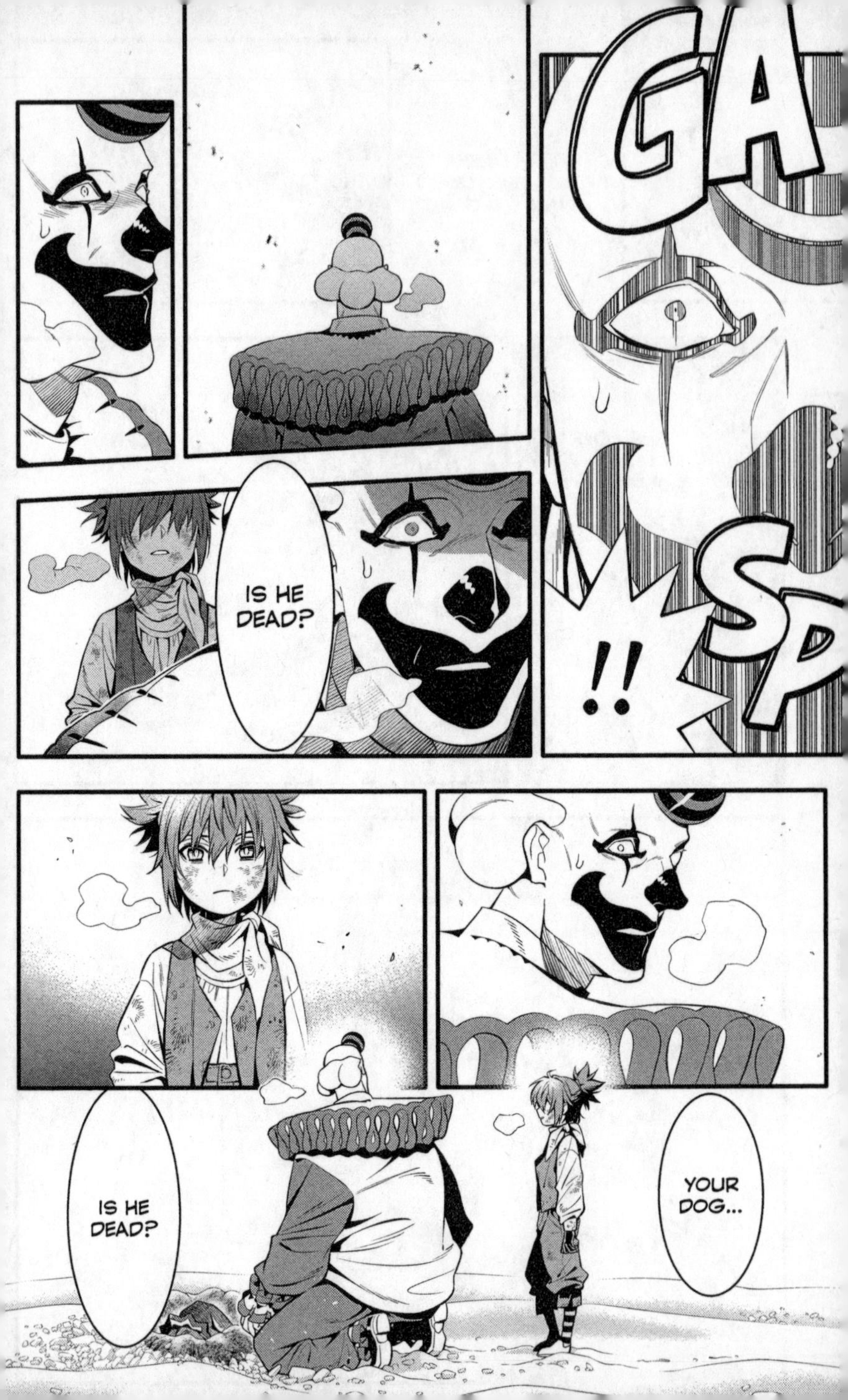
GASP
!!
IS HE DEAD?
YOUR DOG...
IS HE DEAD?

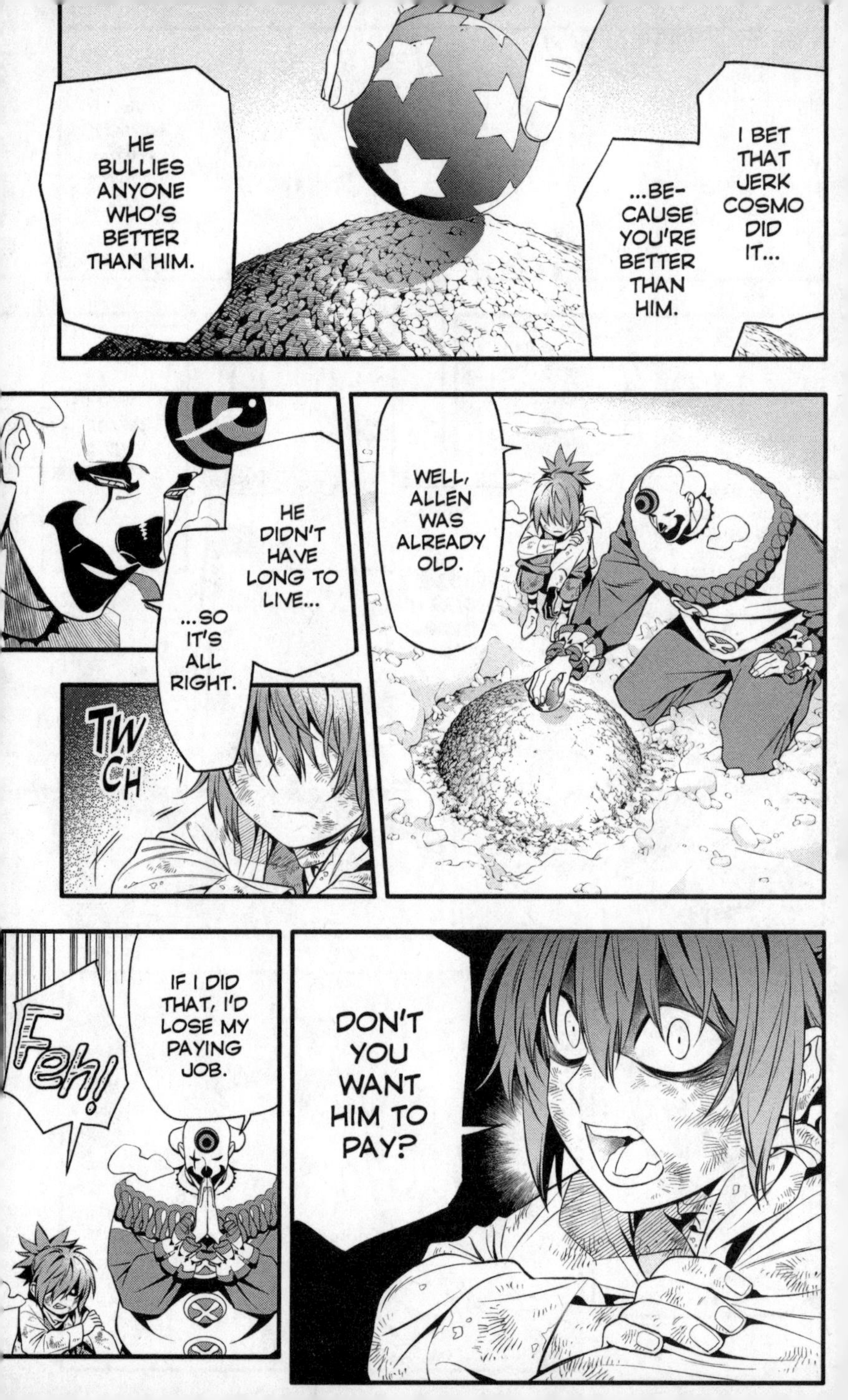
I BET THAT JERK COSMO DID IT...
...BE-CAUSE YOU'RE BETTER THAN HIM.
HE BULLIES ANYONE WHO'S BETTER THAN HIM.
WELL, ALLEN WAS ALREADY OLD.
HE DIDN'T HAVE LONG TO LIVE...
...SO IT'S ALL RIGHT.
TWITCH
DON'T YOU WANT HIM TO PAY?
IF I DID THAT, I'D LOSE MY PAYING JOB.
Feh!

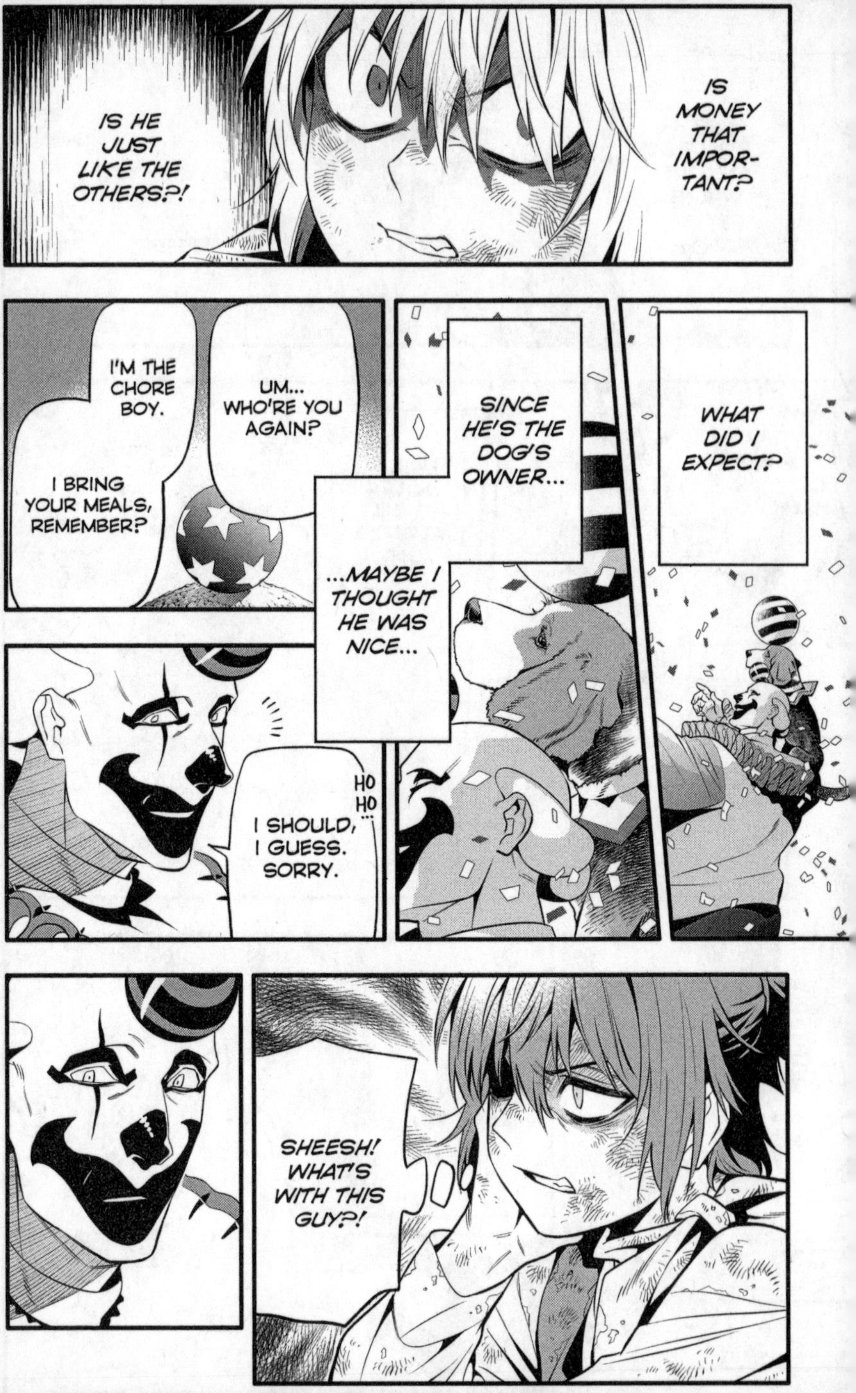
IS MONEY THAT IMPOR-TANT?
IS HE JUST LIKE THE OTHERS?!
WHAT DID I EXPECT?
SINCE HE'S THE DOG'S OWNER...
...MAYBE I THOUGHT HE WAS NICE...
UM... WHO'RE YOU AGAIN?
I'M THE CHORE BOY.
I BRING YOUR MEALS, REMEMBER?
HO HO...
I SHOULD, I GUESS. SORRY.
SHEESH! WHAT'S WITH THIS GUY?!

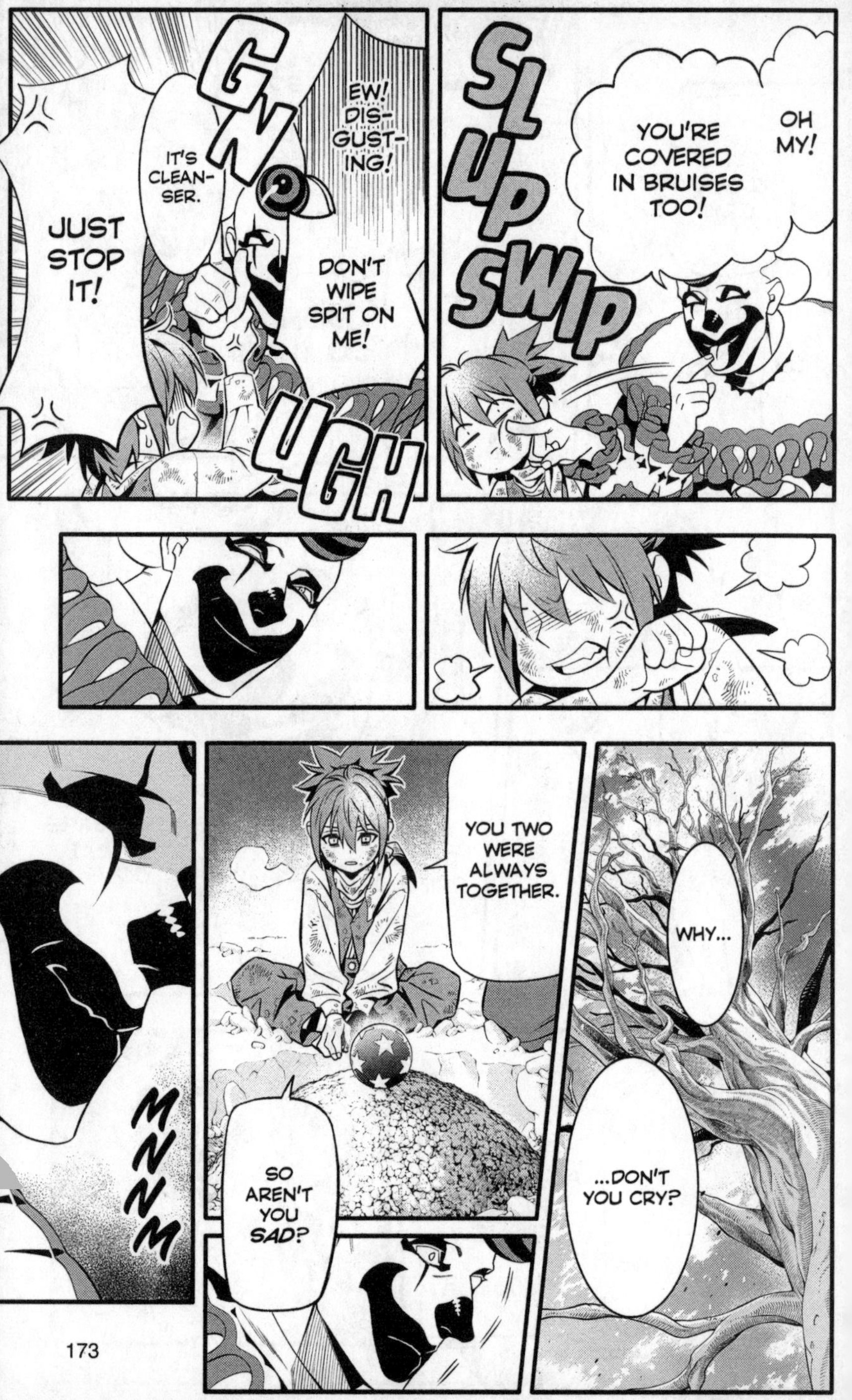
OH MY!
YOU'RE COVERED IN BRUISES TOO!
SLUP
SWIP
EW! DIS-GUST-ING!
DON'T WIPE SPIT ON ME!
GNO
IT'S CLEANSER.
JUST STOP IT!
UGH
...DON'T YOU CRY?
WHY...
YOU TWO WERE ALWAYS TOGETHER.
SO AREN'T YOU SAD?
MNNM

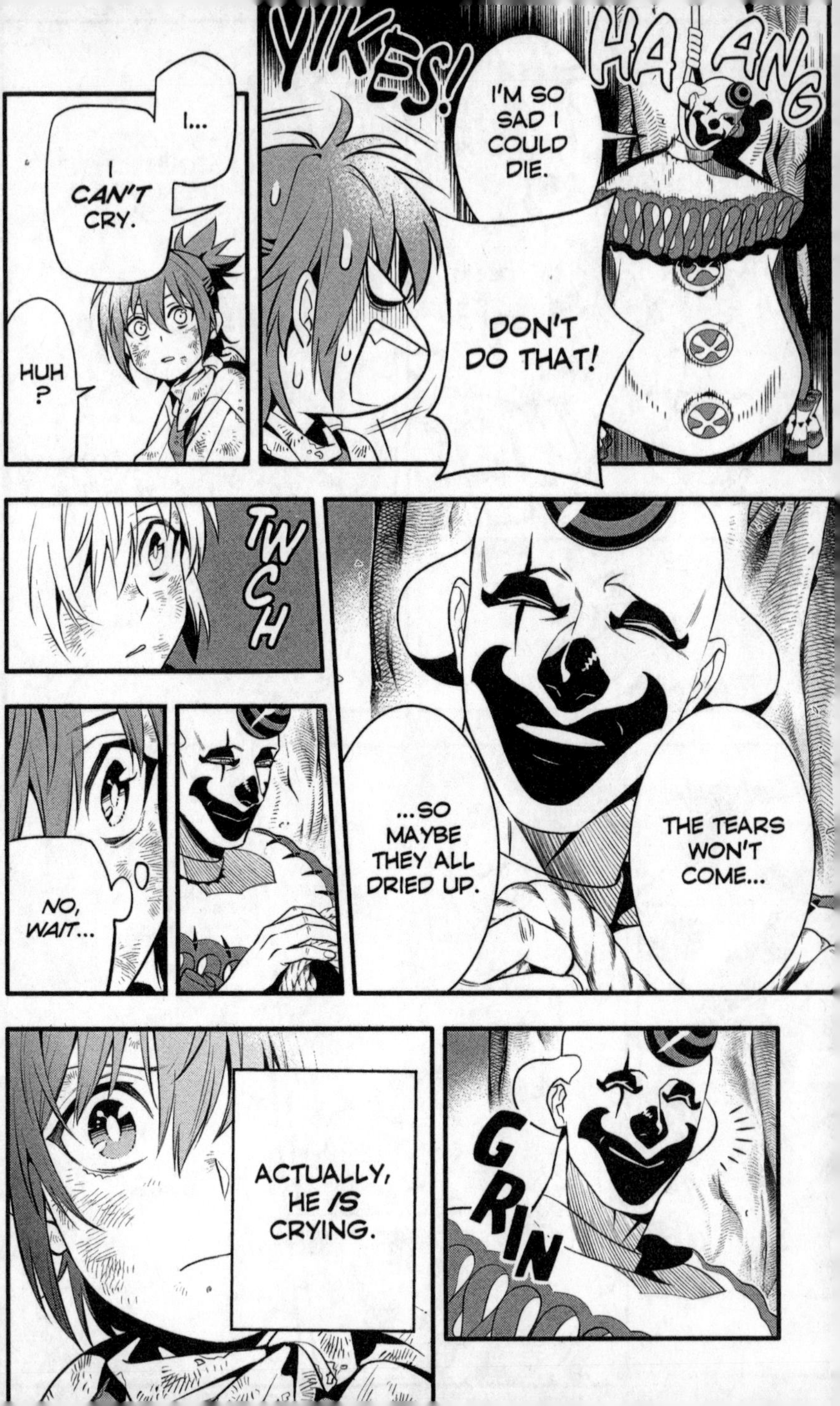
HA ANG
I'M SO SAD I COULD DIE.
YIKES!
DON'T DO THAT!
I...
I CAN'T CRY.
HUH?
THE TEARS WON'T COME...
...SO MAYBE THEY ALL DRIED UP.
TWCH
NO, WAIT...
GRIN
ACTUALLY, HE IS CRYING.

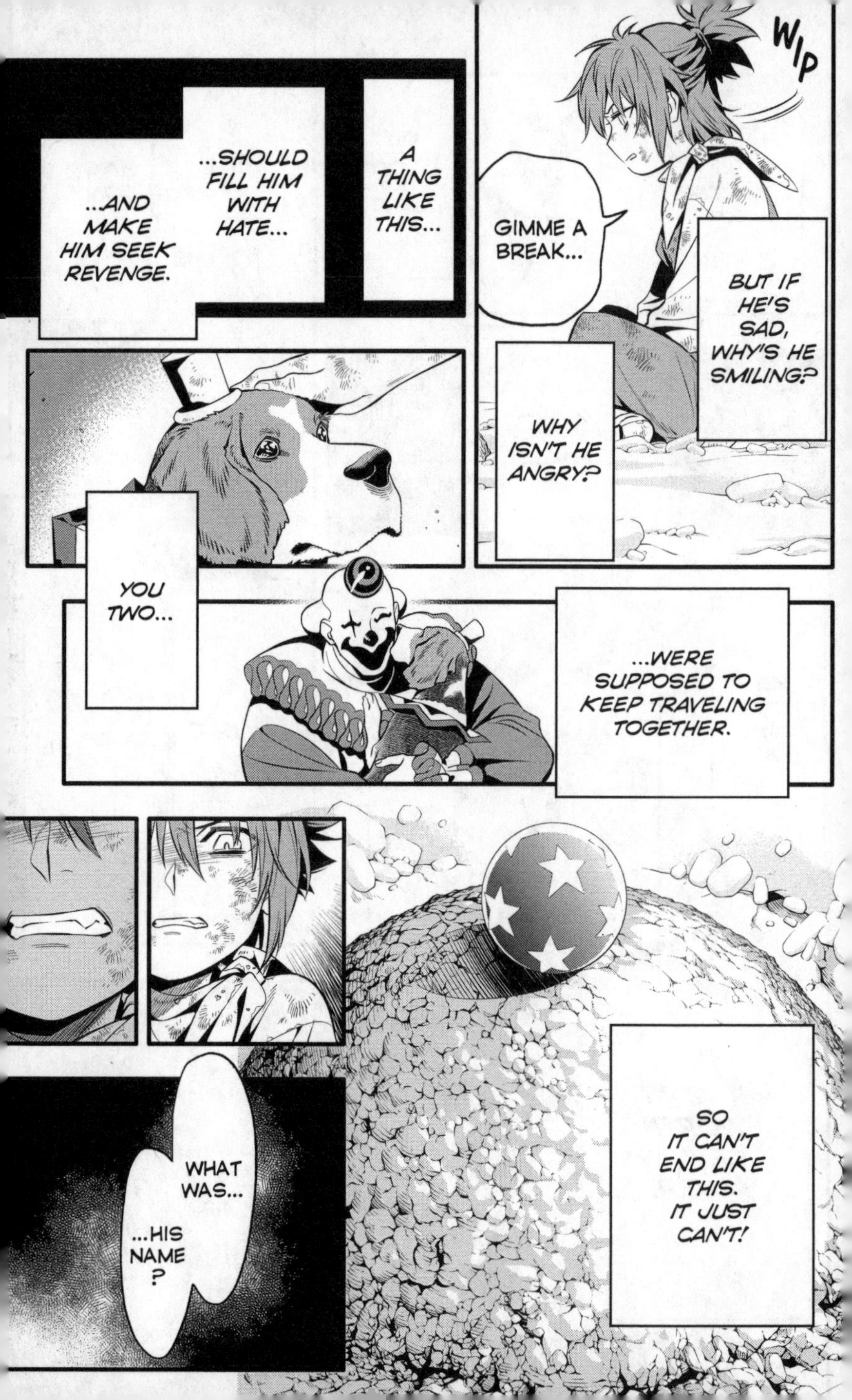
WIP
GIMME A BREAK...
BUT IF HE'S SAD, WHY'S HE SMILING?
WHY ISN'T HE ANGRY?
A THING LIKE THIS...
...SHOULD FILL HIM WITH HATE...
...AND MAKE HIM SEEK REVENGE.
YOU TWO...
...WERE SUPPOSED TO KEEP TRAVELING TOGETHER.
SO IT CAN'T END LIKE THIS. IT JUST CAN'T!
WHAT WAS...
...HIS NAME
?

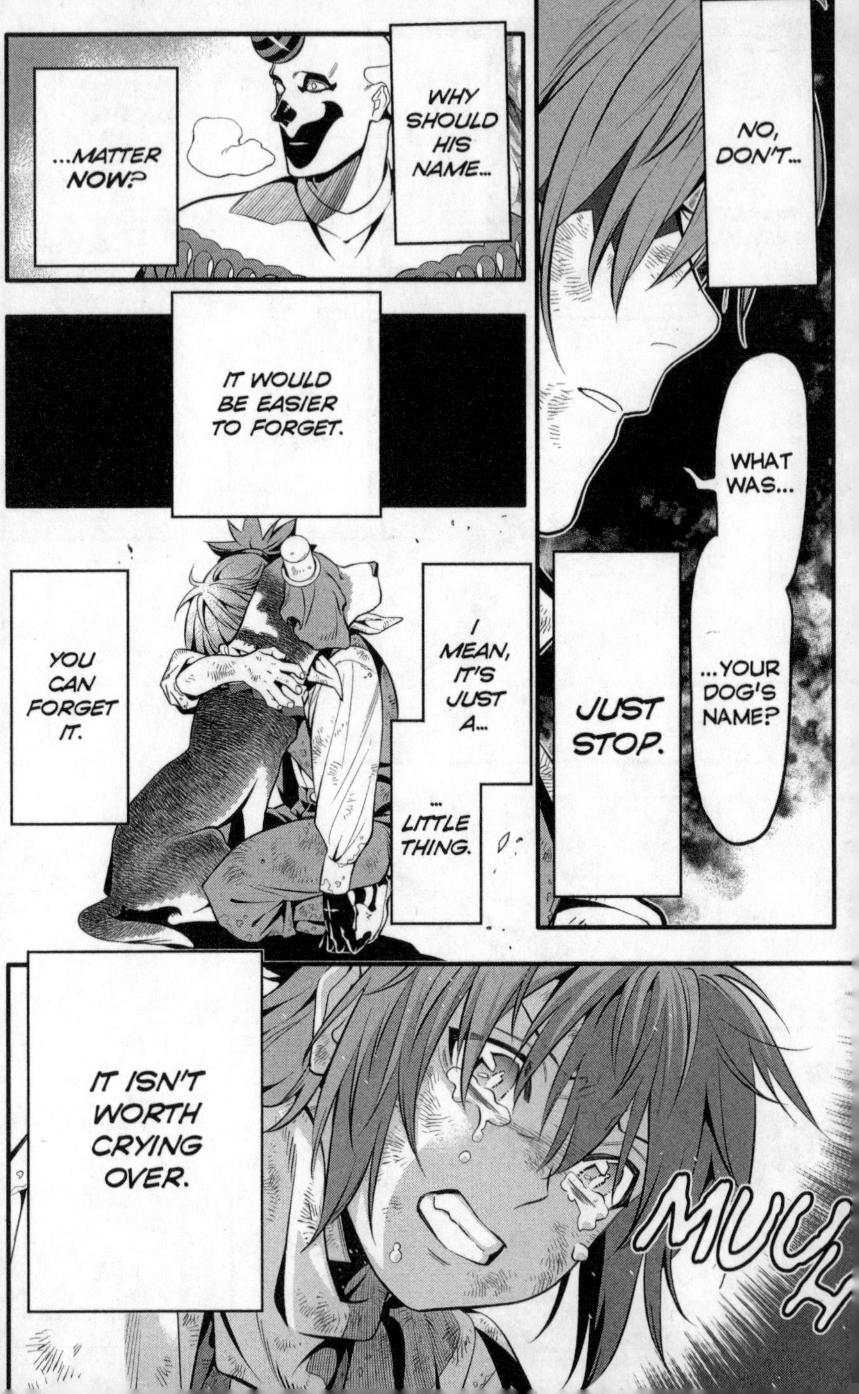
NO, DON'T...
WHAT WAS...
...YOUR DOG'S NAME?
JUST STOP.
WHY SHOULD HIS NAME...
...MATTER NOW?
IT WOULD BE EASIER TO FORGET.
I MEAN, IT'S JUST A...
...LITTLE THING.
YOU CAN FORGET IT.
IT ISN'T WORTH CRYING OVER.
MUU

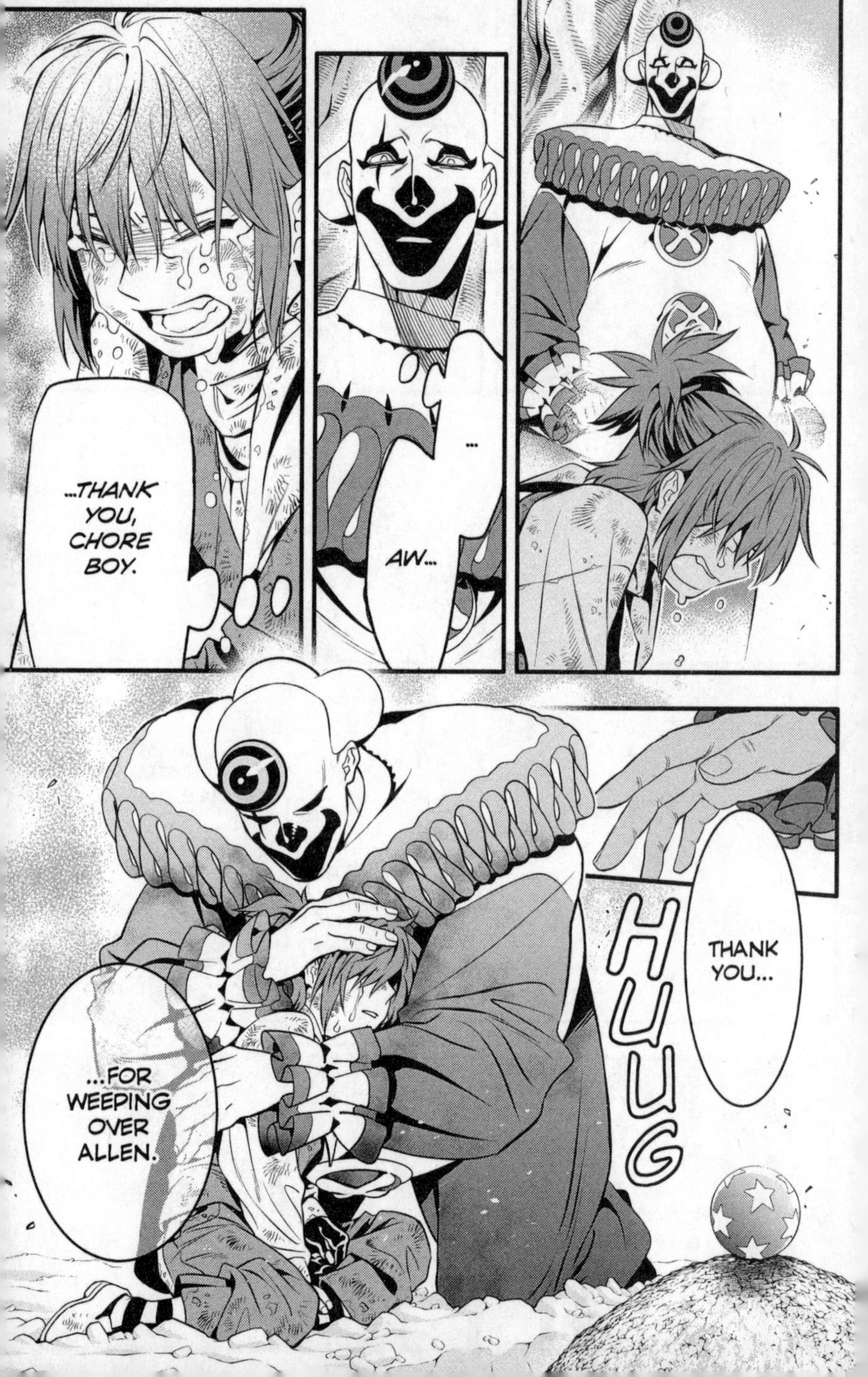
...
AW...
...THANK YOU, CHORE BOY.
THANK YOU...
HUUG
...FOR WEEPING OVER ALLEN.

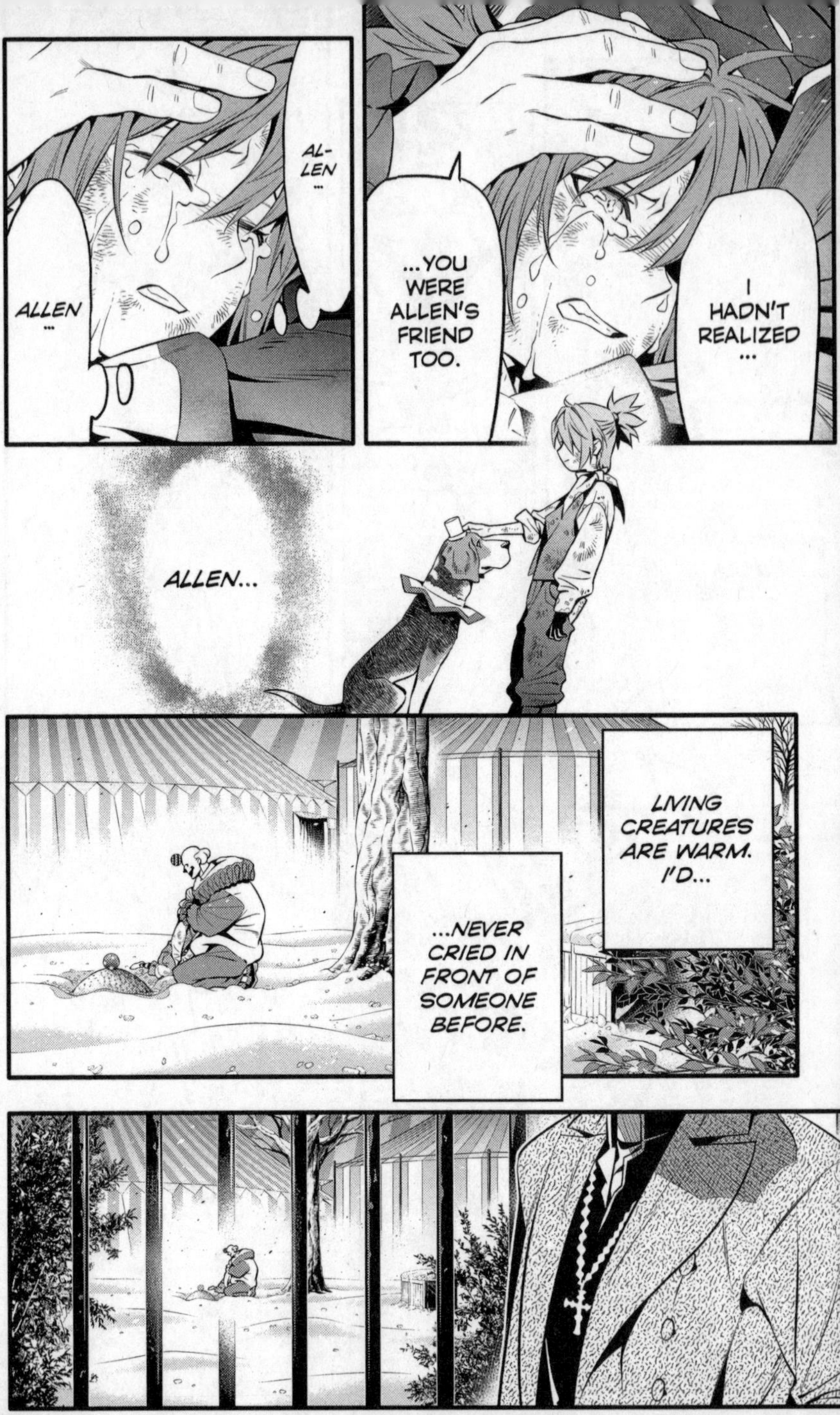
I HADN'T REALIZED ...
...YOU WERE ALLEN'S FRIEND TOO.
AL- LEN ...
ALLEN ...
ALLEN...
LIVING CREATURES ARE WARM. I'D...
...NEVER CRIED IN FRONT OF SOMEONE BEFORE.

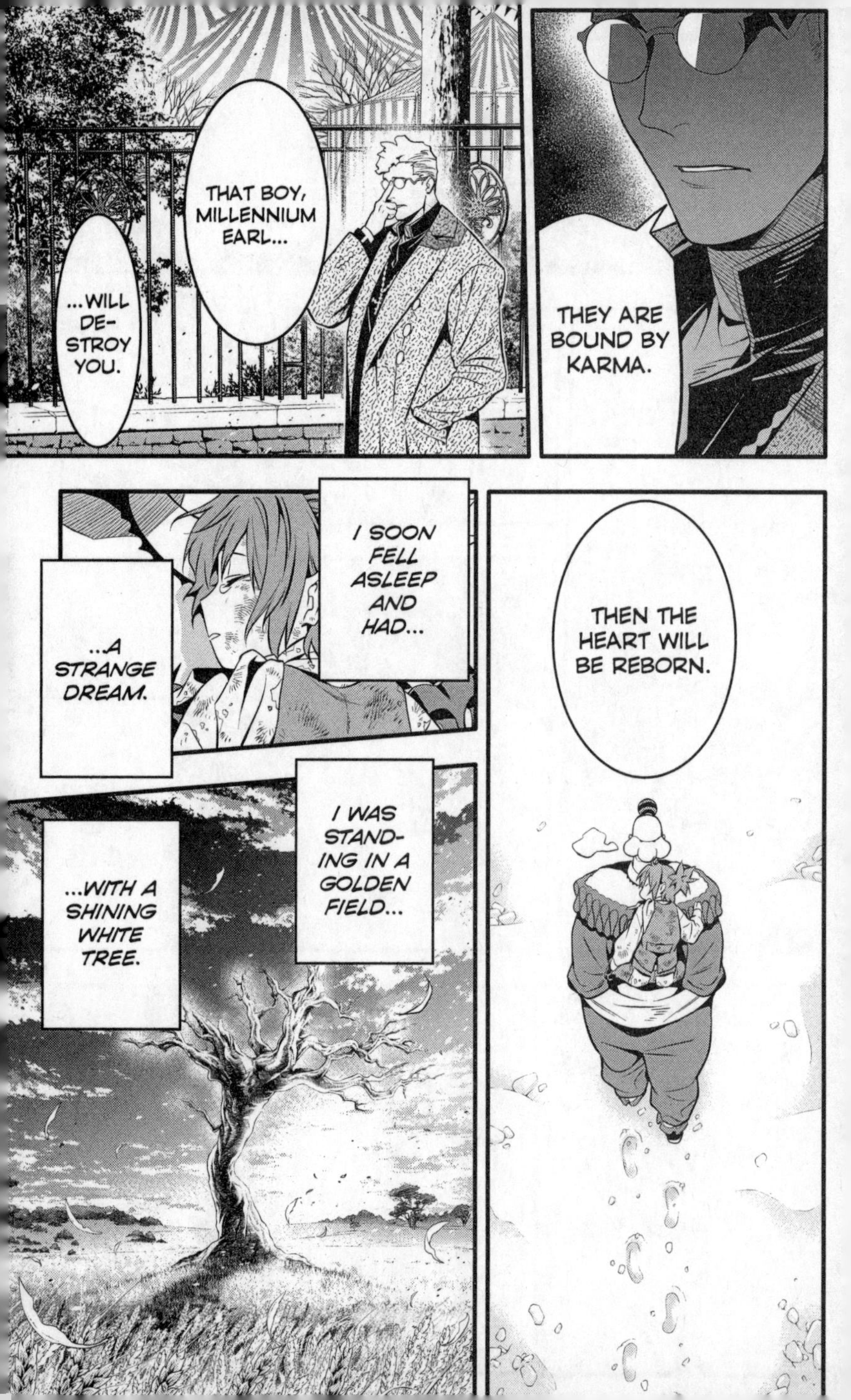
THEY ARE BOUND BY KARMA.
THAT BOY, MILLENNIUM EARL...
...WILL DE-STROY YOU.
THEN THE HEART WILL BE REBORN.
I SOON FELL ASLEEP AND HAD...
...A STRANGE DREAM.
I WAS STAND-ING IN A GOLDEN FIELD...
...WITH A SHINING WHITE TREE.

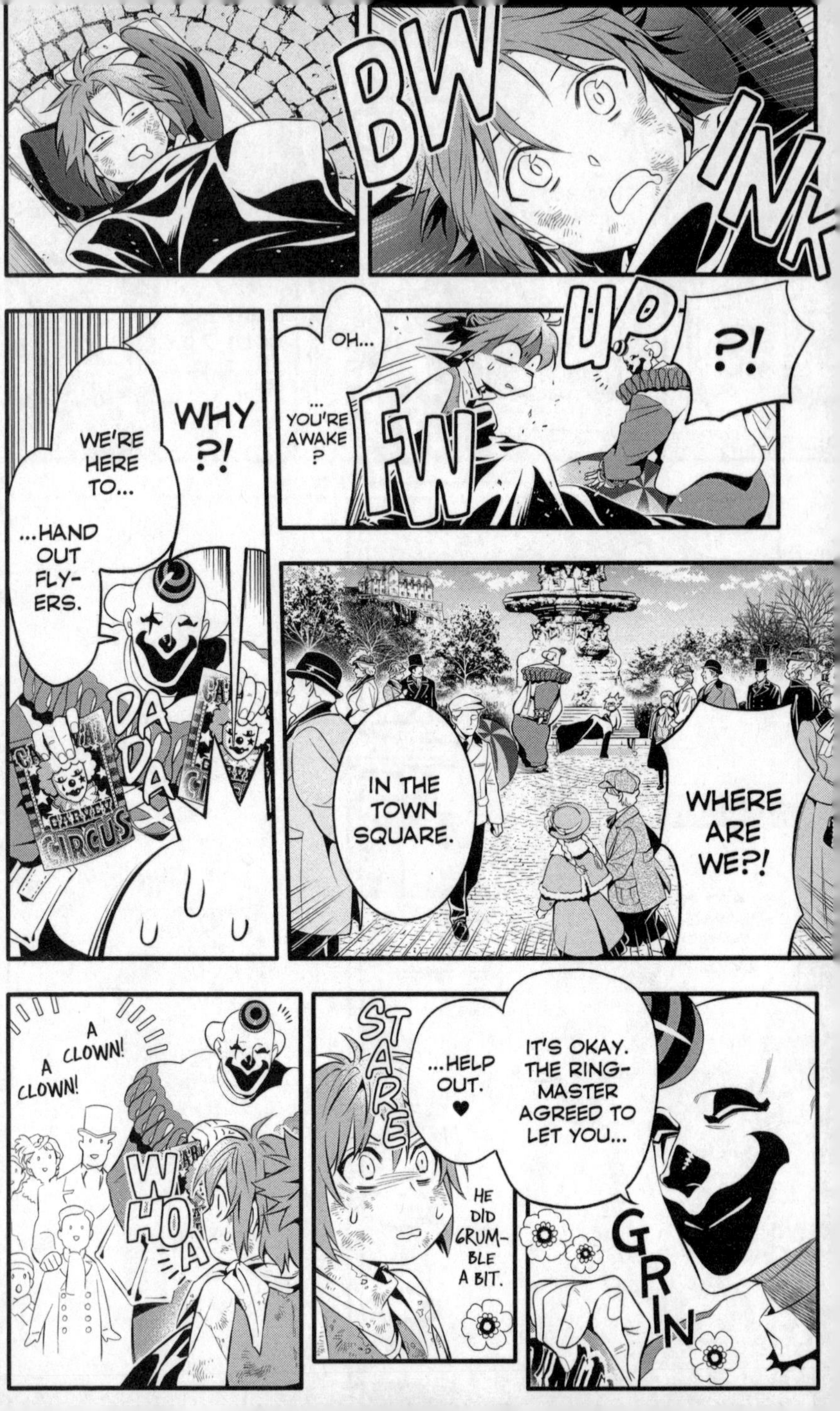
BWINK
UP
?!
OH...
...YOU'RE AWAKE?
FW
WHERE ARE WE?!
IN THE TOWN SQUARE.
WHY?!
WE'RE HERE TO...
...HAND OUT FLY-ERS.
DA DA DA
GARVEY CIRCUS
IT'S OKAY. THE RING-MASTER AGREED TO LET YOU...
...HELP OUT. ♥
GRIN
STARE
HE DID GRUM-BLE A BIT.
A CLOWN!
A CLOWN!
WHOA

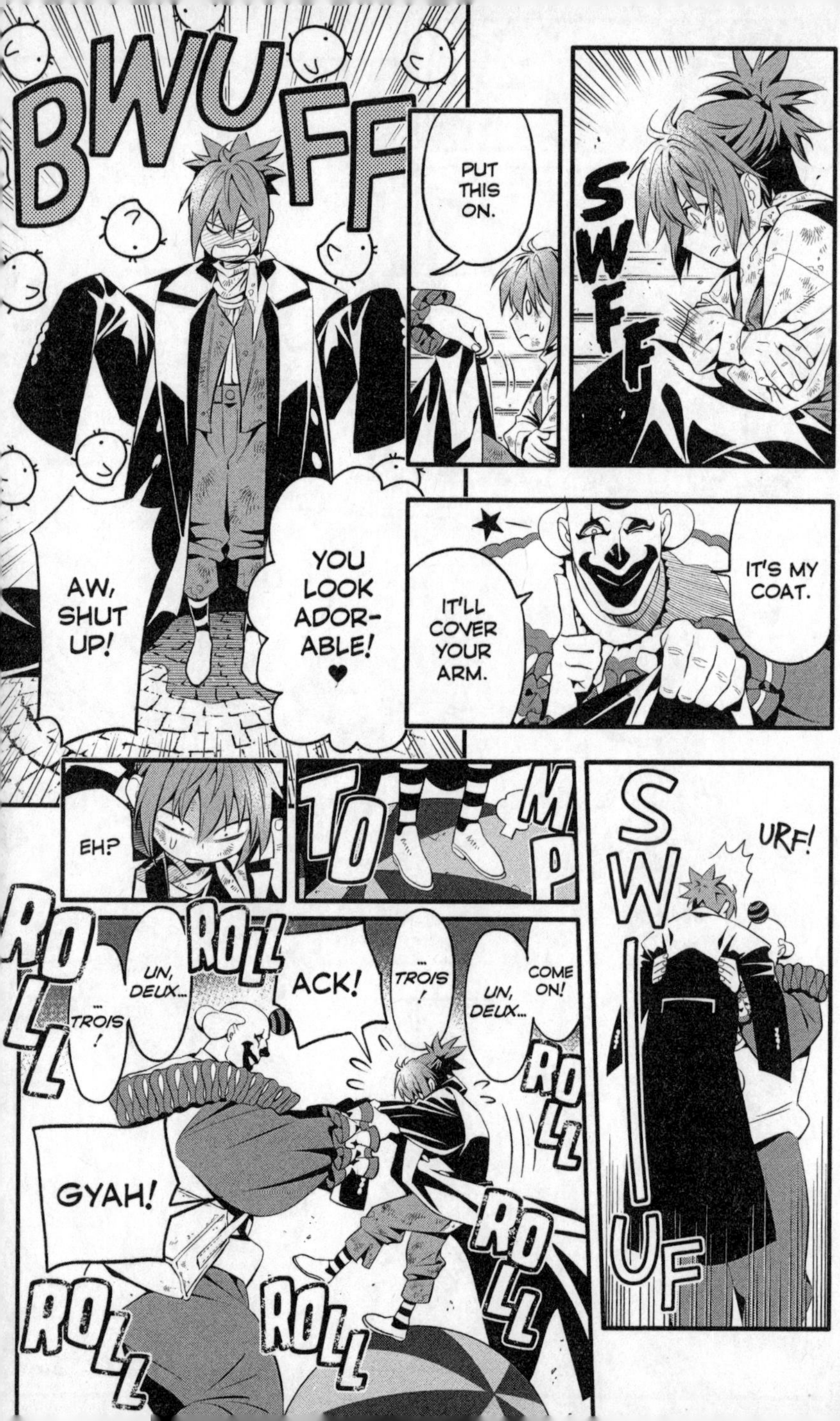
SWFF
PUT THIS ON.
IT'S MY COAT.
IT'LL COVER YOUR ARM.
BWUFF
YOU LOOK ADOR-ABLE! ♥
AW, SHUT UP!
SWUF
URF!
TOMP
EH?
COME ON!
UN, DEUX...
... TROIS!
ROLL
ROLL
ACK!
UN, DEUX...
... TROIS!
ROLL
ROLL
GYAH!
ROLL
ROLL

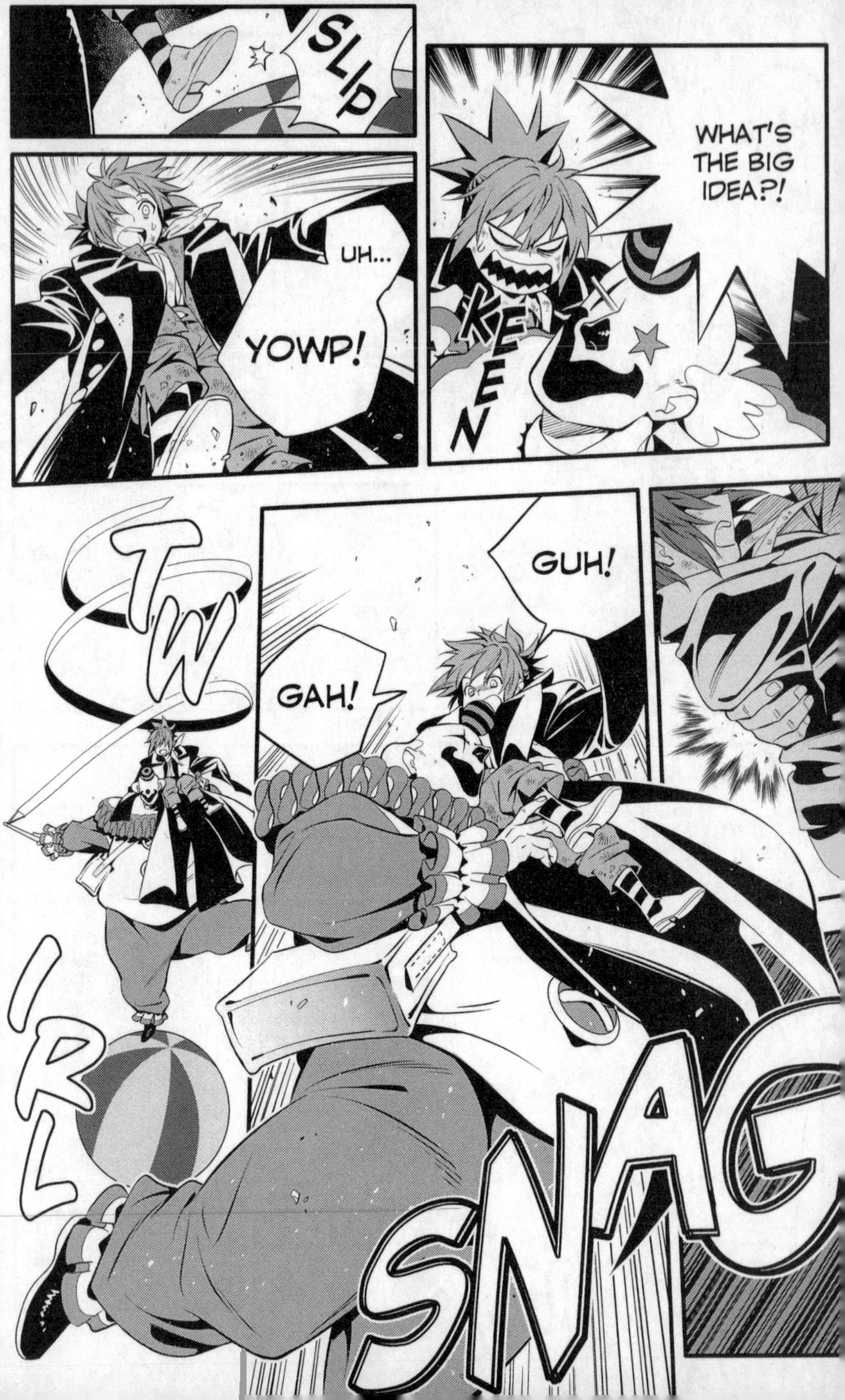
WHAT'S THE BIG IDEA?!
KEEN
SLIP
UH...
YOWP!
GUH!
GAH!
TWIRL
SNAG

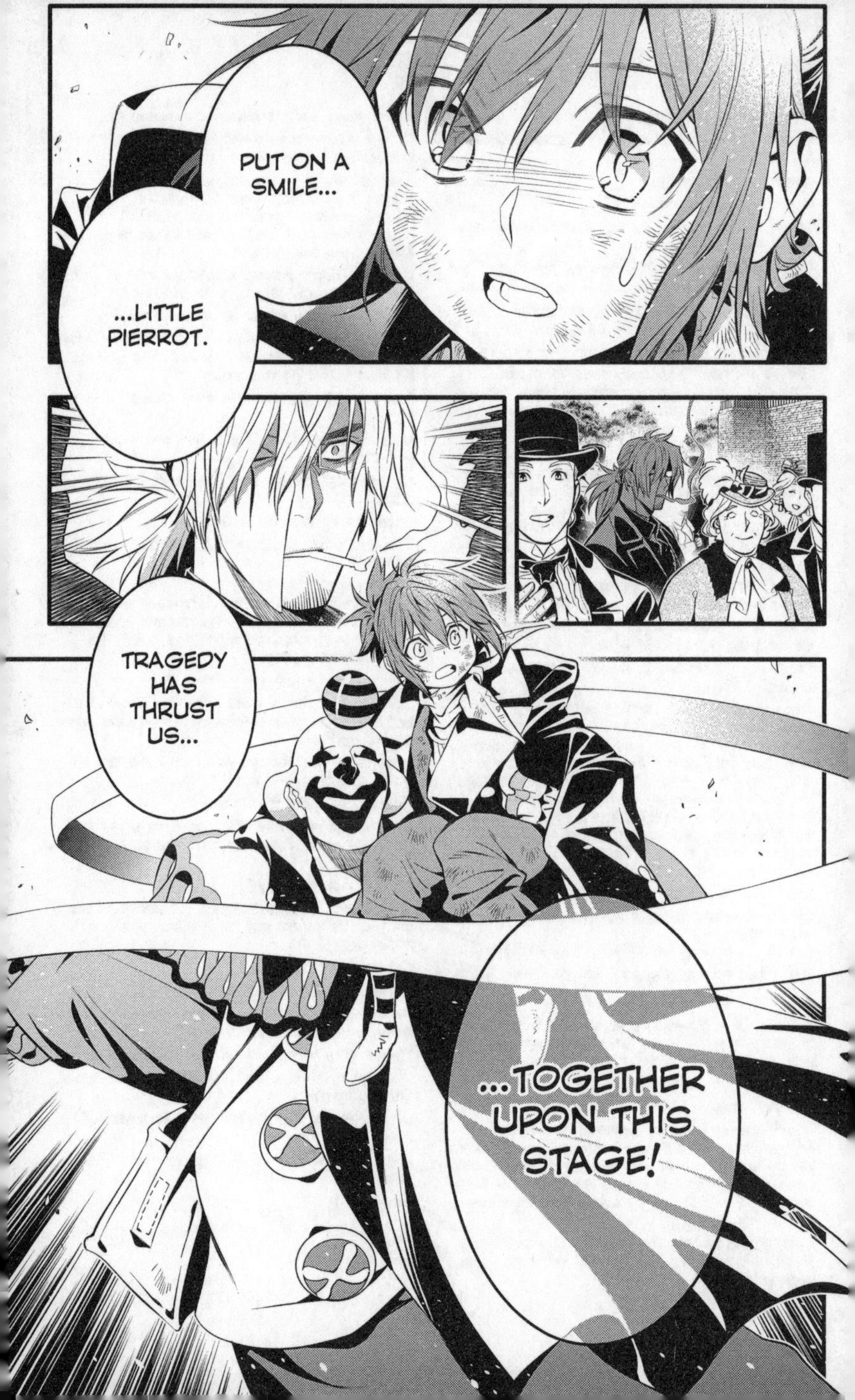
PUT ON A SMILE...
...LITTLE PIERROT.
TRAGEDY HAS THRUST US...
...TOGETHER UPON THIS STAGE!

READ THIS WAY

Kanda: Gggg... Yarrgh!

Tiedoll: Those grunts mean he wants to duel Arystar.

Johnny: I knew it!

Kanda: Arrh... whatever!

Cross: Must be nice having such an untalkative pupil. Mine won't shut up.

Allen: Who do you think made me that way?!

> **@** If Kanda reached a synchronization rate of 100 percent, how did he hide it?

Tiedoll: He hasn't reached that point yet. If he had, Hevlaska would have noticed. He has the potential, but I bet he suppresses it. Right, Yu?

Kanda: Yes.

Cross: Hey, that's impressive. It'd take immense spiritual fortitude to do that. Is that a reflection of how reluctant you are to become a general? I guess it isn't an attractive job though. Ha ha ha!

Johnny: Allen, there's a similar question for you. You reached that point, so why didn't the Order approach you about becoming a general?

Allen: Well, Central Agency put me under surveillance because of that.

Cross: Don't let 'em grab you by the guts, moron!

Tiedoll: It may have partly been because Walker is so young, but being the Pianist, who can operate an Ark—that was the main complication. Central Agency thought he might be an enemy spy or a Noah. Furthermore, his master Marian has a famously terrible reputation. Simply put, they couldn't trust you, Allen, and the big shots value loyalty above all else. I wouldn't worry about it though. The whole thing—every bit of it—is Marian's fault.

Allen: Thank you for clearing that up.

Cross: Sheesh! Being a general's a royal pain in the rump!

> **@** What sort of sleepers are you?

Tiedoll: When Yu was little, he would curl up on his side. It was cute. Now that he's bigger, he still sleeps on his side, usually the right side.

Johnny: Y-you seem to know a lot about it...

Kanda: Creepy old fogey! *(muttering)*

Allen: Johnny used to collapse at his desk or on the floor. He'd lie perfectly still, so I'd poke him to see if he was still breathing. Everyone in the Science Section sleeps like that. The first time I saw it, I thought I'd stumbled on some kind of disaster!

Johnny: Ha ha ha! The labs are cramped and there're lots of us, so naturally we learn to be orderly sleepers.

Allen: No, I don't think that explains it...

Cross: Allen needs something to hold. Otherwise, he complains he can't sleep.

Allen: What're you talking about?! (blushes beet red) When I was little, Tim seemed so big, I got into the habit of hugging him, that's all! It was temporary! Now I sleep like normal!

Johnny: Didn't Inspector Link often tell you not to sleep clinging to your savings?

Allen: That was a matter of sheer survival!

Kanda: I remember when you were in the Order sickrooms you'd sneak in great piles of food. All that munching was noisy.

Allen: Sorry. I'm the type that needs to eat to recover!

Johnny: What sort of sleepers are you, generals?

Cross: Heh! That's only for the ladies to know.

Allen: He splays out. Naked.

Tiedoll: I sleep facedown with my face in my hands. ♡

> **@** Is the symbol on the forehead of the Crows a magical or ceremonial symbol? Or is it a tattoo signifying loyalty to Central Agency?

Johnny: Oh, that's right... All the Crows have red marks on their foreheads. Does that mean something?

Allen: Link was furious when I caught him off guard one time and tried to touch it.

Johnny: Lavi did that too

Cross: It's probably left over from some kind of procedure for turning a normal person into a spellcaster.

Allen & Johnny: Oooh!

Tiedoll: You seem to know a lot about it, Marian. Maybe you're not such a bad spellcaster after all!

Cross: Shut up.

Kanda: How'd you learn magic, huh?

Cross: What's with that tone of voice? Tiedoll, didn't you teach him manners?

Tiedoll: Eh? What did he say? *(oblivious)*

Johnny: I wanna know! Tell me, General! How did you learn?

Cross: Hmph! I *didn't!* This conversation's over. Next question.

Allen: Master always gets angry when I ask about that.

Q Does anyone else use the mysterious language that Lavi and Bookman use?

Allen: Mysterious language? Do they use something like that? Well, Lavi and Bookman are multilingual, so they often use languages I can't understand.

Johnny: Same here. But I heard they do speak a language from an unknown country. Section Leader Reever is a linguistics specialist and he said that's one language he can't identify.

Kanda: Reever's stumped too, huh?

Tiedoll: Hmm... I'd love to find out if it was an ancient dead language or something.

Johnny: You never know with the Bookman Clan. How exciting!

Cross: ...

Allen: What's wrong, Master?

Cross: Nothing!

Q What do you secretly admire about each other?

Johnny: First, Allen and Kanda will answer about each other. And then the two generals will.

Kanda: He's a skinflint.

Allen: He's impatient.

Kanda: He excels at running away.

Allen: He's mule headed.

Kanda: He's a phony.

Allen: He's too ready to whip out his sword.

Kanda: He has no sense of direction, always getting lost.

Allen: His only talent is violence.

Kanda: He's a crybaby.

Allen: He's dark.

Kanda: He's dumb.

Allen: He's a nimrod.

Johnny: Okay, that's enough! (sweating) Now it's your turn, generals!

Tiedoll: He's a bad apple.

Cross: He's too indulgent a parent.

Tiedoll: He's crass and flashy.

Cross: He looks old.

Tiedoll: He's trying not to look old.

Cross: He's too scruffy.

Johnny: Okay, thanks! (sweating)

Q After Yu became General Tiedoll's apprentice, they spent a year traveling around. Tell me something that made a great impression during that time.

Kanda: Can't think of anything.

Tiedoll: What? Didn't we create many beautiful memories together?

Kanda: Don't give anyone the wrong idea.

Allen: What was your journey like?

Tiedoll: At the time, Yu was in need of emotional rehabilitation, so each day I had him engage in casual conversation, interact with plants and animals and gaze upon lovely scenery. I believe that encounters with beauty engender increased connection with the world. At that young age, as a Second Exorcist, he needed to feel kinship with other living things.

Johnny: What a moving account... (crying)

Kanda: Hmph!

Allen: General Tiedoll's love runs deep. I'm jealous. (crying)

Cross: Idjit! I've cleaned up gallons of your pee!

Allen: Stop bringing that up!

Cross: Think about it! Me! Taking care of some snot-nosed twerp's accidents and meals and stuff! Can you imagine that, Tiedoll?!

Tiedoll: No, I can't.

Allen: Okay, fine! Thank you! Now never mention it again!

Cross: I even put your underpants on for you!

Allen: You want me to punch you?!

Q Tell me a childhood story involving Lenalee and Kanda!

Kanda: Feh! Skip this one, Johnny.

Johnny: No! It wouldn't be fair to the person asking!

Tiedoll: Everyone loves tales of Yu and Lenalee when they were little, they're so heartwarming. The two of them together were simply adorable! They were, within the suffocating atmosphere of the Order, like lilies that had suddenly bloomed!

Kanda: Enough already.

Allen: Phooey on Kanda. Tell me about Lenalee! (excited)

Cross: Do you have the hots for her, birdbrain? Don't you already have a woman at the Asia Branch?

Allen: Huh?! D-don't confuse things! Lenalee and Lo Fwa are my comrades! And friends!

Cross: Chill, dum-dum. I wasn't being critical. (smirks)

Allen: This guy is infuriating...

Johnny: Jiji once told me a story about Kanda and Lenalee's childhood.

Kanda: What?!

Tiedoll: Simmer down, Yu. (restraining Kanda)

Johnny: In their early days, no matter how much Lenalee begged him to spar with her, he would refuse because she was a girl. That made her cry.

Allen: You made Lenalee cry, Kanda? Scumbag!

Kanda: Shut up, Bean Sprout!

Allen: My name is Allen.

READ THIS WAY

Johnny: Then Lenalee would go to Section Leader Reever, though she really wanted to see Chief Komui, her brother, who always seemed too busy. She would try, but just ended up weeping at the section leader's desk.

Allen & Tiedoll: H-how cute! *(swooning)*

Johnny: Reever would console her and then Marie would drag in Kanda. Lenalee would pout and hide behind Reever's lab coat, while Kanda just stood there, unable to say he was sorry. Needless to say, Reever wasn't happy to be caught between them. That went on for some time until Kanda gave in and agreed to spar with her.

Tiedoll: How cute you were, Yu! And Marie too for playing big brother! *(swooning)*

Johnny: And once when Kanda had just begun zen meditation and Lenalee returned from a mission exhausted from lack of sleep—

Kanda: There's more?!

Johnny: Huh? Yeah, lots!

Kanda: That's enough, so button it. I'll read the next question!

Allen: Don't interrupt, Kanda! This is just getting good!

Kanda: Shut up! Get lost, bed-wetter!

Allen: *(angrily)* I'm gonna murder you!!!

Johnny: *Gyaaah!* Stop it!

Tiedoll: Hey now, no quarreling.

Q If Allen were to become friends with a Noah, who would it be?

Johnny: *Okay,* you two. Calm down and have some tea. *(sweating)*

Allen & Kanda: HUFF HUFF *(worn out)*

Tiedoll: Come to think of it, Walker, you're buddy-buddy with Tyki Mikk.

Allen: Nuh-uh! He's just way too friendly.

Johnny: Is he always like that?

Allen: Sort of. But I can't imagine being friends with a Noah. Their behavior is rather extreme.

Cross: What about Road? Hasn't she been a bit flirty?

Allen: D-don't say that! Road is...difficult.

Johnny: Are you blushing? She kissed you, right?

Allen: I'm n-not blushing! For her, kisses are like saying hello! *(sweating)* Besides, I think she has her eyes on someone else.

Cross: Oh...?

Q Lenalee and Kanda drank liquid Innocence, which makes me wonder about the taste. I doubt it tastes good, but...

Kanda: It had no more taste than water.

Allen: Huh! I thought it looked bitter.

Johnny: Since becoming Crystal-types, Lenalee and Kanda both have cross-shaped scars on their bodies. What are those like? Do they hurt?

Kanda: It doesn't hurt anymore, though it doesn't seem likely to ever really heal. If my weapon gets damaged, I bet blood from those wounds would restore it.

Johnny: I guess the power of your seal doesn't work on it.

Allen: Do you ever feel light-headed from blood loss? Do you get hungry like Parasite types do?

Kanda: No! Then I'd be weak like you!

Allen: Never mind you. I'm worried about Lenalee!

Tiedoll: You must avoid anemia, Yu.

Johnny: Chief Komui is worried about that too. He gave Lenalee a supplement made by the Science Section. She keeps it in a waist pouch.

Allen: Oh yeah, there was a question about the waist pouches on Order uniforms. What's inside them?

Johnny: I guess we never covered that. The pouches have first aid supplies, like disinfectant and antihemorrhagics. Miranda and Timothy have candies to hike calorie intake and Krory has Akuma blood candy. Lavi and Bookman requested headache medicine.

Tiedoll: We'd never get by without the Science Section.

Allen: Do Lavi and Bookman suffer from headaches?

Johnny: Um...I don't think so. They said they wanted it for a charm.

Allen: Medicine? As a charm?

Cross: It's an occupational disorder from all that record keeping. Makes their brains overheat. Doesn't happen often though.

Johnny: Oh, really? They could've told me!

Cross: It's incurable. They just have to struggle through.

Allen: You really know a lot about the Bookmen, Master! Why is that?

Tiedoll: Yes, Cross, why is that?

Cross: What's it matter? Stop jumping on everything I say!

Q Allen is unlucky, so does he lose at gambling unless he cheats?

Allen: Gambling is about winning, so I use skill to make my own luck!

READ THIS WAY

Kanda: Just admit you suck at it!

Johnny: He's awful at rock paper scissors too.

Kanda: Cheating isn't right. Doesn't it bother you?

Allen: Not a bit. Sure, cheating sounds bad, but I've polished my skills and, besides, I never take from good people. Only from ne'er-do-wells.

Johnny: That's a dangerous way to live, Allen. *(sweats)*

Allen: I need money, Johnny. And, if I get caught, I've always got my Innocence.

Kanda: What would you do with that?!

Cross: He's a chip off the old block after all! Ha ha ha!

Tiedoll: Poor boy, stuck with such a rotten master...

> **Q** When Link was accompanying Allen, did Allen ever see him smile?

Allen: I tried again and again to get him to smile, but he didn't, not once.

Johnny: Inspector Link and everyone from Central Agency must have strong face muscles. They always look so stern.

Allen: Link said that the rest of us are too warm-spirited.

Tiedoll: Look at Rouvelier, their commanding officer! He probably forbids smiling.

Allen: Link was really strict. He'd chide me if I made the slightest mess while eating. When I wrote a report, even if Reever said it was fine, Link would make me redo it because he said my handwriting was sloppy. And if I didn't dry my hair after a bath he'd chase me with a towel, saying I'd catch a cold and hinder a mission. I couldn't even leave my Order uniform lying around unfolded 'cause he'd say it was unbefitting an Exorcist!

Cross: A real mommy type!

Johnny: Yes, he likes to take care of others. I was worried when he was assigned to accompany you, but he fit in well at the Order. And thanks to him, your reports are slightly more legible now. He really did you some good!

Allen: Well, I suppose. Are all mommy types like that?

Kanda: You all trust that guy too much.

Allen: What was that, Kanda?

Kanda: Nothing.

> **Q** Who is faster running at top speed, Komui or Section Leader Reever?

Johnny: I would think Reever, but...

Allen: But Komui has special skills, like Komlin.

Kanda: That cheater!

Johnny: And he's merciless, even toward his subordinates.

Kanda: You should stand up to him. You're the vaunted Science Section, after all!

Johnny: We're doing the best we can! *(crying)*

Tiedoll: At least the place is lively! Ever since Komui became chief, the Order has been more easygoing. Before, it was pretty dark and dour.

Allen: I heard about that from Lenalee. Was the Order really so different then than it is now?

Tiedoll: It was established with lofty aspirations and goals, but became warped over the course of a hundred years. After all, humans are flawed creatures. When you have the chance, you should ask Fo at the Asia Branch about it. She's watched over the Order since the beginning.

Allen: The Asia Branch, huh? I hope I can visit there again sometime. *(glum)*

Johnny: You can! We'll go together!

Allen: Thanks, Johnny... *(crying)* But first I want to eat Jerry's cooking again. *(stomach growls)*

Johnny: You will! I'm sure of it! We both will! *(hugging Allen)*

Cross: Ha ha ha! Good luck with that!

Kanda: Don't you feel the slightest bit responsible?!

Tiedoll: Oops! I forgot about the word count. If we go over again, Hoshino will have to apologize to the designer and the graphic novel editor. Let's wrap this up!

Allen & Kanda: Awesome!

Johnny: *(noticing how happy they are)*

Tiedoll: See ya later, Marian. May you rest in peace.

Cross: Don't get morbid!

Allen: Master, you may be a hallucination born of my weakness, but I'm glad to see you again! *(like in the 222nd night)*

Cross: Feh! Enough goopy sentiment!

Johnny: I hope we haven't gone over the word count this time.

Tiedoll: Me too, or they may clamp down on the discussion room next time. Take care, everybody all over the world! I know you all love Yu, so keep showering him with affection!

Johnny: And thanks for sending so many questions!

Allen & Kanda: Whew! It's finally over! *(panting)*

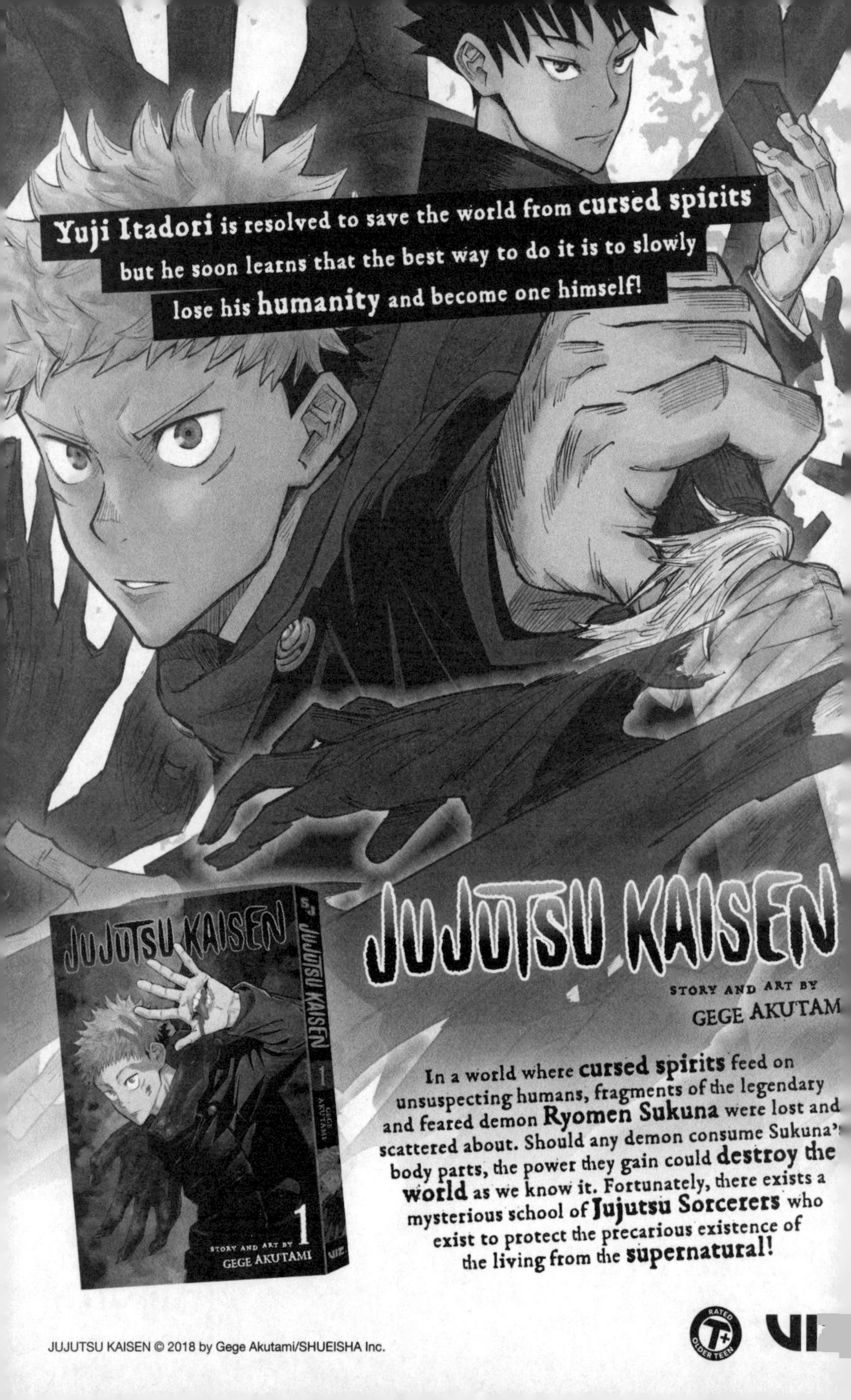
Yuji Itadori is resolved to save the world from cursed spirits
but he soon learns that the best way to do it is to slowly
lose his humanity and become one himself!
JUJUTSU KAISEN
STORY AND ART BY
GEGE AKUTAMI
1
JUJUTSU KAISEN
STORY AND ART BY
GEGE AKUTAM
In a world where cursed spirits feed on unsuspecting humans, fragments of the legendary and feared demon Ryomen Sukuna were lost and scattered about. Should any demon consume Sukuna's body parts, the power they gain could destroy the world as we know it. Fortunately, there exists a mysterious school of Jujutsu Sorcerers who exist to protect the precarious existence of the living from the supernatural!
RATED T+ OLDER TEEN
VIZ
JUJUTSU KAISEN © 2018 by Gege Akutami/SHUEISHA Inc.

**MANGA SERIES
ON SALE NOW**

Rosario+Vampire
ADVANCED

**Tsukune's got
some monstrous
girl problems!**

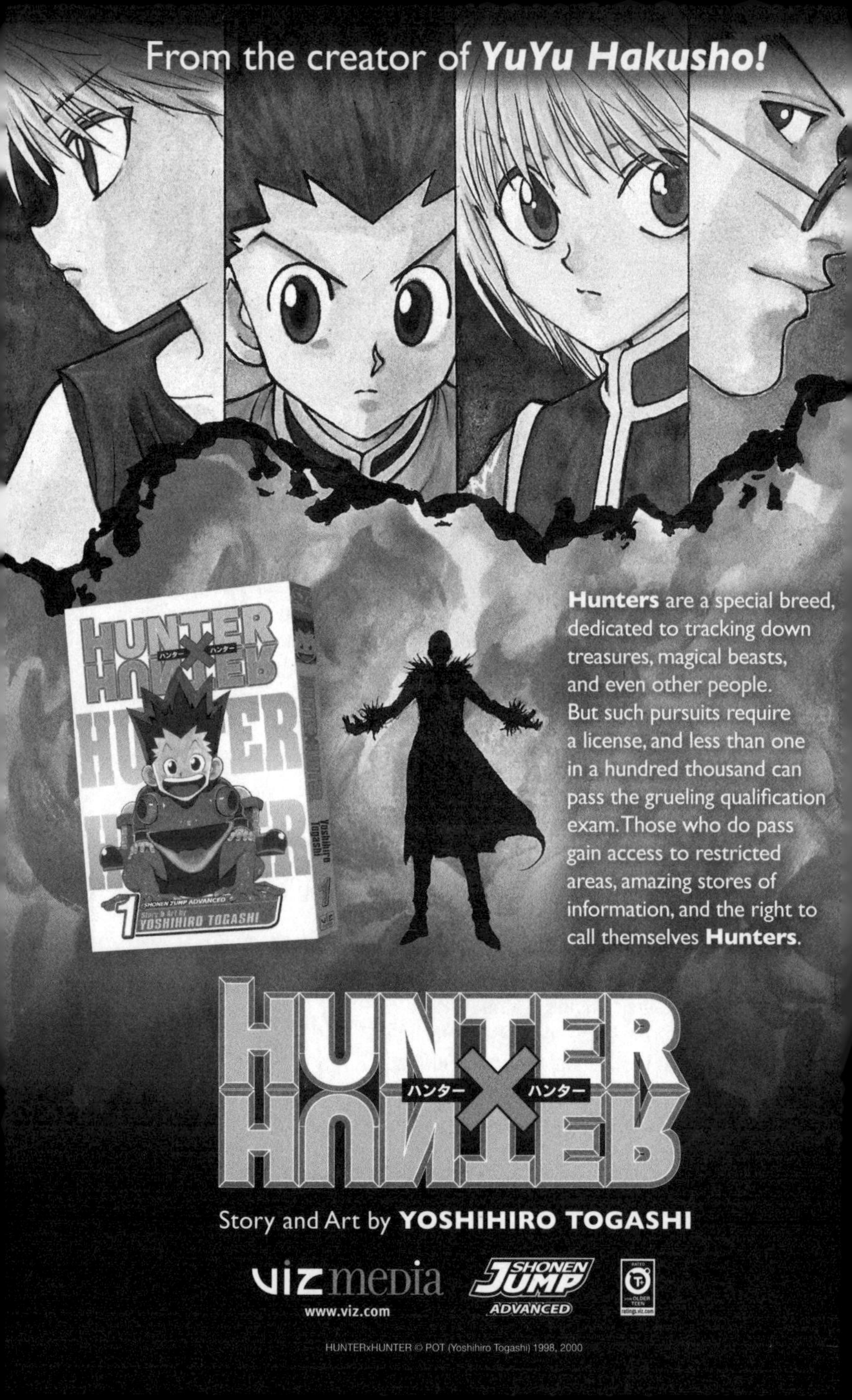
From the creator of ***YuYu Hakusho!***
Hunters are a special breed, dedicated to tracking down treasures, magical beasts, and even other people. But such pursuits require a license, and less than one in a hundred thousand can pass the grueling qualification exam. Those who do pass gain access to restricted areas, amazing stores of information, and the right to call themselves **Hunters**.
HUNTER ハンター × ハンター HUNTER
Story and Art by **YOSHIHIRO TOGASHI**
www.viz.com
SHONEN JUMP ADVANCED
HUNTERxHUNTER © POT (Yoshihiro Togashi) 1998, 2000

You're Reading in the Wrong Direction!!

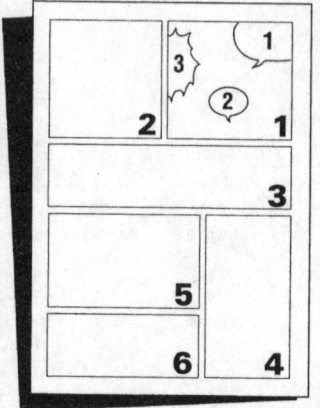

Whoops! Guess what? You're starting at the wrong end of the comic!

It's true! In keeping with the original Japanese format, **D.Gray-man** is meant to be read from right to left, starting in the upper-right corner.

Unlike English, which is read from left to right, Japanese is read from right to left, meaning action, sound effects and word-balloon order are completely reversed... something which can make readers unfamiliar with Japanese feel pretty backwards themselves. For this reason, manga or Japanese comics published in the U.S. in English have sometimes been published "flopped"—that is, printed in exact reverse order, as though seen from the other side of a mirror.

By flopping pages, U.S. publishers can avoid confusing readers, but the compromise is not without its downside. For one thing, a character in a flopped manga series who once wore in the original Japanese version a T-shirt emblazoned with "M A Y" (as in "the merry month of") now wears one which reads "Y A M"! Additionally, many manga creators in Japan are themselves unhappy with the process, as some feel the mirror-imaging of their art skews their original intentions.

We are proud to bring you Katsura Hoshino's **D.Gray-man** in the original unflopped format. For now, though, turn to the other side of the book and let the adventure begin...!

—Editor